published 1988

SC
35-

San Diego Artists

San Diego Artists

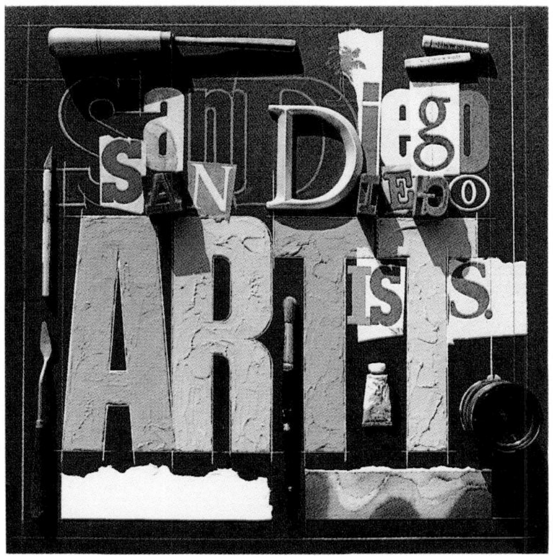

Robert Perine
I. Andrea
Bram Dijkstra

ARTRA Publishing, Inc.

Artra Publishing, Inc.
P.O. Box 575
Encinitas, CA 92024

ISBN 0-936725-02-8
Library of Congress Catalogue Number 88-070826

Book and cover design: Robert Perine
Back cover: *Ode to San Diego (Sunny Side Up)*. . . , Rob Bell, 1978
Typography: Headline Typography & Graphics, Encinitas, California
Graphic Production: Barry Age

Dedicated to the artists and arts supporters of San Diego.

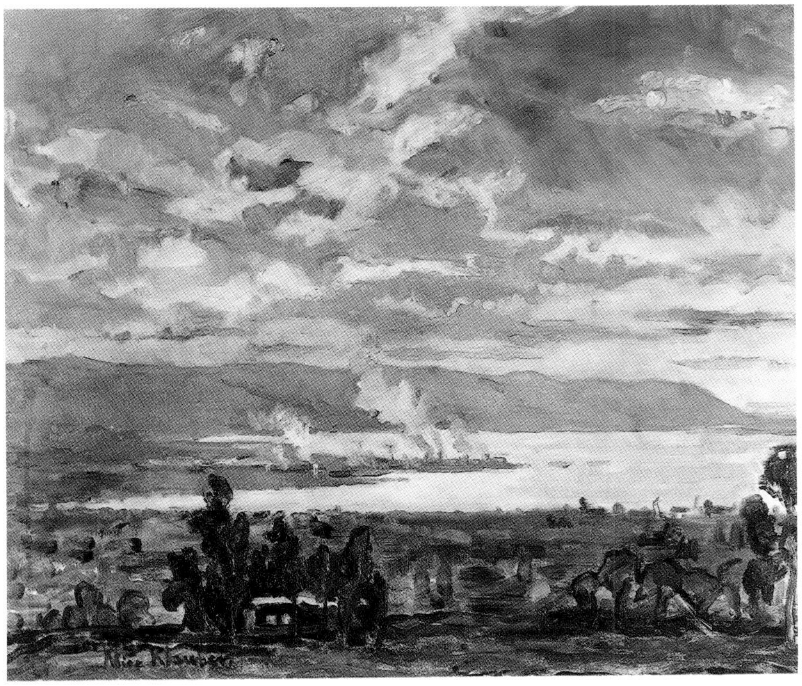

Alice Klauber, *San Diego Harbor*, circa 1920, 19¾"×23¾", o/c

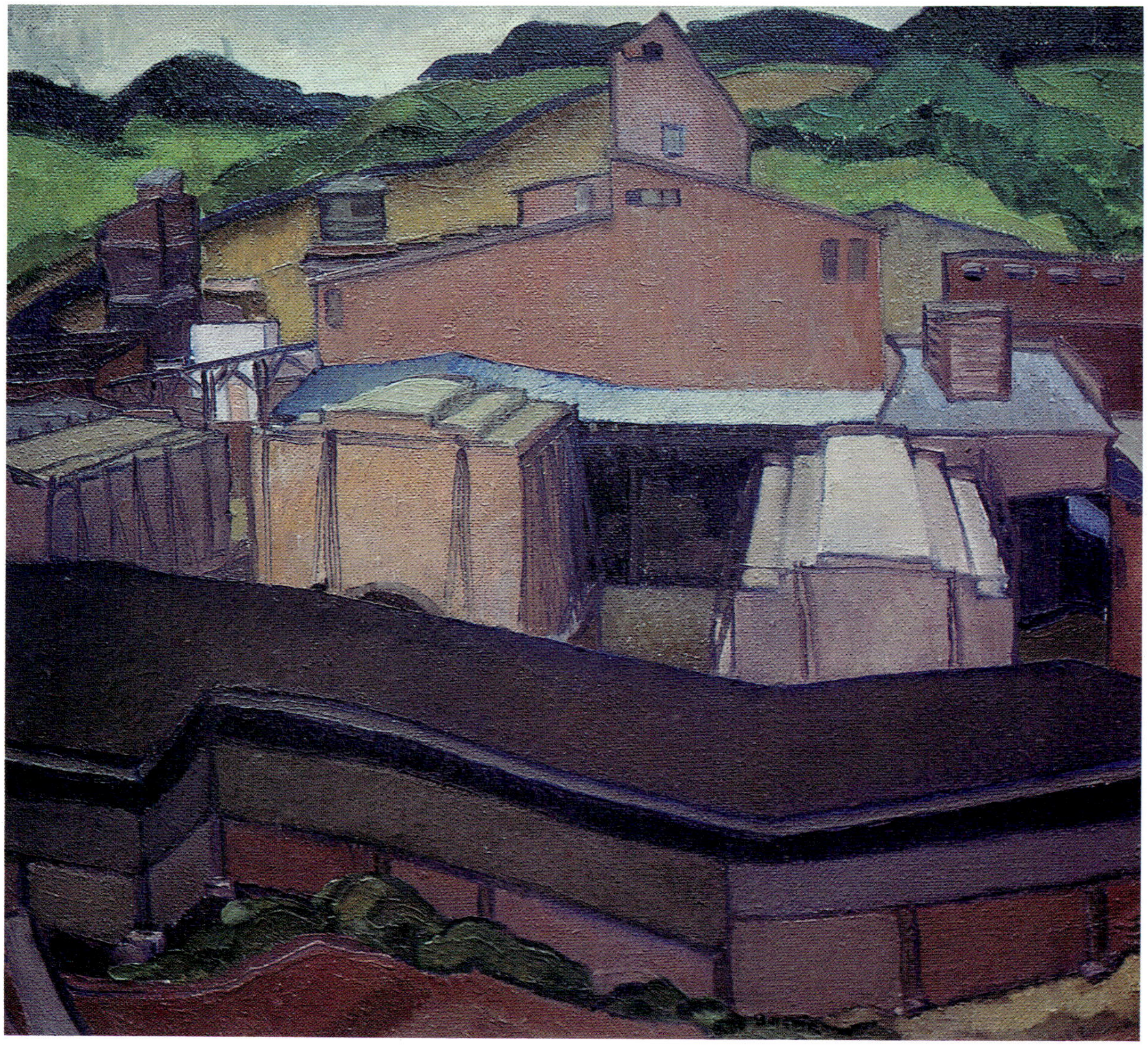

Belle Baranceanu, *The Brick Factory,* 1927, 22" × 24", o/Masonite

CONTENTS

ACKNOWLEDGEMENTS:

We would first like to thank the artists for their cooperation, patience, and willingness to share the deeper, more meaningful parts of their lives and work. Secondly, a thanks to their assistants and representatives who often provided important visual materials for this book. Also our sincere appreciation goes to the following people who contributed in a special way to this project: Mary and David Gaupp, Katherine Sanford, Catherine Bischoff, Alice Culbert Wolk, Kay Wallen, Barbara Herrera, Francesca Rivas, R.N., Ron Smith, Ph.D., and Alexander Jackson. A special thanks to Mary Gaupp for preliminary proofreading of the history and interviews and a big thanks to Blaze Newman who did the final editing of the entire manuscript and whose skills once more came to the rescue.

INTRODUCTION

In the summer of 1986, while in the midst of preparing a history of the old California Watercolor Society, I was reminded that one of the key players in the L.A.-centered, West Coast landscape movement was painter Rex Brandt, a displaced native San Diegan. I realized that for years San Diego-born artists had been leaving their home town for greener pastures. Simultaneous to this summer "revelation" of mine, Elizabeth Kennedy and David Lutz's San Diego Arts Plan was being finalized, and it struck me that this city might soon be ready for a book on its visual artists. Although a number of fine books had been published on the artists of major cities including Los Angeles, New York, and San Francisco, publishers had not yet perceived San Diego as a city full of fabulous artists. Nor had they been very enthusiastic about a community considered to be a cultural wasteland in the visual arts.

My own experience as a transplanted Angeleno (1970) had been far from positive. I learned that being a painter here was a lonely enterprise. There was little serious interplay, either intellectual or financial and, as talented as my local artist friends were, they found few committed sources of encouragement and support, that is, financially stable galleries, sympathetic museums, and serious collectors. Now, eighteen years later, I sense a new spirit in the air. I hear positive rumblings from the art community, a phenomenon related to San Diego County's accelerating growth and the concomitant infusion of more sophisticated art interests.

In late August of 1987, a few months following the passage of the San Diego Arts Plan, I was invited to serve on Mayor Maureen O'Connor's fifteen-member Cultural Arts Task Force. This group spent some sixty hours of intensive investigative research before hammering out the model for the San Diego Cultural Arts Commission. On February 2, 1988 this model was accepted and the ordinance to implement it was unanimously passed by the City Council. Though it was late in coming – comparable cities such as Seattle, Cincinnati, and Houston have had commissions for years – the Arts Commission was a clear signal that the second largest city in California was finally catching up in the cultural arts domain, especially in its weakest area, the visual arts.

Throughout San Diego County other improvements had been occurring. Outlying communities including Carlsbad, Escondido, and La Mesa had already formed their own arts councils, building accessible cultural institutions and facilities and establishing percent-for-the-arts programs. As in Orange County, San Diego citizens were beginning to pressure both government and private interests for more funds for the arts, and art institutions – from large to small – were lobbying for larger pieces of the city-funded art pie. An adequate number of new residents had come here already convinced that a rich culture is vital to the spirit of any metropolitan area, that an art-conscious, art-enriched city pays multiple dividends.

My experience on the Task Force reinforced my belief in the importance of this book. Although Andrea and I were already involved in its preparation, I was more than ever convinced that the time was ripe for introducing San Diego's artists to the art world and to the general public. Since we were both practicing artists and had written professionally, we took on the challenge.

The basic issue, of course, was how to approach this selection process from two personal, private perspectives. How could we deal with our prejudices? The only answer was to be open, to be thorough in our hunt, and to agree on our criteria for selection (see the criteria list, page 10). Basic questions about the art world itself quickly arose: Are the crafts considered art? Do photography, architecture, and industrial design, for example, fit our definitions of art? Where does theater exit and performance enter? Where is the line drawn between visual language and visible language? These and other questions arose which I. Andrea discusses in the second part of this introduction.

Portraying these artists photographically was in itself a challenge for me. Actually seeing them in their studio spaces is often a surprising contrast to the work itself. I wanted to create a photo essay which would capture the San Diego art scene, yet also give each person his or her own identity as a real-life, committed artist. Armed with my two favorite lenses and the current Eastman T-Max system, I zeroed in on the streets, alleys, and trails that led to the homes, studios, warehouses, lofts, garages, lean-tos, or sheds where my artist-subjects waited. While this part of the project proved surprisingly time-consuming and tiring, intriguing conversations resulted; a bit of shop talk or camera talk, discussions over a slide-covered light table, and more than a few offers of food or coffee. When I left Joan Austin's rural Jamul studio, she handed me an oval wicker basket stuffed with home grown fruits. Even the three photographers, whom I approached with great trepidation, were gracious and helpful. One notable highlight was an instructive and productive lesson in night photography from Arthur Ollman.

In the middle of the project, a debate I was having with myself over whether or not to include a brief San Diego art history was finally resolved after talking with Bram Dijkstra. In October of 1986 he had delivered an excellent lecture on "Painting in Southern California, 1920-1950," to the Smithsonian's Archives of American Art seminar entitled "The Visual Arts and the Myth of Southern California – 1900-1950." I was present at the Huntington Art Gallery for that series and made a mental note as to his qualifications to write such a history. A year later we finally met, and, after several discussions with both Dijkstra and Andrea, we decided to divide the history section between them, Dijkstra taking his specialty, the period from 1920-1950, and Andrea bringing us through the 1950s to the present. This supplement, like the book itself, is the first of its kind. I hope it will add to the accurate understanding and appreciation of our art community, giving readers new insights into the sporadic attempts by San Diego artists to shape a better cultural environment for themselves and their neighbors.

I am hopeful this book will also address our serious San Diego collectors. They are essential to the economics of our local art but have tended in the past to leave town to find artists they view as "important." Part of the problem is ignorance of the local scene, an ignorance which is often accompanied by the misconception that because there are fewer artists here, none of them must be very good. Our numbers are as yet few, but our quality and accomplishment measures well against national and international standards. San Diego collectors are therefore well-advised to poke around in their own backyards for worthwhile surprises.

I would like to see this book, in its modest way, help spur on a city that is beginning to support more of its local visual arts talent. San Diego's public arts program should also be venturing into uncharted spaces, pioneering ideas that will invariably prick ears, ruffle collars, and cause not a few out-of-towners to see us as a place of innovation and risk-taking. The city might then be looked upon as the zoo is: as incubator for an endangered species. These kinds of changes call for broader private and corporate support for the arts, accelerated public arts programs through strengthened building codes; broader cooperation between city planners and the Port District, and coordination between the new Arts Commission and the public schools. Like any city with a conscience, we must create a seedbed for future talent.

All of these goals cannot be achieved overnight, or in a decade, but it is clearly time to seriously pursue them. As Newton Harrison wrote in a communique to the Task Force: "Art is slow. Art does not have to adhere to the principles of efficiency. It is slow, it is reflective, and it is necessary. Efficiency is a false savings. It breeds control and reduces the diversity of creativity and does not have the interest of the larger public."

The public, in short, owes its artists space, time, and an ongoing support system. In return, artists must daily commit themselves to their work, singlemindedly executing the ideas and products of their passion.

– Robert Perine, January 1988

"Art isn't easy – any way you look at it."

– *Sunday in the Park with George*, James Lapine and Steven Sondheim, 1985

The artist has gained mythic proportions since the chronicling of Michelangelo's struggle with the popes of Rome and Vincent Van Gogh's emotional upheavals at Arles. Part of the reason for this romanticization is that the end result of these personal struggles – the art itself – takes precedence over the private, day-to-day confrontations each artist has with creativity. The pulse of the art-making process is often out of sync with the other demands on an artist's life. In truth, art isn't easy.

In ancient times the artist's role was considerably different, and significantly less ambiguous. Artists had a clearly defined niche in the culture. They created ritual masks, designed pageants, carved totems, painted cave walls, acted out dramatic folklore, or performed other tasks related to the role of the shaman, or spiritual leader of the clan. Because these societies were uncomplicated and closely held, each clan had its few, especially creative and slightly unusual individuals who were respected and involved in the spiritual and temporal life of the group.

Within modern value systems, which most often place science above spirituality and recreation above art, the artist has been largely deprived of that honored place. Appreciation for individual artistic talent has also seriously declined. The disconnectedness of populace to art and art to ritual also parallels a split taking place between art production and the inner sources of creative impulse that help instruct and widen the scope of an artist's perception. Erich Neumann in *Art and the Creative Unconscious* refers to the ideal artist as "the Great Individual," one who is not just the product of his current values, education, or culture, but one who gives expression to the collective unconscious. The transcendant and universal property which might thus permeate a good work of art also carries it beyond the artist's life, past the tiny world of an individual's home into the larger viewing world of a museum. As Carl Jung describes it, "the work of art is not a human being, but [is] essentially supra-personal. It is a thing and not a personality; hence the personal is no criteria for it. Indeed the especial significance of the genuine art work lies in the fact that it has successfully rid itself of the restraints and blind alleys of the personal and breathes an air infinitely remote from the transitoriness and short-winded excursions of the merely personal." (*Contributions to Analytical Psychology,* 1928. pg 233-4).

Still, a sensitive group of art lovers and collectors seek out information about artists. It is perhaps this group's instinctual cultural need to be involved more closely with the process, to make connections through and beyond the art. This puts a heavier responsibility on today's artist who is also hampered by a culture which has moved away from nature, ritual, and connectedness to the unconscious. The burden then falls upon the reviewers who must translate the artist's meaning as well as stimulate interest in his/her current show. Artists are usually uncomfortable with these limited translations and mis-translations of their work and while they may laugh off the more bizarre interpretations, the alienation they feel can be frustrating.

This alienation, while indigenous to our national culture, is to be understood in approaching art of any kind. I felt that this book, in that sense, must deal mainly with how artists "think" and "feel" about their own work. When I embarked on this project – at Robert Perine's request – I began with another kind of approach, one of allowing the artist to speak. I conducted the personal interviews with two interests. One was my fascination and curiosity with, and respect for, certain fellow artists, some of whom I had been following for a decade. The other was in how the "successful" artist deals with what Jungian analyst Katherine Sanford calls "the cross, the pull of inner and outer creativity on one hand and the nuts and bolts of life on the other hand."

These interests combined to rekindle my old dislike of the art history that separates the art from the artist. The process of identifying art by media, date, period, and style, with a disembodied name attached, was never very interesting to me. Meeting the artist, reading a personal statement, seeing the artist's studio always heightened my sensitivity to the work and gave it new dimension. Somehow, I thought, there must be a way of making this kind of meaningful connection between the art and the artist more available. This book has tried to achieve this goal; in the edited interviews which follow, I heard about the problems and the solutions, the pain and the promise of "art." Not a person failed to affect me on a deep level, whether by their words or, more poignantly, by what was left unspoken.

Far from living in isolated preoccupation with aesthetics, these artists were not especially interested in discussing media, technique, or design decisions. These elements were not considered the essence of their work. Rather, the interviews revealed other common concerns. Issues such as ecology, global environment, discrimination and its forms, and the threat of nuclear disaster were raised repeatedly, reinforcing the old idea that the art conscience must be inseparably connected to the social conscience. Artists, in short, continue to be sensitive and vulnerable to signals from the larger world. In Ezra Pound's words, "The artist is the antennae of the race." It became even clearer to me in these interviews that it is through art that our society confronts its conscience.

The openness of the sharing during this project was beyond what I had expected. There were incisive, in-depth responses to the rudimentary questions I had formulated: "Tell me about what you're doing now and how that relates to what you've done in the past." "When did you decide or know you wanted to be an artist?" "Why do you do art?" "How do you see the artist fitting into our society?"

Robert Perine had given me an initial list of San Diego artists suggested by artist friends he had polled in a wide cross-section of the art community. With few exceptions these "favorites" overlapped to provide a master list. We both agreed that further exploration was necessary and inevitable. The kinds of artists to be showcased also expanded as I sought out suggestions from each person I interviewed. If two or more artists suggested the same name, that person was included in the process.

Unlike curating an exhibit, this selection process required more than a reflection of personal taste. I felt it important that we establish a representative overview of media, personalities, and art currents in the eighties. We were also hoping to create a stylistically, ethnically, gender-, and age-balanced presentation insofar as possible without sacrificing quality. The resulting diversity, we believe, reflects the present local art population.

The criteria were basically simple. Significant characteristics affecting an artist's selection were: 1) an identity in the work which reflects the artist's personal beliefs, a signature through time; 2) continued growth in artistic style; 3) recent and fairly steady creative production (taking into account creative depressions and the practical consideration of earning money); 4) the artist's influence on other artists; and 5) demonstrated involvement and recognition of the artist in the art world both in San Diego and outside this community.

Perhaps there is one final, more elusive criteria: honesty. There is much talk about "honesty" in art, but honesty, it seems to me, remains an ideal until the creator learns to connect with him or herself on a deep, truthful level. Brush strokes, color choice, use of texture, subject matter, and media are not all there is to honesty. Nor is education, exhibition record, or sales. Acquiring true honesty requires more than college or art school or even a long career.

Given the honesty, the art must finally and inevitably stand alone. Whether it takes five minutes or five hundred years to prove the work, its ultimate success ironically may depend on someone else's taste. Final validation also depends on how clearly the artist gave expression to a facet of his or her own unique vision.

– *I. Andrea, December 1987*

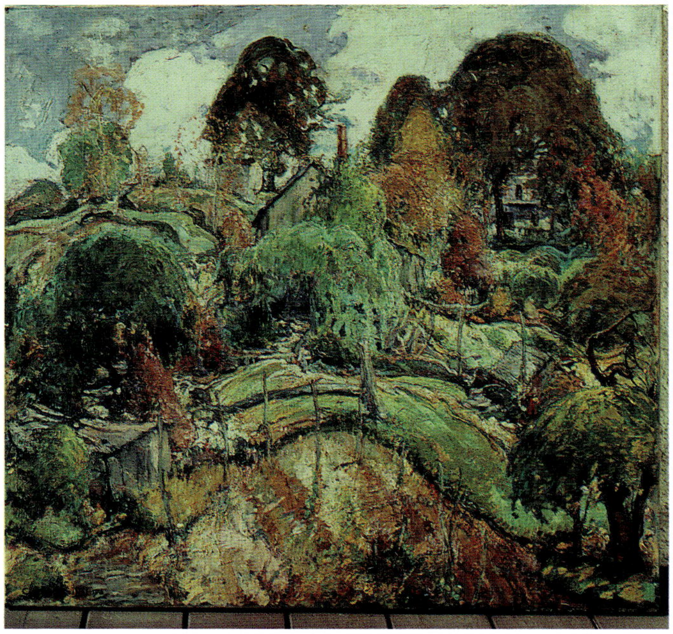

Charles Reiffel, *The Old Farmhouse,* 1916, 34"×37", o/c

REGIONALISM AND AMBITION: SAN DIEGO ART TO 1950

San Diego's attempts to call attention to itself as a cultural center have usually been slightly quixotic: a bit like Woody Allen trying to be Ingmar Bergman. The city's commercial and industrial ambitions have far outdistanced its acumen in the arts. This discrepancy had already become apparent during the Panama-California Exposition of 1915, designed to run concurrently with San Francisco's Panama-Pacific extravaganza. The Exposition symbolized the city's determination to take its place among the country's great urban machines. Indeed, San Diego did everything right in its efforts to present itself as a commercial and industrial region of enormous potential. The Exposition was a huge success, for instead of trying to build mock Eiffel towers or crystal palaces to signal the region's cosmopolitanism, its architects produced the lath and plaster Spanish colonial environment of what was to become Balboa park – a spectacle brilliantly designed to excite the imperialist appetites of potential investors.

But when it came to featuring San Diego as a cultural center, those concerned with the future of the arts in the region produced a display of mock-sophistication that was to set the tone for innumerable subsequent attempts to demonstrate the city's cosmopolitanism in cultural judgment. Alice Klauber (1871-1951), a San Diego native, and a painter of considerable talent who had studied with William Merritt Chase and Robert Henri, invited Henri to visit San Diego in 1914, to plan a major exhibition of contemporary American painting. Their choice was heavily weighted toward Henri's cohorts among "The Eight": painters such as John Sloan, William Glackens, Maurice Prendergast, George Luks and George Bellows – the cream of the progressive wing among mainstream American artists, comparable, perhaps, to a show today that were to concentrate on figures such as Frank Stella, Elsworth Kelly, Susan Rothenberg, and Julian Schnabel.

The limitations of the 1915 San Diego exhibition were immediately apparent to Christian Brinton, at this time America's finest critic of contemporary painting, and a man closely attuned to the eclectic temper of early Twentieth century art. The problem with the art at San Diego, Brinton concluded, in an article for *The International Studio* of June 1915, was that it did not fit with the practical, up-to-date attitude the organizers of the Panama-California Exposition had demonstrated in all other matters. By emphasizing the regional qualities that made San Diego different from the rest of the world, the Exposition had shown itself a good deal more responsive to the modern temper than the art show, which was trying so hard to be "cosmopolitan" in its choices. The welcome absence, Brinton remarked sardonically, "of the customary flatulent and dropsical statuary . . . might well have been supplemented by the exclusion of the pretentious and sophisticated canvas."

In a chapter on San Diego for his book, *Impressions of the Art at the Panama-Pacific Exposition* (1916), Brinton elaborated his point: The San Diego fair had been a success because it had based itself "frankly upon local interest and tradition, conscious of its inheritance and looking with confidence toward the future." The art show, however, had been far too dependent on fashion: "We have for generations been surfeited with ambitious international and universal undertakings," he said – so much so, that by now "the scramble for cosmopolitanism is in itself one of the surest indications of provinciality."

Instead, Brinton insisted, we should now try to "foster individual, independent initiative," without neglecting to "familiarize ourselves with the achievement of our neighbors from overseas." Among artists and art lovers genuine sophistication was the ability to recognize the universal aspects of experience hidden within the structures of everyday life and the elemental forms of one's local environment. Those who wanted to show their sophistication through a pompous preoccupation with the prevailing fashion in art were ultimately as far removed from understanding the real purposes of art as those who, merely as a result of convention, held on to long established forms of expression.

Brinton was astute, scholarly, and undogmatically progressive in his judgments. He admired the work of the early modernist painters, and in his book on the Panama-Pacific Exposition he prophetically announced that in the work of the Cubists he had seen the future of twentieth century art. To him their innovations presaged "a profound spiritual rebirth in the province of aesthetic endeavor." With their radical attacks on conventional conceptions of form, he declared, "they have injected into the pictorial and plastic arts a spirited, energizing impulse which has already proved of immeasureable benefit." It was now up to artists everywhere to feel liberated from convention, and to pursue self-expression in whatever style they might find congenial, just as long as they remained true to the range of their own experience, which was the only source of true sophistication.

Brinton's point of view prefigures the wide-open eclecticism which was to mark the American art scene of the next thirty years. "It matters little, in the end," he insisted, "whether the message of art be conveyed through the employment of lines, dots, dashes, cubes, or spheres. The technical idiom is something that alters with each generation, each decade, almost. What is essential is that the general public, and not a few of the painters, too, be continually awakened, shocked if necessary, into a realization of the fact that art is a living organism which must reflect the temper of its time or degenerate into a sterile and soulless formula."

This is essentially the point of view that would also soon lead poets such as William Carlos Williams and Wallace Stevens to argue that the American artist should above all be concerned with immediacy and honesty of expression. In art "the local is the only universal," they were to insist.

Brinton, in his critique of San Diego's very provincial desire to be "cosmopolitan" which had led it to disdain anything that might be considered "local" in art, astutely pinpointed a problem which has consistently dogged the San Diego art scene to this day, and which has made artistic survival very difficult for most of its finest artists.

II

Even today many otherwise well informed local art lovers find it hard to believe that "provincial" San Diego might actually have had its share of artists of national (let alone international) stature before the second world war. Many of those who most fiercely defend their freedom of choice in lifestyles and politics, are, when it comes to art, content to follow the dictates of a small group of East Coast dealers and critics. They simply refuse to trust their own judgment when called upon to choose the art they are to live with every day. Local critics, too, tend to feed at this East Coast trough – in that respect things have changed very little in more than seventy years.

It is true that at the time of the Panama-California Exposition, San Diego did not have many artists with a distinctive personal conception of the "local" in art. But there were several who were quite as much in tune with the American art scene of their day as most of the painters included in this book are with that of our own time. It was, of course, inevitable that the first painters to gain prominence in a rapidly developing community would be portrait painters, who could properly immortalize the local business elite.

William Thurston Black (c.1810-1893) arrived in San Diego around 1885 after a long career on the East Coast and in the Mid-West, during which he exhibited regularly at the National Academy and the Pennsylvania Academy. His portrait of Alonzo Horton, done soon after his arrival, and now in the collection of the San Diego Historical Society, shows him to have been a forceful and meticulous portraitist, quite capable of capturing the psychological particularities of his sitters. His Alonzo Horton scrutinizes the viewer with a piercing regard. A harsh, unsmiling puritanism tenses Horton's jaws, making it seem as if he has just swallowed his lips. The man's chin clearly has such an aggressive, authoritarian splendor, that his full beard surges over it in a neatly combed wave. There is a monumentality in this portrait that, in its own fashion, is quite as imposing and remarkable as Ingres' famous portrait, *Monsieur Bertin*. There was obviously nothing "provincial" in Black's conception of his sitter. Less imposing is the work of Ammi Farnham (1845-1922), a portrait and genre painter from Silver Creek, New York, who arrived in San Diego in 1888. Farnham's genre work tended toward an academicism that sometimes came to seem impressionistic only because of his somewhat amateurish, smudgy brushwork. As a mediocre exponent of the Victorian academic made popular in America at the turn of the century, Farnham had all the sophistication necessary to be designated the first "dean" of San Diego painters by his local admirers.

That honorary title of dubious merit was transferred after Farnham's death to Charles Fries (1854-1940), who had come to town in 1896. There was an uncanny accuracy of judgment among those who honored him in this fashion, for Fries was no less mediocre an artist than Farnham, and had found his start in art by painting the same sort of marginally competent genre scenes one might associate with Farnham. Upon his arrival in San Diego, Fries commenced a forty-five-year career of painting mountain, arroyo, and desert scenery. His early work in this mode tended to combine the brown tones of the Munich-trained painters, with a subdued range of tonalist color-values. At its best, Fries' mainstream academic sensibility produced landscapes which brought an odd, but rather charming version of Barbizon to the Pacific Southwest. But Fries soon fell into a routine production of scenic back-country views for the tourist trade. The marginal interest of these works as compositions was progressively undercut by the artist's peculiar technique of applying paint, which made them look as if they were painted on butter.

The brief encounter with professionalism in art which San Diego had enjoyed in the figure of William Thurston Black was first renewed through the efforts of several artists who arrived to join the Theosophical Society which had been established on Point Loma in 1897 under the aegis of Katherine Tingley. The first of these, and also the most intriguing, was Reginald Machell (1854-1927), born and educated in England, and trained as a painter at the Acamemie Julian in Paris. In the 1880s Machell began to exhibit regularly at the Royal Society of British Artists, the Grosvenor Gallery, and the Royal Academy, contributing portraits, landscapes and florals, but also works with such telling titles as *Sesha, the Serpent Emblem of Eternity, A Sorceress, Lakshmi*, and *Bacchante*. Given the provocative nature of his spiritual interests, it is not surprising that he soon found himself converted to Theosophy. Before long he was decorating madame Blavatsky's rooms in Regents Park.

Machell arrived at Lomaland in December 1900, and continued to work on enormous, and deliriously complex, symbolist canvases painted in a style that had strong affinities to the work of the Belgian Rosicrucian Jean Delville. They were populated by a host of irridescent angels, courageous souls dressed in knightly armor, flying serpents, and plenty of voluptuous female nudes. The latter undoubtedly signified the dangerous temptations of materiality. However, what makes Machell's work in this manner particularly interesting is the inclusion of a dizzying proliferation of three-dimensionally rendered circles, tetrahedons, octagons, stars, and assorted other mystically charged symbols, all closely keyed to Blavatsky's teachings. Machell, in addition, carved some superb art nouveau inspired chairbacks, standing screens and doors, all endowed with elaborate symbolic meanings. Had he remained in England he would no doubt have carved out quite a reputation for himself among collectors of symbolist art.

Charles James Ryan (1865-1949), came to Point Loma with Machell, and was another British painter who, by doing so, left a promising career behind him in England. He had exhibited in all the right places, and was good enough to be represented in the Victoria and Albert Museum. Ryan, unfortunately, slowly let five years of training with Hubert von Herkomer, as well as a fine sense of three-dimensional form, go to waste at Point Loma in order to teach astronomy and associated subjects to Tingley's followers.

Another painter of merit associated with the Point Loma Theosophical Society was Edith White (1855-1846), a fine painter of traditional flower still-lifes. These she rendered with a vigor that made them resemble the early flower pieces of J. Alden Weir or John LaFarge. White had a predilection for roses, which she often managed to endow with an almost anthropomorphic sense of drama.

Maurice Braun (1877-1941) was – and still is – the most widely known artist associated with the Theosophical Society on Point Loma. He arrived here late in 1909, and became virtually overnight San Diego's main source of civic pride in the field of art – and with good reason, for Braun's work of the 1910's and early 1920's can stand comparison with that of any of the American Impressionists then working. He had studied painting at the National Academy of Design from 1897-1900, and had also worked with Childe Hassam and John Twachtman.

Braun soon developed a distinctive method of applying paint, which made his work instantly recognizable, and which brought interesting new tactile qualities to the products of a compositional sensibility otherwise largely formed by the concerns of late nineteenth century tonalism. Braun's paintings were built up in scuffy, long brushstrokes which gave the impression of being short and stubby, with a grainy texture, because he let his colors overlap instead of applying them in the more customary parallel patterns of conventional Impressionism.

Braun's use of color in his early work is, indeed, distinctive and often quite daring. He was in these works not averse to letting deep greens, cobalt blue, orange-yellow, and white coexist in close proximity. A high mountain range in late afternoon would have him combining hot pinks and blueish purple with ochres and grey haze. Painting a forest clearing at Yosemite, with a blue-white and light-gray, sunlit mountain wall in the background, Braun developed a subtly dramatic, innovative use of the color green among the shadowed redwoods which, in tall verticals, anchored his composition. He made a very unusual, harsh, even slightly poisonous, yet warm, almost irridescent deep green predominate over more conventional color harmonies. By juxtaposing this astonishing hue with touches of milky pink, yellow-green, and warm yellow, Braun succeeded in turning this painting into a joyful tribute to the elemental energies of nature.

Works such as these indicate that Braun was quite aware of the exuberant high color which characterized the work of the Italian Divisionists. These painters, whose work evolved almost imperceptibly into the early Futurist styles of Balla and Boccioni, were being studied quite closely by progressively thinking American artists during the 1910s. Both the Divisionists and the Futurists were amply represented at the Panama-Pacific Exposition in San Francisco, where Braun exhibited three of his landscapes.

In the long run, however, the artist's daring in the realm of color experimentation fell victim to his desire to be understood by a wide public. Most of the official arbiters of taste who saw the work of the progressive Italians at San Francisco, deplored their unbridled celebration of high color. Eugen Neuhaus, then assistant professor of decorative design at UC Berkeley, denounced the "very repulsive color" of two divisionist works by Enrico Lionne. Earlier, in *The New Tendency in Art* (1913), Henry Rankin Poore had stylishly invoked evolutionary theory to combat the cubists' failures in the area of "true" sophistication. "The fact," he said, "that in literature, painting, music and sculpture, American and English art has been practically uninfluenced by 'Primitivolatry' and 'Savageopathy' is evidence that these nations are ascending instead of descending."

Braun was, as a theosophist, a firm believer in spiritual evolution, and such equations between "Fauvist" color and the savage beast still lurking within the human breast must have made him blanch.

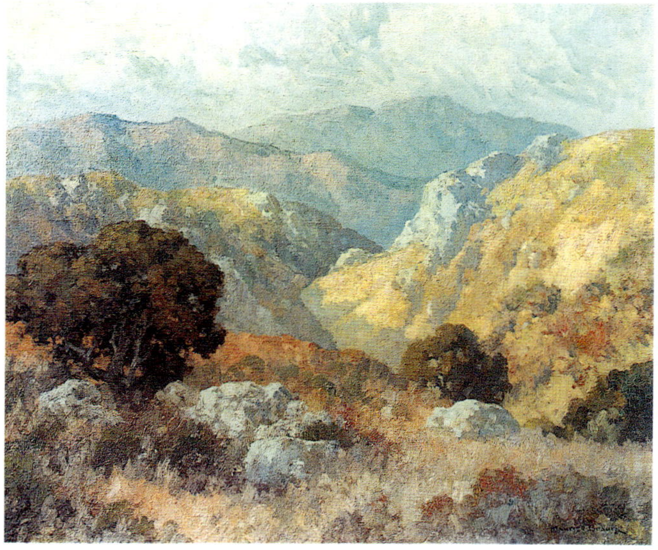

Maurice Braun, *Rocky Heights*, early 1920s, 25"×30", o/c

His audience, moreover, was doing its bit for evolution by demanding as many soothing variations of pink, pale blue, light green, and sappy yellow as he could produce. More and more Braun obliged, and during the last twenty years of his life he managed to fill the drawing rooms of the local high bourgeoisie, whose favorite painter he had become, with countless versions of a handful of very bland, back-country landscape motifs. The interest of those works was not enhanced by the progressive deterioration of his brushwork whose mushy consistency came to rival the very unclarified butter of his friend Fries. Even in his late years, however, Braun occasionally returned to the imaginative qualities of his youth. A group of paintings of desolate, termite-ridden dead oak trees, for instance, took on an expressionist intensity, and were clearly the artist's unsentimental acknowledgement of his own impending death.

Braun was an important figure in the history of San Diego art, and he often succeeded in capturing that "holy spirit of nature" he always sought to express in his paintings. In these works he indeed comes close to justifying William Gerdts recent, and certainly rather extravagant, judgment in his book *American Impressionism,* that he "was arguably the most brilliant landscape artist of his generation working in California." But, ironically, Braun's delight in the harmonies of nature, and his self-professed desire to paint what might be understood, in the long run seem to have exhausted his capacity to evoke those creative links between the soul and nature he had sought to express in his art. There is, after all, danger and conflict as well as concord in nature. Bereft of that recognition, his later paintings rarely recapture the extraordinary vigor of his early work, in which he combined a very personal conception of color with his love for the California landscape, to produce brilliant, eccentric, and oddly appealing dreamscapes of a Pacific arcadia that was not without its poisoned apples.

III

Our conception of what is "new" or "sophisticated" in art tends to conform to the most ingrained prejudices of our culture. Critics praise what they know, and in a society proud of its ignorance of history, knowledge is a computer program designed by a clever adolescent who mistakes the prejudices of his teachers for truth. Most critics now writing about art have only a minimal knowledge of the history of painting before 1950, and hence have very little to work with, other than their crippled (and already "outdated") post-war aesthetic when they set out to determine the "quality" or "value" of painters who worked outside the accepted modernist mold. Yet they judge these artists with the greatest of ease, carelessly dismissing works of art of the highest order, because these works do not happen to fit within the narrow matrix of their capacity for judgment.

In this respect, the most thoughtfully independent artists of our day tend to find themselves in a position not unlike those artists of the past who have been dismissed as insignificant within the prevailing fashions of sophisticated judgment. Artists, of course, cannot escape being of their own time, but only the most bland among them can expect to be fully understood by the reigning arbiters of taste. Artists who seek to minimize conflict produce art of minimal value. But even the concept of conflict itself has become part of the status quo in art – a tool of the prevailing taste, which has thereby succeeded in neutralizing the intent of art, and, indeed, of thought itself. Thus the modernist temper has been absorbed by the dualistic structures of our dominant value system. That system habitually pitches polar opposites against each other, not to transcend them, but to paralyze our search for viable alternatives. Thus our culture has turned the process of experimentation itself into a harmless game with astonishing rewards for those who play it best.

Fortunately our best artists almost invariably show a far greater catholicity of taste, when it comes to studying the art of the past, than most critics can muster. Good artists see the past as part of the continuity of experience which must shape the future, while their critics are caught in the narrow present of an aesthetic judgment blandly tied to the post-war glorification of form and gesture for its own sake.

It did not take long for the most astute among our early Twentieth century artists to recognize the fundamental contradictions in a value structure which demanded that they prove their "individuality" by lining themselves up at either pole of a dualist system. Instead they forfeited the game and resigned themselves to the minimal rewards of genuine artistic independence. Before the second world war, California was still very remote from the art wars which were developing on the East Coast. But during the Twenties it had already become evident to most artists that if you yearned for national fame you must go to, or stay in, New York. On the other hand, if you were a loner, if you looked upon the wide open spaces of the West as a source of raw materials for the imagination rather than as a range of empty bleachers in the vast stadium of potential stardom, you came to Southern California and settled in some outlandish place such as San Diego, Cathedral City, or Santa Monica, and you doggedly set about doing your own thing.

Southern California thus became a haven for many artists of genuine originality, who had deliberately chosen to abandon the competitive East Coast art environment, not because they could not have held their own in that environment, but because they cared more about art then about recognition. Born, bred, and trained on the East Coast or in the Midwest, and usually keenly aware of what was being done by even the most experimental painters of their time, they could hardly be accused of genuine provincialism – though the art public and critics who have persisted, then as now, in deriding, ignoring, or in blandly dismissing their work, perfectly match Christian Brinton's profile of the provincial mind.

Charles Reiffel (1862-1942), who was perhaps the most doggedly independent of this group of early modernist loners, settled in San Diego in 1926, thereby forever removing the city from the roster of artistic backwaters, although this fact escaped most of its good citizens, who paid the artist little mind and did what they could to avoid buying his paintings. Sherman Trease, in an undated newspaper clipping from the late Twenties which Reiffel pasted in his personal scrapbook, noted that, although the painter had been awarded a list of prizes as long as his palette by his fellow artists, "his work is not particularly popular with the majority of people."

In fact, a rather sardonic myth developed early that Reiffel had actually set out to join the artist colony of Santa Fe, New Mexico, but had been waylaid by a snow storm which made him change his itinerary and end up in San Diego, that tartarus of artists. It is a lovely story, but another newspaper article in Reiffel's scrapbook printed in a Norwalk, Connecticut newspaper not long after his arrival in San Diego, and obviously planted there by Reiffel or his wife, simply records that "Mr. and Mrs. Reiffel left Wilton last fall, by auto, for the West coast, taking a leisurely route through New Mexico and Nevada. At present they are at the Beck ranch near East San Diego, Cal., where they will remain a number of months." Apocryphal or not, the snowstorm story was probably fostered by the artist himself, who, although fascinated by the local landscape, probably felt less than kindly toward the townspeople who looked upon his paintings with hostility and suspicion, and who carelessly allowed him to sink progressively further into poverty.

Reiffel was born in Indianapolis, Indiana. In his mid-twenties he became a lithographer, first in Cincinnati, then in New York. He continued to earn his living as a journeyman lithographer for most of his life, taking his trade to Europe in the early 1890s. In 1893 he visited Tangiers, Madrid, Lisbon, Marseilles, and Paris, making oil sketches wherever he went. At the Munich Academy he briefly attended the painting classes of Carl Marr (1858-1936), an American, born in Milwaukee, Wisconsin, who had become a major figure on the German art scene.

By 1898 Reiffel was back in Cincinnati and exhibiting at the Spring Exhibition of American art there. He soon moved to Buffalo, where he remained for more than a decade, becoming a local celebrity as a painter and frequently entering the national juried shows. The Corcoran bought his *Railway Yards, Winter Evening,* a small, brilliantly executed, loosely painted tonalist-impressionist work with strong conceptual affinities to Alfred Stieglitz's *The Hand of Man.*

Early in this century, Reiffel became a weekend commuter between Buffalo and Silvermine, Connecticut, where he had bought an old farm. But he was very disappointed when he discovered that Silvermine was developing into a thriving artists' colony: "I like artists," he told Arthur Millier, "but one at a time." By the early 1910s, already about fifty years old, Reiffel finally risked devoting full time to his art. In the decade preceding his arrival in San Diego, he gained a major East Coast reputation as a painter of particularly tempestuous and idiosyncratic, proto-abstract Post-Impressionist landscapes. His work soon became a familiar presence at the National Academy Exhibitions, the Carnegie Institute Internationals, the Corcoran Biennials, and the American annuals at the Art Institute of Chicago.

Conservative critics hated his work, but fellow artists and supporters of modernist art became his champions. In its June 1916 issue, for instance, the *International Studio* reported that at the Allied Artists of America's Third Annual his paintings had attracted considerable attention: "Reiffel . . . is represented with a couple of decorative landscapes in the purest of pure colour." A vermillion barn in one takes its place capitally in the colour scheme. An old and famous painter looking at it said: "I have never seen that coloured barn, but I like it, I like it."

The work referred to here may well have been Reiffel's *A Bit of Silvermine – The Old Farmhouse,* of 1916, a brilliant painting typical of the artist's proto-abstract conception of landscape. In this work the high horizon characteristic of most Impressionist landscapes becomes merely a secondary factor in what is essentially a boldly abstracted composition constructed of flattened, undulant layers of paint which yet succeed in remaining organic and representational. Reiffel was compared to van Gogh by the critics of the 1910s, and to such American contemporaries as Ernest Lawson or George Bellows. Discussing another of Reiffel's paintings shown at the winter exhibition of the National Academy of Design that same year, the prominent critic Charles Caffin described the artist's work as characterized by "a superior structural building up of the several planes of the scene. From the background upward are interlocked relations of the part[s], which in connection with the rhythmic use of lines, gives a sense of mounting growth to the whole composition." A similar method of composition is operative in *A Bit of Silvermine.* It makes the painting come alive with elemental power. Long, fettuccini-like strands of paint loop past rainbow clusters of dots and dashes. Colors rush in torrents over the canvas, creating uncanny suggestions of sentient tensions, not only in plants and trees, but even in the inanimate forms of rock and soil. There can be no doubt that Edgar Allan Poe would have loved Reiffel's work.

A year later, at Chicago, Reiffel received a silver medal for his *In the Hills,* a work of similar force, in which the artist went even further toward the abstracting and flattening of his picture plane by eliminating any suggestion of a horizon and of conventional perspective. Again organic matter circles, rolls, and churns fiercely over the entire picture plane in a visual world that retains only the barest hint of conventional perspective. This work is every bit as adventurous and revolutionary in conception as anything being done at this time by the avowed American early modernists, but because Reiffel insisted on combining a very organicist, humanist conceptualization of nature with his experiments in planar abstraction, the revolutionary implications of his experiments in landscape painting were generally ignored by the supporters of modernism who found it easier to understand the simple mechanistic deconstructive compositional theories of the early cubists. The fact, moreover, that Reiffel was of the age group of the first wave of American Impressionists, and continued – though with very little actual stylistic justification – to be lumped with them, has not helped his still lagging recognition as an important transitional figure with pronounced early modernist tendencies.

Thus Reiffel was, almost as if by his own design, destined to remain a misunderstood loner. Just before his arrival in San Diego he had gained his greatest measure of recognition on the national scene. But instead of trying to consolidate and improve his position further, he chose to explore the elemental hills of San Diego county and the Southwest for the rest of his life, painting canvases in which he made the local landscape lope and surge with an eerie, almost preternatural tension. The wealthy citizens of San Diego, who were buying the works of Maurice Braun with impressive regularity, refused to probe the meaning of these strange masses of paint turned into undulating waves of primal matter. A compulsive painter, Reiffel resorted to selling his work for a few dollars, or to giving it away. Finally, while never abandoning his serious work, he found himself often painting potboiler landscapes for the tourist trade, simple of color, with fairly conventional perspective, bland. These brought him a very modest income. As a result, many of the younger artists, who knew little about him, tended to dismiss him as a somewhat odd, if skillful, painter of impressionist landscapes. Those, however, like Belle Baranceanu, who came to know him, could not help but recognize his exceptional qualities and speedily revised their opinion.

In fact, even during the last years of his life, nearly eighty years old, dirt-poor, while his wife of more than forty years was slowly disintegrating into paranoia and death, Reiffel continued to experiment whenever he could. In the late Thirties he even began to explore the field of pure abstraction. Several of these experimental canvases were included in the San Diego Fine Arts Gallery's memorial exhibition of 1942, but none seem to have been preserved. It is not difficult to imagine what they might have looked like, however, since most of his major works contain large patches of abstract work, in which the scratchy, stringy, splashy coherence of the paint anticipates the post-war preoccupations of the Abstract Expressionists.

In addition, a good proportion of Reiffel's late representational work conveys an intensely imaginative, moody, expressionist sensibility, an almost gothic mood replete with haunted towers, membrane-like mosses, and anthropomorphic trees: the House of Usher brought to San Diego! That a painter of such imagination and power should still be so completely neglected by the city in which he died, that the San Diego Museum of Art should have a number of the man's most powerful late works, yet refuse to place any of them on permanent exhibit – preferring to hang minor examples from the oeuvre of "big name" European painters – is a sad demonstration of the continued prevalence in San Diego of a truly provincial conception of sophistication.

Things were much better in this respect when Reiffel first arrived here in 1926. The paintings by pre-World War II San Diego painters owned by the San Diego Museum were nearly all acquired under the guidance of Reginald Poland. He had arrived in San Diego only weeks before Reiffel to take on the direction of the newly established San Diego Fine Arts Gallery which opened its doors on February 27, 1926. The Gallery was the outgrowth of years of effort by members of the San Diego Art Guild, particularly Alice Klauber, to establish a permanent, non-commercial exhibition gallery in town.

Poland, judging from all available evidence, was an ideal choice to be the Gallery's first director, and in the twenty-five years of his tenure he built the Gallery into a museum and exhibition space of fine quality. From the very first he combined a concern for the development of a representative historical collection, particularly in Hispanic and American art, with a lively interest in the support of good local artists.

Poland had an excellent eye and was quite eclectic in his taste. When he spotted a painting of quality available for purchase, he would goad wealthy members of the San Diego community into buying it and donating it to the Fine Arts Gallery. Many of the best works in what is now the San Diego Museum of Art were acquired under his direction. He recognized the potential of the eccentric

Putnam sisters as donors to the Gallery and carefully guided them in their purchases, until a Los Angeles art dealer, first introduced to the sisters by Poland, reportedly succeeded in turning them against the Gallery's director. Pressure from the Putnam sisters resulted in Poland's dismissal in 1950.

During the years of his tenure, however, the Gallery organized countless one-person shows by the more prominent local painters, and deserving members of the old guard of San Diego's art community who died were, without fail, given a fitting tribute in the form of a memorial exhibition. Within months of the Gallery's opening, moreover, it sponsored what was to be the first of a series of yearly juried exhibitions of "Artists of Southern California," which included many of the Southland's most prominent painters and sculptors.

Thus, partly as a result of the active involvement of Poland and the San Diego Fine Arts Gallery, a perceptible community of good, professional artists was developing. Some of the better known among these, eager to separate their wheat from the chaff, banded together in 1929 to form the "Contemporary Artists of San Diego." In his foreword to the catalogue of the first exhibition of this group to be held at the Fine Arts Gallery in 1930, Reginald Poland emphasized that its eleven members were all "men whose status is national, as is proved by their election to membership in other organizations throughout the country, purchases of their work for public or private collections, or the awards given to them."

The group included Fries, Braun, and Reiffel, as well as Leslie Lee (1871-1951), an elusive painter of landscapes, portraits, and genre themes, born in Manchester, England, whose mixed tonalist and Barbizon palette could not but give his often sombre, atmospheric, well-composed canvases underdog status among the candy-color-seeking art lovers of Southern California.

Leon Bonnet (1868-1936) was an indifferent painter of marines, who followed in the ample wake of Frederick Judd Waugh's dramatically composed symphonies of surf and rock, but who was unable to reproduce Waugh's crisp, shimmering realism, and instead tended to smuge his outlines, thereby obviating much of the noisy visual muscle-flexing that made Waugh's works boardroom favorites.

Bonnet and James Tank Porter (1883-1962), a sculptor of marginal merit, could lay considerably less claim to being worthy of inclusion in this "elite" of San Diego art than a number of the women artists and sculptors working in the area in 1929. The all-male constituency of the group demonstrates the prejudice against women in the arts still rampant at that time. The sculptor Anna Valentien (1862-1947), had arrived in San Diego in 1908 with an armful of major honors. Her larger-than-life-size *Ariadne* had been exhibited at the World's Columbian Exposition in Chicago in 1893. She had studied with Rodin, exhibited at the Paris Salon, and won a Gold Medal at the Atlanta Exposition of 1895. Valentien thus would have been an obvious choice for membership. This is particularly true since, in addition to being a fine sculptor, she had taken up painting in the summer of 1920 and had, by the end of the decade, developed into a fine landscape painter of the California Impressionist variety.

Anni Baldaugh (1881-1953), who had moved to San Diego from Pasadena in the late 1920s – perhaps encouraged to do so by the enthusiasm Reginald Poland had shown for her work – would also have been a fine candidate for membership. She painted strong, broadly sketched, gritty, and brightly, yet harmoniously, colored portraits and lands capes. Her *Donna*, acquired through Poland's efforts for the Fine Arts Gallery, is a fine example of the flair and daring of her portrait work, a wonderfully sympathetic character study of a modern young woman who, quite visibly bristles with intellectual vitality and imagination. The inherent psychological presence of this portrait is so strong that we seem to see a young woman, not of the Twenties, but of today. Baldaugh's landscapes, too, have a very contemporary quality. Her *Poplars*, for instance, now also part of the San Diego Museum's collection, is a work that could have been painted yesterday. In it, landscape becomes primarily a vehicle for the exploration of color, texture, and form while never relinquishing its local specificity.

Margot Rocle (1893-1981), like Baldaugh, had become a figure of considerable prominence in the Southern California art scene by 1930, with a series of strongly painted scenes of European peasant and village life, in which she combined a fine sense of composition and form, clearly inspired by Gauguin, with a very modern use of simplified volumes and a strong emphasis on rhythmic line.

In addition to Valentien, Baldaugh, and Rocle, there was, of course, Alice Klauber, who had probably done more for the promotion of art in San Diego than anyone else. She worked in broad strokes, allowing paint rather than outline to suggest form, and this gives canvases such as her *San Diego Harbor* a very contemporary quality. Her well-structured impressionist landscapes should have made her certainly as eligible for inclusion in the group as most of its actual members.

Other legitimate candidates for inclusion might have been Hope Mercereau Bryson (1887-1944), Annie Pierce (1877-1951), Martha Jones (1870-1945), Hazel Shoven (1884-1969), Sarah Truax (1872-1959), Ollie Montgomery Perry (1881-1964), and Elizabeth Sherman (b. 1896), who were all very active on the Southern California art scene during the Twenties. They were certainly good enough to be included regularly in juried exhibitions throughout California, and, for that matter, to serve on those same juries right alongside the all-male membership of the "Contemporary Artists of San Diego." Unfortunately, however, and clearly as a direct result of their marginalization, relatively little is, as yet, known about most of these women artists and their work.

Among the remaining members of the "Contemporary Artists" group, Elliott Torrey (1867-1949), a relative of the man who gave his name to the Torrey pine, also liked to paint marines, and did so with considerably greater success than Bonnet. He had followed a career trajectory not unlike that of Reiffel, having also been a frequent contributor to the national painting annuals before he arrived in San Diego – not long after first settling in Pasadena in 1923. His marines tended to be studies of wave and surf, constructed in an undulant, layering fashion clearly indebted to Reiffel, though not nearly as daring. He also liked to paint children, whose spontaneity he often captured quite successfully, first in a rather academic style, later in a much more broadly painted, almost calligraphic version of Impressionism.

Otto Schneider (1875-1950) is particularly intriguing for his almost chameleonic ability to shift styles. He began painting lands capes in a tonalist-impressionist manner under the influence of Twachtman, studying and painting in Buffalo during the same period Reiffel was there. In 1910 he went to Paris to study at the Academie Julian where he continued, sometimes quite successfully, to paint landscapes in a very Gallic impressionistic mode. He arrived in San Diego two years before Reiffel and became an instructor at the San Diego Academy of Fine Arts in Balboa Park, directed by Eugene and Pauline De Vol, which had succeeded the San Diego Art Academy, started in 1911 by Maurice Braun.

In San Diego Schneider continued to develop a progressively looser impressionist style, which by the late 1920s had begun to congeal into a calligraphic linearism not unlike that of Torrey's, and equally indebted to Reiffel, though Schneider's forms tended to be awkward and stiff. His work was very uneven, bouncing back and forth between an amateurish modulation of forms and a very shrewd sense of color.

In the long run a series of six large canvases, now owned by the city of San Diego, painted during the construction of Boulder Dam (Hoover Dam), will undoubtedly prove to have been among his best work. In these he combined an expressionist sense of industrial form influenced by the social realists of the Thirties, a Southwestern post-impressionist color sense consisting primarily of bright orange, ochre, and a wide range of dusty blues, and a now fully developed, virtually entirely two-dimensional emphasis on the delineation of simplified, monumental forms. This complicated mixture of influences, characteristic of the mood of the eclectic Thirties, ultimately produced a series of canvases with a very contemporary "post-modernist" feeling.

Alfred Mitchell (1888-1972) was, after Fries, the first of these artists to settle in San Diego. He arrived in 1908 and began to study with Maurice Braun in 1913, later also attending the Pennsylvania Academy of Fine Arts. Mitchell was essentially a realist painter who was, except in his earliest work, more influenced in his conception of the picturesque by the masters of the Pennsylvania school of landscape painting (and particularly Edward Redfield), than by Braun. This influence is most noticeable in his Eastern snow scenes but is also easily detectable in his Daniel Garber inspired cross-bay-view compositions of San Diego. Mitchell's paintings have a tendency to look like stage settings: seeing them one often gets the feeling that their true raison d'etre – the play for which they were designed – is missing. Images without eccentricity, compositions without bite, they remain much too often merely picturesque: nicely painted postcards which are sometimes, though not often enough, rescued from banality by strong, luminous color or by the painter's fondness for large, interlocking, single-hued planes of light and shade. In Mitchell's best work these qualities invite the viewer to think about landscape in abstract terms, thus allowing the interplay between form and content to become their real subject matter.

The youngest member of the group was Donal Hord (1902-1966), who arrived in San Diego in 1916 from the Midwest. He received his first training as a sculptor in the night school modeling class of Anna Valentien. Hord was a dionysiac, often esoteric, and always astonishing talent, who clearly was ecstatically in love with the masculine form, seeing it as emblematic of the elemental forces of nature. He tried to capture eternity by creating a sculptural mode in which the hardest rocks taken from the body of the earth might become the raw materials for a human form made infallible through the artist's superhuman efforts to transcend the flesh. "The artist in this, the extreme southwestern corner of the United States, lives in an environment that is concerned less with people and an industrialized landscape than with the strong light beating on ancient, granitic, and sparsely watered hills," he declared. "I learned to carve here in Southern California where sunlight is intense and shadows are harsh." He believed that to be a sculptor in such a primal environment one had to match force against force: "Stone teaches one thing to the artist – that agonies and fears and posturings should not be beaten into a boulder that has kinship only with serene eternity. Stone sculpture should not carry a shape foreign to the spirit of timelessness. The actual physical execution of sculpture in hard stone is long and arduous. Its shaping is timed by months rather than by days." In keeping with his theory of struggle, Hord despised the weakness of clay, was indifferent to limestone and marble and, whenever possible, worked only with obsidian, diorite, and granite.

Whatever one may think of the sculptor's fantasies of elemental force and the symphonies of bulging masculine muscle they engendered in his work, there can be no doubt that his unique conception of form, in combination with his extraordinary level of technical ability, made Hord an artist of national significance, as the Museum of Modern Art recognized when he was featured in its *Americans 1942* exhibition. The remarks by Hord quoted here are from his personal statement in the catalogue for that exhibition which also featured reproductions of his *Aztec* (1937) and several highly stylized Mexican peasant subjects. These, and other sculptures, such as his *Spring Stirring*, are simple, monumental forms carved painstakingly and with incredible elegance of detail from stones of immense weight. They are true masterpieces, works of lasting importance. As Homer Dana (Hord's co-worker and devoted friend for more than forty-five years) has pointed out: "They are not based on Indian legends nor are they ethnic types, but rather figures representing the seasons, the elements, and the moods of this country."

The emotional universality, and the psychological tensions embedded in these works make them as good as anything ever done by an American sculptor. In many of Hord's other works, however, subtlety of statement gives way to an extravagant Art Deco sensibility. When joined with the sculptor's appetite for muscular excess, that decorative impulse unfortunately frequently led to brilliantly crafted works of sensuous kitsch.

Everett Gee Jackson (b. 1900), represents the bridge between the "California Impressionist" sensibility predominating among the older members of the group, and the figurative, expressionist mood which was to pervade the American art world during the Thirties. After an initial flirtation with Impressionism, Jackson's work began to take on some of the linear precision of the American modernists of the Twenties and of such German expressionist realists as Christian Schad, although it is clear that Jackson, who had travelled widely in Mexico, had received his principal inspiration from Diego Rivera's linear modernist forms.

Under Rivera's influence Jackson moved away from landscape and began to develop a spare, quasi-documentary style whose realism was tempered by a sophisticated, cubist-inspired, flattened perspective achieved through minimal shading. This made his sharply delineated, angular forms dramatic participants in a figure-ground dialogue between interlocking two-dimensional planes. In these works colors tended to be subtle variations on a single hue. His subjects, too, gained a topicality usually shunned by his older San Diego colleagues: sailors on leave, fishermen, industrial sites. Cool, distant, and precise, their ironies are rather Kafkaesque in what was otherwise a predominantly Brechtian age.

During the later years of the Thirties, Jackson became strongly influenced by the monumental muralism of Orozco, whose fresco of Prometheus at Pomona, and whose contributions to the *New Masses* were easily accessible to Jackson even while tending to his teaching duties at San Diego State. Jackson's invited contribution to the contemporary art exhibition of the Golden Gate International Exposition of 1939 in San Francisco, *Embarkation*, is an intriguing, daringly composed, and prophetic, semi-abstracted representation of sailors embarking on a warship. As they enter into the metal monster which is to be their home, they seem to duck instinctively while passing under the threatening cannons of the ship, until their heads disappear between their shoulders. Their sailor's caps become pie-like shapes, as if flattened by the brute force of authority.

The work is painted in a manner closely approximating Orozco's charcoal-sketch method of delineating form. The subject matter of the painting would seem to indicate that Jackson was coming under the influence of Orozco's world view as well. But, as was to be the case with so many American artists, the coming of the second world war appears to have succeeded in changing all that.

Jackson began to concentrate more and more on the delineation of Mexican folk motifs. His work lost the declarative energy it had obtained during the Thirties, and his colors weakened. A disturbing pseudo-ethnicity, not unlike that of Jean Charlot, began to pervade his work, until his canvases came to resemble shelves in a museum of natural history on which nearly the entire range of Mexican folk culture was to be placed for safe keeping. Jackson's work of the Thirties, in contrast, continues to astonish with its immediate, expressionist energy.

Another San Diego painter who came into his stride during the 1930s is Ivan Messenger (1895-1983), who like Jackson, worked in the field of lithography in addition to being a painter. Messenger, who was born in Omaha, Nebraska, received a master's degree in languages from Stanford. He first studied painting with Henri de Kruif in Los Angeles and, after settling permanently in San Diego, he studied etching with Leslie Lee. By the mid-Twenties he had begun to exhibit locally, and when Reiffel arrived in town, Messenger became his student and friend. After Messenger and his father completed building a house near Julian in the late Twenties, Reiffel and his wife became frequent guests. The two painters did a great deal of sketching and plein air work together and at one time the Reiffels, who, since they arrived in San Diego had never been very far from indigence, stayed in the Julian house for about six months while Messenger and his wife Evelyn were travelling.

Messenger, who had a subtle and wicked sense of humor, was a superb observer of everyday life. He had a special knack for the representation of gesture. In one of his lithographs he caught a prim and proper lady, stiffly perched on a wagon under the eyes of thousands, trying desperately to maintain her composure while steering two show horses through their paces at a Coronado horse show. His paintings documented family picnics, freeway scenes, West-Indian women doing their washing, and the main street of Julian in 1935 caught on a lazy summer afternoon with old geezers snoozing in the sun and young ones tooling at their old jalopies. He liked better to paint the teeming throngs at the side-shows near the California-Pacific International Exposition of 1935 than the pomp and circumstance of the show itself. The hardships of the Depression years did not escape him and he caught the throngs at the State Emergency Relief Administration (SERA) as the unemployed and homeless waited for a chance to work.

Messenger's work is every bit as busy, calligraphically inventive, and colorful as that of Maurice Prendergast – to which it bears a close thematic and stylistic resemblance – though in an updated Thirties style. His forms have a cheerfully caricatural quality which allies them to those of comic strip artists such as George McManus whose work he obviously admired. This aspect of his sensibility injected joyful laughter into much of his oeuvre.

Messenger was also a great chronicler of the life of cats, whose relaxed, self-indulgent sense of being clearly spoke to him. Ironically it is primarily through his unpopulated landscapes, and a few affectionate but touristy views of San Diego's missions and parks, that he is still remembered, although these form by far the weakest link in his output.

In the early Thirties, under the influence of such figures as Baldaugh, Jackson, and Messenger, the artistic climate in San Diego was changing, along with that of the country as a whole, toward an eclectic humanist expressionism, which blended influences from modernism with a populist concern for "recognizable images." The local version of this movement took a perceptible leap forward in 1933 with the arrival of Belle Baranceanu whose art soon came to define the modernist temper in San Diego.

IV

The 1920s had been a period of consolidation and reconsideration in American art. The avant garde's move, during the 1910s, into cubist and futurist forms, and into such varieties of color abstraction as the synchromism of Stanton Macdonald Wright, attracted the attention of many of the talented younger painters, who proceeded – not to imitate these styles to the letter – but rather to adapt them to their own purposes. These painters developed variegated, eclectic modernist modes of expression in art. Their very real and lasting achievements, however, have until recently been all but buried in history as a result of the narrowly focused, authoritarian mentality that came to prevail in the American art world during the Fifties and Sixties. The argument was, essentially, that only actual examples and immediate prefigurations of post war abstraction should be regarded as "good" art.

During the Twenties a much more open and broadly creative approach prevailed. The younger painters liked to combine influences from Gauguin, Cezanne, and Fauvism, as well as from much earlier figures such as Giotto, El Greco, and the Mannerists, or from Asian and African art. The term "primitivism" became a designation of praise rather than of opprobrium. These artists did not militate against abstraction, as hostile post-war critics have insisted, but argued instead, quite justifiably, that they used the principles of abstract art in organizing their otherwise representational canvases. They never doubted the fact that they were "modernists."

Although one is hardly likely to discover this from a reading of the standard histories of twentieth century American art, which seem to hold to the position that Georgia O'Keeffe was the only woman worthy of note in the field of painting during this period, the Twenties and Thirties in fact produced a superb array of women artists whose work was at least as rich and imaginative as that of their male counterparts. Belle (Goldschlager) Baranceanu (1902-1988) was among the most brilliant of these adventurous early American modernists.

Born in Chicago, a few months after her parents' arrival from Rumania, she studied at the Minneapolis Art Institute and the Art Institute of Chicago. During 1927, and part of 1928, Baranceanu lived in Los Angeles. She then returned to Chicago, finally settling in San Diego in 1933.

Under the tutelage of her teacher (and, eventually, her lover) Anthony Angarola, she, and another student of Angarola's, William S. Schwartz, developed personal versions of Angarola's linear, expressionist mode of representation. Baranceanu had an uncanny ability to distill the forms and structures of the material world into compositions of essential line and color. In such early works as her *Leafbud* of 1925, she brought her work close to abstraction. Paintings such as this combine the close-up sensibility of O'Keeffe's flower studies with a forceful interest in the formal properties of color, plane, and line.

But Baranceanu's love for the shapes of nature made her turn away from complete abstraction toward the creation of canvases in which superbly controlled sequences of line recorded the volumes and textures of everyday experience. Equally comfortable with landscape, figure painting, and still-life, she brought her determinedly individualist sensibility to bear upon a portrait of her sister, painted in Los Angeles and shown that same year at the Los Angeles Museum's Annual American Painters and Sculptors exhibition under the title *The Yellow Robe* (a brilliant work, now hidden in the basement of the San Diego Museum of Art). In Baranceanu's composition the regal figure of her sister gains strength and independent authority from carefully balanced horizontal and vertical patterns of complementary color. These simplified forms and pure colors strongly anticipate Milton Avery.

The following year Baranceanu exhibited a view of Los Angeles from her hilltop house close to the downtown area. *From Everett Street* is very European in sensibility, although Baranceanu never visited Europe. In this work there is a striking stylistic affinity with some of the angular, stylized, flattened cityscapes Egon Schiele had been painting during the 1910s, although Baranceanu had, almost certainly, never seen these works of Schiele.

From Everett Street is part of a splendid series of paintings and lithographs produced by the young painter during her sojourn in Los Angeles. These paintings vary from Cezannesque explorations of the local landscape as a series of receding planes in subtly complementary blues and greens, to brilliantly colored industrial images whose conception parallels Charles Sheeler's explorations of geometric form in the American workplace. She was able to bring an angular poetry to the streets of the city and, in some of her delineations of the Hollywood Hills, she dramatically pitted the tensions of nature against the encroachment of city life in a manner not unlike the poetic semi-abstractions of Arthur Dove.

However, no matter what associations one may be tempted to make between Baranceanu's work and that of other American or European painters of her time, she was always, first and foremost, her own person. Her work is instantly recognizable as hers and all of it has the stamp of an extraordinarily creative and yet very carefully organized imagination. When she arrived in San Diego she was ready to become involved in a new phase of her development as an artist: mural painting, a form with which, under the influence of Rivera and Orozco, she had already begun to experiment in Chicago where, before her departure, she had developed quite a local reputation as a painter.

The timing of Baranceanu's arrival in San Diego was crucial to her subsequent development as a muralist. Preparations for the California-Pacific International Exposition, to be held in Balboa Park during 1935 and 1936, were already well underway and Baranceanu lost no time in securing commissions for a large mural depicting, in very Thirties fashion, *The Development of Man*, for the Palace of Education at the Fair (now the Balboa Club). This striking visual narration (one of only two of her murals still in situ at this writing), is, given its enormous proportions, a truly remarkable feat of coherent compositional organization. The mural's various narrative details are outlined in a flattened, linear manner, expressive of a near-abstract conception. Yet all these separate sections interact and arch inward, to form a superbly balanced and easily understandable delineation of humanity's great feats of artistic, intellectual, and industrial progress.

While she was completing her *Development of Man*, Baranceanu also won the competition for a fresco for the west entrance to the Fine Arts Gallery. The artist, who loved music, designed a Debussy-inspired, Matisse-like linear pattern of a nude young woman accompanied by a deer in a forest glade (now destroyed). Hazel Boyer Braun remarked in her "Comment on Art" column for the *San Diego Tribune* of May 18, 1935 that Baranceanu was "now the busiest girl in San Diego."

This was particularly true since she had also won a commission to paint a mural for the La Jolla post office, under the auspices of the Public Works of Art Project of the Works Progress Administration, a program which had been instituted late in 1933, the very year of her arrival in San Diego. The post office mural (still in situ) is a splendid example of Baranceanu's conception of landscape. It manages to fit a very wide, panoramic, stylized, yet instantly recognizable view of La Jolla into a very awkward and cramped space. A series of linear patterns, both angular and undulant, interact to reach a miraculous balance of form and line just above the door leading into the postmaster's office. Varieties of green, blue, and grey predominate in a composition which can be looked at with equal interest for its subject matter and for its patterns of abstract design.

The terrible ravages of the Great Depression made it clear to many, including many artists, that the American Dream of the self-made man was not what it might have seemed in an earlier time. They came to realize that you cannot attempt to pull yourself up by your own bootstraps if those in power have forced you to walk on bare feet. That realization made the prevailing contention that artists should only produce art for art's sake seem very hollow to many of the painters of the Thirties. Moreover, when the WPA established its "New Deal" for artists, many quite understandably felt called upon to express their gratitude to the common people, the fruits of whose labor were ultimately the source of this subsistence wage for needy artists. Where a fascination with industry and energy characterized the work of many artists in the Twenties, the common people and their plight now came to occupy the painters' attention.

The snobbish emphasis given by post-war art critics to abstraction, as the only "pure" art, has served to brand the populist concerns of the artists of the Thirties as "unsophisticated." The social concern and consciousness of place characterizing the work of many of these artists was equated with the mythic rural America of Thomas Hart Benton and Grant Wood and came to be summarily dismissed as "Regionalism." But there is a world of difference between the jingoistic conception of America, such as was to be found in the fairy-tale world of Benton and Wood, and the expressionist humanism of the social realist painters. The latter, inspired by a genuine understanding of the plight of the common people, followed the example of the great Mexican muralists in painting works which, while they maintained their inherent integrity as works of art, might yet be accessible to every one, be "recognizable images." It was the primary goal of these artists to demonstrate that in a humane society concerned with the development of a qualitatively better future a desire for beauty must coexist with a knowledge of pain.

The spirit of eclecticism which characterizes the Thirties is also expressed in the lively interest among artists for the work of folk artists, untrained, but dedicated to self-expression through art. In San Diego this interest led, through Elliott Torrey, to the discovery of the naive paintings of Josephine Joy (1869-1948) who had moved to San Diego in 1924. After her husband died in 1927 she had begun to paint. In 1936 she joined the California Art Project. Landscapes (Balboa Park, Mission Valley Farms) and fantasmagoric narratives were her subjects, meticulously detailed on a flat ground, virtually without any attempt at perspective. These images existed precariously on the picture plane, conveying the sense that everything on the canvas might, at any moment, slip down to the lower edge of the frame. Joy found enthusiastic supporters of her work in Lorser Feitelson, Roland McKinney, and Reginald Poland, who brought her work to the attention of Sidney Janis, and he included a chapter on her work in his book *They Taught Themselves, American Primitive Painters of the Twentieth Century* (1942). Joy won a prize at the 1940 Art Guild Exhibition for her painting *My Gift to You*, and in 1942 twelve of her paintings were exhibited at the Museum of Modern Art. That same year she left San Diego to return to the town of her birth, Peoria, Illinois, where she died six years later.

In San Diego, the early (mid-1934) roster of the Public Works of Art Project included some of the area's best artists: Belle Baranceanu, Charles Reiffel, Dorr Bothwell, Donal Hord, Foster Jewell, Elliott Torrey, and Sarah Truax – a sad indication of the correlation between true artistic independence and material poverty. The pay received by each artist was, at about 52 dollars a month, a bare subsistence wage, but it allowed them freedom to work in dignified poverty. Good art simply did not sell. Hazel Boyer Braun reported in her column of May 23, 1936 that in San Diego many of the artists who were not yet part of the federal relief programs "virtually have given away their work, have rented it to private homes for a few dollars a month and often sold their work on the monthly payment plan or have traded it for necessities."

By 1936, too, the State Emergency Relief Agency's curriculum project for the San Diego schools was employing 83 local artists. Ninety paintings by Reiffel alone were deposited with the local authorities. Baranceanu and Reiffel, moreover, were painting important murals for the local schools (all since destroyed or placed in storage – from whence several have only recently been rescued though the efforts of Bruce Kamerling of the San Diego Historical Society). Even in his old age, Reiffel managed to get into hot water with the local arbiters of taste. In 1940, 78 years old, he aroused the ire of several city council members over murals he had painted for the council's chambers. The *San Diego Union* of April 4, 1940, reported that several on the council had complained that Reiffel's murals were not "harmonious." A retired navy officer turned councilman, Herbert Fish, in particular, denounced the artist's rendering of battleships for a port scene as "terrible. They are out of proportion; they are grotesque." Reiffel was unperturbed and pasted a series of clippings about the controversy in his scrapbook. Two years later he was dead. San Diego forgot about him. City and county officials stored or destroyed his work and "sophisticated" art lovers complained about the absence of "quality art" in the region.

V

With the advent of World War II and the deaths of Charles Fries, Maurice Braun, and Reiffel by 1942, the early period of San Diego art was coming to a decisive close. The Thirties in particular had been an exciting, busy, though obviously not very lucrative, period for San Diego artists who in the eclectic spirit of the time had learned to coexist, interact, and exchange ideas in a new and exhilarating fashion. A charming newspaper article by Etta Mae Wallace (later "Ettilie" Wallace) from around 1937, preserved in Reiffel's scrapbook, depicts Baranceanu, Charles Reiffel, and Dan Dickey, certainly artists of widely divergent styles and generations, doodling together on paper napkins at a chinese dinner in the Spanish Village Art Center, discussing methods and exchanging anecdotes.

The Spanish Village section of Balboa park had become an art center in 1936 upon the close of the Exposition, at the instigation of Sherman Trease, Hazel Shoven, and Leda Klauber. Artists such as Anni Baldaugh established studios there and participated in a lively dialogue with others. Ivan Messenger's wife, Evelyn, ran an arts and crafts shop at the center where she also exhibited the work of painters such as Reiffel and her husband. Another art center, Los Surenos, had found space in Old Town. The eclectic temper of the American art scene had led to the establishment of separate juries for "conservative," "centrist," and "progressive" categories of painting at the major national annuals. Following this trend, the San Diego Art Guild in 1934 offered prizes for "center," "right," and "left" styles of painting. Clarence Hinkle won among those judged to be representative of the status quo in art (center), while Braun was first among the conservatives. The "leftist" prize went to Tom Lewis of Los Angeles and Laguna Beach who was to move to San Francisco in 1935.

The Forties were clearly a period of transition. Representation still predominated, but now amid the return to prominence of strict "art for art's sake" convictions, the latter – no doubt at least partially instigated by a swelling tide of wartime patriotism and post-war McCarthyism – made it dangerous to express social convictions in art. Abstraction, though, at first, itself often suspected by the ideologues of Americanism of harboring none but dangerous subversives, soon became an attractive refuge from the all-too-easily interpretable messages of representational art.

During the 1940s Dan Dickey (1910-1961) was generally regarded as the most progressive painter in town. He was born in New York City, studied at the Art Institute of Chicago, and came to San Diego in 1935. He participated in the Federal Art Project from 1937-1939, directed at this time in Southern California by Stanton MacDonald Wright and Lorser Feitelson, with whom he felt an artistic kinship. Dickey's work was heavily imbued with the transitional features of Forties art. Though he was primarily a figure painter, his figures were, like Donal Hord's sculptures, always symbolic. In addition they were introspective, moody, usually female, and heavily under the influence of Picasso's blue and rose periods. Dickey's line drawings seem often especially close to Picasso's conception, while in his paintings his own voice tends to predominate in the monumentality of his forms, their weighty three-dimensionality, and their often exquisite dark – yet luminous – tonalities. In essence Dickey was a poet, a painter of visual elegies in which he captured stillness, sadness, and the inexorable passing of time. In his use of line he was "post-war," in his forms he courted abstraction, but in his preference for introspection and in the uneasy humanism of his imagery, he remained rooted in the Twenties and Thirties.

The rigid institutionalization of abstraction during the post-war years did incalculable damage to the creative spirit of many of the serious painters who had matured during the eclectic artistic environment of the years before the war. Often they tried to force their very personal styles into an abstract mold, with disastrous results. Dan Dickey spent the last decade of his life fruitlessly attempting to give abstract expression to his reflective humanist sensibility, but most of his work in this fashion is listless, unformed, forced. Baranceanu returned to abstraction in the early Forties, but her strength of line was more suited to representation and her late experiments with "non-representational" art lack the strength of her earlier work. She must have realized so herself, for she virtually abandoned painting in the early Fifties to devote herself to teaching.

A similar trajectory was followed by William Newport Goodell (b. 1908), who had developed a highly impastoed style of figure and still-life painting which won him the First Hallgarten Prize of the

National Academy of Design in 1933. Goodell's method of using thin streaks of purple, red, or green, in each case mixed with white, to suggest shading in the outlining of forms, uncannily prefigures Wayne Thiebaud. But when he arrived in La Jolla in 1950 Goodell could not find a public for his work and, like Baranceanu, was unwilling to compromise his vision. He gave up painting altogether.

Only Beatrice Levy (1892-1974), a Chicago artist who had already exhibited some very Whistleresque prints at the 1915 Panama-Pacific Exposition and who had developed a strong, personal style of landscape painting during the Twenties and Thirties, proved able to adapt fully to the new art when she moved to La Jolla in 1942. Her abstract work of the Forties and Fifties is subtle, beautifully organized, and full of complex textures and shading. Fred Hocks (1886-1981) was another painter whose modernist sensibility had first been stirred on seeing the Futurist works which were exhibited at the Panama-Pacific. He had lived in the San Diego area since the early Thirties and also became an early convert to abstraction. Like Levy he was able to do convincing work in this field.

The San Diego painter who perhaps stands poised most securely between the art scene of the Thirties and the post-modern temper – that new eclecticsm so evident among the contemporary artists featured in his book – is Jean Swiggett, whose work may be said to represent both past and present. Born, like Dan Dickey, in 1910, Swiggett was brought to Long Beach, California, from the Midwest when he was two. He attended Chouinard in 1931, then studied at San Diego State with Everett Jackson, graduating in 1934. During the next ten years he worked as a painter and muralist in the Long Beach-Los Angeles area, first on the Federal Art Project, later independently. In 1946 he joined the faculty of San Diego State where he remained until his retirement in 1977.

Swiggett's style of painting is firmly grounded in the eclectic realism of the Thirties, and in his early work the influence of Everett Jackson is clearly noticeable. A sometimes ironic, but more often ambiguously obsessive, fascination with the objects and shapes of the material world runs through the entire body of his work. A subtle suggestion of the existence of symbolic relationships among the objects he depicts takes his paintings out of the realm of simple photographic realism. Forging ahead on his own, he developed ever more meticulous patterns of naturalistic representation, working in isolation through the abstract years, as well as the years of the "new realism" of the Seventies. His style may at first suggest surrealism, but it has remained too precisely a record of the everyday to be surrealistic in effect. There is in his work too great a taxidermic fondness for the objects he portrays, and not enough fear. Viewers and critics have tried to cope with his large, strange, yet very sensibly arranged, cold and classical looking canvases with their hard out lines and their sometimes almost blinding colors. Most often they have dismissed him. But Swiggett has continued to paint in his own manner, and now, it seems, fashion in art is finally getting ready to catch up with him. The critics have found a word for him. What, after all, better defines Swiggett's style of painting than the term "double coding?" Whose work better expresses that ironic sincerity, abstract realism, cool line and hot color, distant eroticism, and mock-historical emphasis on "timeless" immobility which characterizes the now stylish "Post-Modernist" movement in the arts?

Indeed, his work in many ways closely resembles, but long predates, that of the current star of official Post-Modernism in painting, Carlo Maria Mariani. Swiggett was out of fashion for decades, and his work, like most of the art produced by San Diego's earlier painters has, almost as a matter of course, been dismissed as "provincial." But now that the future seems to be catching up with him his art is beginning to look very "sophisticated" again.

As Christian Brinton already pointed out more than seventy years ago, the true provincials are those who let fashion dictate what they must like, who rarely make their own decisions, and who are unable to see the world of art that flourishes in their own back yard. For such narrowly determined sophisticates, even the work of San Diego's very best early artists, Maurice Braun, Charles Reiffel, Belle Baranceanu, Donal Hord, and Dan Dickey, will have to remain of no importance – at least, that is, until East Coast critics rediscover them, or new fashions in art revalue their work. Then the San Diego Museum of Art, which currently does not deign to put the work of any of these local artists on permanent display, will undoubtedly take their legacy out of storage. After all, even true provincialism has its seasons.

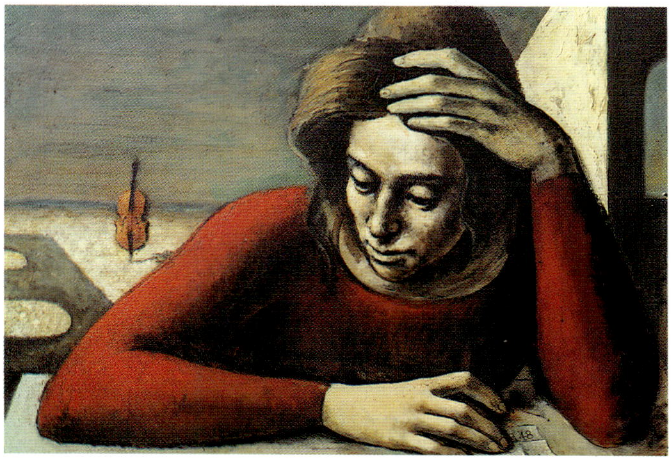

Dan Dickey, *Woman in Red*, 1948, 20″×30″, o/board

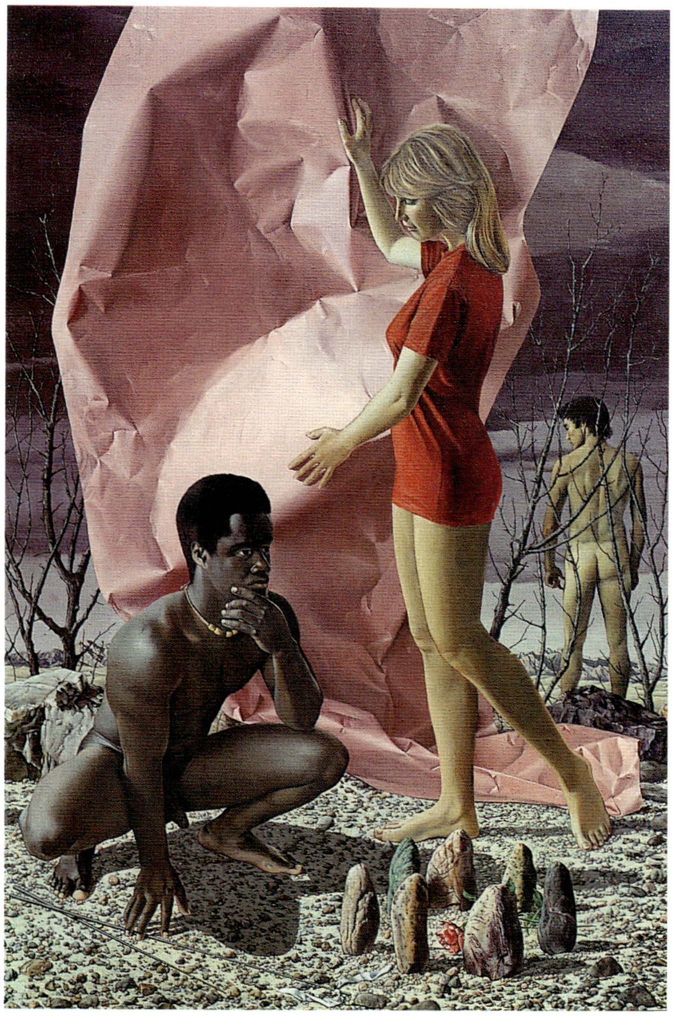

Jean Swiggett, *Mythic Circle*, 1975-76, 72″×48″, o/c

N.B.: Representative works by most of the painters discussed here can be found at the San Diego Historical Society, in many local private collections, and, as noted, in storage at the San Diego Museum. Bruce Kamerling, Curator of Collections at the Historical Society, has, for many years, been the principal champion of early San Diego art. He has done superb work in documenting and preserving the work of these pre-war painters, and I am heavily indebted to his expertise and cooperation. Martin Petersen, of the San Diego Museum of Art, has also done valuable work in this area. Much of their research has been published in the *San Diego Historical Society Quarterly* over the past decade, and anyone interested in the early history of San Diego art will find an ample documentation of the subject in the pages of this journal. I would also like to thank George Stern, who allerted me to the existence of Charles Reiffel's scrapbook, and who, more importantly, rescued it from possible destruction.

– Bram Dijkstra, February 1988

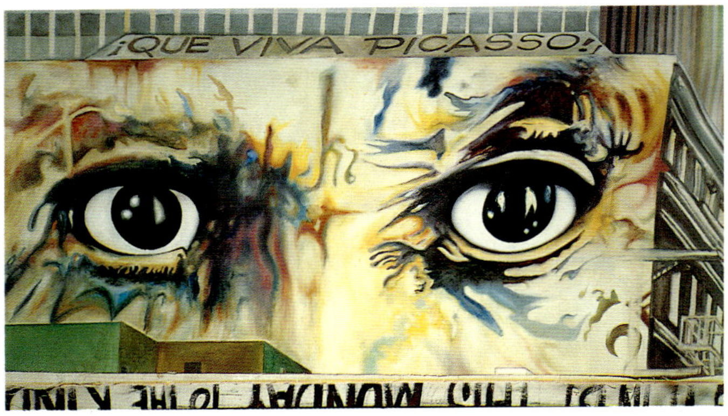

Mario Torero, *Picasso's Eyes*, acrylic/canvas billboard, 2'×6', 1986

SINCE 1950

Stories of San Diego's slow cultural leak have become part of its folklore. Martha Alf's success in Los Angeles and New York and John Baldessari's move from Southwestern College in Chula Vista to the cover of *Artforum* could have been chapters in any other city history that is not New York or Los Angeles.

But these stories of exodus are more than balanced by the number of recognized artists who have been drawn to San Diego and remain here. For them San Diego offered the last fresh cultural soil in which to grow without fighting the cold temperatures of New York or the traffic and pollution of Los Angeles. This was a last frontier where they could escape the social expectations and pressures of the larger art world, but still be within a few commuting hours of Los Angeles. A nucleus of established artists were brought in by the University of California, San Diego when its Visual Arts department was launched in 1967. As it grew, UCSD helped breathe life into an art community unevenly nourished by San Diego State University, the San Diego Museum of Art, and the La Jolla Museum of Contemporary Art. Although there was little direct UCSD involvement in San Diego's art concerns, the city's larger body of artists were stimulated by what "those guys on the hill" were doing.

The evolution of art in San Diego since the 1950s has been sporadic and uncertain, a holdover phenomenon akin to the regionalism in the 1930s and 1940s. As in any growth process, many individuals and institutions have played roles in the on-going, sometimes painful, formation of an art community trying to find its place in a city more obstreperous than charitable.

THE MUSEUMS

Since the 1950s the national media has enlarged its interest in, and coverage of, art and artists, thus stimulating social awareness, piquing the curiosity of a growing art audience. Expectations for museums to stay abreast of contemporary art have increased. Higher standards in collecting, connoisseurship, and conservation, accompanied by skyrocketing facilities and administrative costs, have forced museum trustees to look carefully at ways to boost their attendance figures. Public education programs have been beefed up; crews of docents stand ready to shepherd and teach. To attract larger numbers of presumably more sophisticated art lovers, impressive shows known as "blockbusters" have become popular. Commensurately, museums have learned to deal with the larger crowds; like Disneyland, long lines are a tolerated annoyance. All of this indicates one thing: growing interest means expansion and that means more public and private funding.

San Diego museums have not been immune to this national trend toward packaged art. To meet the high costs of shipping works and fabricating exhibits, museum boards have looked to their administrators to perform magic. In the post-1950s scenario in San Diego, for example, newly appointed directors first commit themselves to energetic fundraising. Then follows the new addition. In a half dozen years or so, as if expendable, the director moves on and, with his own brand of leadership, tackles the needs of the next beleagured museum. Personal style and taste are the earmarks of the system. Over the past thirty years art institutions have been impacted in this manner, resulting in continued expansion.

THE SAN DIEGO MUSEUM OF ART (Fine Arts Gallery)

The city's oldest art museum – originally called the Fine Arts Gallery – was opened in 1926 with Dr. Reginald Poland as its director. In 1950 he retired and was replaced by Thomas B. Robertson who served until 1955. Warren Beach was then appointed and he effectively guided the Balboa Park facility through difficult changes in size and scope, though not without several serious conflicts. Beach was replaced by Henry Gardiner in 1969.

As early as 1959, art patrons Anne and Amy Putnam were concerned about administrative changes at the Fine Arts Gallery. With San Diego architects Frank L. Hope and Associates, they began discussions on a $1.250 million plan for a private museum. It was to be known as the Timken Gallery, opening its doors in 1965 at its Balboa Park location adjacent to The Fine Arts Gallery. Earning its reputation as a "jewel" of a museum, the Timken maintains a permanent collection of fine Italian, French, Spanish, Dutch, and Flemish paintings, as well as three hundred or so Russian icons from the 17th and 18th centuries. Many well known works at the Timken have previously been on loan to the The National Gallery in Washington, D.C., The Metropolitan Museum in New York, The Art Institute in Chicago, the Fogg Museum at Harvard University, and at San Diego's Fine Arts Gallery.

Despite the loss of many prestigious works to the Timken next door, the Fine Arts Gallery opened a new West Wing in 1966. Designed by San Diego Architects Robert Mosher and Roy Drew, the $1.654 million, 50,0000 square foot addition included a library and an auditorium. The exhibition space for the permanent collection and for future contemporary acquisitions was also extended. The slender concrete columns and decorative fence on the exterior were designed and executed by Malcolm Leland, an artist currently living in the border town of Potrero. He is also the creator of the Civic Center's Bow Wave fountain.

Martin Petersen, a graduate of the University of Iowa with an additional degree from UCLA, was given his first museum position as the educational curator under Beach in 1957. Petersen stayed on and is currently curator of American Art. He has been with the museum more than thirty years.

Harvard-trained Henry Gardiner followed Beach as director from 1969 to 1979. He immediately oversaw the completion of the Asian Courtyard with the assistance of Asian Art curator Lennox Tierney. With assistant director Ron Hickman, now director of the Phoenix Museum, he completed the 25,000 square foot sculpture garden in 1972. It was landscaped by architects Wimmer and Yamada and houses works by Henry Moore, Louise Nevelson, and Barbara Hepworth.

In 1979 the Fine Arts Gallery changed its name to the San Diego Museum of Art, forced Gardiner's resignation, and moved from Gardiner's conservative style to the innovative approach of a young Steven Brezzo. Gardiner had recently hired Brezzo away from the La Jolla Museum of Contemporary Art where he was filling his first curatorial museum position.

Brezzo's directorship at SDMA was soon focused on enlarging the museum's financial base of operations. He and his wife Dagmar Grimm, a public relations director at UCSD, brought a social thrust to the Museum aimed directly at attracting a young audience. Brezzo originated several popular exhibits including "The Muppets," "The Cowboy," the illustrations of Dr. Seuss (La Jolla resident Theodor Geisel), and the Laurent de Brunhoff illustrations from the Babar children's book. Travelling exhibits like the Peruvian Gold collection and "American Women Artists 1830-1930" found appeal for all ages.

In the early 1980s, when other U. S. museums were beginning to develop exhibition policies sensitive to the artists of their community, The San Diego Museum of Art made several moves to lessen the visibility of the contemporary San Diego artist. The Art Sales and Rental Gallery, which had been showing the juried work of local artists from San Diego and Los Angeles, was phased out. The popular Allied Craftsmen exhibit which had been held annually since 1949 – showing such artists as Svetozar "Toza" Radakovich,

Tom Hatten, Larry Hunter, Irina and Erik Gronborg, Joe Nyiri, and Phyllis Wallen – was also discontinued in 1979 by Brezzo. The annual juried exhibition of the Artists Guild (a 64-year-old, 250-member organization formed to support the museum) was relegated to a minor space. The annual "Young Artists" exhibition of San Diego's school children has, nevertheless, continued.

Under former curator Grant Holcomb III a few exhibits in the early 1980s highlighted the work of contemporary San Diego artists, including an installation by Patricia Patterson and another by Ann Inman and Robert Bradford, visiting British artists-in-residence at SDSU. Otherwise the museum has been unresponsive to the needs of the San Diego art community despite the fact that its widely acknowledged artistic talent is probably in its richest period.

THE LA JOLLA MUSEUM OF CONTEMPORARY ART (La Jolla Art Center)

Built on a bluff overlooking the Pacific Ocean, and fronted on Prospect Street, the La Jolla Art Center opened in 1941. Its clean lines were the concept of Irving Gill, an architect who designed it originally as a home for Ellen Browning Scripps in 1915.

On opening, the Center offered art classes and housed an eclectic collection of gifts. Patrick Malone was the first director from 1955 to 1959. Although he garnered the support of the distinguished art collector and actor, Vincent Price, Malone was regarded as disorganized and controversial by most of the board members. Described by arts writer James Britton, Malone "unquestionably put first emphasis on the work of the experimental, the living, breathing, and bleeding artists. He was most at home with . . . people who shrugged off the pretensions of organized society." (*San Diego Magazine*, May 1959).

After Malone was forced to resign, Don Brewer served as director from 1959 to 1968. Brewer, a shy man who was a painter, initially worked as registrar at the Art Center in 1951 and became a curator under Malone in 1955. Another artist, Guy Williams, was considered for the position but, typically, moved to Los Angeles to further his painting career.

Under Brewer the museum expanded, adding Sherwood Hall auditorium and twelve huge classrooms. On the school faculty were artists who are now familiar names: Fred Holle, Malcolm McClain (who writes as Mac McCloud), Sheldon Kirby, and Guy Williams. Of the teachers at the La Jolla Art Center only Rhoda Lopez, a ceramist, remained in San Diego when the Art Center merged with UCSD Extension in 1964. This move precipitated major changes in philosophy and atmosphere at the Center.

In 1966 the name was changed to The La Jolla Museum of Art, a decision based on Brewer's determination to attract more significant exhibits. As he was departing in 1968 to take a position in Fresno, Lynn Fayman died. Fayman, a supporter of the visual arts and a respected photographer, was long active as a La Jolla Museum trustee. His views on the museum's possibilities were perpetuated and realized by his youthful and energetic wife, Danah Fayman.

From 1969 to 1972 Thomas Tibbs served as the museum's director. He was assisted by Lawrence Urrutia, who succeeded him as interim director. In 1971, under Tibbs, the name was changed to The La Jolla Museum of Contemporary Art and the exhibition focus was narrowed to art since the 1950s. One of the more memorable exhibits during this period was "Earth: Animal, Vegetable, and Mineral" (1971) which included works by Guy and Laddie John Dill, Vija Celmins, and Newton Harrison. The local press, shocked by the new, denounced it as "criminal."

When Sebastian "Lefty" Adler became director in 1973, "controversial" soon became the common description of the museum's new head. Unconventional in his approach, Adler began acquiring Minimalist art, an art movement little understood locally but which soon contributed to building the museum's national and international reputation. In the 1970's the collection reportedly grew from an estimated value of $500,000 to $2 million, an astounding 400 percent increase.

In the mid-1970s, under Adler, the museum underwent an extensive $3.5 million expansion. San Diego architects Mosher, Drew, and Watson executed a design which would expand the facilities from 3000 to 13,000 square feet. This included raising ceilings five feet to accommodate large scale works. The upgraded museum opened with a Sol LeWitt exhibition, followed by solo exhibitions of artists Agnes Martin, Craig Kauffman, Charles Garabedian, Leo Rabkin, Robert Smithson, and Christo.

When the long standing Art Sales and Rental Gallery was discontinued, just previous to the museum's redesign, there followed no clear policy for showing the work of San Diego artists. Locals Robin Bright, Russell Baldwin, Faiya Fredman, Russell Forester, Reesey Shaw, Toza Radakovich, and others, were instead selected by Adler for modest one person shows.

Adler became known for his shocking and autocratic style, depending heavily on staff for writing the catalogues his curating demanded. He had an undeniable ability to pick talent and gave many young curators their first museum positions. Among these were: Richard Armstrong, who eventually became a curator at the Whitney Museum of American Art in New York; Christopher Knight, who became an award-winning art critic for the *Los Angeles Herald Examiner*; Steven Brezzo, who became director of the San Diego Museum of Art; Martha Winans, who had formerly directed Heron Gallery of Purdue and Indiana universities and is presently director of the Evanston Art Center in Illinois; Robert McDonald, who became director of the deSaisset Museum of Santa Clara University in northern California; David Lewinson, who became an art critic for *San Diego Magazine* and other publications; Burnett Miller, who directs Burnett Miller Gallery in Los Angeles; and Lynda Forsha, who began as a registrar and is currently a curator at the Museum.

Adler was forced to resign in mid-1983. Backed by museum trustees Danah Fayman and Vance Kondon, he was chosen to direct the San Diego Art Center, a short-lived attempt to create a center for the arts downtown. Plagued by financial problems and a frustrating search for a suitable space, the Center closed its temporary Horton Plaza facility and floated uncertainly in limbo without a director. As of this writing a lecture series continues and fundraising events are held in hopes of reopening the Center.

At the end of 1983 Hugh Davies became director of the Museum. As former head of the art gallery of the University of Massachesetts in Amherst, Davies brought to the museum a more scholarly approach. In an effort to meet the needs of the community, especially its artists, one of his first exhibits was the quickly assembled "A San Diego Exhibition: Forty-Two Emerging Artists" (1985) which elicited the wrath of numerous highly visible and vocal artists who had been overlooked. Reaction took the form of "salon de refusees" style exhibits which were quickly organized by curator and educator Ellen Phelan and artist Marjorie Nodelman to draw attention to the number and quality of artists in San Diego. This drew wide media attention because the exhibition focused on the lack of an ongoing museum policy reponsive to the local art scene.

Davies was able to effect some of Adler's dreams, such as the development of annex spaces downtown to access a wider audience and mount wider varieties of exhibits. From 1986 to 1987, "Parameters 8" was established in a modest space as proof of the Museum's desire to mount cutting edge shows. It was replaced by a 1000 square foot, second story space on "G" Street called "LJMCA Downtown" which opened with an architectural installation by San Diego artist James Skalman. LJMCA Downtown has plans to continue including artists from the community in its scheduling.

The museum in La Jolla is currently planning a major expansion designed by the noted architect Robert Venturi. The grand opening is scheduled for 1991, the museum's fiftieth anniversary.

THE MUSEUM OF PHOTOGRAPHIC ARTS

The most recent addition to the city's museums is The Museum of Photographic Arts. Originating as the Center for Photographic Arts, spearheaded by Danah Fayman, it functioned for eleven years as a "museum without walls" and sponsored photographic exhibits in various places, including the La Jolla Museum. Then, in 1983, the Center found a home in Balboa Park and opened under the directorship of Arthur Ollman, well-known photographer.

Exhibitions which have received the attention of *Time Magazine* and other national press include the works of Ansel Adams (1984), an exhibit entitled "Arnold Newman: Five Decades" (a 1986 travelling show originating in San Diego), and "William Klein: An American in Paris" (1987).

Among the local photographers included in group shows at the Museum are: Barry Bell, Faiya Fredman, Harley Gaber, Suda House, Pablo Mason, Duncan McCosker, Han Nguyen, Philipp Scholz Rittermann, and David Wing.

ART GALLERIES

In the 1970s and 1980s watching the openings and closings of San Diego art galleries was like watching life signs on a respirator. Each sporadic blip brought new hope, attracting art-starved audiences to crowded openings. But since the city's more affluent collectors were already purchasing San Diego's top artists from Los Angeles and New York dealers, many San Diego galleries, thus bypassed, were struggling for their existence. Though this phenomenon was only part of the problem leading to gallery failure, it is worth mentioning a few dedicated survivors who made a mark in the community: The Thomas Jefferson Gallery, Mary Moore Gallery, and the Scott Youman Gallery, all centered in La Jolla in the early 1970s; the Casat Gallery, Wenger Gallery (now in Los Angeles), Sedar/Creigh Gallery, Triforium Gallery, Thomas Neumaier Gallery, Celebrations Gallery, Deicas Art, and the Maple Gallery, all short-lived in the 1980s; and the more recent galleries like Quint Gallery (showing Manny Farber, Ming Murray, Italo Scanga, Ernest Silva, Peter Stearns, and others), Patty Aande Gallery (which included Janet Cooling, Amanda Farber, Gillian Theobald, Wick Alexander, and others), Natalie Bush Gallery (which featured Hispanic artists), and Anuska Gallery (which featured Marjorie Nodelman, Philipp Scholz Rittermann, Deborah Small, and Erika Suderberg).

As of this writing Thomas Babeor Gallery and Gallery Eight (both of La Jolla), Installation Gallery, Spectrum Gallery (an artists's cooperative), Sushi, Inc., Wita Gardiner Gallery, and Dietrich Jenny Gallery (all downtown), and Henry Vincent Gallery (formerly Nivada Gallery), are the main sources of cutting-edge art in San Diego, a small minority of the hundred plus galleries listed each week in San Diego's newspapers.

The San Diego Art Institute cannot be ignored as another part of local history. This gallery space, which fronts on the southeast corner of the house of Charm, Balboa Park, serves a five hundred member group of artists living within the county. It emerged in 1941 as the San Diego Business Men's Art Club and became the San Diego Men's Art Institute in 1951. Shortly thereafter it began including women as associate members. In 1953 the city provided the present 4,800 square foot facility which faces the San Diego Museum of Art. Two years later the name was changed to the San Diego Art Institute.

Under the direction of Leafy Mayhew (1970 - 1977) and Shirley Viennese (1977 - present), the Art Institute has presented and promoted rather uneven exhibitions of juried contemporary art ranging from student illustration to truly innovative painting and sculpture. Until the mid-1980s the Institute offered art classes, but inadequate heating and limited upstairs space forced a discontinuance of the school. Occasionally, over the years, the Institute has brought in a prestigious juror/curator such as Henry Hopkins of the San Francisco Museum of Art and Richard Koshalek of the Los Angeles Museum of Contemporary Art. Among the artists who have shown in the Art Institute's juried and invitational shows are Vicki Cole, Jesus Dominguez, John Edwards, Tom Frankovich, Beth King, Hiroshi Miyasaki, Ellen Phillips, Richard Allen Morris, Allan Morrow, Barbara Weldon, Michael Wheeldon, Marie and Ed Wordell, and W. Haase Wojtyla. It has continued to be one of the few galleries where both younger and mature artists can show together and be exposed to a wide audience. Art Institute attendance has been counted at more than 350,000 visitors annually.

These, then, were the only galleries – other than the museums, community colleges, and the Jewish Community Center – with a reputation for exhibiting the area's best contemporary artists. The universities later opened their upgraded gallery spaces – UCSD's Mandeville Gallery (1974), directed by Gerry McAllister, and the San Diego State University Gallery (1977).

THE PRESS

Commiserating over the lack of public support for their art, artists and artist's groups sporadically point to poor coverage by the local press as the underlying source of their recognition problem.

"The critic analyzes works of art, evaluates them, sometimes just calls them nasty and lets it go. But if he's a thoughtful critic he indicates what he finds favorable or unfavorable in the work of art and points out good things that the artist himself may not have known, at least that the audience probably would not have known without the sensitivity of the critic," according to John Hospers, philosopher of art and aesthetics from the University of Southern California. Using this standard, there was plenty to complain about.

San Diego Magazine consistently ran noteworthy art features and stories relevant to the city's museums and their personalities. Writers James Britton and Marilyn Hagberg were among the staff from the 1950s to the mid-1970s who showed insight and style. *San Diego Magazine's* monthly format, however, provided a bare minimum, offering only a cursory taste of what was being offered in the local scene.

Leadership at the Copley newspapers – *The San Diego Union* and *The San Diego Tribune* – had no understanding of the need to have writers trained in art history and criticism. The *Tribune* assigned underqualified beat reporters to be art critics until the late 1970s. Richard Reilly, chief curator of the James S. Copley Library from 1966 to the present, was assigned double duty, acting as art critic for the *Union* from 1974 to 1983. It was a position he was widely known to feel uncomfortable with and which often took him to other cities looking for art he could review.

Conservative art coverage reflected more appreciation for the traditional landscapes, wildlife paintings, and Western art of local artists Frederic and Eileen Whitaker and Olaf Weighorst than the abstract and non-objective art that was the focus of art magazine criticism in major cities.

The establishment of *The Los Angeles Times* San Diego County Edition in 1978 inspired an interest in better art coverage for San Diego. A call was put out by the *Times* for knowledgeable art writers and in 1978 Elise Miller and I were among the first to cover the visual arts for them. The policy to review only, not to criticize, was restricted to exhibits not "important" enough to be covered by the regular *Times* art critics William Wilson and Suzanne Muchnic.

Miller reviewed for the *Los Angeles Times* San Diego County edition (1978 to 1982), as well as *San Diego Magazine* (1978 to 1983) and *Art News* (1982 to 1984), until she took a full time position in Publications at SDSU. Following Elise Miller were a string of writers including Roger Rose, Jeff Kelley, Robert McDonald, and Leah Ollman.

Keeping up with what *Tribune* editor Neil Morgan called "The Outatown Times," both Copley newspapers finally acted to hire qualified art writers. Morgan had become associate editor of the *Tribune* in 1977 and, with editor Barbara Herrera, recognized the need to improve arts coverage. I was brought in by the *Tribune* to consult and later write an art column and various features (1979 to 1981), and was followed by artist/writer Mark-Elliot Lugo. Only recently were well-trained art critics Robert Pincus of the *Union* and Susan Freudenheim at *Tribune* installed as full-time staff.

THE ARTISTS

Just when it seemed San Diego art and artists were never to fly, unconventional, influential forces on the San Diego art scene began lobbying for increased support in the arts and for stepped up interaction among artists. These artists were soon encouraging each other to be more vocal and politically involved, joining forces in an effort to change the old patterns of passive interest. Small arts organizations came forth to lobby, as did medium and large institutions. So many desperately needed increased funding. COMBO (Combined Arts and Education Council of San Diego County, 1964), a private fundraising group, was forced to relinquish the control it had exerted over distribution of the city's T.O.T. tax fund allocation earmarked for the arts. This was primarily due to the work of PAAB (Public Arts Advisory Board) and of Jennifer Spencer, chair of COVA (Combined Organizations for the Visual Arts). Since visual artists and smaller performing arts organizations are now learning to more effectively win their share of the funding pie, which heretofore went to the more dominant performing arts groups and larger institutions, the visual arts in San Diego may now begin to flourish without affecting the needs of the old line organizations. The new Cultural Arts Commission, with broadened fund-raising skills, will be the tool for bringing the city and the county abreast of other major metropolitan areas. As this goes to press, the San Diego Cultural Arts Commission greets its new director, Victoria Hamilton, former director of commissions in Santa Barbara and the State of Washington.

In the 1970s and 1980s, increased networking within arts groups and between individual artists gradually acheived momentum. In addition to small supportive groups of artists, such as the Afro-American Artists Coalition headed by artist Jihmye Collins, there have been several major forces producing significant change in the city's art. Among these are:

CENTRO CULTURAL DE LA RAZA

An artist's collective known as Toltecas en Aztlan was organized by Salvador Torres in 1969 out of the frustration Mexican-American artists felt trying to break into established art institutions. In 1970 the city gave this group the Park Boulevard watertank in Balboa Park to use as their permanent home. They named it Centro Cultural de la Raza. Both emerging and established artists are given exhibitions here, including performing arts programs and literary events. From the beginning the Centro aimed at attracting works related to the Chicano cultural community, involving artists living from the border region all the way to Los Angeles. San Diego artists exhibiting in the Centro include David Avalos, Mario Lara, Lourdes Becker, Aida Manzanillas-Doyle, Victor Ochoa, and Roberto Salas.

Founder Salvador Torres and Mario Acevedo Torero, long active in the cultural development of San Diego, have occasionally exhibited in the Centro group shows. Besides establishing the Centro Cultural de la Raza, for example, Torres was also the initiator of the Chicano Park murals beneath the Coronado Bridge, now a San Diego landmark. He received his art training at the California College of Arts and Crafts in Oakland and one of his early project ideas was to create, with his fellow artists, the attention-getting wooden sculptures on Interstate 80 in the San Francisco Bay mud flats near Berkeley. A committed artist, Torres continues to work in his Logan Heights studio. He is chairperson of the Chicano Park Arts Council, working to preserve these community murals and to eventually realize his dream of a waterfront Chicano art center.

Mario Torero has also drawn attention to the talents of the Mexican-American and American Indian artists in the larger Southwest region, from Los Angeles to Taos. With his wife, former SDSU professor Rita Sanchez Acevedo, Torero founded Solart Gallery in Golden Hills (1977 to 1980) which moved to 10th and "E" Streets downtown (1980 to 1981). They have been co-directors of Acevedo Gallery in Mission Hills since 1983, showing internationally respected Hispanic artists.

Torero's mural "Picasso's Eyes" (1978) was destroyed when the historical Knights of Pythias building – which also housed Community Arts – was torn down in 1982. His murals on the Estrada Court housing projects (1974 and 1978) were featured with photographs in *Time* (April 7, 1975) and *Newsweek* (January 1, 1989). Other mural commissions include works done in Amsterdam, San Francisco, Los Angeles, and St. Paul, Minnesota. Torero's Martin Luther King mural at 26th and Market Streets is his latest work. The son of artist Guillermo Acevedo, Torero will exhibit his latest studio paintings on the theme of world peace early in 1988.

WEDNESDAY MORNING ARTIST'S BREAKFAST

In the winter of 1976, a Wednesday morning gathering of artists at Mr. T's boardwalk restaurant in Solana Beach turned into a weekly affair known as the "Wednesday Morning Artist's Breakfast." Robert Perine initiated these coffee clutches with artist friends and with Artist Equity activist McNeil Sargent (formerly Jean Braley) lending her support.

The breakfast has continued for twelve years, drawing between six and thirty artists each Wednesday to share anything from the latest New York exhibition catalogues to creative solutions for depression. Artists who have regularly dropped in over the years are Stephen Beck von Peccoz, Rob Bell, Marianne Childress, Monroe Eisenberg, Russell Forester, Faiya Fredman, Nancy Livesay, Martha Matthews, Anne Mudge, Carl Provder, Jennifer Spencer, and Playboy cartoonist John Dempsey.

THE ATELIER

The Atelier is a printmaking studio founded by internationally known artist Francoise Gilot in 1984. McNeil Sargent is the present director of these thirty plus printmakers who take part in the ongoing programs at the Sorrento Valley location. One of the trustees of The Atelier, Martin Petersen of the San Diego Museum of Art, curated an exhibition of prints by Sir Stanley William Hayder, the "father of modern printmaking," at the San Diego Museum of Art in 1988.

The Atelier sponsors speakers and exhibits and has plans for exchange exhibits with Germany and France in 1988. Among the artists at The Atelier is SDSU Professor Emeritus Paul Lingren, who has led printmaking workshops throughout the Middle East and India, and who curated a travelling exhibition of contemporary Indian prints for the Festival of India in the United States. Other Atelier printmakers include Catherine Collins, Maria Gardiner, Penny King,

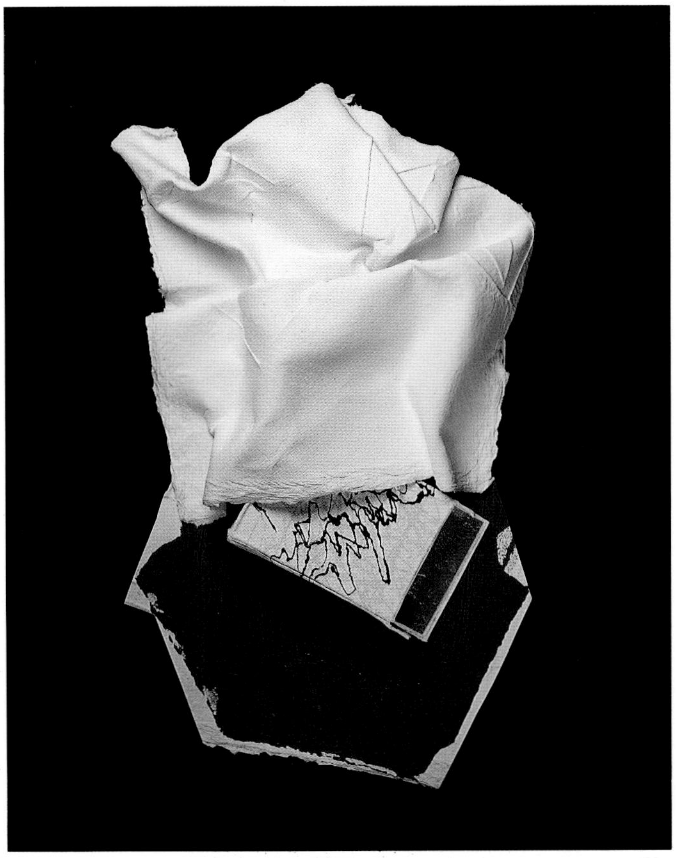

Ed Pieters, *Scanner*, 1987, 24" × 30", paper sculpture

Julie Ricksecker, Anita Shaw, and Angelica Villagrana.

COMMUNITY ARTS

Another coalition of artists calling themselves Community Arts developed between 1978 and 1980. This was a government funded (CETA) program headquartered downtown and was headed by June Gutfleisch. Gutfleisch eventually left to become director of the California Confederation of the Arts in Los Angeles. Community Arts attracted young, energetic artists in the early experimental stages of their careers. In 1980 Community Arts's assistant director and grants writer Lynn Schuette moved on to found Sushi, Inc., a downtown performance space. Community Arts attracted artists to inexpensive downtown loft space, creating a center for meetings and discussions. Grassroots artists-work-here exhibits and performances grew out of the friendships and communal support that developed at Community Arts. The downtown art scene was suddenly alive with the vitality of off-beat, shoestring-budget spaces such as Richard Sigmund's Gallery 552 (painter Sigmund now lives in New York), Jay Johnson's Pawn Shop Gallery, and Gary Ghirardi's Installation Gallery.

MAPLE CREEK STUDIO

Also having an impact on the San Diego art community was the formation of Maple Creek Studio (1980) on Kettner Boulevard near the airport. Ed Pieters, a dynamic former San Diego State University instructor, developed Maple Creek Studio as a center for papermaking. The large space, excellent equipment, and Pieter's reputation for kingsize handmade paper reliefs enticed artists Paula Matthei (now married to Pieters), Martha Chatelain, David Zapf, and others. Maple Gallery was a natural outgrowth of Maple Creek Studio and its excellent exhibitions successfully recognized the art community's needs. These group and solo shows were always crowded; Maple was an excellent place for local artists to connect into the network. Financially strained, Maple Creek Studio and Maple Gallery were forced to close in 1985, then, with Pieters' renewed enthusiasm, reopened in 1988 as Mapleworks.

Pieters, while exhibiting his work nationally, continued to take an active interest in the local scene, becoming an outspoken advocate of San Diego artists as chair of PAAB. With the assistance of artist Jennifer Spencer, head of COVA, Pieters lobbied strongly and in 1985 succeeded in getting San Diego's One Percent for Art passed. The passage of this statute stipulates that one percent of city building costs go to artwork. This was long overdue, trailing major cities like Seattle and Portland by more than a decade.

Eleanor Antin

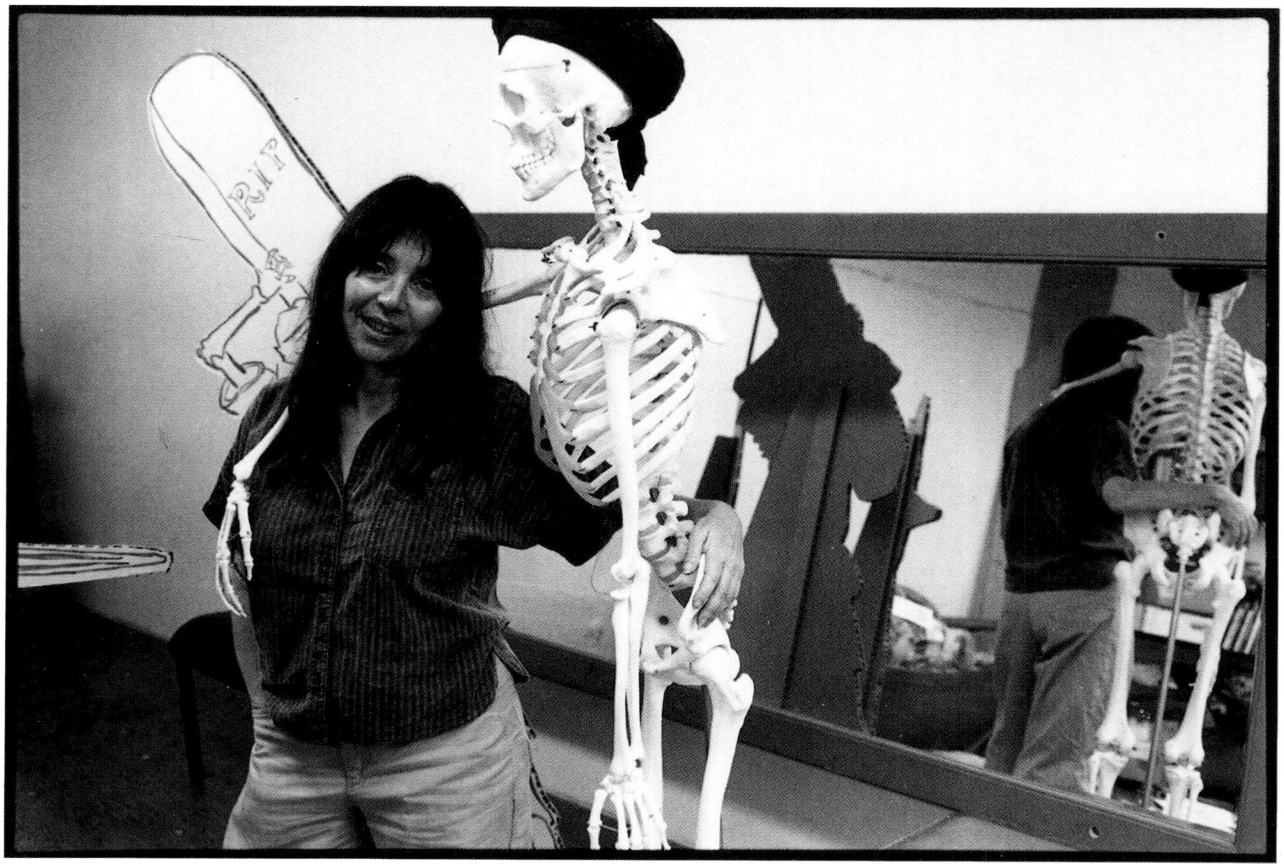

I tried to find a self that would fit those other parts of myself that were very wretched and humiliating to me. It was between a nurse and a stewardess.

Clad in a T-shirt and jeans with her long dark hair hanging loose, Eleanor Antin is as animated talking about her many art forms as she might be in a performance. The costumes she wears in these performances are displayed in numerous posters and book jackets and on hangers scattered around her Water Tank studio at UCSD.

Antin has earned an international reputation through her multicultural and multimedia works. She recently completed her first theater works, writing and directing other actors. This is a departure from her prolific video and performance works that at times saw her playing as many as forty roles. She has been most highly visible as Eleanora Antinova, whom she has lived, written about extensively, and seen through several stages of evolution since 1973.

She and her sister, a pianist, grew up in New York, attending the Music and Art High School. Her parents divorced when she was young. Her mother was an actress in the Yiddish theater in Poland and, after coming to the United States, worked in and owned various hotels and "colorful, nutty" summer resorts.

Eleanor Antin is married to David Antin, a poet, critic, and professor in the Visual Arts Department at UCSD since 1968. They have one son in college.

My work is always formative in impulse. You might say that it's performative in its structure and nature. I started with performances many years ago and even from the beginning they'd be saying, "Oh, it's too theatrical." What's the difference between theater and art? Why is this art and not theater, or why is that performance and not theater? I've never worried about these things. I used to fight being a performance artist because I knew that my work had so many different faces and all of these different works have to be considered on their own, as well as part of the overall thing, but everyone insisted on calling me that and I realized if that's what they're thinking, they must know something and why fight? I just go along with it. I just use the term to encompass a much broader scope. What I do is just a little more fantastical than what most people do.

I was doing a number of pieces that were related to my own body and feelings and personal experiences. I started realizing that if I could playfully invent my body, I could playfully invent my soul as well.

I was curious to see if I were a man, what kind of man I would be. Which is not a feminist question at all, but I was just playing with the idea, talking about putting hair on my face to be the handsomest man I could be. I couldn't be like Hemingway because I don't have any of his facial characteristics. But I could be sort of cavalier and that was the right kind of beard for me. I really looked quite like the Van Dyke portrait of Charles I. I read about Charles I. He was a very Hamlet-like king, the only English king to be axed. They chopped off his head because he was stubborn and a romantic and a drag – things that I am. I've always been political, so he was my political self, obviously, and my male self.

Then I wondered who's my most wonderful woman self and knew obviously there's a ballerina in my life. I mean, every little girl has a thing for ballerinas. I had studied some, actually more modern dance, and I'd had a scholarship at the Martha Graham School at one point. So that was my Ballerina. I taught myself to be on toe and then realized I came from a Russian Jewish background filled with fantasies of noble Russia and also leftist. Somehow I just gravitated towards the Ballet Russe, the Russian Ballet. Of course they were a bunch of White Russians, aristocrats, but that's amusing too, because they're exiles.

My king is a deposed king, so he's in exile. When we moved from Solana Beach because developers were destroying it by putting up condos, my king went into exile because he used to be King of Solana Beach. "Battle of the Bluffs" is a piece I tell and act. I took it to Venice in 1976. In the Battle we were trying to stop the developers who had just taken down the last of the Torrey Pines and were going to build the Independent Order of Foresters building that's there now. I led the very old people, the ones who played shuffleboard at the community center, and the young people on their skateboards. The old people were my infantry and the guys on the skateboards were my cavalry. We had a great battle and we almost won. We won, actually, but then we were betrayed.

It was a friend of mine, Mel Freilicher, a professor at San Diego State University and publisher of *Crawl Out Your Window* magazine who said, "Your friends are so grand. Oh, your selves are so grand!" And I said, "No," and I tried to find a self that would fit those other parts of myself that were very wretched and humiliating to me. It was between a nurse and a stewardess. The Nurse turned out to be this marvelous figure who is incredibly creative, plays with paper dolls, and has romantic fantasies. She opened the whole theater area for me. She also represented that nurturing and caring part of me which is one of the marvelous roles that women have.

A little earlier I also knew that I had been a black movie star. That didn't work out as a self, but as a role. A movie star just plays a role. So I just played the King, the Ballerina, and the Nurse as a movie star, which means I'm black. They all turn black. All it means is that self disappeared. All that means is my King, my Nurse, and my Ballerina are black, are becoming black. The Ballerina is already black; she's been black for years. The King was black a couple of years back, though in the Battle of the Bluffs he wasn't black. I like to be black with my light eyes.

You see, my Ballerina self is iconic, like "A Ballerina," you know, and once she became black she became a person. She became humanized very precisely. She became Eleanora Antinova, a famous black ballerina with the Ballet Russe. It's funny how much richer and more personal and human they become once they're becoming black.

SELECTED BIOGRAPHY

BIRTHPLACE

New York City

EDUCATION

City College of New York, BA
New School of Social Research, graduate work in Philosophy
Tamara Daykarhanova School for the Stage, certificate of completion

TEACHING

University of California, San Diego, 1975 – present

SOLO EXHIBITIONS AND PERFORMANCES

"100 BOOTS," Museum of Modern Art, New York, 1973
"Battle of the Bluffs," performance, Thirty-eighth Venice Biennale, Italy, 1976
"The Ballerina," Whitney Museum of American Art, New York, 1978
"The Nurse and the Hijackers," 1977; "Before the Revolution," 1979; "Recollections of my Life with Diaghilev," 1980; "El Desdichado," 1983; "Loves of a Ballerina," a filmic installation, Ronald Feldman Gallery, New York
"Help! I'm in Seattle," (premier) LACE, Los Angeles, 1986

GROUP EXHIBITIONS

"Art as Photography/Photography as Art," travelling exhibition, Tiroler Landesmuseum Ferdinandeum, Innsbruck, Austria, 1979 to 1980
"Directions, 1979," and "Content: A Contemporary Focus 1974 to 1984," Hirshhorn Museum, Washington, D.C.
"American Narrative/Story Art: 1967 to 1977," 1977, travelling exhibition; "Other Realities: Installations for Performance," 1981; "Video: Heroes/Anti-Heroes," 1984, Museum of Contemporary Art, Houston.
"Revising Romance: New Feminist Video," travelling exhibition, American Federation of Art, 1985 to 1987
Video Festival, American Film Institute, Los Angeles, 1987

PUBLICATIONS

Before the Revolution, a ballet of Eleanora Antinova, Santa Barbara Museum of Art, 1979
Being Antinova, a journal of experiences in New York, Astro Artz Press, Los Angeles, 1983
The Antinova Plays, Sun & Moon, Los Angeles, 1988

GRANTS AND HONORS

National Endowment for the Arts
VESTA Award for Performance Art, Honoring women who have made significant contributions to the Arts in Los Angeles, given by the Women's Building, 1985

COLLECTIONS

Museum of Modern Art, New York
San Francisco Museum of Art
Long Beach Museum of Art, Long Beach
Sol Lewitt Collection, Wadsworth Athenaeum, Hartford
Walker Art Center, Minneapolis

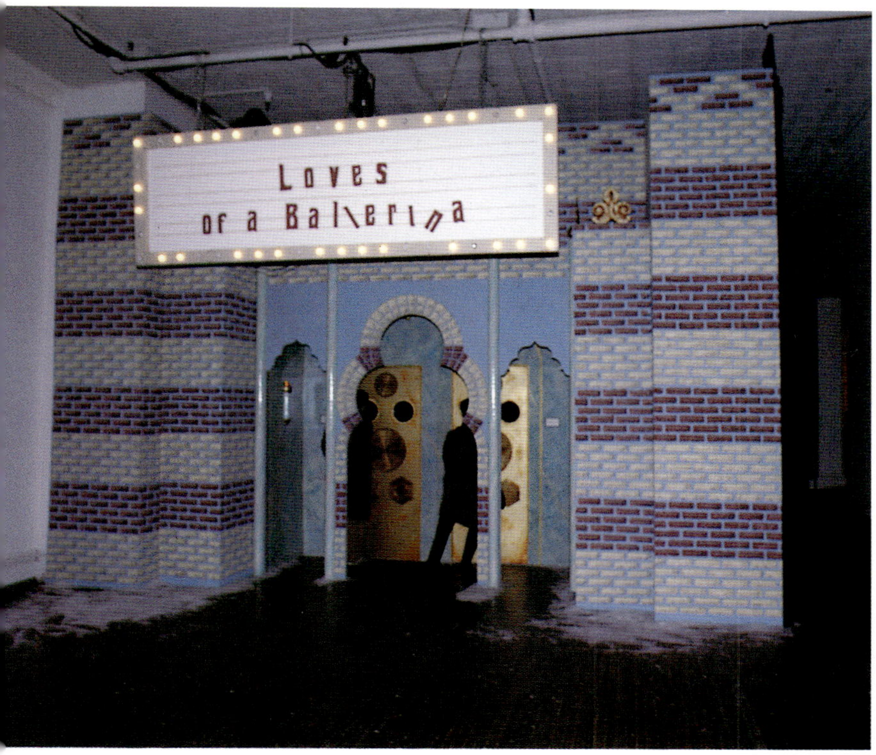

Photos by Becky Cohen   Courtesy of Ronald Feldman Gallery, N.Y.

s of a Ballerina, installation, Ronald Feldman Gallery, New York, 1987

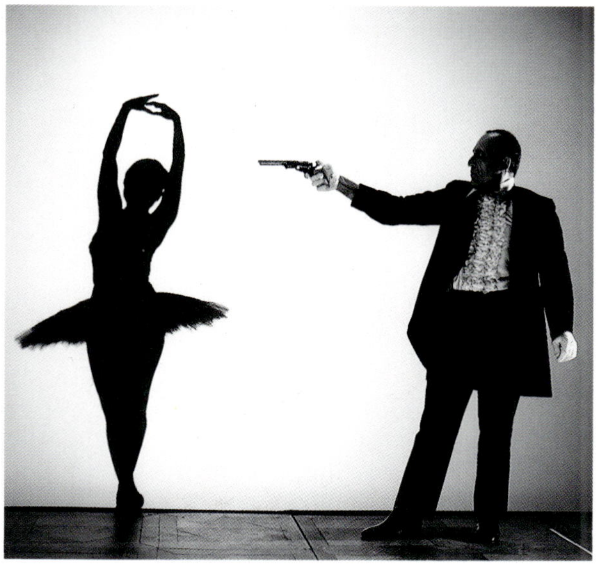

Love's Shadow, 16mm film, B&W (with Eleanora Antinova and Luke Theodore Morrison)

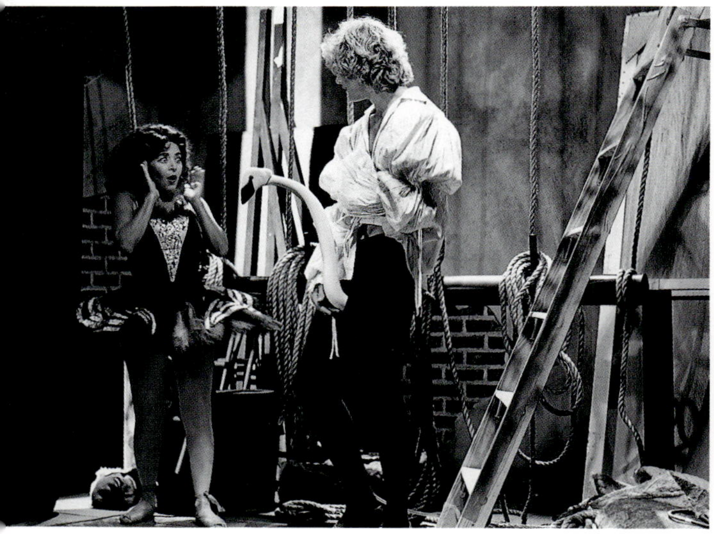

n Lake, 16mm film, B&W (with Eleanora Antinova and James Tackett)

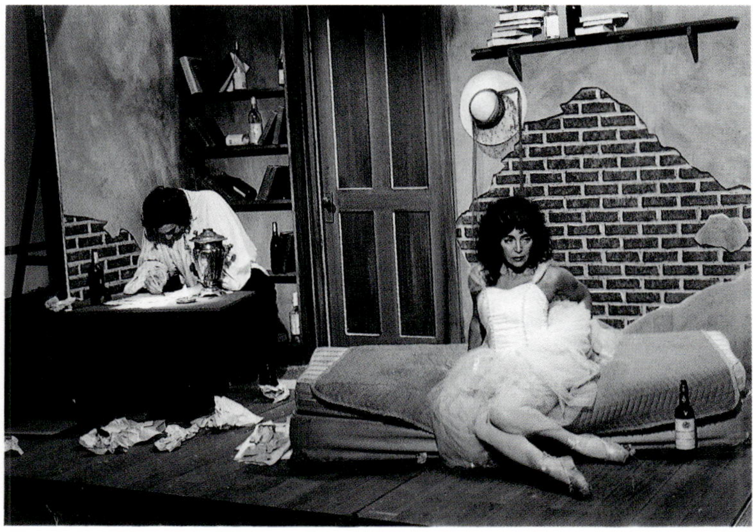

The Ballerina and the Poet, 16mm film, B&W (with Eleanora Antinova and Sheldon Nodelman)

Joan Austin

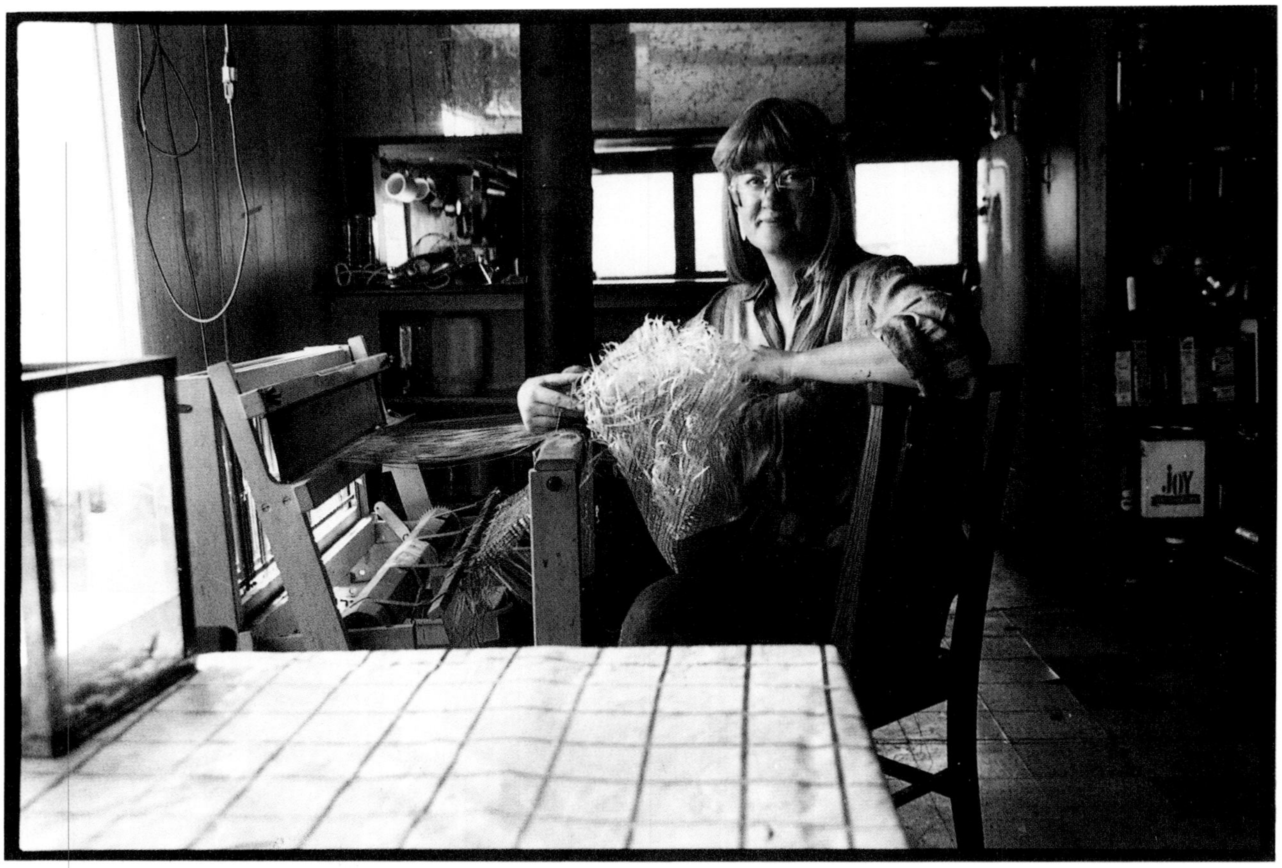

Everything I do tends to have some element of difficulty. I . . . struggle with it. I like that struggle, the little give-and-take battle back and forth.

The frames of looms nearly obstruct Joan Austin's vision whether she is in her office near the weaving studio at SDSU or in the studio/living room of the trailer she and her eight-year-old son Jonathan call home. Her approach to weaving is emotional, sensitive, and far from traditional, which could also describe her individualistic lifestyle.

Austin lives past Jamul, an hour's drive from SDSU down a dirt road, on land she bought ten years ago. Her jerry-rigged construction trailer is surrounded with fruit trees, vegetable gardens, and a grape arbor. Her father, in his seventies, has lived down the road since the death of Austin's mother.

Austin spends little time interacting with other SDSU faculty and dedicates her life to weaving, teaching, and caring for her son. Her interest in experimenting with materials and exploring the sources in nature are clearly the sustaining forces in her creative expression.

My dad was a commercial fisherman for over fifty years. As soon as I was big enough to walk around, my mom and my sister and I went commercial fishing with him. We'd fish for albacore in the summer for two or three months. I went fishing with him for about fifteen or twenty years. Every summer my friends would be off to parks and parties and I would get on the boat and go fishing. It's real exciting because you're out on this big pancake of water and you really feel like you're on your own island and there's nobody else around. We went from Long Beach to Catalina and San Clemente. Sometimes we were 200 miles out. At the beginning of the season we'd stop in San Diego for a while and by the end of the season we'd go north to Morro Bay or Monterey, but seldom north of San Francisco.

As a kid I'd pull fish out of the water and sketch fish and since I had a camera I started photographing fish and gills and scales. In grade school I didn't find success in writing and math and all that academic stuff, but the art was real exciting. My teachers always said I had admirers and the drawings would disappear.

For a lot of years I went alone with my dad because my mom and sister got seasick. They didn't want to be part of it. It was a way for me to make money to buy clothes, art supplies, paper, and to go to graduate school. I drew on the boat, did a lot of watercolors. In graduate school I took books and learned while I was there, made sketches of what I wanted to do. I also took fleece and spun it.

I've always made three-dimensional vessel forms. Twenty-five years ago my things were derived from tradition, from looking at vessels from different cultures like African, Japanese, the American Indian. Now I don't look back to those sources; I look more to sources that are about where I live and what I do. The ocean has been important to me. The mountains, growing things are important. I want to say something about that with structure, with form and color and transparency. And I want the materials to be as important as the form. The materials come into play as they help me to capture the quality of light, of water, of reflection. I've done a lot of experimenting and right now I'm trying to find what would work by going back and sitting at the beach, looking at water, looking at waves, trying to pick out what it is that makes that happen, that quality of color and reflection, and then trying to duplicate it through lots of experimentation.

For the last few years I've used mylars and plastics, spray paints, sand, glue, adhesive, anything. I want to do something that's unique and different and fits the work, but I don't think you can claim anything as your own for very long.

We think of sculpture as being permanent, large scale, monumental, forever. Maybe it's more, something about form and shape and light, maybe not meant to last forever. I'd like to be able to visualize something that has a wonderful exterior form and interior form, and that really grabs the viewer to look, walk around, look inside, feel something. I want to feel and I want other people to be reminded of some special experience or of something atmospheric, not just something pretty.

My imagery is staying the same but my materials have changed. Maybe you just have to be gutsier and do what you think is right. I like weaving and I like the history behind it and I see there is a tremendous amount of potential for making creative works that are beyond what's ordinary. What I do with the weaving could make some contribution to the field. If I give that up I won't make a contribution.

Everything I do tends to have some element of difficulty. I sit there and struggle with it. I like that struggle, the little give and take battle back and forth. I guess it's a communication. I want to communicate with the materials, find out what they can do, their response, and then see what I can make them do that they haven't done before. But it's not meditative. I've never found that I can just sit there and think of one thing and do something else.

SELECTED BIOGRAPHY

BIRTHPLACE

Huntington Park, California

EDUCATION

California State University, Long Beach, 1966
Cranbrook Academy of Art, Bloomfield Hills, Michigan MFA, 1969

TEACHING

San Diego State University, 1970 to present

SOLO EXHIBITIONS

Galeria Del Sol, Santa Barbara, 1972
Boehm Gallery, Palomar College, San Marcos, California, 1986
Cabrillo College Gallery, Aptos, California, 1986
Cerro Coso College, Cerro Coso, California, 1987

GROUP EXHIBITIONS

"Craftsmen USA 1966," Two National Merit Awards, Los Angeles County Museum of Art and The Museum of Contemporary Art, New York, 1966
"Pulp," travelling exhibition, City Art Gallery, Wellington, New Zealand and Australia, 1980 to 1982
"Basketry Now," University of Wisconsin at Green Bay, 1985
"The Art of Basketry," Ninth Annual Invitational, Liberty Gallery, Louisville, 1986
"Fiber Invitational," Wita Gardiner Gallery, San Diego, 1987

COLLECTIONS

National Handicraft Collection, New Delhi, India
Robert Pfannebecker Collection, Lancaster, Pennsylvania
Leonard Vitzer, San Diego
Francoise Grossen, New York
Fern Jacobs, Los Angeles

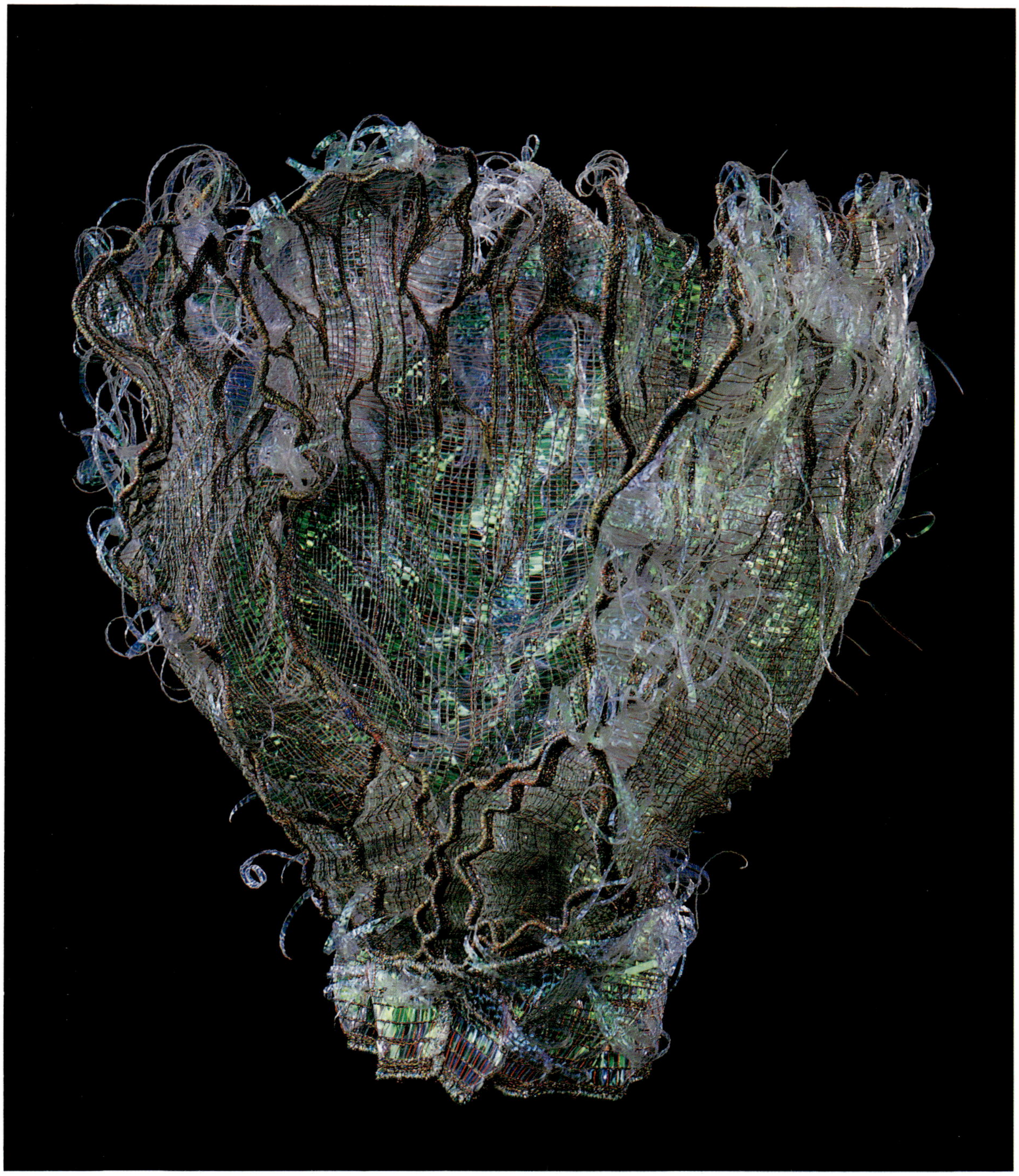

The Mermaid's Jewel Box, mylar and linen wire, 18" × 12", 1987

Photo by Nick Juran

David Avalos

I see connections between art and society, between religion and sexuality. My work tries to deal with these different aspects.

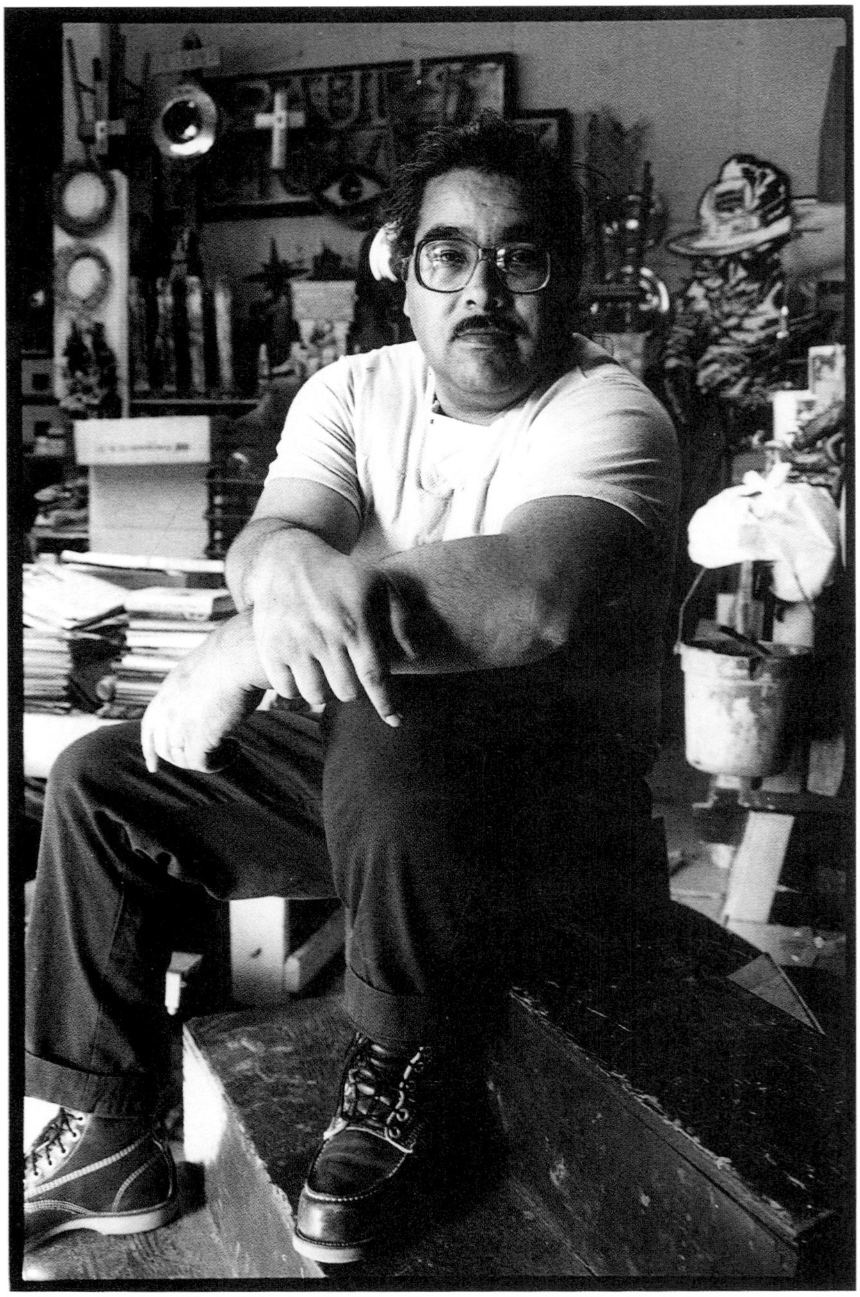

In his work space in the Centro Cultural de la Raza, a large water tank in Balboa Park, David Avalos is surrounded by materials and art which evidence both his Mexican-Catholic heritage and his political activism. He usually dresses in jeans and workboots with his long hair in a ponytail.

On the wall hang hubcaps he has used to create assemblages he calls Milagros *(miracles) that shine with "cultural fetishes" such as the cross, the heart, and the revolver. Nearby is his best known piece, "The Donkey Cart," which received national press because a local judge ordered it confiscated when it was placed in front of the Federal Court House. The case was taken up by the ACLU and, as of this writing, is being heard in Los Angeles.*

He has participated in several mural projects and has long been involved in civil rights. Avalos has created posters, political cartoons, and flyers. One of his most recent posters, created for San Diego city buses with artists Elizabeth Sisco and Louis Hock to coincide with Superbowl XXII, elicited extended public debate because of its political slant. A co-founder of Voz Fronterizo, *a UCSD Chicano newspaper, Avalos has worked for more than a decade with the Committee on Chicano Rights.*

He was born in San Diego of parents from Mexico. He and his five brothers and sisters were raised in National City, where he still resides with his wife and three children.

I did the first model for the donkey cart sculpture back in 1983. I had this image of an undocumented worker being apprehended by a border patrol agent with his hands up and it looked like a crucified image without the crucifix. The donkey cart was represented as an altar.

I see altars everywhere. If you conceive of an altar as a location or an investment of passion that has a certain structure then a lot of things become altars. The donkey carts in Tijuana are altars of Mexican culture. On them you see the geometric designs that have been passed down since the Aztecs and other Pre-Columbian civilizations, the flora, the images of Mexican life like the *charro* serenading a woman by her window. Then the tourists climb up on them to have their photographs taken. I've taken those pictures too. I think they're fun. But at another deeper level it's like sitting in one of the largest cities on the West Coast of North America, a modern urban center with about one and a half million people, and you're on this cart that's on wooden horses so the wheels don't even touch the ground. So you bring back your photograph as a souvenir and tell your friends that you were in Mexico. This has nothing to do with the contemporary reality of Mexico. Art has the capacity to divert by being so seductive. By being so attractive it diverts our attention from realities.

I'm a university-educated person, but I feel that I'm a self-taught artist. I'm very insistent that I be seen as a Chicano artist because I think that gives me a certain perspective within U.S. society. I think that we need to accept the fact that different people in this society have different perspectives. We're not a multicultural society in the sense that everyone is able to appreciate everyone else completely. We're unable to penetrate people's pasts and community histories, but I think that we can enjoy each other's differences and benefit from them if we're able to create forms that allow these different perspectives to contribute to a social dialogue that moves us away from the status quo and into the exploration of other possibilities.

I think my perspective, the materials I use, my palette, is very much influenced by what I saw around me when I was growing up. It's influenced by the abstract communication of images. Visually one of the things that had an impact on me was my mother's Bible that was illustrated with works from the Italian Renaissance. I would go through the Bible and there would be a place with twenty color plates and I'd look at them for the longest time. I was just amazed at all the detail that was involved and what was conveyed visually.

My dad is an incredible storyteller. He used to come home from work and sit right down at the table which would be set and ready with six of us kids waiting. And then we'd have dinner and he'd tell us about what he did that day. He could impersonate all the guys he worked with on his pipe-laying crew. I always saw my dad working with his hands, plumbing. I'd see him out there melting lead, plastering, and pipefitting. I worked with him a little bit as I got older and so I'm used to being around power tools, wood, a lot of different materials.

I recently took a fifty-foot section of eight-foot-high chain link fence and made a Moebius strip out of it. I read about this guy August Moebius, an Austrian scientist who had reached the height of his career in 1848 when he was appointed head of the observatory in Vienna, the same year the U.S./Mexican border was established. If you and I stood separated by the fence, we would still be on the same side as the Moebius strip has only one side, defying our intuitive understandings. Some scientists now say that the universe may be in the shape of the Moebius strip.

The driving force of my work is not to isolate myself as someone who's different. What keeps me doing art is that it enables someone who would probably be a hermit to connect with other people, to connect with other ideas. I see connections between art and society, between religion and sexuality. My work tries to deal with these different aspects.

My art has to do with the future. If it makes reference to my childhood or my history, it's only for the purpose of saying, "Hey, let's get some things resolved." Whenever I bring up the past, the history of the United States and Mexico, people say, "Oh, I like to be more positive," or "I think we've got to move beyond that." And yet in personal relationships I don't know of any therapy in which someone is told to forget this source of trauma, forget this historical point at which your perception of yourself and this other person changed.

SELECTED BIOGRAPHY

BIRTHPLACE

San Diego

EDUCATION

University of California, San Diego, BA in Communications, 1978

SOLO EXHIBITIONS

Galeria Posada, Sacramento, 1985
Robert Else Gallery, California State University, Sacramento, 1986
Grand Rapids Art Museum, 1986
Intar Latin American Gallery, New York, 1988

GROUP EXHIBITIONS

"A San Diego Exhibition," La Jolla Museum of Contemporary Art, 1985
"Streetworks," Federal Building, Sushi, San Diego, 1985
"Chicano Expressions: Grafica/Urban Iconography," Intar Latin American Gallery, New York, 1986
"Southern California Assemblage: Past and Present," travelling exhibition, Santa Barbara Contemporary Arts Forum, 1986
"Lo Del Corazon," travelling exhibition, Mexican Museum, San Francisco, 1987

GRANTS

California Council for the Arts, Artist in Residence grants
National Endowment for the Arts, Visual Artists Fellowship

COLLECTIONS

Amy and Philip Brookman, Washington, D.C.
Tomas Ybarra-Fransto, San Francisco
Armando Cid, Sacramento
Michael Schnorr, Imperial Beach, California
Margaret and Ted Godshalk, National City, California

Photo by Manuel Cavada

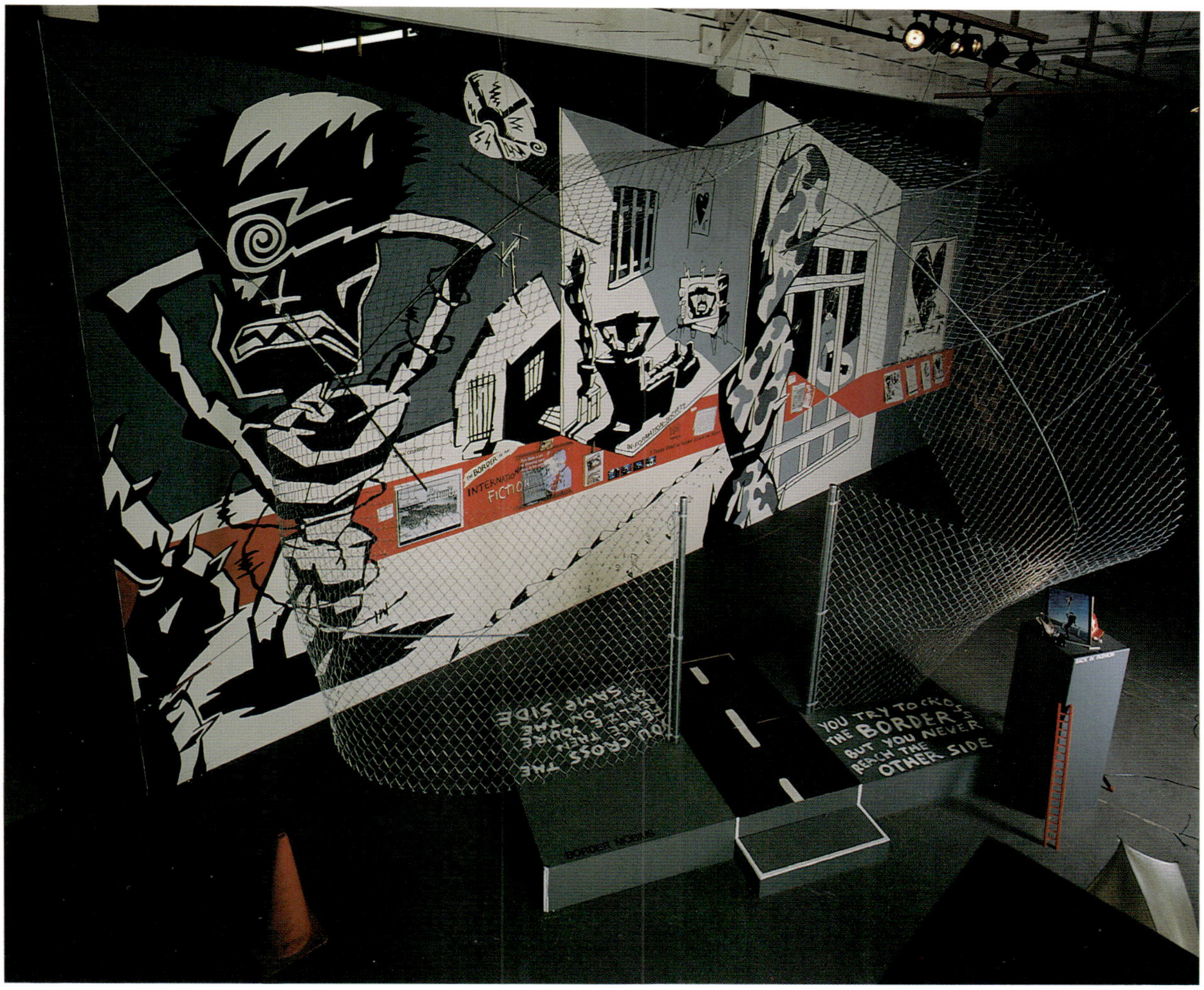

Border Fence as Moebius Strip, Installation with sculptural and mural components, Mural: 15'5" × 38', Sculpture: 16' × 10' × 6', 1987

Richard Baker

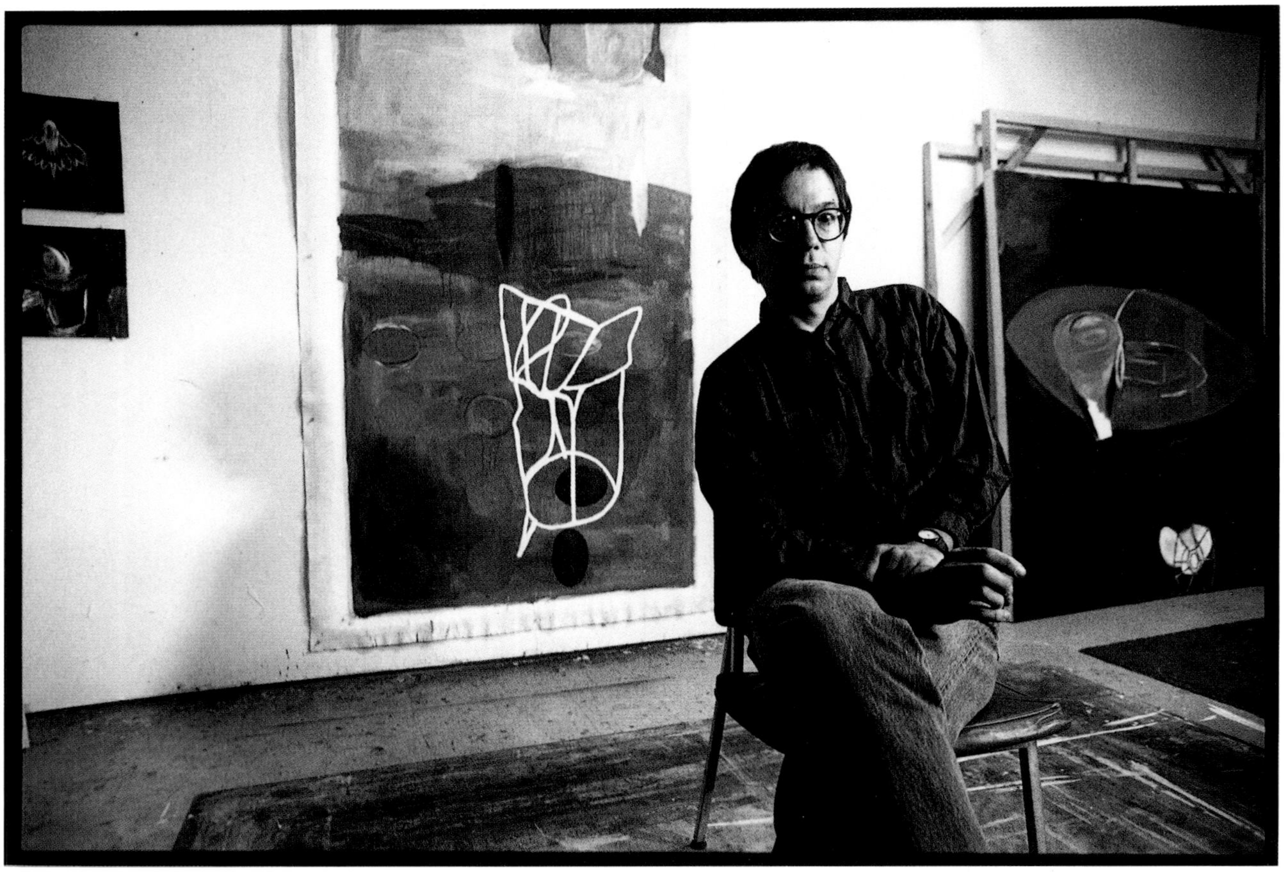

I don't think my paintings are beautiful. They're about potentials, about possibilities.

Tall, slim, and soft-spoken, Richard Baker works in a studio behind Sushi, a downtown San Diego performance gallery. He moved here recently after giving up a studio he shared in Los Angeles. Against a high-ceilinged wall lean many of his large canvases, some of which are survivors of his yearly "spring cleaning, getting rid of material goods."

Baker met his Japanese-born wife Yoshiko, who is also an artist, when they were in school. In the mid-1970s they went to Japan to live. There, influenced by the landscape, the sculptured trees, and the Japanese flair for design, he began to change his work. Upon moving to San Diego in 1978 to teach at SDSU, Baker made even more radical changes, based on his rethinking of many vital issues. No longer married, he spends his time creating works which are the result of his introspection – somber and moody.

Baker grew up in the Midwest, drawing and cartooning as a boy. While stationed with the Army in Washington D.C., he made his choice between art and classical guitar. He has a sister ten years his senior who is a costume designer in Tucson, Arizona.

For quite a while in my work I've been concerned not with what's going on around me but with my *awareness* of what's going on and trying to process what I, we, all go through in trying to understand the world around us. It's not so much what is going on out there as what I do with it inside, how I sort it, catalogue it, classify it, manipulate it. I can manipulate it here any way I want. That process has been interesting to me for a long time; I can date it to 1979. I had an experience then when I completely dried up and couldn't continue working. I didn't have any motivation for painting for three or four months, which doesn't sound like a lot to some people but – because I've been so used to working steadily in a very disciplined way – for me it was devastating. It was catastrophic for me, like bottoming out completely. It forced me to reevaluate everything. I found that my life had not been what I had hoped for. I found that if I could stop painting that easily then there was something wrong. It made me question why I was doing it in the first place. I realized that I had to connect a lot closer to my day-to-day living.

I started painting about death, putting things in front of me I didn't understand, that were not comfortable, to see what it was all about. The paintings got to be more about internal phenomena than external phenomena. That was really the beginning of my work about what art critic Jeff Kelley called "the psychic body" in a review in the *LAICA Journal*.

I'm pretty disciplined. I really believe the only way I'm going to accomplish anything is if I work from nine to five. Sometimes the most productive periods are those when I don't feel like working at all. I know for myself I don't wait for inspiration. I believe in it but can't wait for it to come to me. I have to go to it. And the only way I can do that is by working through drawing, through any kind of visual activity. It's not necessary that I have a brush in my hand. Usually the way I generate that excitement, that motivation, is through drawing. Somehow drawing has become a kind of meditation. There's a certain disciplined activity that I have to go through in order to arrive at a certain point. In fact when I start thinking about it I usually get into trouble. But it's almost like mindlessly going through the motion. It's action that's important. Making those movements, seeing those parts go down, feeling the pen. After a while something begins to be generated and I focus more and more. The more I do it, the more focused I become, until I find I'm thinking anyway, despite the discipline, in a way that uses more faculties. Then I start asking questions and finding answers. I put ideas down from outside sources and then work through those ideas and remove myself by stages from the outside sources. That's the crossover. You take it from out there and bring it inside one or two drawings through stages. You break that down and then break it down some more. And all the time you're breaking down you're building up, too, because you're putting things in that come from other sources inside which have been fed from the outside. It's a cyclical form.

Is there really a difference between inside and outside? We can make that stuff out there what we want by manipulating it. We can wake up one morning in a great mood and see things that we wouldn't see if we'd awakened in a glum mood.

I don't think my paintings are beautiful. They're about potentials, about possibilities. In a way, that's a disturbing factor because they don't define themselves as being part of a familiar territory. I never look at them as art. I never question them in terms of art. I question them in terms of whether there is power or not, whether I'm being honest or not. They're possibly ugly for some people, but I also see something quite restful in them too, and something accepting. Accepting in that there can be a form that doesn't give you clear answers, that doesn't fit, that doesn't have a place already made for it, but is left suspended. Such a form can be as important as a form that already has a niche carved out.

With these paintings there is a sense of being left hanging without answers. That's fine because I never did much believe in answers anyway.

SELECTED BIOGRAPHY

BIRTHPLACE

Columbia, Missouri

EDUCATION

Yale University Summer School of Music and Art, 1968
Kansas City Art Institute, B.F.A., 1969
University of Cincinnati, M.F.A., 1971

TEACHING

San Diego State University, 1978 to present

SOLO EXHIBITIONS

Tucson Museum of Art, Tucson, Arizona, 1975
Tokyo Central Art Museum, Tokyo, 1977
Installation, Los Angeles Institute of Contemporary Art, 1984
Cirrus Gallery, Los Angeles, 1982, 1983, 1985, 1987

GROUP EXHIBITIONS

"Newcomers 1981," Los Angeles Municipal Art Gallery, 1981
"Sunshine and Shadow: Recent Paintings in Southern California," curated by Susan Larsen Martin, University of Southern California, Los Angeles, 1985
"A San Diego Exhibition," La Jolla Museum of Contemporary Art, 1985
"The Capitol Group: Selections from a Corporate Collection," Fine Art Gallery, University of California, Irvine, 1987
"Abstractions of the Eighties," Mandeville Gallery, University of California, San Diego, 1988

COLLECTIONS

University of Cincinnati
Capitol Group, Los Angeles
Dr. Yohkazu Ito, Chiba, Japan
Dr. Patrick Culbert, Tucson, Arizona
Wita and Ed Gardiner, San Diego

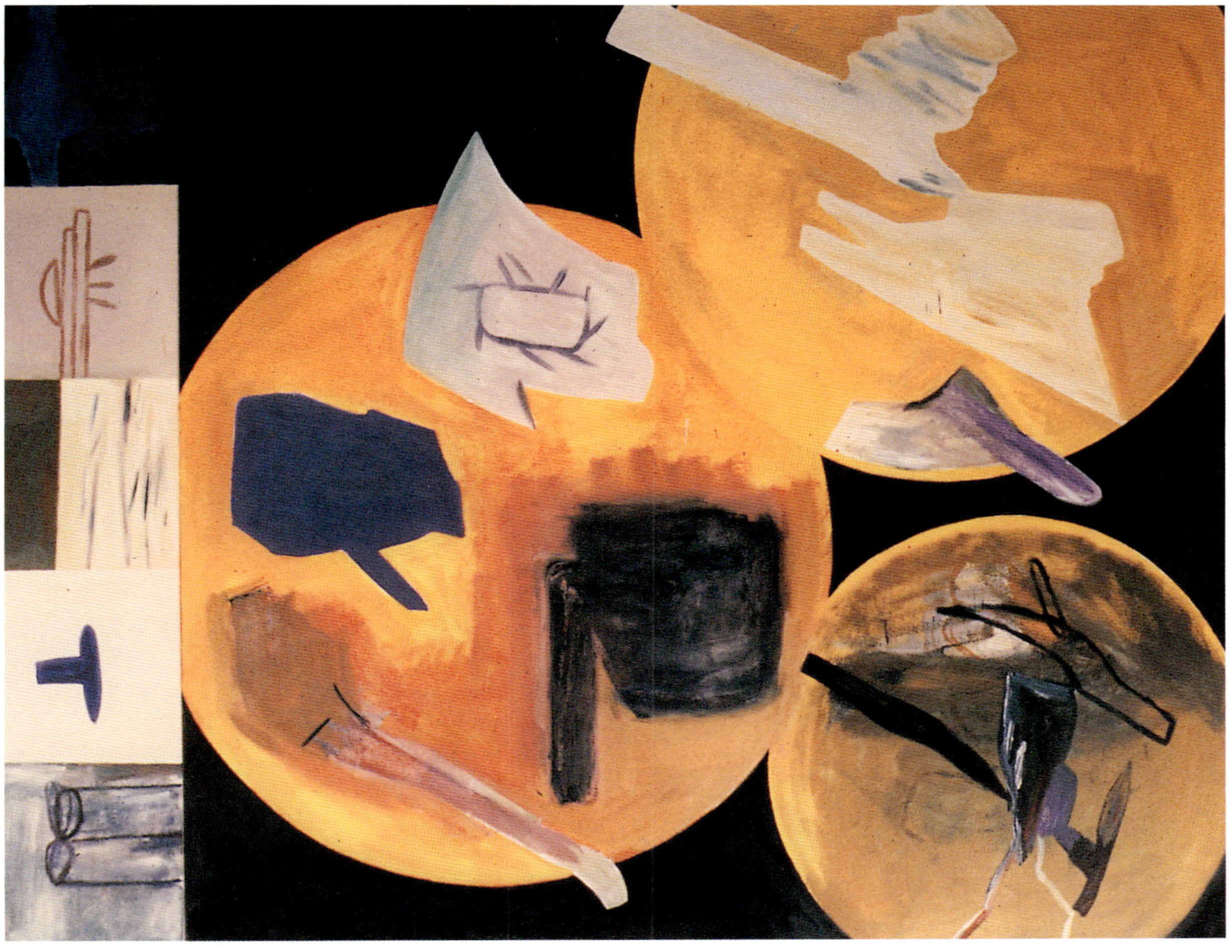

Parts Display, oil/canvas, 60″×78″, 1986

Border Art Workshop/Taller de Arte Fronterizo

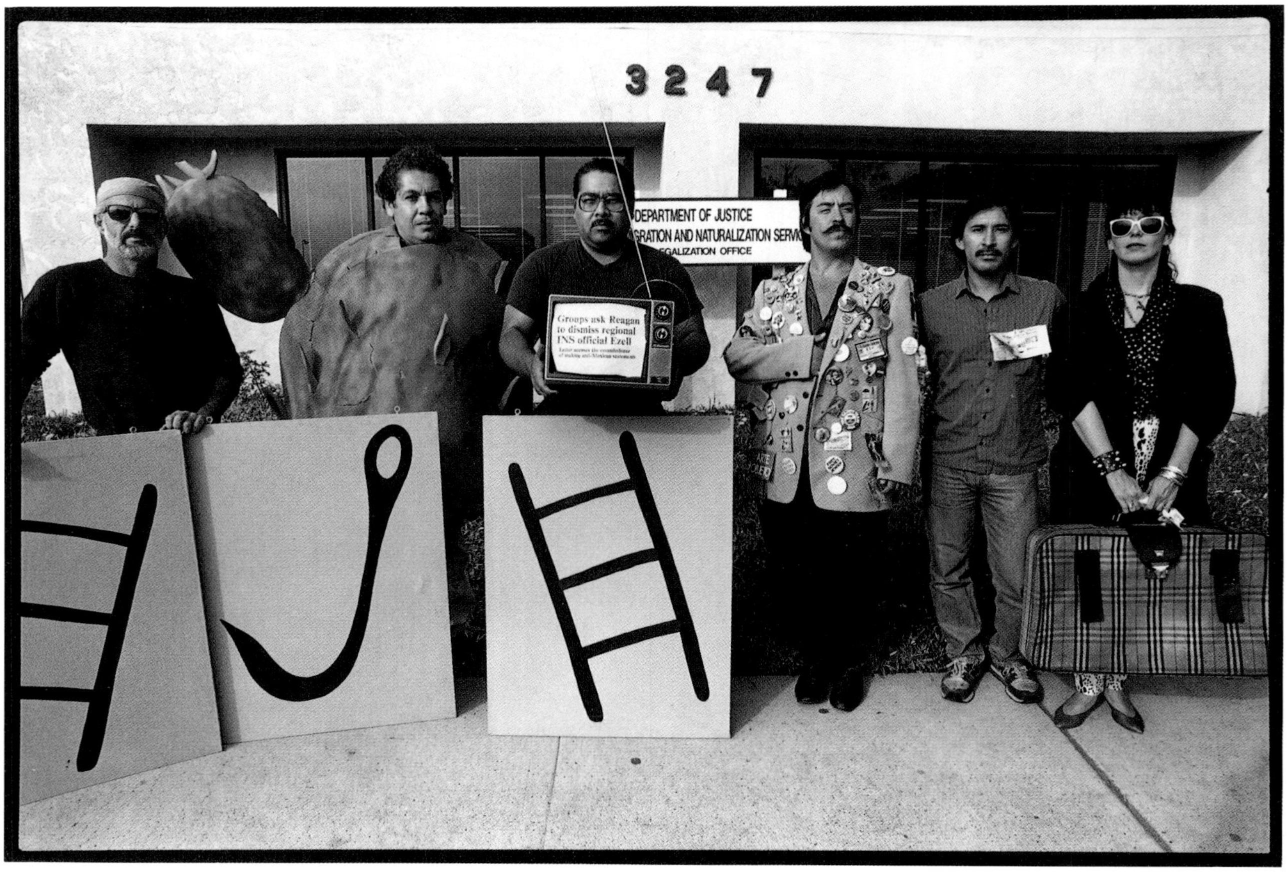

Left to right: Schnorr, Ochoa, Avalos, Gomez-Peña, Sanchez, and Hicks.

see 42 P.16 (8)
see 42 P.30 (28)

I see the Border Art Workshop as citizen diplomacy, a group of artists who are doing what consulates and cultural institutions are not doing. . . .

The Border Art Workshop was co-founded in October 1984 by David Avalos, Guillermo Gómez-Peña, Michael Schnorr, Victor Orozco Ochoa, Isaac Artenstein, Sara Jo Berman, and Jude Eberhard. It is a flexible group of multi-talented artists, writers, and performers from San Diego and Mexico who are committed to stimulating thought about borders and encouraging the exchange of ideas on topical border issues. Current participants in the Border Arts Workshop are:

DAVID AVALOS: see page 32.

GUILLERMO GÓMEZ-PEÑA is an interdisciplinary artist, actor, and writer from Mexico City who received his BFA and MFA at the California Institute of the Arts. He founded Poyesis Genetica Troupe, a troup which travels throughout the U.S., Mexico, and Europe.

EMILY HICKS completed her Ph.D. in Comparative Literature at UCSD after art studies at the San Francisco Art Institute. She writes for Artweek *and is co-editor with her husband Guillermo Gómez-Peña of the journal* La Linea Quebrade/The Broken Line. *She is completing a book on border culture.*

VICTOR OROZCO OCHOA is a co-founder of Centro Cultural de la Raza, which he directed from 1970 to 1973, and co-initiator of Chicano Park Community Murals. He is an Artist-in-Residence, working on mural projects with the San Diego city schools.

ROBERT SANCHEZ received his MA from the University of New Mexico and did postgraduate studies at Cornell University. He has taught at Mesa College since 1981 and recently has been a visiting lecturer in art at UCSD and SDSU.

MICHAEL SCHNORR has been a professor of art at Southwestern College since 1970 and is currently Summer Director at Santa Rapparata Graphic Art Center in Florence. He attended the Royal Academy of Art in Stockholm and received MAs in Printmaking and Art History at Pope Pius XII Institute of Fine Arts in Florence.

Michael Schnorr: There's much positive energy gained from cooperation, from internal discussion in which people are challenging each other's ways of making their statements. Otherwise it would be a piece of dead meat as far as I'm concerned. For me, it makes art making and social responsibility as an art maker fit very well. It makes me have a kind of willingness to plod though certain things in art that I don't necessarily like.

This is not just a community of artists. It is a community of people who have some direct involvement with a real life situation.

Guillermo Gómez-Peña: When I came here the first thing that had become apparent to me was that this place was a laboratory for U.S.-Mexican relations. It's very easy now to move one's cultural context as a creator and I knew it was the place for me to be. I was interested in issues that range from bilinguality and biculturality to bicultural dialogue of aesthetics and cultural misplacement. Since 1983 the border has been my home; I have become a border citizen. The Tijuana-San Diego metropolitan area is the place I claim as my city. It's an excellent place to be networking. In many ways Tijuana/San Diego becomes a spiderweb of communication.

Another thing that fascinates me about this region is the vernacular culture. I am not that much interested in the galleries, the museums. I am interested in the series of subcultures that create this fascinating mosaic that is the border culture: the streets of Tijuana, the Tijuana nightlife, street performers, the biker culture and, in some bizarre ways, the surfer culture which is an exotic phenomenon to me as a Mexican.

I see the Border Art Workshop as citizen diplomacy, a group of artists who are doing what consulates and cultural institutions are not doing; that is, to really create a cultural dialogue between the two sides of the border. It is really functioning well as a form of cultural diplomacy that comes from a civilian effort and that excites me a lot.

Robert Sanchez: Before the Border Art Workshop there wasn't much concrete reason to make a piece that wasn't charcoal on paper or acrylic on canvas. It's opened me up to try other forms of artmaking, other than the traditional approaches I'd used in my own two-dimensional artworks.

I also had a desire to get closer to other artists who were identified with Chicano art. My father was in the Navy and I lived in a lot of Navy towns that were separated from the Chicano community. There were mostly Black artists at the Memphis College of Art where I first studied. Later, at Cornell, I found myself doing papers on Chicano Art and the Chicano movement. When I came into contact with the Centro, I started to feel a much closer connection and finally was at a point where I could really start to feel comfortable doing work that was identifiably Chicano.

David Avalos: What I get from the group is a lot of energy. I've been encouraged to do things and to experiment with things that maybe I wouldn't do if I was hanging out in my studio operating alone. We share the same attitude which is that the border is a very exciting place. We're fortunate to be at a place and time in the States where a great many elements of history, politics, culture, and society are intersected right here at this point [San Diego], and we're here in the middle of it. I think we share an attitude of curiosity, inquisitiveness, fascination, fear, and stimulation.

Emily Hicks: In the performance work we try to present images that are extremely ambiguous and which will create very strong reactions. But the images are accessible because if something is so threatening that someone just says, "No, I don't want anything to do with it," there's no way to get a dialogue going.

I would say we all have very different viewpoints. There are times when – because I have familiarity with certain reference codes that differ from some members of the group – I can at least get the person to listen for a few minutes. Not to agree, but at least to listen. I don't think I'm successful very often!

Victor Ochoa: I don't see the Border Art Workshop being something that only lasts one more year and if we don't get funds or any projects the group disbands.

I'm really interested in taking things to the East Coast, trying other places, taking the whole Border Art Workshop to Germany and to borders in other places in the world. I hear people talking about other places and they say certain things are similar or that there are *pachucos* in Turkey, or that certain reactions relate to what we experience here. I would enjoy seeing some Turkish border art. I'd like to see what the similarities are, if they like oldies-but-goodies, if they have low-riders, how they comb their hair and if they wear their T-shirts down to their knees.

SELECTED BIOGRAPHY

FORMED

1984, Centro Cultural de la Raza, San Diego

EXHIBITIONS

"Border Realities," multi-media event including video, sculpture, painting, performance, and an outdoor mural, Galeria de la Raza, San Francisco, 1985

"Border Tableau," (included in La Frontera: The United States Border with Mexico by Jay Dusard, photographer, and Alan Weisman, Harcourt Brace Jovanovich, Inc., 1986,) Border Field Park, U.S.-Mexico Border, 1985

"A Tri-Cultural Street Event," performance within a light and sculpture installation, Sushi, San Diego, 1986

"Border Realities, Part II," installations and performances, Centro Cultural de la Raza, San Diego, 1986

"End of the Line," installation and performance, U.S.-Mexico Border, Columbus Day 1986

"Border Realities III," installations, Centro Cultural de la Raza, 1987

"911 – A House Gone Wrong," installation and performances, La Jolla Museum of Contemporary Art, Parameters 8, San Diego, 1987

DIALOGS

"Cafe Urgente" sculpture and light installation for presentations by U.S. and Mexican humanities scholars and artists: Tomas Ybarra-Fransto, Ph.D., James D. Cockroft, Ph.D., Alan Weisman, Felipe Ehrenberg, David Marciel, Ph.D. and Border Art Workshop, Centro Cultural de la Raza, 1986

"Parameters 8," four informal panels including Tijuana publisher Rosina Conde, The Tribune editorial page editor Joe Holley and Pulitzer Prize editorial writer Jonathan Freedman, Chicano activist Herman Baca, Mexican researcher Jose Luis Perez, director of the Institute for Regional Studies for the Californias Paul Ganster, The Tribune art critic Susan Freudenheim and art critic Leah Goldman, Java Coffe House-Gallery, San Diego, 1987

"Is the Border on Your Mind, on the Ground or in the Media," 30 minute event, Society for Photographic Education, 24th National Conference, San Diego, 1987

GRANTS

National Endowment for the Arts and Rockefeller Foundation grants to LACE, Interdisciplinary Artists grant

California Arts Council

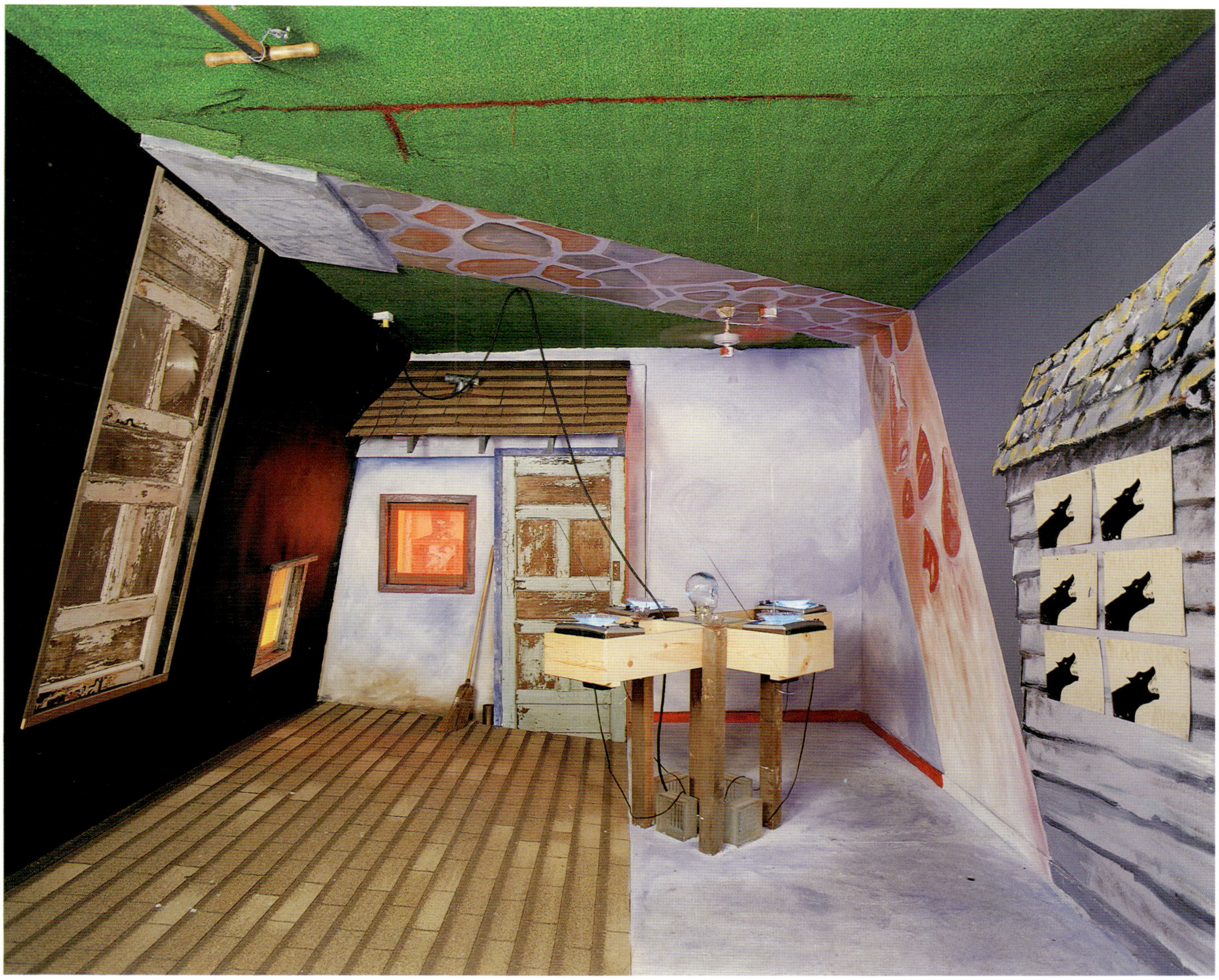

911, House Gone Wrong, mixed media installation, La Jolla Museum of Contemporary Art, Paramaters 8 Gallery, 14′×20′×8′, 1987

Dan Camp

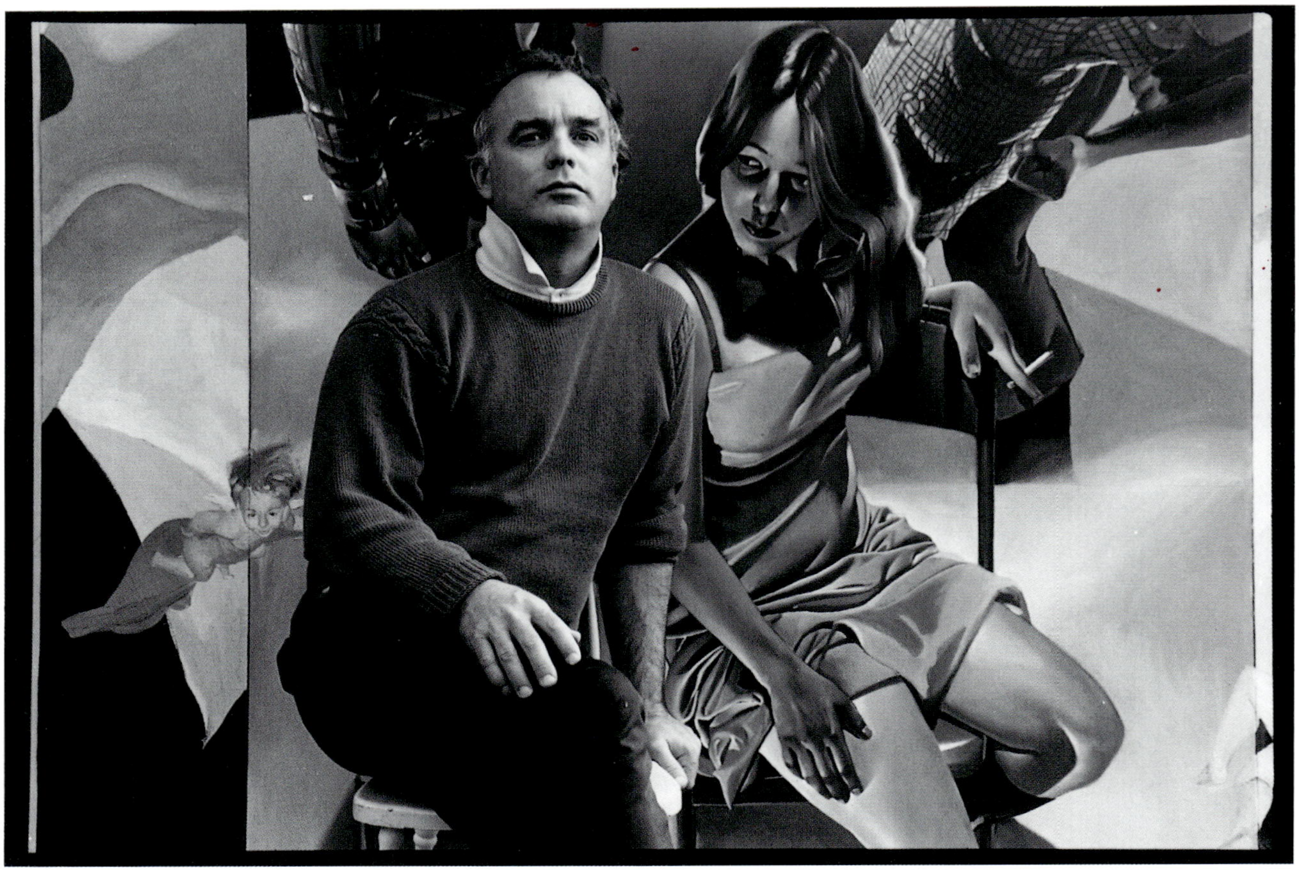

If I have any objective in painting it's to be able to paint in a tuxedo with perfectly shined shoes and just not move a hair.

With paintings that have strong, sensual, foreboding contrasts much like his views on life, Dan Camp is a highly complex personality. Intense and mercurial, he is stoically serious about art one moment and whimsically playful the next. Although he often travels throughout the U.S. to complete portrait commissions, Camp has recently been adding a new studio onto the Encinitas home he shares with his companion Nilly Gill, an Israeli-born painter and poet. An innovative watercolorist, he has taught painting at Mira Costa College for the past ten years.

Camp's father, a night editor for the San Francisco Chronicle, *died when Camp was less than a year old. His mother, who later remarried, raised him and his two older brothers, one a musician and the other a nuclear plant quality controller. Camp has two teenage daughters.*

A lot of what I've been concerned with is time, the issue of time in paintings. When I was in graduate school I gave up on the idea and started making movies. I couldn't deal with trying to pinpoint time. Now I add side panels for another frame and do paintings in series. I figure if I worked in a triptych (three panels) I could have the side panels simultaneous to the center painting. I added the triptyches to the main painting after I saw the Medici Chapel in Florence. That work's all about time.

I did a painting about Bernard Goetz, taking an incident that happened and making more out of it, making much more far-reaching issues from just that one incident. I tried to work it like a metaphor by bringing in the Three Graces and the Judgment of Paris for a framework. I really would like to work that big again. It was a monumental effort to paint on it and to move it. I figured the monumentality of the size required some monumentality of subject matter. It's kind of hard for me to do the things I want to do, like the Bernard Goetz. My mother, who has been real supportive of my art, looks at it and goes "tsk tsk" and shakes her head and says, "I'll be so glad when you're doing your little watercolors again."

In the third grade she put me in a portrait painting class in south La Jolla. The teacher was an old guy named Major Willoughby. He was at the Pennsylvania Academy of Art in its hey day. That's how I got interested in John Singer Sargent. He was flipped out on Sargent because Sargent once used Willoughby's studio in Philadelphia to paint a portrait.

I do a lot of portrait commissions. They really wipe me out. If there's a lot of money offered you've just gotta do it. The worst part is that people are paying for something and they don't know what it's going to look like. There's a lot of faith on their side. That gets to me. The old puritan work ethic, you know? It's their money so they should have something they like. I can't get away from that. I want to get paid. If I'm even going to stretch the canvas I want to get paid. But I also want to make it a good painting. I really have to draw the line. I'm going to do this my way, and that's the way it is. It's gratifying. I usually always like it. The last one I did almost killed me, really threw me for a loop emotionally and physically, because I think I'd reached the point where the desire to please was so important that I was fighting with my sense of what I wanted to do.

I think sensuality is definitely a part of portraiture,

but it's a matter of covering it up. Like in our lives. It's like what we do in our lives. We cover up certain things or we flaunt certain things. Sargent just let it slide right off as soon as the brush hit the canvas.

I have to pretty much see it before I do the work. I saw the whole Goetz painting before I did it. It's pretty easy with watercolor; I can do anything I want with it. Painting is just a lot of work. I get at it as soon as possible and rush through it because I don't really like the process, especially oil. It's so messy, filthy. It's really working in trenches as far as I'm concerned. Watercolors are dandy, dandy.

I kind of like the idea of the 19th century painter William Merritt Chase who came into the class wearing his waistcoat and he never got anything on him until one time one of his students dropped some prussian blue on his foot and he said, "No more prussian blue in this class." Or Manet who painted with his top hat on. If I have any objective in painting it's to be able to paint in a tuxedo with perfectly shined shoes and just not move a hair. I admire that. My hands get all dirty. If I can just do that I'll be happy. Without getting messy.

Actually, my objective is to have assistants like Reubens, like some of the university professors who have all these graduate student flunkies. Only my flunkies would have to know how to paint. And I'd pay them.

Other than the fact that I paint what I see, I'm not part of any kind of movement. I don't read art magazines much except when I don't have anything to do and I go over to the library to see if the new issues are in. But it kind of strikes me that people who are making art these days always have to tell you what they're "involved" with. "I'm involved with the arms race," or "I'm involved with crimes against women." I'm at a point where I don't care what anybody else is involved with. I don't care to see their viewpoints put into an aesthetic framework where they expect me to like it. Although I do that, I don't want anybody to do it to me.

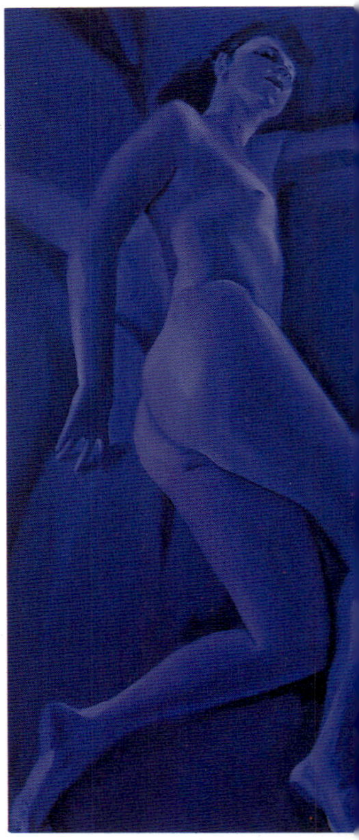

SELECTED BIOGRAPHY

BIRTHPLACE

Berkeley, California

EDUCATION

Principia College, Esah, Illinois, BA, 1969
Pennsylvania Academy of Fine Arts, 1970
University of California, San Diego, MFA, 1976

TEACHING

Mira Costa College, Oceanside, CA, 1977 to present

SOLO EXHIBITIONS

Memorial Union Gallery, Arizona State University at Tempe, 1977
Capitol University, Columbus, Ohio, 1978
Cygnus Gallery, San Diego, 1981
Gallery 129, La Jolla, 1986
Lyceum Theater, San Diego, 1987

GROUP EXHIBITIONS

California-Hawaii Regional, San Diego Museum of Art, 1971
National Watercolor Society, 1972 through 1975
Four States Biennial, Phoenix Art Museum, AZ, 1976
Summer Show, Anuska Gallery, San Diego, 1986

COLLECTIONS

Twenty-eight paintings, Combat Art Collection, U.S. Marine Corps, Washington, D.C.
Senator John Warner, Washington, D.C.
Principia College, Esah, Illinois
Capitol University, Columbus, Ohio
Mira Costa College, Oceanside, California

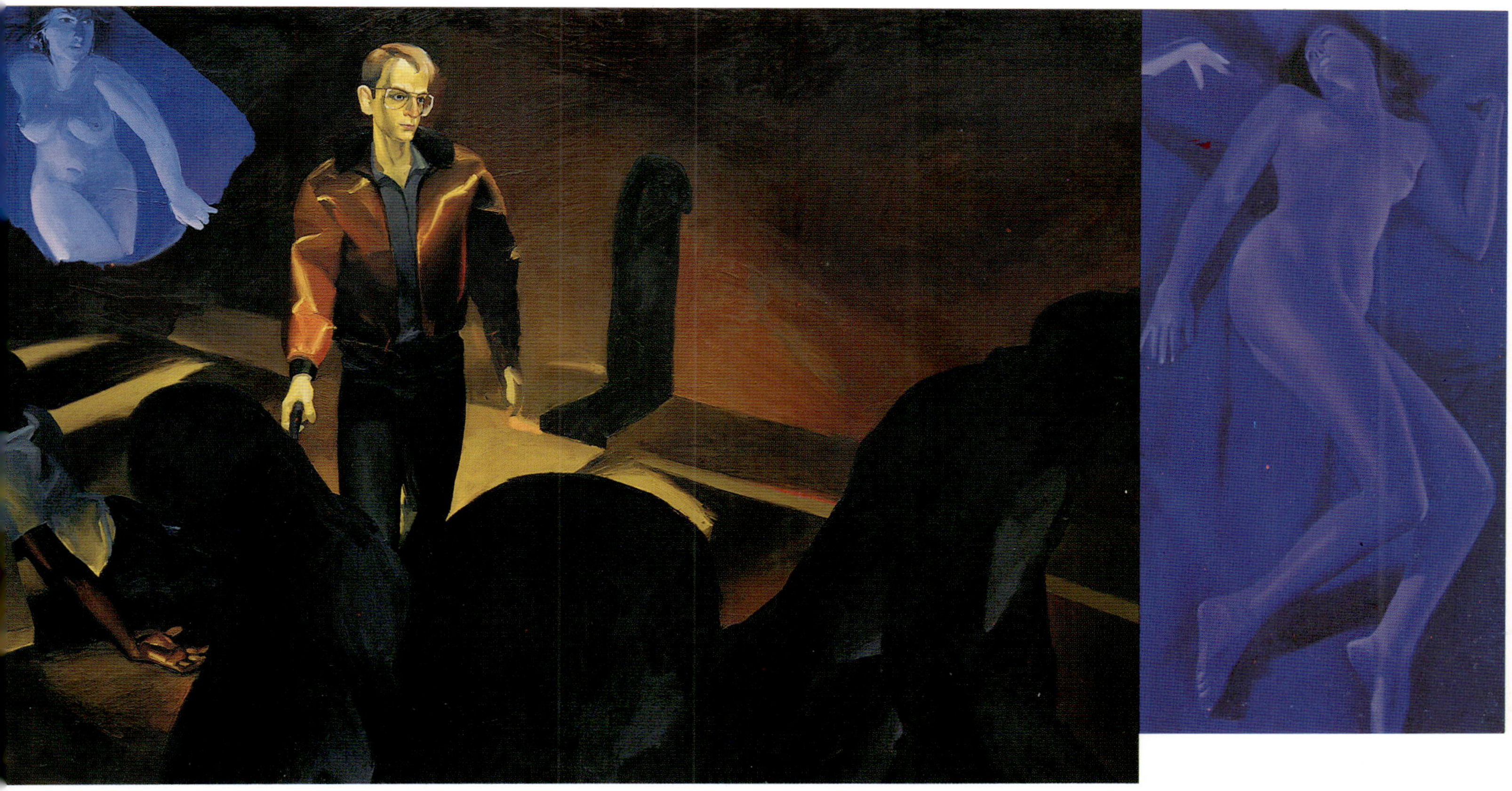

Judgement of Paris, oil/canvas, 204" × 84", 1986

Collection of the artist   Photo by Nathan Stimson

Kenneth Capps

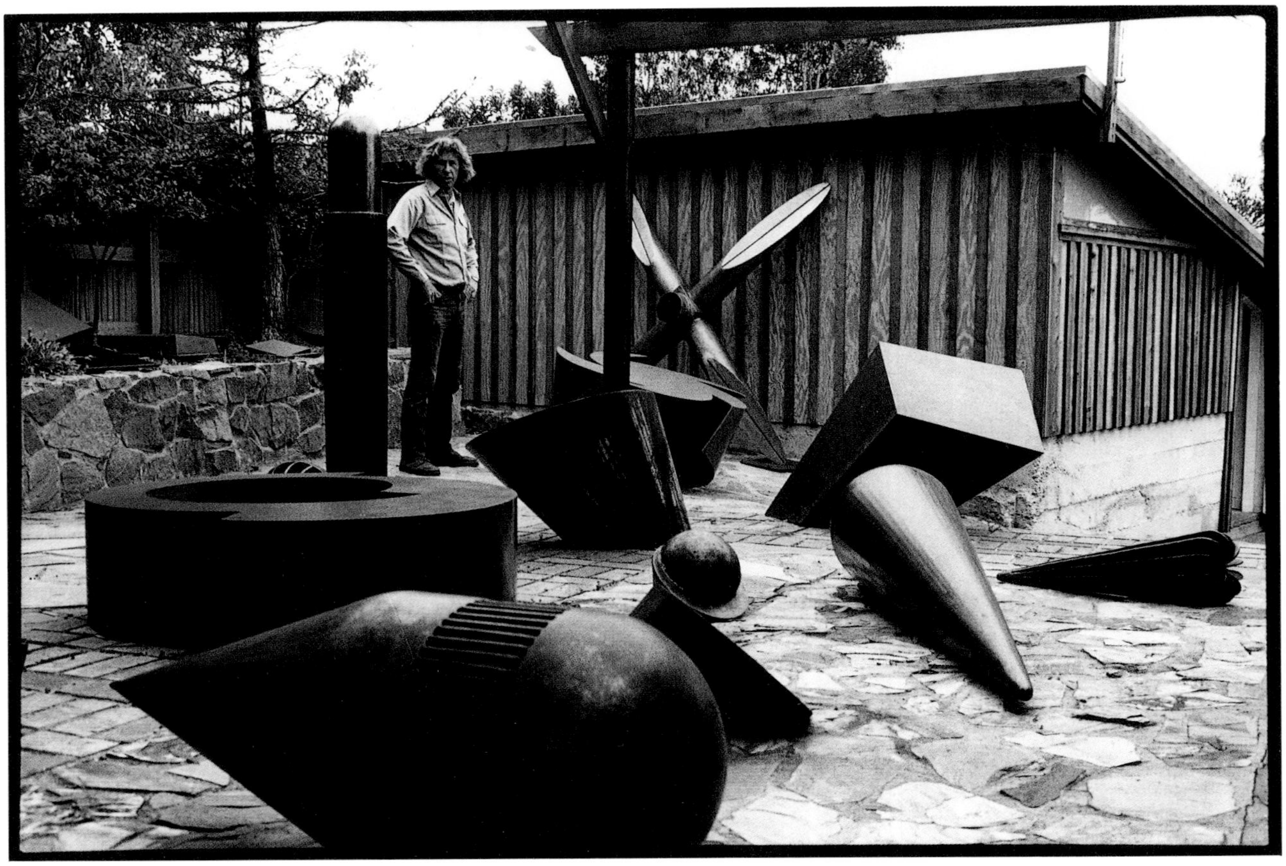

I have no problem with destroying a whole body of work, wiping out tons of steel, two years of work. I think it gives you new kinds of energy and new kinds of space and clarity that you can't get any other way.

Kenneth Capps is guarded with visitors, protective of the way his sculpture is seen, and adamant in his convictions about art and life.

Heavy-gauge steel work surrounds his Carlsbad home, strewn like bombs waiting to be defused. His sensibility to light, landforms, and placement is evident. Separated from the main studio and other work areas, a white display room houses the best of Capps's most recent sculptures. These metal forms utilize compressed air which is blown through their dramatic yet simple configurations, issuing subtle, haunting calls to the quiet listener.

Capps's development as an artist draws from an adventurous background. Before coming to San Diego to study art he had, among other things, gathered rocks for geologists on the Alaskan North Slope and herded musk oxen for anthropologists near the Bering Sea.

He lives with Katy, his wife of nearly twenty years who is an elementary school teacher, and their two teenagers in a hillside house overlooking the Pacific Ocean and the Aqua Hedonia Lagoon.

I remember one piece I did, a piece with a chain and two logs that were each twenty feet long and eighteen inches in diameter. I know even now my greatest joy and satisfaction above all else was when I tightened the thing down, really cranked it down and I didn't know if it was going to hold and I took the clamp off and ran because if it came down it would have wiped me out. You scrounge materials here and there and you put this thing together and you don't know how it's going to work. There was this risk involved and that kind of entry was very exciting. That gave me energy for probably a month after that.

This continuum of edge is very much connected to the way I used to ride motorcycles. As a kid I did art in many ways, motorcycles primarily. Bending, twisting, turning, tuning and then trying to ride. I probably had twenty bikes in my yard when I was sixteen. I used to sleep and eat bikes. That was my work, my life, my world. I was consumed just like I'm consumed with my work now. I'd ditch school and ride these dunes. I used to just love to hit a dune and try to hit it to the next dune. . . to glide through the air, almost like flying.

When I was sixteen someone had cut the back side off one of the dunes with a bulldozer to make a shooting range. I went off a thirty foot drop, no crash helmet, and it just wiped me out. I don't remember anything. I didn't remember being out there riding those dunes. The bike broke in five places, the frame disintegrated when it hit. Luckily I left the bike and went end over end. Sand was stuffed up every crevice of my body. I was in a coma for three days. My recall before that is a chance guess. In a coma you break with your history totally. It's the ultimate drama. Breaking.

I still have this instinct, no matter what has happened in the past I still try things out. I like to work the edges. A lot of time has passed since that accident but it's funny how the coma didn't take that out, that core is still there. But to me it just makes life much more alive when you exist that way. Life is exciting for me. If I removed that I might as well die.

I'm very hard on my work. I like to break with my past. I have no problem with destroying a whole body of work, wiping out tons of steel, two years of work. I think it gives you new kinds of energy and new kinds of space and clarity that you can't get any other way. When you cut something off and destroy it, you also conceptually destroy it. The break isn't just physical, it's very conceptual too. I think those breaks are very essential. I'm not nostalgic. I don't believe in nostalgia. That's not part of my identity.

Although some of my works I call sound pieces or sound sculptures, I don't think of them as that. The closest thing I can describe is that everyday we're in this environment and there's a bombardment of messages that we're taking in. Most of it goes right through us like a wave length. But if we could hold onto all this we wouldn't handle it anyway because mentally we couldn't exist with it. One of those waves came streaming through me when I looked at a certain form and thought, "How would it be if air came out of this? Maybe air should come out of it." But the fact was it was the idea for a new body of work. I don't like to talk about the sound works. In fact I'm very guarded about what I want to know about it, what I want to discuss about it, because I don't want to know too much. I want a naive element to be there.

I feel like I'm competing with every artist out there. When you're competing it's hard to maintain a real good friendship, especially with an artist you're competing with. You're both guarded. You don't want him to know your secrets and you don't want to know his. You don't want this kind of reference. So I'm very guarded about looking at art magazines, reading about other people's work, about knowing too much. I didn't used to be that way. I used to like to read everything, every article in *Artforum, Art in America*. At UCSD I got so crammed with knowledge I was just overloaded. But now I look at information quite differently and I'm very calculating about how I take in new information. Certain things I don't want to see. I don't want to be influenced. To maintain my own clarity I discriminate with people, with images, with things I see. I'd much rather discuss a profound movie or profound music.

I treat life with priorities. It's the way I approach work, the way I approach a day, the way I approach my existence. Making art is a priority in my life. To me it's taken on many levels. It obviously won't all get in. Every time I do a new body of work, I realize how much longer ago that should have been done and how much further I have to go. Not only do I not have a choice, but I have only one choice and with that one choice I have no way to do it justice. There's no other time for anything else. The essence is time. There is no other choice. This is it.

SELECTED BIOGRAPHY

BIRTHPLACE

Kansas City, MO

EDUCATION

University of California, San Diego, BA and MFA, 1975

SOLO EXHIBITIONS

O.K. Harris Gallery, New York, 1976 and 1977
Quint Gallery, San Diego, 1982 and 1984
Boehm Gallery, Palomar College, San Marcos, California, 1985
"Metered Atmosphere" installation, Brandstater Gallery, Loma Linda University, Riverside, California, 1987
Saxon-Lee Gallery, Los Angeles, 1987

GROUP EXHIBITIONS

"Public Sculpture Urban Environment," The Oakland Museum, Oakland, California, 1974
"Sculpture in California 1975 to 1980," San Diego Museum of Art, 1980
"Constructed Metal Modern Sculpture," College of Creative Studies, University of California, Santa Barbara, 1984
"A San Diego Exhibition," La Jolla Museum of Contemporary Art, 1985
"Sculpture Arenas," Mandeville Gallery, University of California, San Diego, 1987

GRANTS

National Endowment for the Arts, Visual Artists Fellowships
Pollock/Krasner Foundation

PUBLIC COLLECTIONS

Storm King Art Center, Mountainville, New York
Sculpture Park, Alfred Schmela, Dusseldorf
Aldrich Museum of Contemporary Art, Ridgefield, Connecticut
Kaufman and Broad Collection, Los Angeles
Oakland Museum, Oakland

Meter X8A and *Meter X8*, steel, both 200"×68"×20", 1987

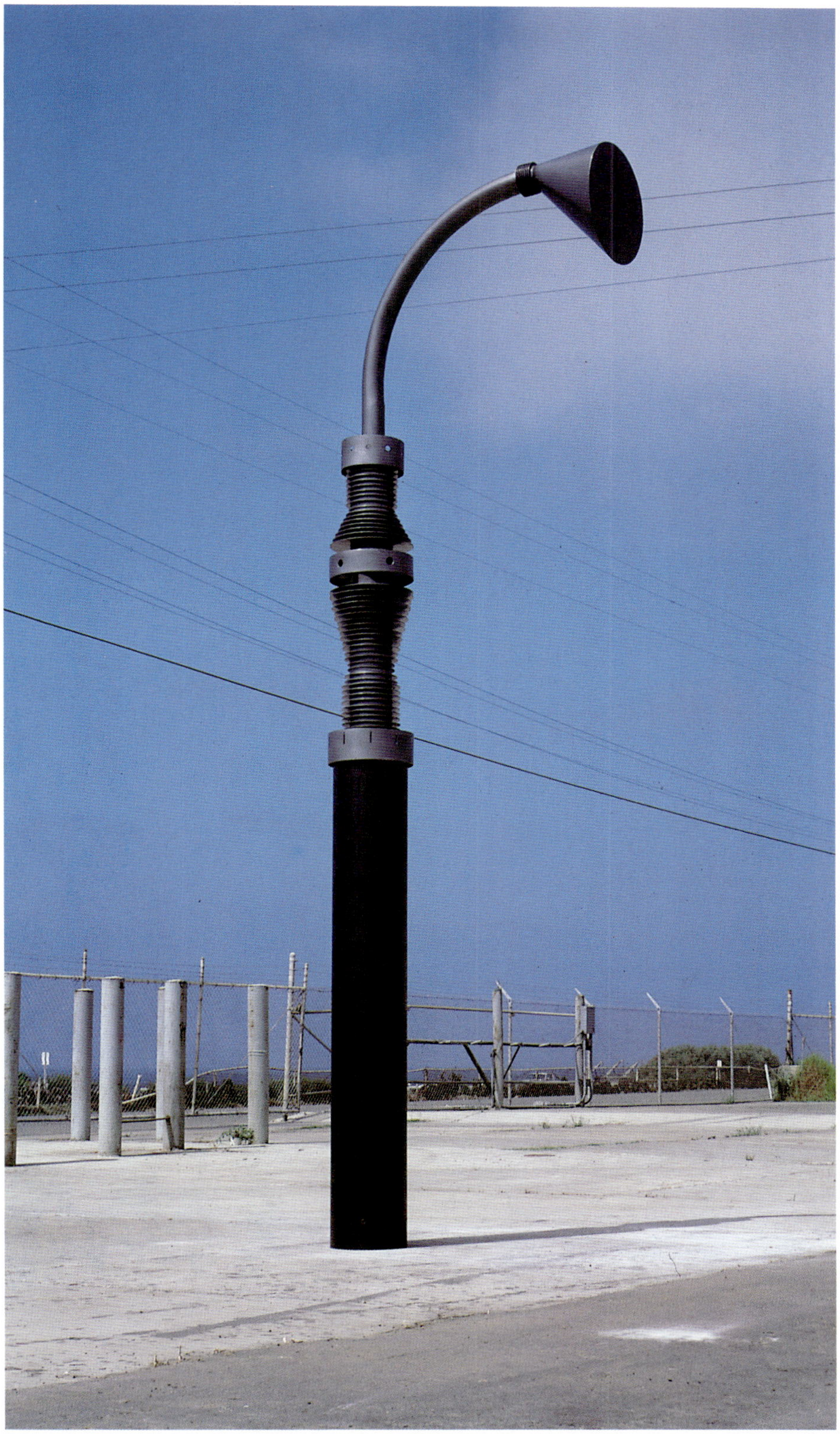

Meter X8, steel, 200″×68″×20″, 1987

Harold Cohen

I'm an extraordinarily lucky person because this is the only moment in history in which what I've done could have happened.

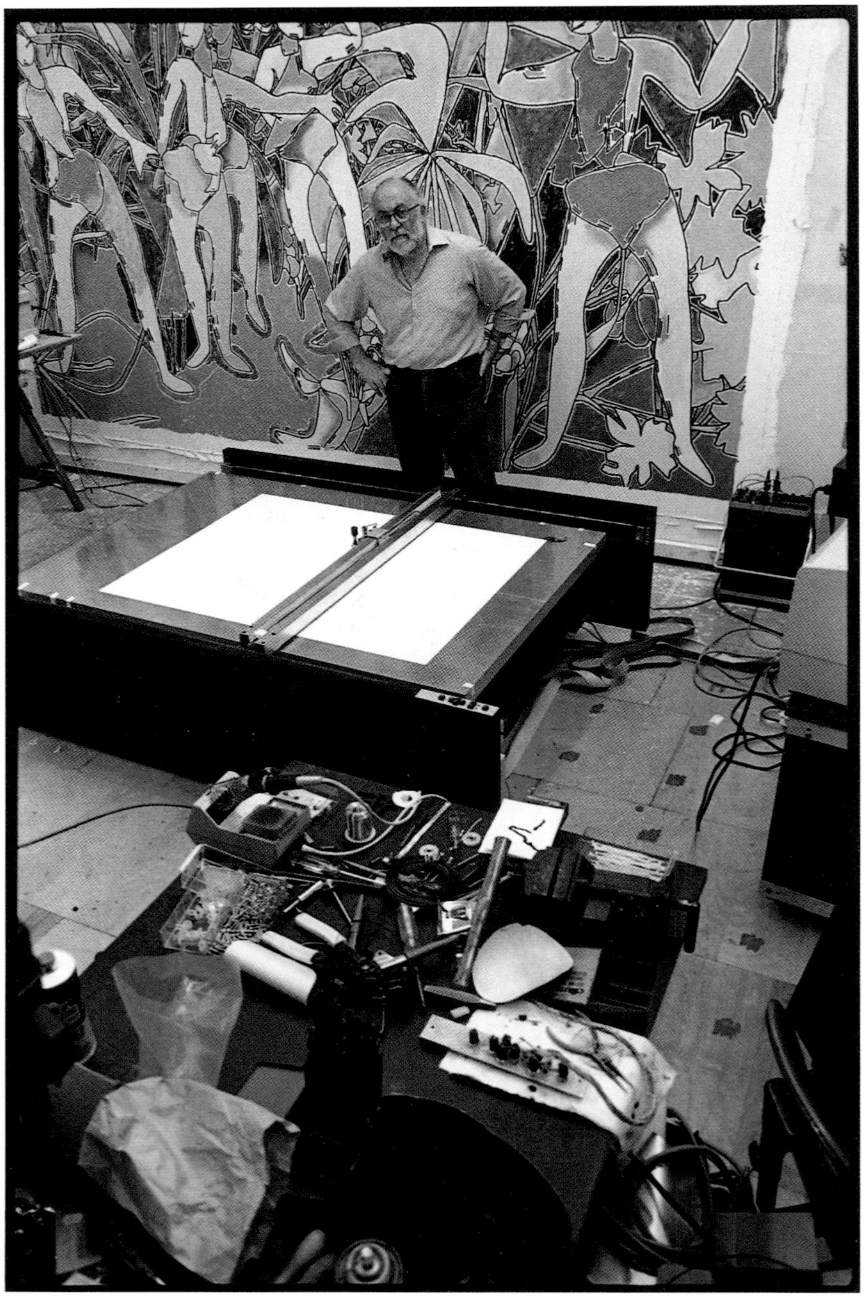

In his busy Water Tank studio at UCSD, with the help of a few assistants, Harold Cohen is preparing to ship two of his hand built, computer-driven drawing machines to Boston museums. Meanwhile another assistant applies brilliant color with an artificial finger to a nine-by-twelve-foot painting of several figures which takes up part of the studio wall.

Speaking in a soft British accent, his greying hair pulled back in a ponytail and shirt-sleeves rolled up, Cohen chooses words patiently and carefully in explaining his interest and explorations into artifical intelligence. In no uncertain terms he disavows any interest in mundane "computer art" which utilizes pre-packaged, "instantly wonderful" programs. He is concerned only with art theory and the development of cognitive processes.

In coming to teach at UCSD from London, where he had left behind a highly successful career, he found himself involved in exploring the potentials and challenges of computing. Now firmly settled in his lab in one of the Visual Art Department Quonset huts, Cohen is proving that his explorations are not only of great fascination to art students but worthy of further academic exploration.

He was raised in London by parents from Russia and Poland. His older brother took over the family hardware stores and his younger brother has become a successful British artist. Cohen has three grown children. His second wife Becky Cohen, is a respected photographer.

I've never been so engaged in my life as I am now by what I do. The problem for me with painting is that I have this sort of insatiable, quite unreasonable need to understand how things work. And the trouble with painting as I practiced it – it is probably more true of the late twentieth century than at any other time in history – was that there was nowhere to put my mind. You can sort of intuit your way around a painting, you can inspire yourself around a painting, you can passionate yourself around a painting. But you probably can't think your way around a painting. I found that very disturbing. It was as if I was not allowed to use all of myself.

Right through the 1960s my work really had to do with the whole problem of representation, of why we can make marks and people assign meanings to those marks. I was doing it and I was, if you like, getting better and better at it, but never feeling that I was understanding anything more about it. I wasn't finding my way to a field theory of representation. I felt like a sort of inspired idiot or something, doing all this stuff. There was nothing wrong with the work. I look back on my work in the sixties and think it was pretty good. I was actually living off my work as a painter, but something about what was going on wasn't really satisfying.

It was pure chance I got involved with the computer when I came to San Diego. I was in some disquiet about my work when I came here, it didn't come on overnight. I had become more interested in the perceptual side of how we see things rather than the cognitive issues having to do with what they really mean. I had the feeling that there are more interesting things going on outside my studio than inside my studio. In fact, I still believe there are more interesting things going on outside the artist's studio than inside the artist's studio.

The biggest single difference between what I am doing now and what I was doing previously is that the new drawings are manifestly figurative. That is not merely a break with what I was doing with computing up to a year ago but a break from anything I've been doing since I was drawing from life in art school some thirty-five years ago. Immediately prior to this figurative work were quasi-figurative drawings as if they were things of the real world, people-like entities, rock-like entities. The critical turning point came before that, however, when I introduced the idea of overlapping.

It seems to me that there are two main

paradigms in art-making and painting. One is what you might call the "rock art paradigm" where everything in the image occupies its own space, nothing ever overlaps anything else. You go out of your way to avoid an occlusion. The other paradigm is what we might call a "window paradigm" under which Western art has been operating for the last five hundred years. In that, the edge of the frame is an analog for the frame of a window through which you're looking at things in the outside world where things do overlap each other, things do occlude each other.

So then I introduced the notion of overlapping to the computer program so that things occluded each other. And the program started producing this quasi-visual space. The pressure on me to make things in the drawings more object-like simply increased to the point where I had no alternative but to give the program real knowledge of the things in the world. There is in fact a smooth transition from non-figuration to what we call figuration. I had moved through that transition simply by changing the state of the program's knowledge.

What I'm doing now challenges the mind on so many levels. I think the reasons I got involved with computing in the first place – quite a long time before it occurred to me that it would have anything to do with art-making – was the sense of having my mind expanded. Programming called into play intellectual muscles that I didn't know I had, it was so long since I'd used them, if ever. And now I have to be able to deal with the very broad range of conceptual issues on a large number of different levels. I find that very challenging.

If you don't value what you've got you might as well dump it. My willingness to put my painting career aside allowed me to find new and more powerful strategies for dealing with the things that had really concerned me, from which I had found myself increasingly separated during the 1960s. I was perfectly aware that most of my buddies thought I'd gone completely bonkers. I was prepared to chance a real long shot. What I've got now is worth infinitely more than I've lost. I'm an extraordinarily lucky person because this is the only moment in history in which what I've done could have happened.

SELECTED BIOGRAPHY

BIRTHPLACE

London, England

EDUCATION

University of London, Diploma in Fine Arts, 1951

TEACHING

University of California, San Diego, 1968 to present

SOLO EXHIBITIONS

Retrospective, Whitechapel Gallery, London, 1964
"Three Behaviors for the Partitioning of Space," Los Angeles County Museum of Art, 1972
Stedelijk Museum, Amsterdam, 1977
"Harold Cohen: Drawing," San Francisco Museum of Modern Art, 1979
The Tate Gallery, London, 1983

GROUP EXHIBITIONS

Thirty-third Venice Biennale, representing the UK, 1966
Documenta III, 1964 and Documenta 6, 1977, Kassel, Germany
"Artists at Curwen," 1977; "Images of Ourselves," 1980; "The Kelpra Studio: Artists Prints 1961 to 1980," 1980; "Landscape: The Printmaker's View," 1980, The Tate Gallery, London
"TSUKUBA-EXPO 85," World Fair, one of four exhibits in the US Pavilion on the theme of Artificial Intelligence and Communications, Japan, 1985
"The Age of Intelligent Machines," travelling exhibition, Boston Museum of Science, 1987 to 1989

PUBLICATIONS

The Homecoming, Edition de Luxe of the play by Harold Pinter, Designed and illustrated by Harold Cohen, 1967
Drawing for Machine and Four Hands, with Becky Cohen, limited edition photo-record, 1976
15 Flower World Variations, Poems by Jerome Rothenberg and drawings by Harold Cohen, Membrane Press, 1984
The First Artificial Intelligence Coloring Book, with Becky Cohen and Penny Nii, William Kaufman, 1984

GRANTS AND HONORS

National Endowment for the Arts, Research grants
Digital Equipment Corporation
Fujitsu America Corporation
Kurzweil Foundation
Research Awards, Creative Arts Institute, University of California, Berkeley

COLLECTIONS

Tate Gallery, London
Victoria and Albert Museum, London
British Petroleum, London
Mural, Ontario Science Center, Toronto, Canada
Mosaic mural, Computer Science Department, Stanford University, Palo Alto

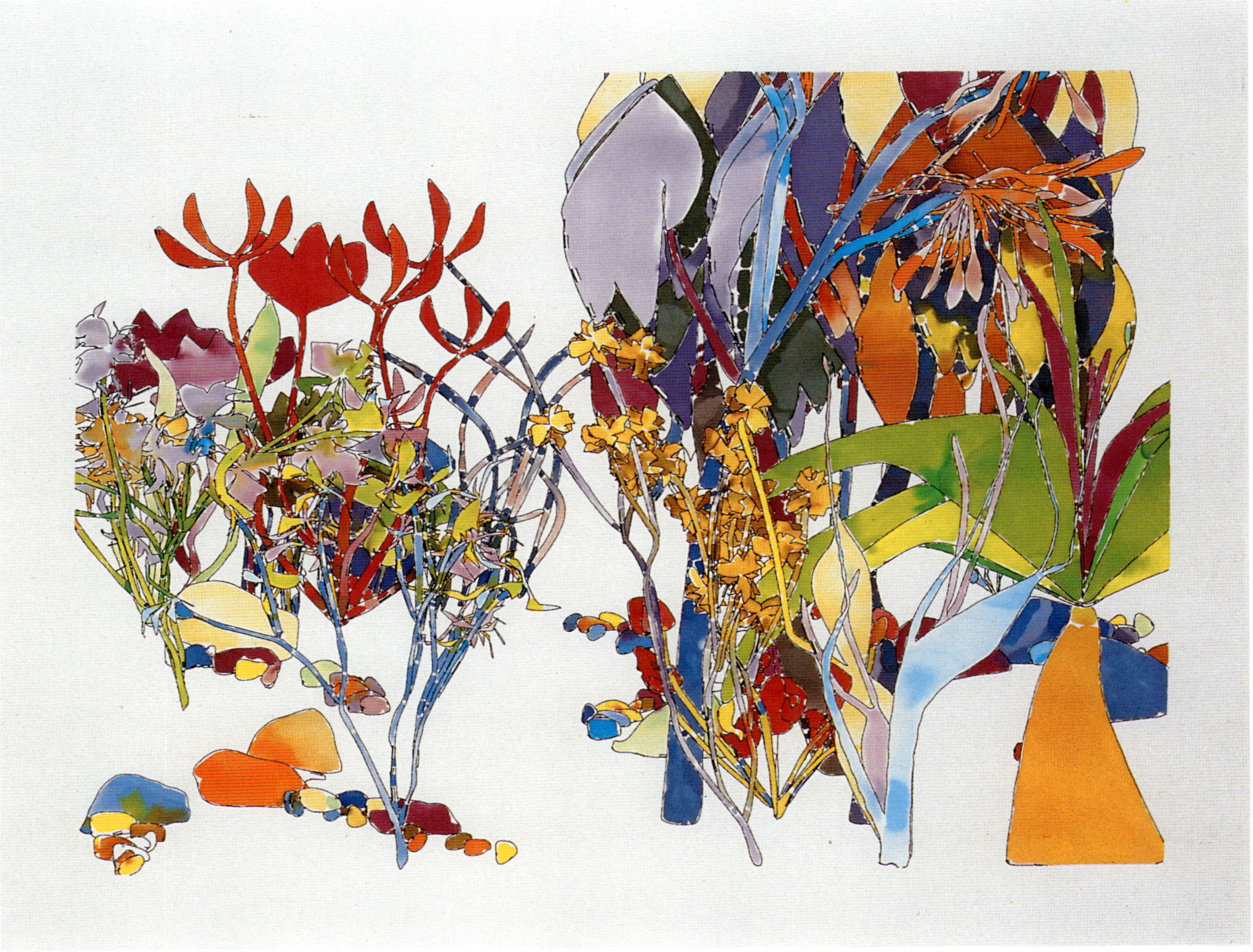

LW13 753, hand-colored computer-generated drawing, 38″×50″, 1987

Photo by Linda Winters

Janet Cooling

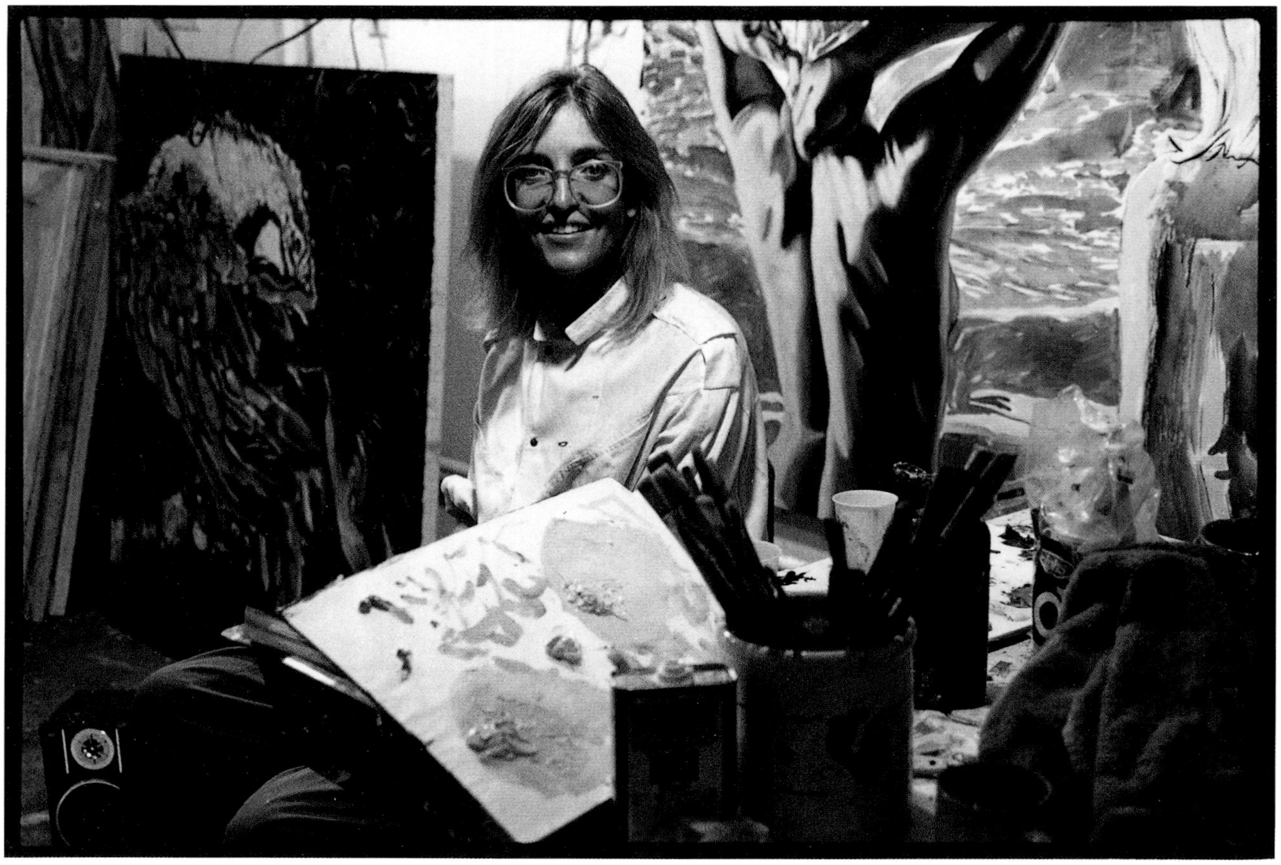

A lot of anger has been present in my work. I'm trying to get away from that and deal with female power instead of victimization.

Talking in her kitchen, Janet Cooling seems oblivious to the loud, constant stream of sound effects and smatterings of conversation offered by Roscoe, her Yellow Nape Amazon parrot, who she affectionately refers to as "my animal ally." Roscoe is her constant companion as she paints in the studio just off the kitchen.

Cooling has been preparing for a twelve-year retrospective in Chicago and her energy runs high as she talks about the struggles and vision of her new paintings. She has recently decided to give up her Los Angeles studio, clearly an important choice which forced an assessment of her spiritual and artistic focus. While her earlier works, which had commanded critical acclaim in Chicago and New York, were considered "sexually shocking," she has become best known in San Diego for her use of exotic high color and rich texture in animal and human close-ups.

Cooling grew up in Pennsylvania with an older brother and a sister two years younger. With Jacqui Corlin, a friend since 1981, she has recently bought a home near San Diego State University where Cooling teaches.

I'm working on inner images more than portraits. They're not really portraits at all. The way I paint is kind of visceral. My work is very, very passionate. It's a very, very hot type of work. I think the energy is really embodied in the stroke. And my use of color is real intuitive. It almost goes back to people like Gauguin and Van Gogh. It's very hot, exotic and sensual. It's one of my powers as an artist.

My mother could have been an artist. She was a thwarted, powerful person and like a lot of women of that generation she got stopped. She had a real love of nature and a real sense of the magic in it. The house was filled with paintings. My mother made a lot of things and I think her interest got transmitted to me. My father wanted to be a musician, but he started out as an engineer and ended up as a labor negotiator on the side of the company, not on the side of the people. I got a lot of my political material from him, but more as a reaction. I went way beyond my family. As a little kid I read a lot of books. I remember reading Thoreau, *On Civil Disobedience*, in the seventh grade. I was really nourishing myself with books. I would sit at the dinner table and talk about these ideas.

I think growing up in Pennsylvania was a real influence for me. I had a lot of magical experiences with nature. We used to live at the shore and I would go swimming in the ocean every single night. Also in the back yard we had a swamp and an orchard. I just ran free. I would have encounters with snakes all the time and was constantly encountering animals. A lot of my work is informed by that.

Animal imagery has been in my work since I began putting them in landscapes, magical landscapes surrounded by nature images. There I was in New York painting these nature images and God knows where that was coming from. It was just a longing. I knew on an instinctive level to get out of New York. I knew that I needed to try something different. For one thing, I'm not interested in that particular type of glamour, in that type of relationship with people where it's like feeding on each other's blood. It's awful. Some people love it. I hate it. And the lack of connection to nature was a very serious issue. Living like a caged animal was too much for me.

In the past I've worked with really little baby rabbits, little creatures like deer, very vulnerable and tender, potentially victim symbols. I'm working now with wolves and scavengers, tigers, snakes, birds, eagles. They are power symbols, much more like really wild, wild things, not little vulnerable things.

At times I was dealing with a more political consciousness, working against nuclear energy, war. A lot of anger has been present in my work. I'm trying to get away from that and deal with female power instead of victimization. I'm really consciously phasing that out, at least not putting it into my art.

At this point I'm thinking more about what a symbol is, what I am really conveying. Anything to do with my art before was pure feeling, pure science fiction. But this simplification process is interesting. It's something I've never been attracted to before. It's real hard. It's almost kind of reductive to a certain extent. I think in order to convey that kind of passion, that kind of heat, with that kind of exotic color, everything else has to be stripped down to those elements.

The process I'm going through now is one of real clarification. I'm thirty-five and I think that women go through this stage between thirty-five and forty where they fall in and take a long hard look and a re-centering. That's what I'm doing, re-centering, and looking to go to the next level. And the only way I can go to the next level is through working.

SELECTED BIOGRAPHY

BIRTHPLACE

Chester, Pennsylvania

EDUCATION

Pratt Institute, Brooklyn, NY, BFA, 1973
School of the Art Institute of Chicago, MFA, 1975

TEACHING

San Diego State University, 1984 to present

SOLO EXHIBITIONS

Roger Litz Gallery, New York, 1982
Nancy Lurie Gallery, Chicago, 1979, 1980, 1983
Getler/Pall/Saper Gallery, New York, 1985
Feature Gallery, Chicago, 1985 and 1986
Twelve year retrospective, Beacon Street Gallery, Chicago, 1987

GROUP EXHIBITIONS

"Young Americans," Allen Art Museum, Oberlin College, 1981
"Extended Sensibilities," The New Museum, New York, 1982
Forty-first Venice Biennale, Venice, Italy, 1984
"Disarming Images: Art for Nuclear Disarmament," travelling exhibition curated by Nina Felshin, ICI, 1984 to 1986
"Going Fishing," Graham Modern, New York, 1987

COLLECTIONS

Bank of America, San Francisco
Prudential Insurance, New York
Chemical Bank, New York
Allen Art Museum, Oberlin College
Illinois State Museum, Springfield, Illinois

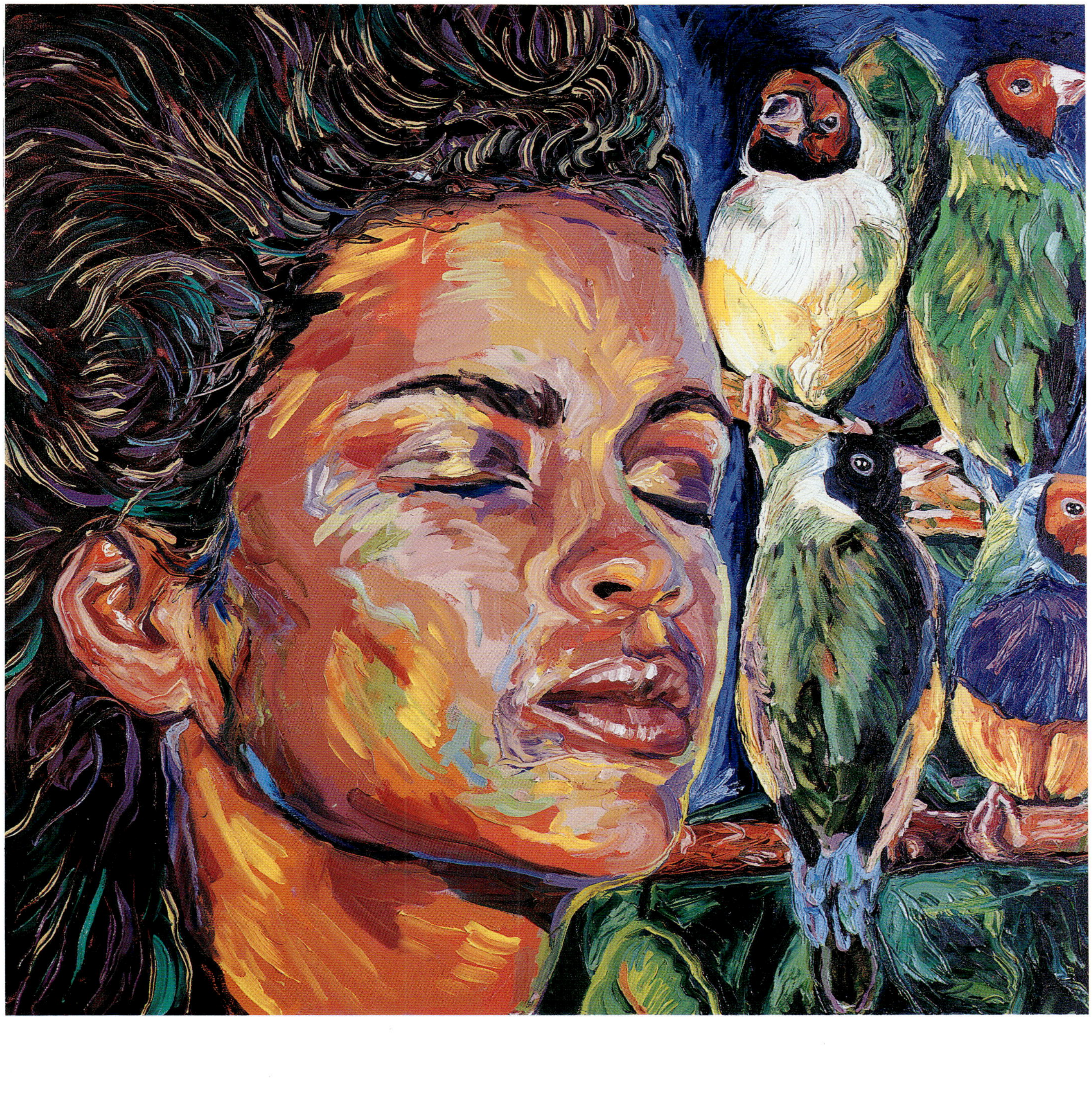

Untitled, oil/canvas, 48″×48″, 1987

Joyce Cutler-Shaw

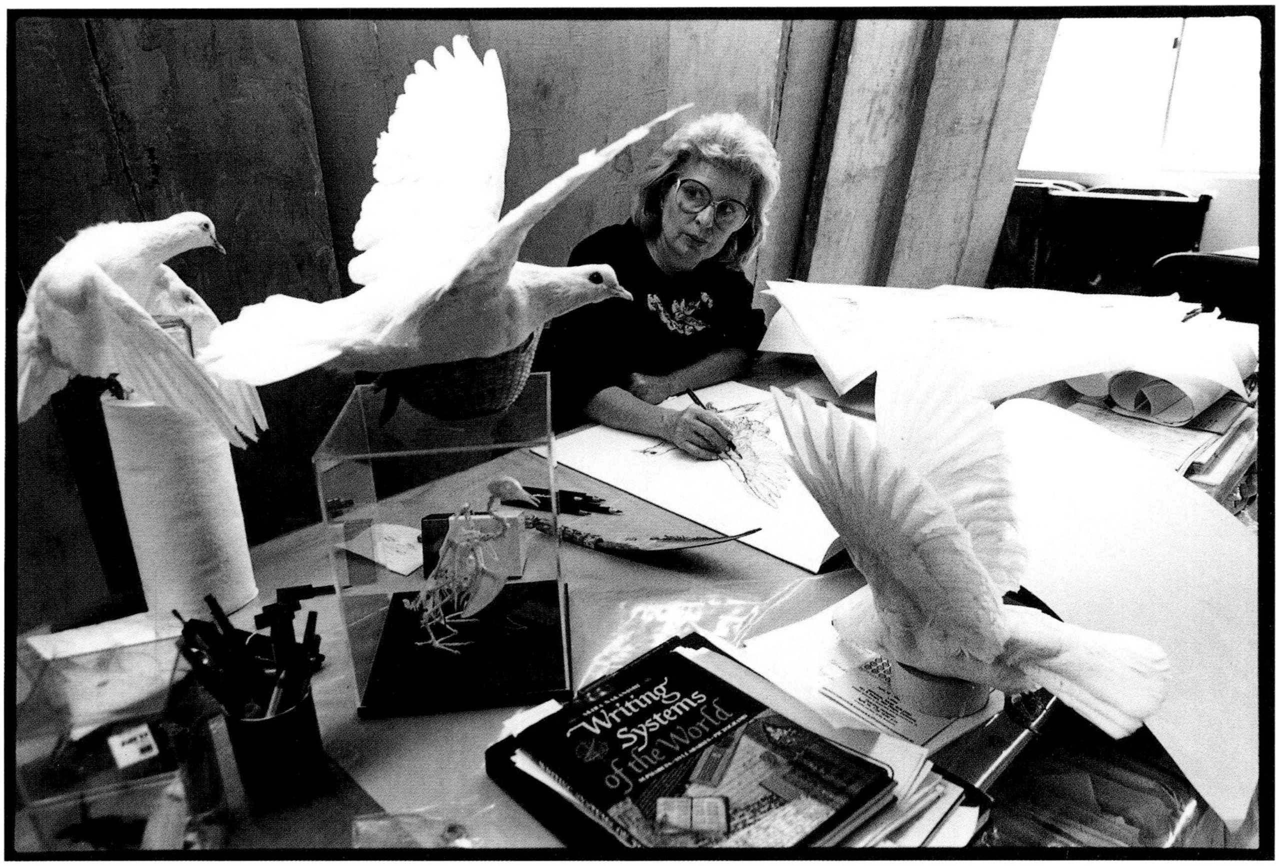

The artist must be open and free and responsive. . . . the artist is the messenger of hidden messages, of things that are underneath the structure.

In a non-descript Kearny Mesa office complex Joyce Cutler-Shaw develops her ideas and seeks to create new languages to communicate her sensitive and passionate feelings of the inner and outer world. She is committed and energetic in her approach to realizing projects even if they require acres of land and congressional approval.

Her ability to communicate in many media has led to public forums as diverse as the Los Angeles International Airport and the United Nations Plaza. Using birds, ice sculpture, and names written over and over, Cutler-Shaw is no stranger to using whatever means best realizes her visions. To continue the development of her multifaceted work "The Alphabet of Bones," she has recently begun rising at four in the morning to practice Chinese calligraphy. These techniques have been taught to her by Ming Yi Feng, a Chinese dramatist and master calligrapher visiting UCSD from Beijing.

From 1979 to 1982 Cutler-Shaw hosted one of a rare series of locally sponsored PBS Television programs entitled, "Art and Artists: Art of the 80's," interviewing foremost U.S. artists. She is now busily engaged as Project Director for The Museum of Seasonal Change. She lives in La Jolla and is married to Jerry Shaw, a businessman. She has three grown children.

The Alphabet of Bones condenses what not only my work but my life is about. It is about the concern for language, for a medium of communication between oneself and the other, ourselves and each other, between nature and human nature, the internal self and the external world. It's a search for communication.

I'm very much aware that we're mortal, we die, but that life is really very sweet and beautiful in the most devastating situations. Perhaps that's something that's been my own saving grace through a very difficult childhood, a very painful adolescence, a very distraught and unhappy young adulthood; there's always a distance, an objectivity. In the worst of times I had an ability to see the situation as a painter, as a graphic artist, as a drawer, as someone who wanted to represent this scene, this situation in its immediacy, in its full terms, but also in its visual terms. That part of me that stood apart to observe – the observer. I think this is the essential characteristic that made me have to be an artist. And then the problem was discovering not what to say, because that's there, but how to find a language to communicate these thoughts, these feelings, this set of connections. It inevitably had to be a multilevel work. I started out writing. I was always drawing and writing as a child in this private language, this private on-going dialogue with myself in lieu of the other.

My mother was a very talented woman. She left school when she was in the third grade but she was trained as a milliner. She was an illegal alien from Canada. I think she married my father because she thought he was an American citizen. He said he was born in Chelsea, Massachusetts; it turned out he has born in Russia. He was illegal and had come over when he was a very young boy. He was not a provider, he was a gambler. She left him when I was less than a year old.

When I was three she went to New York to make her way. She got jobs managing shops, ladies ready-to-wear. We never lived any place more than three years. I still find every move a trauma. We lived in furnished rooms, not even apartments, and that was a way for somebody to take care of me. I had some rather dreadful experiences. I had some rather lovely ones, but I had some rather dreadful ones. Except every Sunday was my day with my mother. She would buy me a gardenia corsage. We went to Central Park and then we went to the Museum of Modern Art and then to the Metropolitan Museum and then we would go out to eat some place. Later, some of her boyfriends were very wealthy. She would work twelve hours a day and then go out dancing at the nightclubs, the Copacabana. I started going to nightclubs when I was about eight years old. They would take me. Her boyfriend would take me to Best's and buy me three piece outfits. He would sit there with a big cigar and say, "What have you got for this little girl?" And the lady would bring out all these outfits. I was extremely shy.

There is also this internal person who is very bold. It really has to do with an objective, something I wanted to do. It's the same thing now. I want to do a Museum of Seasonal Change. If I get an idea, I want to realize it. There's this kind of determination, this sense of discovering a permission process and realizing it. I get carried away. I don't give up in time on some things. I certainly relate to Christo in the sense that he gets a very grand project, works it out completely, does not compromise his concept, and he realizes it. It may take years and there are some that he does not realize, but it's a matter of not giving up. Not giving up.

The artist must be open and free and responsive. That's The Messenger. The artist is a messenger of hidden messages, of things that are underneath the structure. I could draw the figure well. I was interested in gestural drawing and I didn't know what was inside. So I thought I'd sketch the internal structure. We're an integrated system.

I want to say what it meant to experience a birth twice, death twice, the pain of being a survivor. I know what it is to be a survivor. I can tell everything about everything that I can do or experience if I find a new language. The Alphabet of Bones is a search for communication, this coincidence of form and image. It has imagery that everyone understands. Everyone understands a bone, a bird, and flight and feathers. A bird is a perfect image.

My *zaddeh* (grandfather) called me *Feigeleh*. It meant bird. He'd say, "The things that I've written are true. They're all true." I'd leave him to go back to my mother and he'd say, "My *feigeleh fliegen*." And I would fly away. I didn't think of it for years until I went to a pigeon show and saw how we take a natural phenomenon and we so shape it that there is an exquisite aesthetic in the feathers, the things you can judge and compete with. But also they have beaks so short that they can't even feed their own young. Their capacity for natural existence has been distorted. Everything in the image of the bird has manifestations of the real world and can express the range of human experience metaphorically and factually.

SELECTED BIOGRAPHY

BIRTHPLACE

Detroit, MI

EDUCATION

New York University, BA, 1953
Columbia University, graduate studies, literature
University of California, San Diego, MFA, 1972

SOLO EXHIBITIONS

"The Lady and the Bird," Fisher Gallery, University of Southern California, 1976
"The Lady and the Bird VI," Apropos Gallery, Luzern, Switzerland, 1979
MESSENGER, "Wingtrace," San Diego Museum of Natural History, 1985
MESSENGER, "Wingtrace/The Sign of Its Track," Johnson Museum of Art, Cornell University and National Academy of Sciences, Washington, D.C., 1986
MESSENGER, "Its Song, Its Call, Its Cry," Intersection, San Francisco, 1988

GROUP EXHIBITIONS

"Three Directions," Newport Harbor Museum of Art, Newport Beach, California, 1976
"American Women Artists," Museu de Arte Contemporanea, Universidade de Sao Paulo, Brazil, 1980
"Artreder/82," Muestra Internacional de Arte Grafico, Bilbao, Spain, 1982
"To the Astonishing Horizon, L.A.V.A.," curated by Peter Frank, Los Angeles Design Center, 1985
"Letters," The Clocktower, New York, 1986

PUBLIC PROJECTS

Namewall, Los Angeles International Airport
Charity Namewall, Charity Hospital, New Orleans
Messages from the World/Waters of the Nations, United Nations Plaza, San Francisco: opening event for the International Sculpture Conference, 1982
Namewall and three installations, Volt Corporate Park, City of Orange, California
Landmark Art Collaborative, "Urban Meadow, Urban Mesa, Museum of Seasonal Change," Three environmental sculpture projects for the City of San Diego

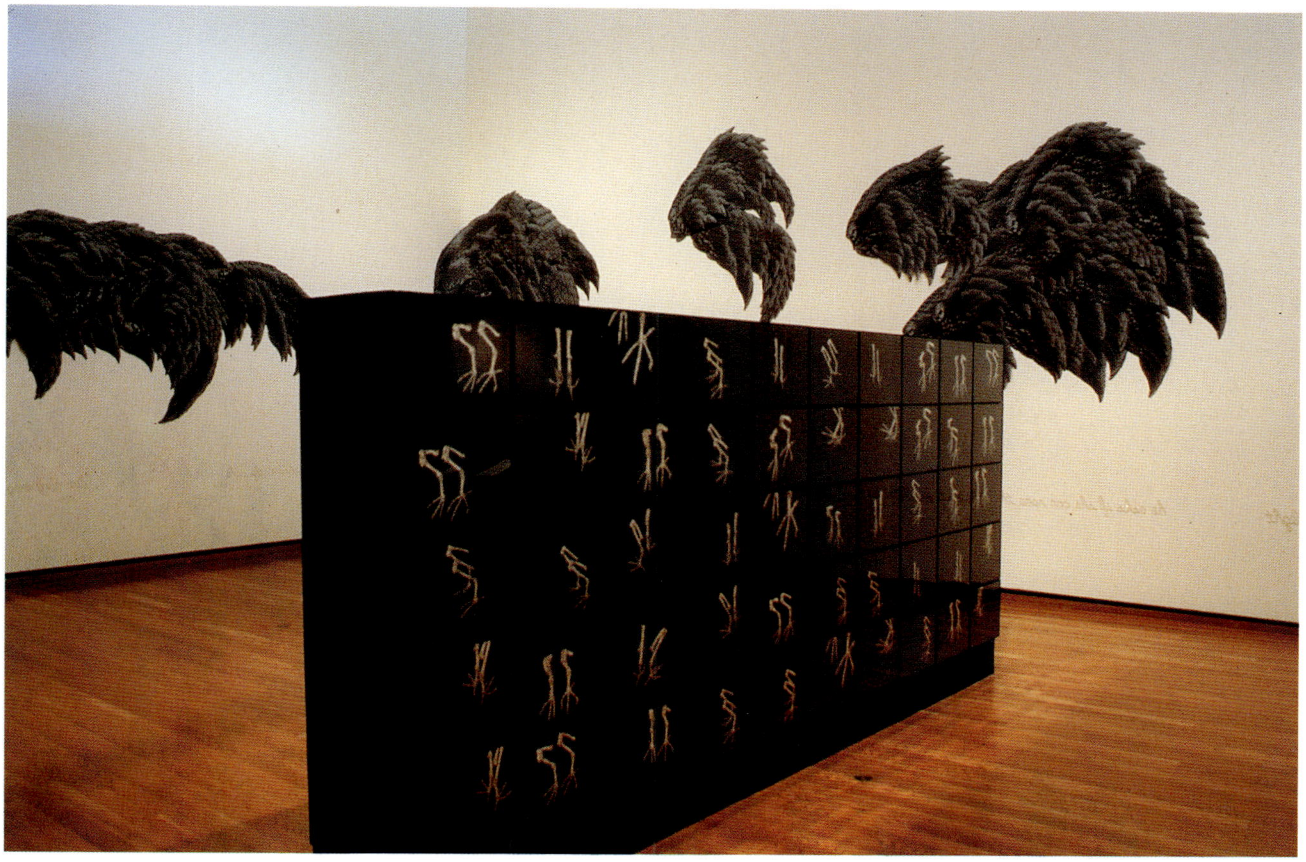

Wingtrace/The Sign of Its Track, installation Johnson Museum, Cornell University.

Alphabet of Bones and Wingwall, installation, 65″×150″, 1986.

Photo by Emil Ghinger

Manny Farber

The landscape that I live in is very important, just as the language that I decided on as a critic was excruciatingly important.

–From an interview with Richard Thompson in *Film Comment,* May-June 1977

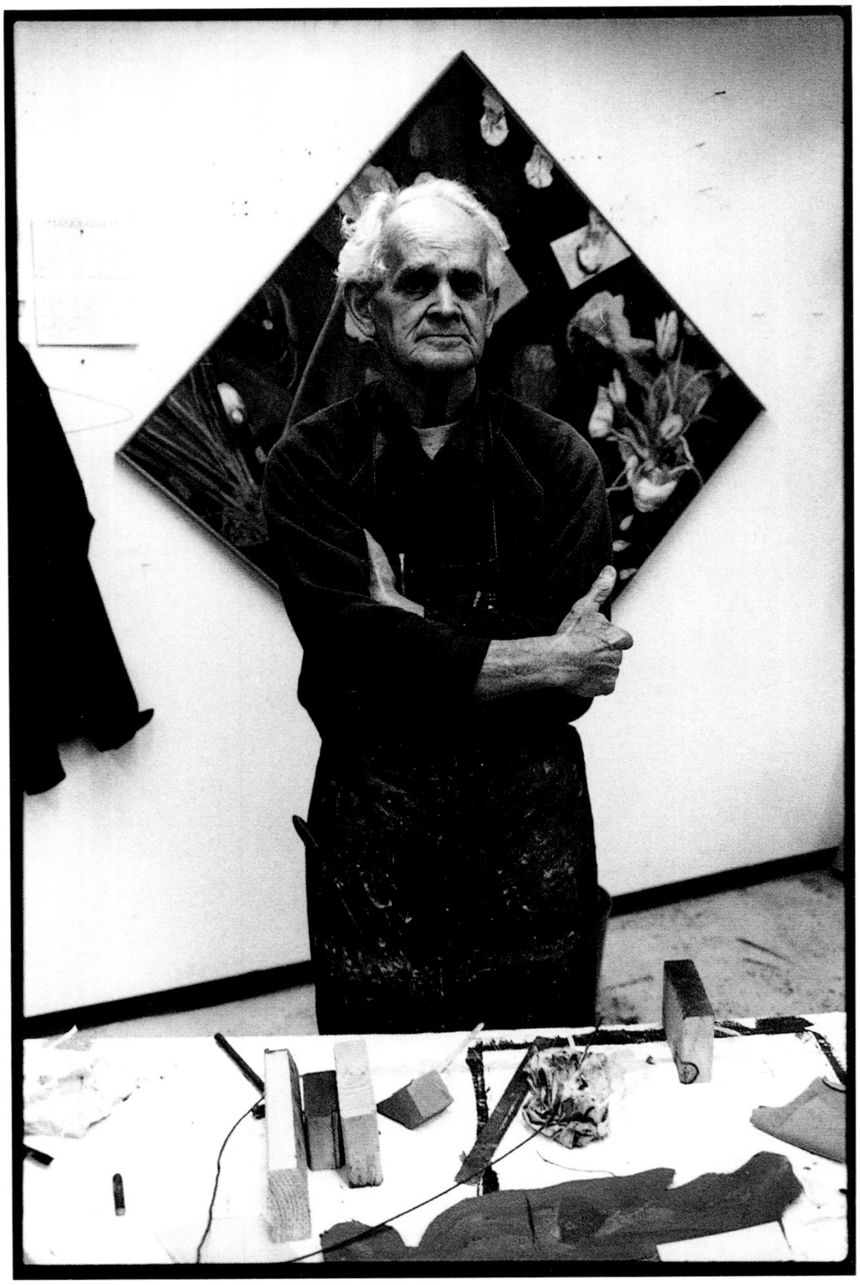

Manny Farber holes up as much as possible in his studio, eschewing conventional niceties. He is curt and has a reputation among colleagues and students as a sort of curmudgeon of an artist, though a brilliant one.

In New York during the 1940s and 1950s, Farber established himself as a tough, slangy film and art critic for The New Republic *and* Nation *magazines, writing with visceral intensity about grade B movies and abstract expressionism. During that time his friends were Jackson Pollock, Robert Motherwell, Hans Hoffman, and Clement Greenberg.*

Farber came to San Diego to teach at UCSD for a few months in 1970 and stayed, becoming the Visual Arts Department's first Professor Emeritus in late 1987. During the mid 1970s Farber's work shifted from large scale abstraction to complex narrative still life. Done from a bird's eye view, the richly colored and textured paintings are packed with references to films, autobiographical allusions and diaristic notes.

Farber has said of his work:

*"Most of what I liked (in the movies, art and criticism) is in the termite area. The important trait of termite – fungus – centipede art is amublatory creation which is an act of both observing and being in the world, a journeying in which the artist seems to be ingesting both the material of his art and the outside world through horizontal coverage." (*Manny Farber at the Movies*, 1971.)*

"The things I do – painting, criticism and teaching – all crawl along the termite path I promulgated years ago." (Interview with Richard Thompson, Film Comment*, 1977.)*

"The best examples of termite art appear. . . where the spotlight of culture is nowhere in evidence, so that the craftsman can be ornery, wasteful, stubbornly self-involved, doing go-for-broke art and not caring what comes of it." (Quote from James Wolcott's "Manny Farber's Termite Art," Vanity Fair*, May 1986.)*

Farber lives in Leucadia with Patricia Patterson, his third wife. They share space in the recently built studio she has designed. His daughter Amanda Farber is a graduate of UCSD and exhibits her paintings and sculptures.

I hate interviews almost as much as I hated my parents.

SELECTED BIOGRAPHY

BIRTHPLACE

Douglas, Arizona

EDUCATION

University of California, Berkeley, 1934
Stanford University, Palo Alto, CA, 1935
California School of Fine Arts, San Francisco, 1936
Rudolf Schaeffer School of Design, San Francisco, 1937

TEACHING

University of California, San Diego, 1970 to 1988

SOLO EXHIBITIONS

O.K. Harris Gallery, New York, 1969, 1971, 1972, 1977
Retrospective, La Jolla Museum of Contemporary Art, 1978
Solomon R. Guggenheim Museum, New York, 1981
Oil and Steel Gallery, New York, 1985
Museum of Contemporary Art, Los Angeles, 1985 to 1986

GROUP EXHIBITIONS

Peggy Guggenheim Group Show, New York, 1951
Clement Greenberg Group Show, New York, 1952
Annual Painting Exhibition, Whitney Museum of American Art, New York 1970
"19 Artists, Emergent Americans," Exxon National Exhibition, Guggenheim Museum, New York, 1981
"American Still Life: 1945-1983," Contemporary Arts Museum, Houston, 1983

PUBLICATIONS

Film critic, *The New Republic,* 1942 to 1947
Art and film critic, *The Nation,* 1949 to 1954
Articles in *Commentary,* 1952 to 1963; *The New Leader,* 1958 to 1960; *Artforum,* 1967 to 1973; and more
Negative Space, Manny Farber at the Movies, Praeger, New York, 1971; re-issued as *Movies,* soft-bound, 1974

GRANTS AND HONORS

Guggenheim Fellowship
National Endowment for the Arts, Visual Artist Fellowship
National Endowment for the Humanities
Film Scholarship Award, Los Angeles Film Critics

COLLECTIONS

Solomon R. Guggenheim Museum, New York
Whitney Museum of American Art, New York
La Jolla Museum of Contemporary Art
Worcester Art Museum, Massachusetts
Robert Rowan, Los Angeles

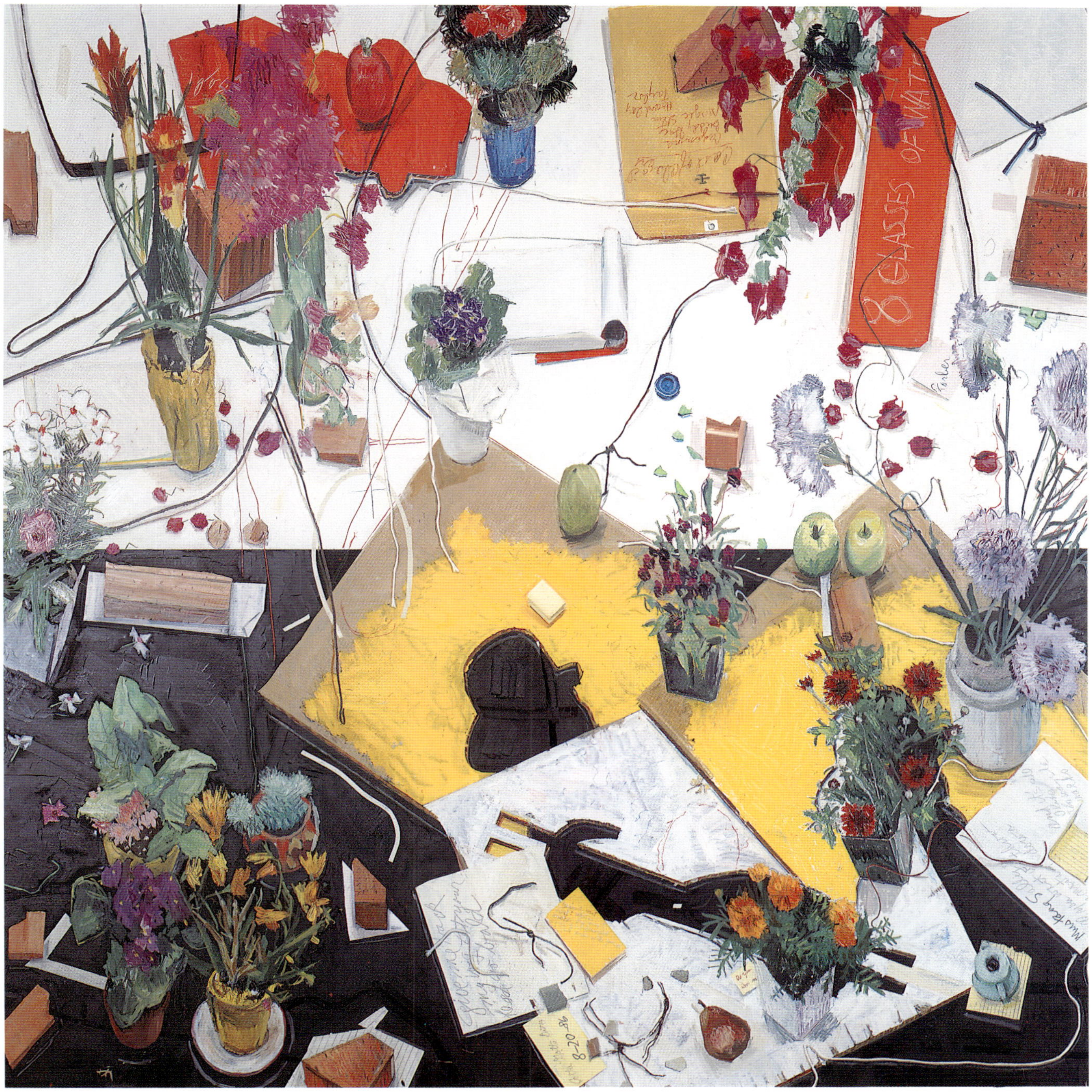

Photo by Roy Porello

Cezanne Avait Ecrit, oil/board, 72" × 72", 1986

Collection of Robert Rowan

Arline Fisch

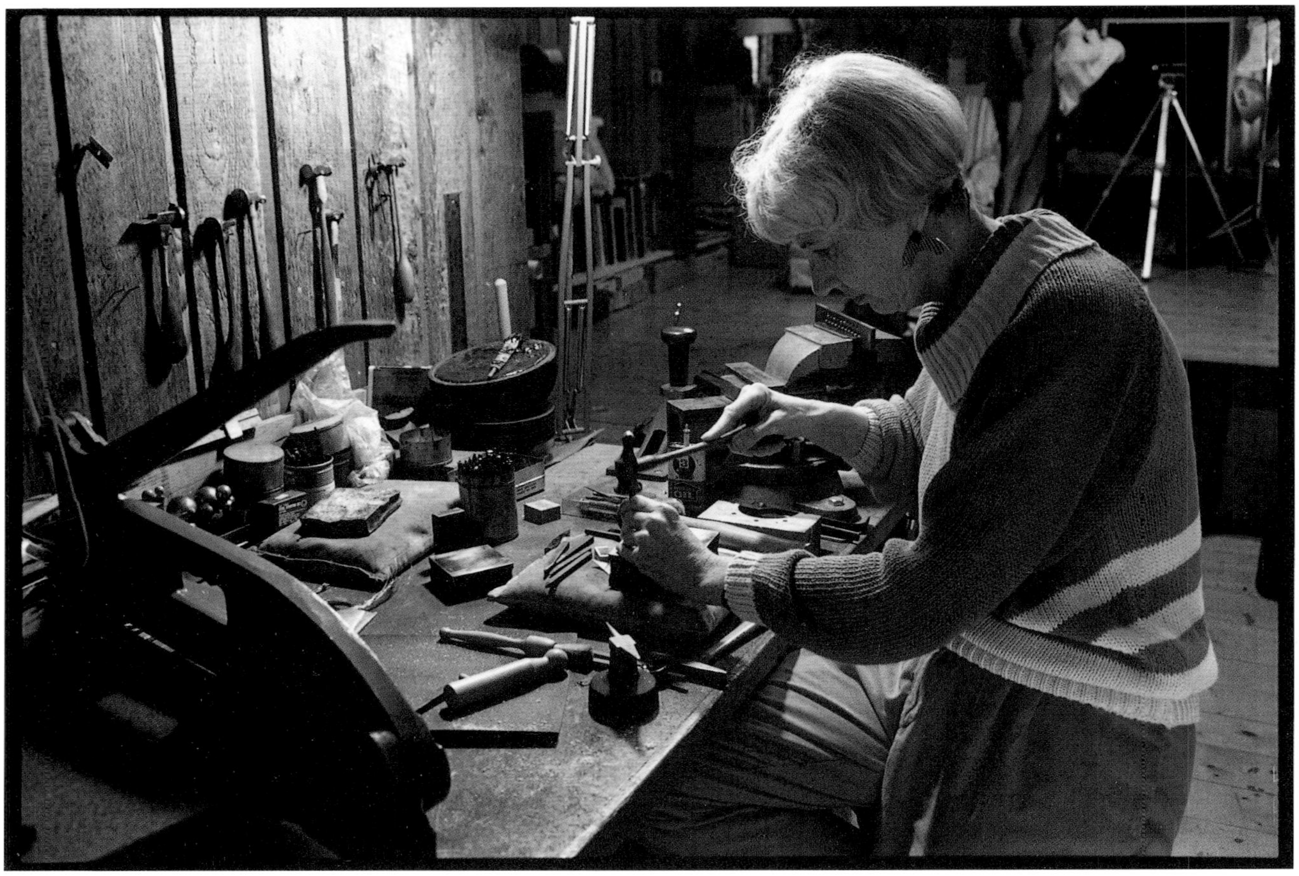

My decision was that if I could travel I could survive in San Diego. Now I find it's very productive to be here.

On a Mission Hills canyon hillside, surrounded by native plants and large Eucalyptus trees, Arline Fisch works in her contemporary redwood studio. Unlike the main house a dozen steps above, which displays brightly colored accents from her collection of crafts, the studio has a restful, no-nonsense sophistication which seems a true reflection of this artist.

As early as 1956, when she was on a Fulbright grant to the School of Arts and Crafts in Copenhagen, Denmark, Fisch knew that she wanted to do more in the field of jewelry than traditional approaches would allow. Today Fisch's niche as a vanguard jeweler has been reaffirmed by a number of American Craft Magazine *features, by books, and by prestigious grants and awards. She has developed a rare ability to interrelate textile approaches to metalwork, giving her forms an unusual dimension which combines fantasy and fine technical achievement. Many of her own creations provide the source material for her recent textbook on knitted and woven jewelry and body adornments.*

A professor at San Diego State University for almost three decades, Fisch is nevertheless a private person who has remained aloof from the local art community in favor of focusing on international conferences and playing important roles within national and international crafts associations.

Since the collection I did before this was knitted, I decided this time I would use weaving. And because weaving provides the greatest amount of surface and reflection, it makes more sense to use gold. You can see a surface reflection and the kind of color interchange and subtlety of reflection of which only gold is capable. What comes off the loom is basically rectangular and I decided to concentrate on working with a square plane and either curving it, or folding it, or cutting it. Basically I used the woven plane as it exists, and so the collection has grown based on that idea.

Because gold is more expensive, I don't have quite the freedom to generate masses of raw material so I've had to take a much more considered approach. I did go ahead and weave, but I had to take more time in figuring out what to do. I don't normally use stones, but when I saw the woven material, the accents of dark or clear stone made a significant difference. So I've used stones, but only as accents and all non-precious. I could say, well I'll just throw some diamonds in here, but I really don't like diamonds and I really don't like the combination. Gold is very soft and diamonds are very hard. What I'm using instead is onyx and hematite, which are both essential stones but they're not cut with special edges.

I studied weaving when I was teaching at Skidmore, because the weaving professor was retiring and she asked me if I'd like to take over that program. I found it very fascinating although I knew that's not what I wanted to do. However, when I came to San Diego State University, it turned out that they didn't have a weaving program. From 1961 until 1970 I taught both weaving and jewelry and in fact created quite a large program.

My interest in weaving was always in the research aspect rather than in the making aspect. The whole time that I was teaching was sort of like having a research lab. I gave all the ideas and thoughts to the students so it was a real rich experience as I had a lot of rich information stored which never would have gotten used.

The impetus for my textile works in metal came absolutely from the fact that I had to learn about weaving for other reasons. I became fascinated and saw possibilities because of the historic things that I looked at. In 1970, when I was on sabbatical in London and working at a friend's workshop I could only work during certain hours and I had to work at home. I took the time to try some of these things that I had put off and I did my first woven and knitted jewelry and body adornments that year, even though I was primarily doing other things.

I'm just not a beach person. Once a year I have to go to the beach. And I'm not a pool person and I 'm not a jogger. I don't run at all. My decision was that if I could travel I could survive in San Diego. Now I find it's very productive to be here. I can work without a lot of local involvement. I have been very involved with the World Craft Council, Haystack as a trustee. All of that was intended as an outreach program for me. I accepted all that responsibility because it enabled me to reach out and it also meant that the work wasn't constant.

I have tried very hard to keep the studio separate from the other pressures of teaching and writing. I don't do any of those things in the studio. I don't do any classroom preparation or phone calls there. For many years I didn't have the telephone there. I had a telephone hour from eight to nine on Monday, Wednesday, and Friday when people could reach me. At nine o'clock I went out into the studio and if the phone rang, too bad. That's where I do my thinking. So there's a place to sit, to read, to draw, to photograph the work. But I do all the packing and shipping and cleaning in the house because that's onerous stuff. I hate doing that. I try not to put things that are unpleasant in the studio and I try not to use it as a storage place for leftovers. It is a big space and it would be easy to fill up with extraneous stuff.

I don't like working for deadlines. I can work under pressure, but I don't do my best work that way. I find it very stressful. So I always end up with a lot more work than I need for a show. I start far in advance. I do still feel that kind of frantic push at the end when things have to be shipped. I'll ship what I've chosen and what's finished. There will be pieces that are not finished and I will not stay up all night and finish a piece. The world doesn't know about the piece that isn't done.

I like working on a lot of different things at the same time. I like coming into the studio with something to work on. Even if I go away I try to leave unfinished things so that when I come back I don't have to start cold. I don't ever walk into the studio with a blank slate, even when I've been away for a year. There's something either I've brought home with me that isn't quite done or I left something that I look at with a fresh eye and I think, that would be nice, I think I'll finish that. I never feel trepidation. There's always something sitting down there. It isn't that I don't get stuck. I do. But then I just move on to something else.

SELECTED BIOGRAPHY

BIRTHPLACE

Brooklyn, New York

EDUCATION

Skidmore College, Saratoga Springs, New York, BS, 1952
University of Illinois, Urbana, 1954

SOLO EXHIBITIONS

Museum of Contemporary Crafts, New York, 1968
The Egg and the Eye, Los Angeles, 1969
Goldsmiths Hall, London, 1971
Wita Gardiner Gallery, San Diego, 1987
Electrum Gallery, London, 1983 and 1987

GROUP EXHIBITIONS

"Form and Quality," Gold Medal, International Jewelry Exhibition, Munich, 1971
"Craft, Art, and Religion," Vatican Museum, Rome, 1978
"Good as Gold," Renwick Gallery, Smithsonian Institution, Washington, D.C., 1981
"Contemporary Jewelry," National Museum of Modern Art, Kyoto, Japan, 1984
"Craft Today: Poetry of the Physical," American Craft Museum, 1986

PUBLICATIONS

Textile Techniques in Metal, Van Nostrand Reinhold Company, 1975

GRANTS AND HONORS

Fulbright Grants
National Endowment for the Arts, Arts Craftsman, Research and Apprenticeship Fellowships
American Craft Council Fellow
Trustee, Haystack Mountain School of Crafts, Deer Isle, Maine
Declared "Living Treasure of California"

COLLECTIONS

Vatican Museum, Rome
American Craft Museum, New York
Worshipful Company of Goldsmiths, London
Objects: USA, the Johnson Wax Collection
National Museum of Modern Art, Kyoto, Japan

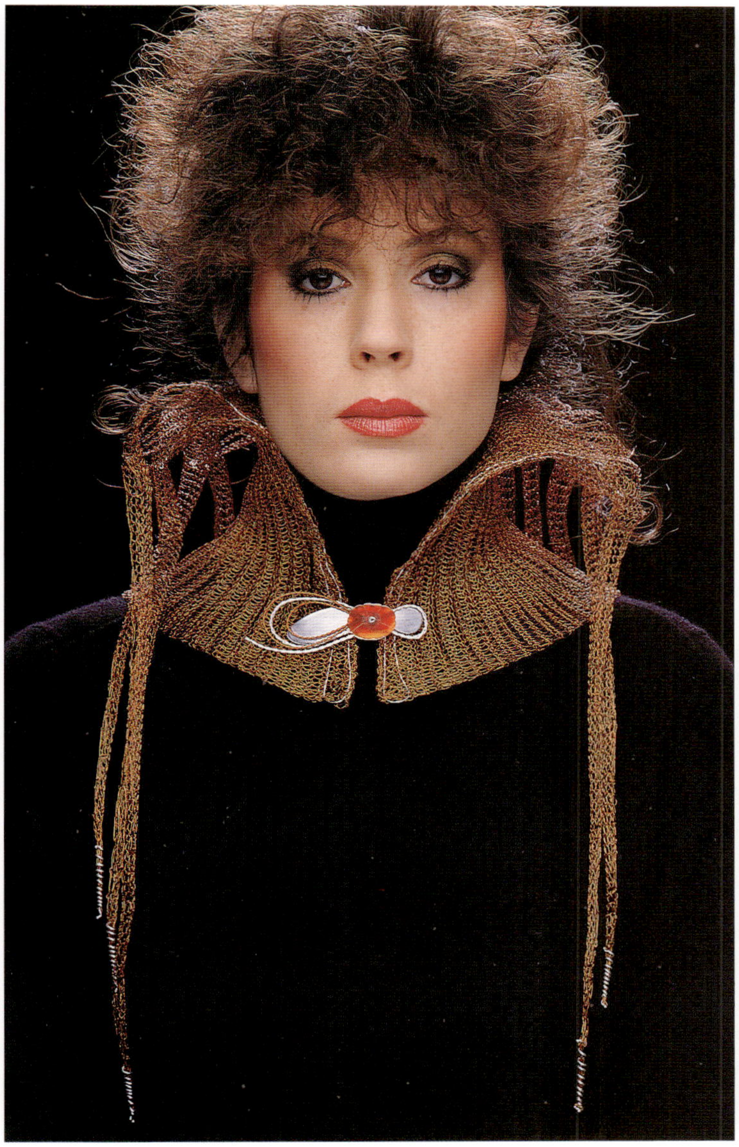

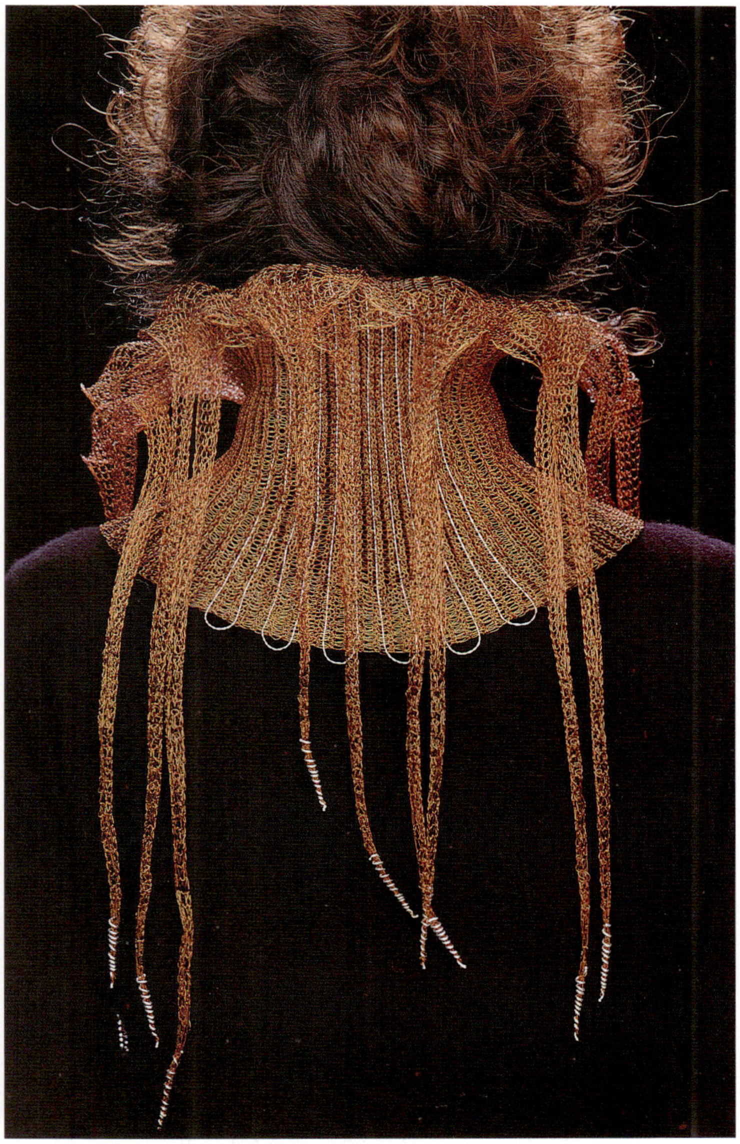

Collar, coated copper with clasp of sterling and carnelian, 9½" to 6½", tendrils hang to 14", 1985

Photos by William Gullette

Russell Forester

I'm basically afraid of the dark and I think that's why I'm doing the things that have light in them. They're strong during the night and very weak during the daytime.

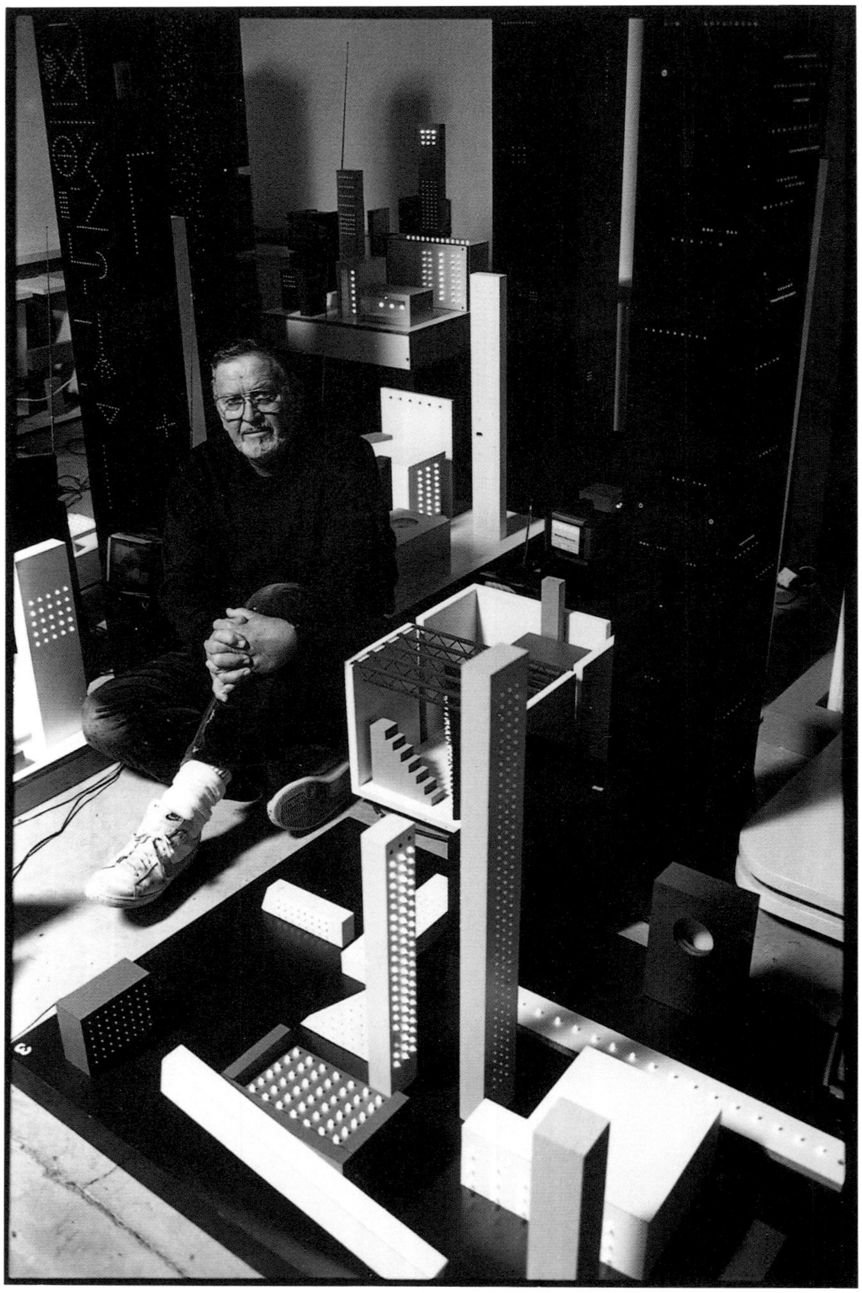

Working in a studio where unique skylight shutters can be drawn closed to darken the space, Russell Forester weds practicality with creativity using skills ingrained during his highly successful career as an architect. In the darkness small LED (light emitting diode) lights shine in tiny dots, creating secret symbols which lace his six foot mini-skyscraper prototypes.

A bear of a man with a close-cropped beard, an earring in one ear, and his characteristic loose-knit sweater, Forester manifests a strong sense of design and technical curiosity in all aspects of his art and life. Strong colors, neon lights, and TV images are used as punctuation, these ideas traceable to his early architectural designs as well as the detailed black and white drawings, large gauze paintings, and sewn lead works of his recent past. These transitions in his art have always been respectfully received by international collectors and his peers in the art world.

Forester and a brother four years younger were raised by their mother, a librarian at Scripps Institution of Oceanography. His father – an architect and designer of several French war memorials – left them when Forester was five years old. His younger brother is a chemical engineer in California. Forester recently discovered a French half-brother, also a chemist, living in France.

He and his Swiss-born wife Marie-Christine, an architect and self-described "catalyst," live in the high-ceilinged La Jolla home they designed together. His daughter, Lynn, is a chemical engineer with a Ph.D. from Cal Tech.

I've been using tiny LED computer panel lights for about six or seven years. I started out with a bang – I used one light! I never intended to use lights but such purity of color comes from them. My feeling is that all things influence us and you don't know how they're going to spring out into your art. My brother-in-law was here a while ago and we drove by an apartment I did in La Jolla twenty-three years ago. He said, "Did you see the ceiling in the entry?" I said, "No, why?" He said, "It has hundreds of little lights!" I'd done it, filled the ceiling with tiny little round bulbs, hundreds that go down the hall, exactly as I'm doing now and I didn't even think about it. Isn't that funny, you don't get away from yourself. You're doing them, but you're doing them in a different way than you might think, almost by rote.

A Swiss architect was here recently and wanted to look at my drawings. After looking at drawers of them, since I've chosen not to sell them, he said he couldn't believe how the drawings and my use of lights fit together. I hadn't really thought of it that way, but my drawings are little lines filled with little dots, like little dots of light. I don't think there's a thing I've ever done that hasn't led to something else. I've got twenty pieces in my head right now that I want to make. I know where I want to go.

I've been dealing in my work with issues like loneliness, personal and introspective kinds of things that deal with how you feel in relationship to other people, how the world treats you, how your relationship to the world is. I started doing these interior boxes with real TV sets and chairs where there are no people. They're empty, but the machines go on. A reaction to one of my shows was that the machines go right on without us. And actually that's what I see; the world does go on without us.

I've often felt that one of the problems with sculpture is that when the sun goes down the sculpture goes off. The sculpture isn't seen once the sun is down. I've thought of doing pieces that are just the reverse, pieces that turn on as the sun goes down and become much more solid and visual than during the day. It's something like whistling in the dark or whistling through the graveyard. Art is like a beacon that you have seen, something of an anchor. It can give you something to hang on to. I'm basically afraid of the dark and I think that's why I'm doing the things that have light in them. They're strong during the night and very weak during the daytime.

I have a very hard time having a serious talk about art. I have a sense that all of us have a thing within us that thinks it's lonely. I think we're all frustrated in many ways by our inability to handle the whole world. So much is thrown at us. The more that's out there the more withdrawn we become. The more you become yourself inside, nobody's going to know about it. Outside we all appear the same way. It's kind of like when somebody you love or know commits suicide or gets divorced, you think how come I didn't know that? How come I didn't know that about this person? And you start realizing that you don't know anybody really. You hardly know yourself, what you are. I think there are times when I don't really know who I am.

I'm not a good communicator. I think that's why I do art. I think I'm a private person. Sometimes I'm witty, sometimes the wit becomes lost and becomes trite. I hate that. But it's very hard to look at yourself and really know what you are. Sometimes it's easier to say I don't like that, than it is to say what it is you like, because you judge it. You say, "I don't like that." And then you answer, "If you don't like that then what do you want to do?" And you say, "Well, I don't know." I think I've spent most of my life being lonely, afraid. Afraid to be the one person who stands up and says, "Hey, I don't like this."

One of the marvelous things about getting older is that you gain strength in your ability to express what it is you don't like publicly. Most of my life I spent hiding, not saying what I liked, feeling that it would hurt me or people around me. I don't know why, that's the way my life went. I don't want to be the person that stands on the corner and becomes the local nut because you don't like anything. I think in my later works I show more of what I am.

SELECTED BIOGRAPHY

BIRTHPLACE

Salmon, Idaho

EDUCATION

Institute of Design, Chicago, 1950 to 1951
Registered Architect, State of California, 1960
Registered Architect, National Council of Architecture, 1965

SOLO EXHIBITIONS

Willard Gallery, New York, 1973
Everson Art Museum, Syracuse, 1977
La Jolla Museum of Contemporary Art, 1972 and 1979
Herbert Palmer Gallery, Los Angeles, 1982
Bertha Urdang Gallery, New York, 1985
G G Modern Art AG, Zurich, 1988

GROUP EXHIBITIONS

The Albright-Knox Gallery, Buffalo, 1971
The Solomon R. Guggenheim Museum, New York, 1977
Maurer Gallery, Zurich, 1977, 1979, 1980
Laguna Art Museum, Laguna Beach, California, 1985
La Jolla Museum of Contemporary Art, 1978, 1979, 1981, 1983, 1986

AWARDS

Honor Award, American Institute of Architects, 1966 and 1972
Merit Award for Sculpture, American Institute of Architects, 1968

COLLECTIONS

The Solomon R. Guggenheim Museum, New York
La Jolla Museum of Contemporary Art
Aerojet-General Corporation, La Jolla
Bank of America, San Francisco
McCrory Corporation, New York

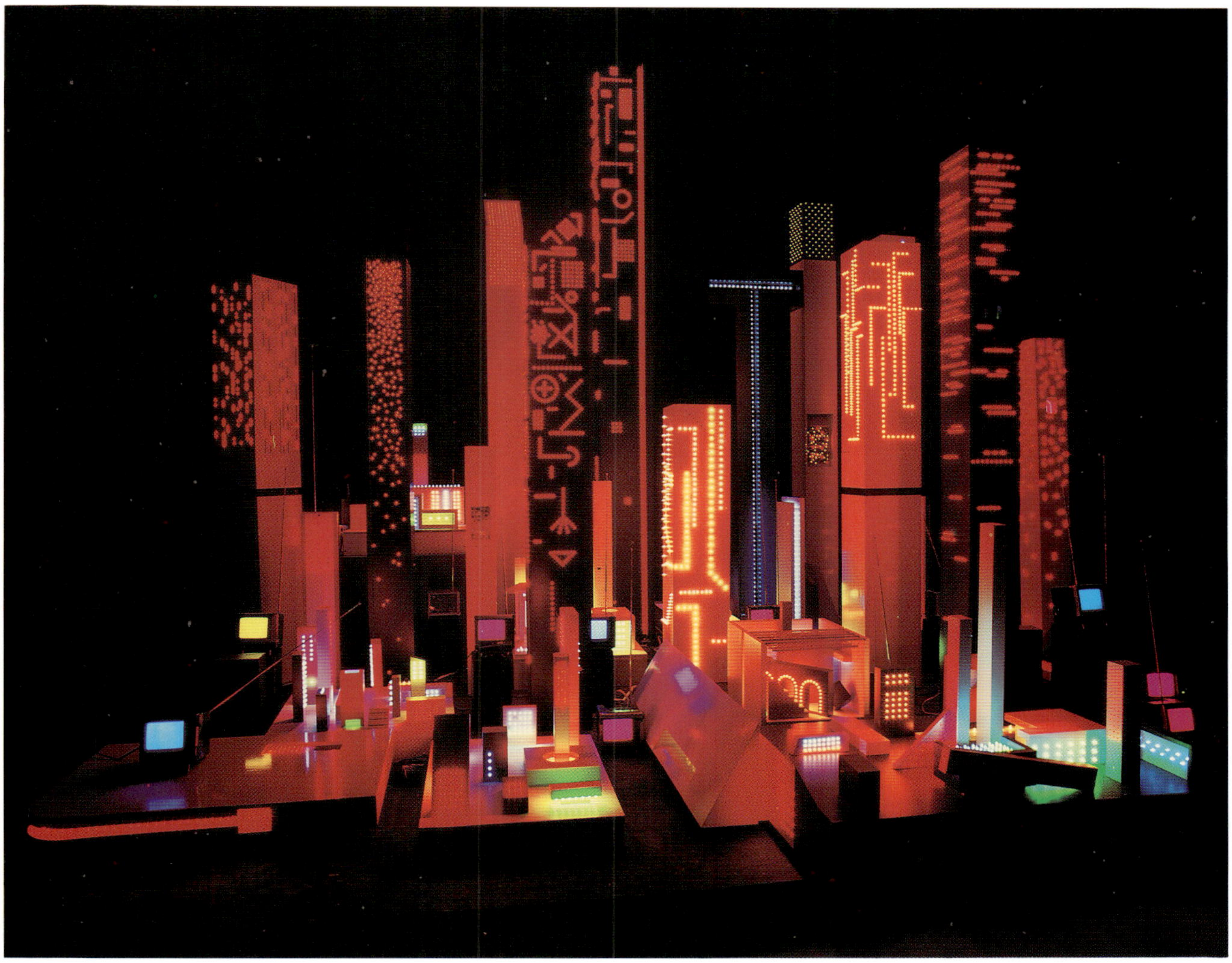

City untitled, Color Cor, LED lights, neon bulbs, two sound systems, and sixteen television sets, 16′×12′×10′, 1987

Faiya Fredman

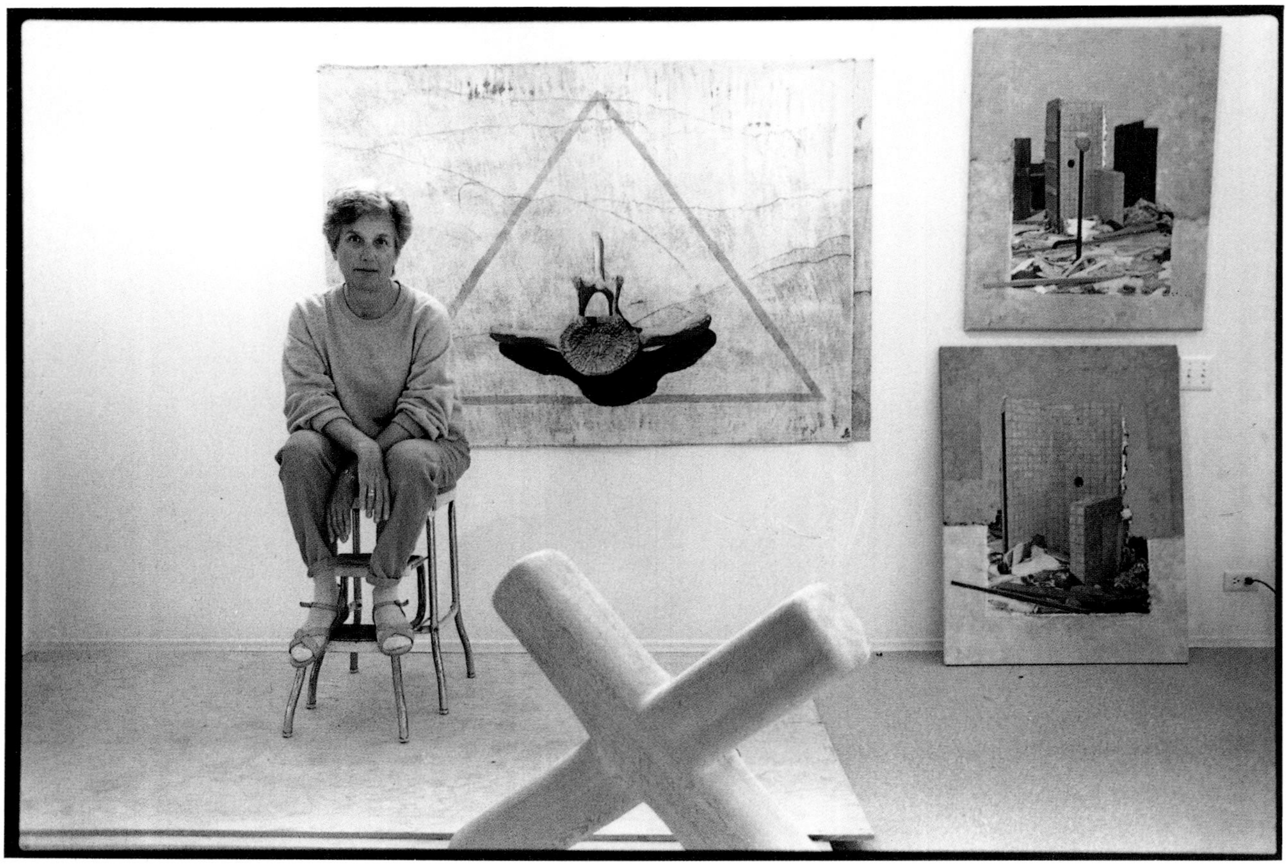

One of the things I really want to express in my work is silence, because silence is so little felt in our society and it's such a beautiful experience it should be a part of people's lives....

Faiya Fredman's personal style is understated, expressed in her clothes – muted greys, beiges, and browns – as well as in her art, that subdued, nature-toned palette she loves. Providing the richest source material for her, the ocean played a major roll in her paintings during the last fifteen years of a Del Mar beachfront residency and continues today as she works in her newly-built studio overlooking the rooftops to La Jolla cove.

Her canvases are often textured with gently sprinkled sand, evoking an elusive kind of beauty. This subtlety is perhaps a visual paradox since her subjects – tide lines, beached fish, and ancient and contemporary ruins – deal with destruction and decay.

After raising two children, Fredman spent some years painting her way through the changes in the art world in order to catch up. In the process she developed innovative solutions to artistic problems and is continually evolving ways to express her sense of environment and time. Her statements have a philosophical simplicity; they remain independent of cultural trends, express a sensibility attuned to the interactions of the man-made and natural worlds.

Fredman lives with her husband Milton (Mickey), a lawyer, in La Jolla. They have a daughter trained in social work and a son who is a poet teaching at Notre Dame University.

When I was a little girl we homesteaded out in the desert when we lost everything in the Depression. To give me something to do my father, who had been an architect and contractor, bought me an easel. I don't know whether I would have been an artist or whether he preordained it by setting me up with an easel. It was a regular easel for grown ups and I worked on it as a little kid with anything that happened to be around. As I got older everything I did revolved around art.

One of the greatest influences on my art was Professor Abramovitch at UCLA. She came up to me and sat down and spent about two hours with me when I first got up there. She said, "Look, either get yourself into this work or get out. You're just standing on the outside. You're not putting yourself into your work." This was like a revelation. From then on my work changed. I had a sense of freedom that I had never had.

At that stage the women's movement hadn't been dreamt of. At UCLA they had already set me up to be in a graduate program when I met my husband and we got married right away. So that finished that up right there; that was expected. I had two children right way. Life puts limits on you. Of course, one can change one's life. I feel that I live within my choices. There are many men who would love to be artists who have become dentists or surgeons. I think that they've totally diverted their art for a life that they feel will help them provide for a family. I don't think you can say that women are the only ones to sacrifice. I think they're choosing to lead what one person will call a full life and another who doesn't choose that life would not. I chose a life that incorporates husband, family, art, and all of the things that are associated with that. I answer to both calls. At different periods you have different responses to that. With time one gains more understanding of that issue. It's a tough issue, but it's determining what you're doing with your life.

My Tide Lines series definitely reflected the life I was leading when I lived on the beach. Everyday I would walk on the beach and every day I saw those lines. I'd think of the continuum of the ocean and the never ending resources of the line constantly being redrawn, of being able to capture just a moment in time. The line is there for such a short period of time and then the wave comes in and takes it out again. As I used to walk along I'd think a great deal about that. I started using thirty foot long canvases on which I would place a thick string. I would paint a liquid adhesive on the canvas and put the string down, sprinkling some sand with a little sieve over the entire canvas. Then I pulled the string off and this beautiful line occurred. At a Palomar College exhibit I lit the line and as people came in I requested that they just follow the line and try not to talk, just to come up with a response to the feeling that was created.

One of the things that I really want to express in my work is silence, because silence is so little felt in our society and it's such a beautiful experience it should be a part of people's lives, I think.

Once Mickey and I were sailing on the Aegean Sea in a small boat. We came to the island of Santorini but didn't enter from it's normal side. On the maps we kept seeing that there were some ancient ruins. I was just overwhelmed when I saw the village of Akroteri, because here was a village that was covered with volcanic ash. There is a quiet about a space that had been covered like that. One of the things that I tried to express in the Akroteri series was the feeling of ash sifting down. I like to express continuum, flow, timelessness. Although I call them Akroteri pieces, and it is a specific site, I actually painted out anything that would take you to that site. There are none of the huge water jugs. I wanted it to be non-specific.

Then it was natural to go from the past and show what our society is producing as far as ruins are concerned. So that's how I got started on the sites I've been working on recently. The pipe pieces evolved from a house I saw in Del Mar that was demolished along the beach near the cliff area. It was torn down so another house could be built. What is so peculiar is that people used to live in houses for centuries and in some countries they still do. We take houses that are twenty years old and demolish them. Time is so relative.

It all sifts down to the same thing. You have a roof on a house, and then it doesn't have its roof left after the demolition. That's pretty ironic, I think. We're all trying to protect ourselves and cover ourselves up and then whenever things start to wash away, the roofs immediately go. The walls remain and the roof gets stripped away. It's pretty interesting.

SELECTED BIOGRAPHY

BIRTHPLACE

Columbus, Ohio

EDUCATION

University of California, Los Angeles

SOLO EXHIBITIONS

Galeria Chapultepec, I.N.B.A., Mexico City, 1976
Thomas Babeor Gallery, La Jolla, 1981
La Jolla Museum of Contemporary Art, 1968, 1974, 1981
"Akroteri Series," travelling exhibit, University of California, San Diego, Irvine, Riverside, 1984 to 1985
Ruth Bachofner Gallery, Los Angeles, 1985

GROUP EXHIBITIONS

Newspace, Los Angeles, 1978
"New Artists in New York," Alex Rosenberg Gallery, New York, 1979
Sao Paolo Museum of Contemporary Art, Sao Paolo, Brazil, 1980
La Jolla Museum of Contemporary Art, 1972, 1973, 1978, 1979, 1986
"Introductions: The Extended Image," Museum of Photographic Arts, San Diego, 1987

COLLECTIONS

University of California, San Diego
Arizona State University at Tempe
La Jolla Museum of Contemporary Art
Security Pacific Bank, Los Angeles
Cedars-Sinai Hospital, Los Angeles

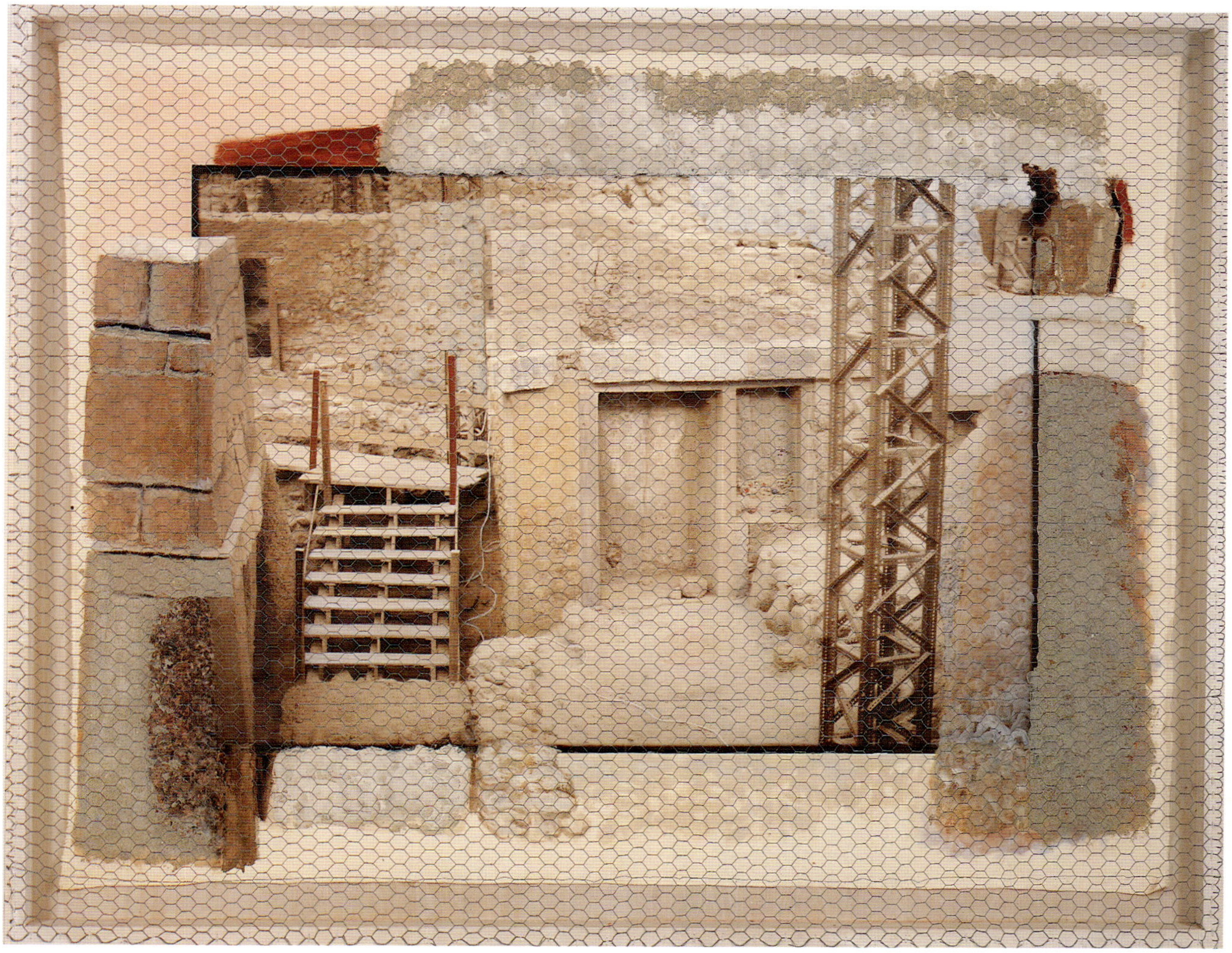

Akroteri #11, photo, acrylic, sand, wire mesh, and wood on canvas, 67″×86½″, 1985

Photo by Kimball/Nanessence

Gary Ghirardi

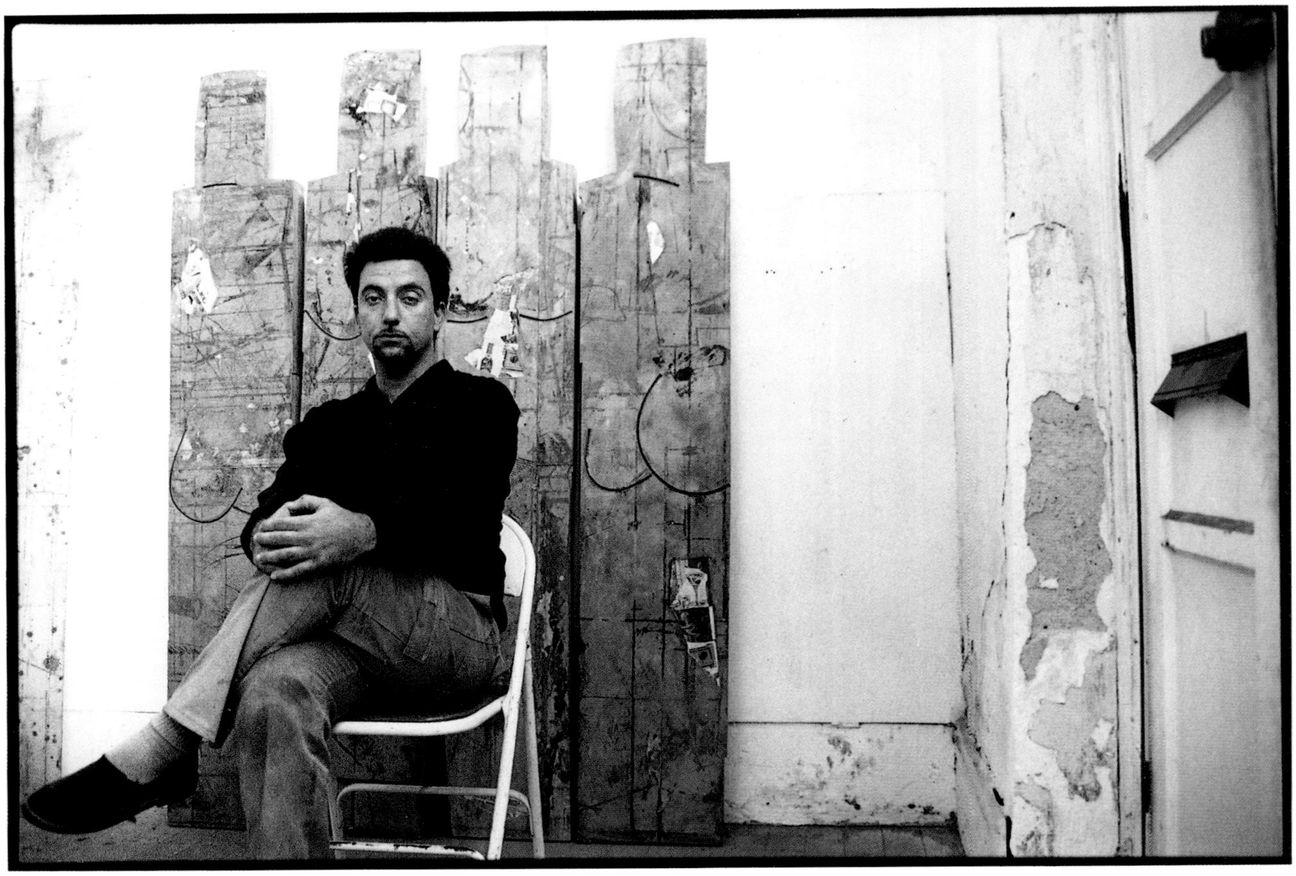

I'm kind of a bebop artist. I like and write jazz and I think my work is kind of jazz oriented. I've always been interested in that fringe motorcycle, not the mainstream.

A bright red door on Island Avenue – near the downtown produce markets – marks the place where Gary Ghirardi has his studio-living space. He has just finished working on a vintage motorcycle and maneuvers around an electronic piano keyboard to ascend a ladder. This delivers him to his loft to brew a strong pot of coffee before we talk.

Ghirardi has experienced many personal changes in both his art and as founding director of Installation Gallery downtown. His latest architectonic sculptures are the result of concentrated explorations into form and experiments with media. Concurrently he supports his art by designing exhibits for large trade shows, primarily jobs from San Francisco.

Until he was seven years old, Ghirardi lived with his parents and younger sister in a New York Italian neighborhood which afforded him a well-remembered bedroom window view of the Statue of Liberty. After moving to the San Diego environs, where his father became a city school administrator, Ghirardi began drawing on shopping bags with graphite "while the other kids got in trouble."

He and his wife, social worker Carol Roskos, have been living together in various downtown lofts since 1979. He frequently commutes to San Francisco to develop his trade show projects and reconnect with artist and musician friends.

I had started Installation in 1980 to have a place for artists in San Diego to show since the museums weren't doing much. Gallery 552, Installation, and then Alternative Space Gallery all played off each other pretty well around the early 1980s. The others closed. Installation went full term and Pawn Shop opened. They had quite a group at 552, about twenty artists ready to start programs but then the building inspector closed the building. Lynn Schuette, William Allen Morris, Gillian Theobald, Richard Baker were part of it. There were some good people getting ready to gear up. It could have been quite a gallery if it had stayed the course.

Originally the idea was to set up an installation space for site work. The first thing on the agenda was to survey artists of merit, so that took two years with shows every two weeks. In the first two years thirty-six artists had shown. It came out of Carol's and my pocket. We lived in the back. About eight months into the program Dan Wasil came on with me and we split the schedule, alternated shows. We had different sensibilities. His orientation was more scholastic than mine.

There were sales, but not a great deal, to people who said, "I want that." It wasn't a commercial gallery. We had a policy of no repeat shows, so that kind of limited the artists and they put their best and their most outrageous foot forward. If you went back and looked at those shows they don't look that outrageous compared to what we have now. I'm glad lately Installation has Dan back as director with a big space on Broadway and it is again site-oriented – not really dealing with object orientation.

The work I'm doing is process work that develops from different techniques I would associate with monoprints or monotyping where you prepare a plate, ink it and run it through the paper and each one turns out different. I do the same thing only upside down and with some unusual materials. The pieces start down on the ground, backwards, like drawing on a mirror. I start with a mold, create a shape, build an armature on it. I make certain decisions about the plaster, cement, wood, broken glass, rubber, plastics, color inlays, and sifting oxides. I don't know how it's going to happen till it happens.

I've always been interested in cracks, in places between known quantities. I've been functioning between sculpture and painting and it's scary turf, but yet I'm intrigued by it. I want to continue the dialogue between painterly imagery and sculptural form. It's a hard place to be, but it's an interesting place, a unique place.

I began doing trade shows for Hughes Aircraft in 1976 and in 1984 I got a big one, a thirty by thirty foot trade show for a small start-up computer company. I did it like an artist instead of like a trade show designer and out of 700 exhibits everybody flocked to our booth. To me these are very much site pieces. They're kind of like stage sets. I think it's more in line with architecture than painting. You could do a booth based on painting but it would look like nothing that's ever been done. I proposed one in two huge meetings and got shot down.

I feel like the art I'm doing now is getting closer to what I want it to be. More than anything I hope to make the immediacy of the process more functional, have more things going and a large work load emerge from that. I think that'll create more dynamics. I won't be so invested in a piece if I have four things going and I can risk trying things.

I want to build up the studio to the point where I can have full time paid employees. All the major artists have help. Nobody can produce enough work to have three one person shows a year and do it by themselves. Right now I do about twenty pieces a year. You need to get it up to like fifty, sixty a year. It sounds really commercial, but I've been doing research and there isn't one artist out there that doesn't work that way that's successful. The idea of being in your studio in a small space is no way to make money at it. When I sell a piece, half is immediately split with the gallery and half my money goes into materials the next day. Ultimately I want to quit doing commercial work completely.

I'm kind of a bebop artist. I like and write jazz and I think my work is kind of jazz oriented. I've always been interested in that fringe motorcycle, not the mainstream. I'm not that interested in making money, never had the cultural necessity that most people seem to have about it. I've always hung out with misanthropes. Money isn't an issue, it's more the interaction of art, of trade shows that I find exciting. I like starting a project, finishing it and being done with it to start a new one. I like resolution.

The older I get the more freedom I gain, learning to control what I'm doing. When you don't have control of something you don't know how to turn, you don't feel free, you feel locked in.

SELECTED BIOGRAPHY

BIRTHPLACE

Jersey City, New Jersey

EDUCATION

No institutional fine arts training

SOLO EXHIBITIONS

"Flag Room 1," Pawn Shop Gallery, San Diego 1981
"New Views of Non Reality," 1982 and "Second Wave Non Realities," 1983, Thomas Neumaier Gallery, San Diego,

GROUP EXHIBITIONS

"California Contemporary Artists 14," Laguna Art Museum, CA, 1983
"Sculptural Tendencies from San Diego Galleries," San Francisco Museum of Art Rental Gallery, 1984
"A San Diego Exhibition," La Jolla Museum of Contemporary Art, 1985
Patty Aande Gallery, San Diego, 1984, 1986
"Street Sets," Sushi, San Diego, 1987

AWARDS

Onion Award for Fifth and "G" Street Mural, American Institute of Architects, 1982

COLLECTIONS AND PROJECTS

Mural at Fifth and "G" Street, San Diego
Rudick, Platt, and Victor Law Offices, San Diego
Telephone Pole Piece (Stolen) at Eighth and Island, San Diego
"No Context" installation, empty building at Sixth and Island, San Diego

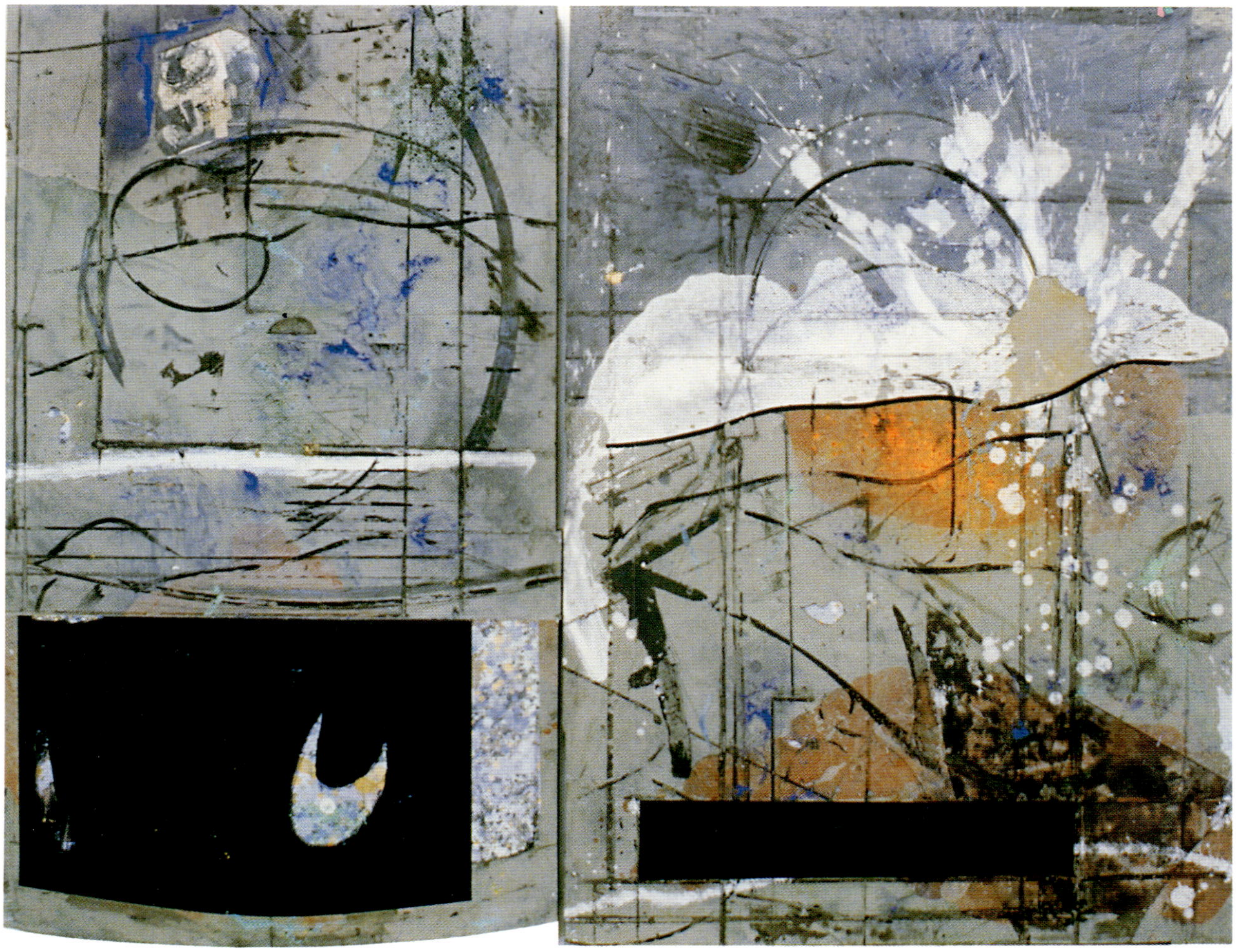

Calvin's Complaint, cement, plaster, rubber, oxides, enamel, plexiglas, and collage – diptych, 52.5″×40″×2.5″, 1986

Robert Glen Ginder

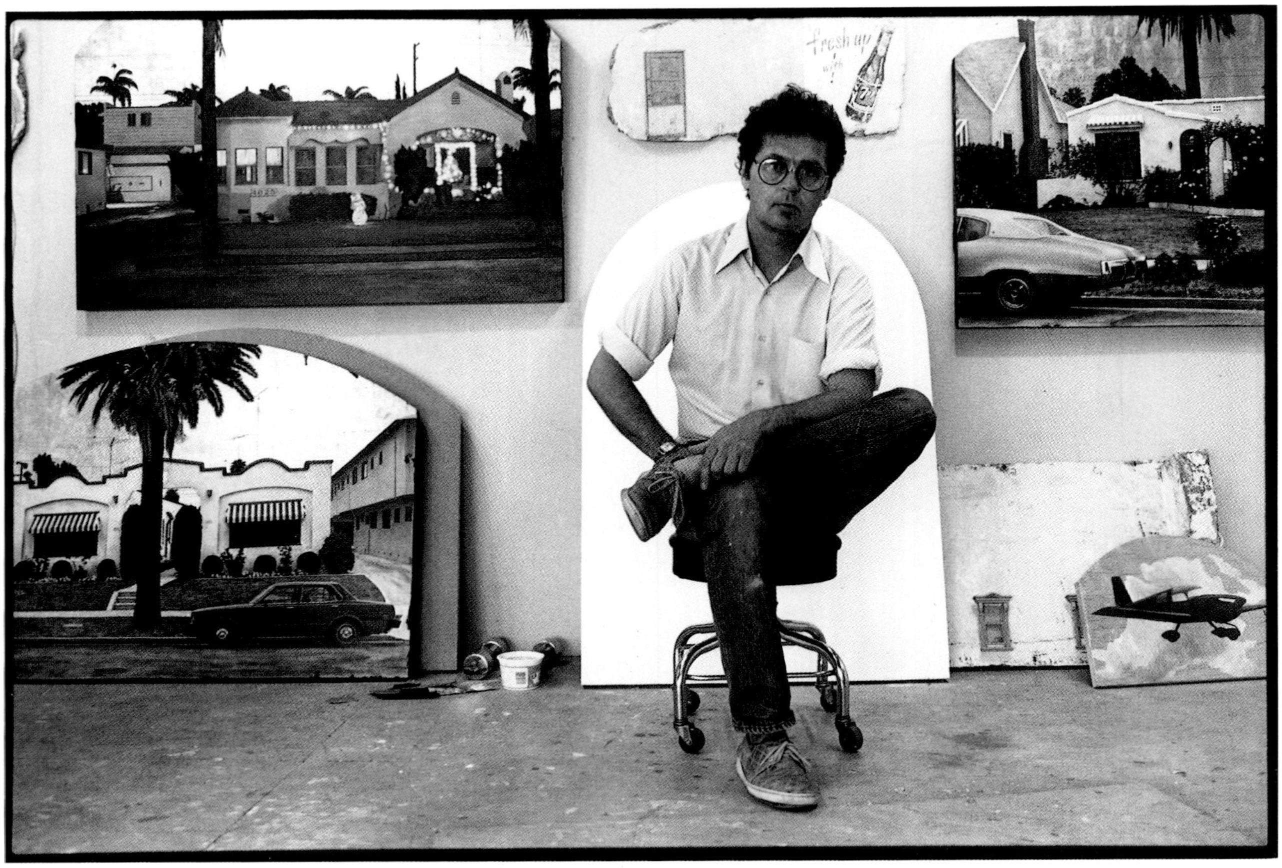

How could I be angry about not being accepted in New York if I'd never been there and tried it?

A few doors from the Belly-Up Tavern in Solana Beach, Bob Ginder works in his studio. He is contemplative about each contemporary icon he labors months over in order to capture the rich, aged look of subjects from the 1940s and 1950s.

Ginder was struck by the timelessness of the art and architecture he saw on a trip to Europe in 1978 and on his return to San Diego began studying the gold-leafed Russian icons at the Timken Gallery and the Italian Renaissance works in the San Diego Museum of Art. He had set out to explore in his own way the shapes and techniques that captured and held his attention.

Architectural fragments that were common in his youth, like old fresco-style advertisements on plaster walls or the classic California bungalows he now places beneath a crackled gold-leaf sky, are among the mundane subjects Ginder memorializes and whimsically salutes as a part of recent history.

He grew up and lived for eighteen years in the same house, sharing life with an older brother, a drummer, in a Los Angeles suburb. His mother worked for a construction company after divorcing the undependable designer/father when the boys were small. Ginder thought of making a career out of art when his kindergarten teacher held up his picture of trees as an example for the second graders, and at eight years old he was profoundly affected by a major Van Gogh exhibition he attended with a drawing teacher.

Never married, Ginder has lived in his second story Solana Beach studio since 1984, a studio whose rent was originally paid by trading for art. He has recently had a sell-out showing of his work at O.K. Harris Gallery in New York.

There are no people in any of my paintings, but I'm not so much painting architecture. If you don't paint the people, if you paint their effects, the architecture they make, where they live, all the little things that they do that are surrounding them, these are pictures of people. I'm painting little things that people do.

I grew up, until I was about eighteen, in Southeast Los Angeles. I've always seen the type of houses with this lumpish quality they have that's really rooted there. You drive by and there's this kind of anchored look to them. There's something appealing to me. The curved arches work well with the shape of board that I'm painting on. But I think the overall thing in my intuition is the way they hold their own space when you're driving around. They have this real solid kind of feeling to them and they make a nice metaphor for a house, for a shelter in general. They're kind of humble looking.

When I left college after a year and a half, I didn't know what I was going to do but I knew I was going to be an artist. I knew no matter what other jobs I took to do it, that it was going to be a learning experience for me. I decided to go out into the world because I thought the people I admired, like John Steinbeck, really did their best work when it was from real life. It wasn't from when they learned how to spell and write and from theory. You know, even James Joyce did the same thing. Plus a lot of my friends were musicians who had jobs and were writing music on the side and they were playing gigs and that seemed natural to me. I started to hang out with them.

For a long time I avoided any type of artistic community because I wanted to research my own feelings about art so I wouldn't be influenced by any other art. I wanted to have a very organic, personal art come out. So I cut myself off from it. During the 70's I felt like the Lone Ranger. I did it on purpose, but it wasn't easy, because virtually the only people I'd really talk to had no idea what artists did. It's hard to talk to friends who lay bricks, or drive a truck or a cab. Although they may like art, you can't really talk about certain things. It was sort of a slow process. By the late 70's, I felt I was in an unshakeable position. I felt that I had resolved something, found a mature direction. I wasn't blown by every wind that was coming by. Then I felt, okay, I've resolved what I was trying to do by cutting myself off and getting into things that aren't necessarily considered fine art, like sign painting, scenic art, graphic art, and jobs that had nothing to do with art, tending bar and all that – not in an art bar either, but in the Belly Up in Solana Beach, next door to my studio. I felt I couldn't be alone without talking to other people involved in art anymore. It had been too long. Then I went to an opening for Ken Capps at Mark Quint's gallery, so I met them and Jay Johnson.

I went to New York and did some reconnaissance a couple of times and looked at what everybody was doing and mainly what the galleries were showing. I got a simpatico feeling with one and got a feel of where they were going and felt it was similar to what I was doing. It sounds simple, but it's real important to do, because it's kind of insulting to them to be showing them something that has nothing to do with what they're trying to do. They're serious about a direction they're trying to show. I mean, the gallery directors and curators are like artists, in a lot of ways.

So when I found a place – O.K. Harris – I eventually went back there when I had a body of work that I felt was significant enough to show. I went with my knees shaking and showed it to them, and they liked it. It sounds easy, but it's not. The first time I took slides and Ivan Karp said he wanted to see the actual work. The way he said it was, "Well, if these are ever within ten miles of here and I'm still alive, I'd like to look at them . . . hunh, hunh." And then he leaned back and smoked his cigar, kind of vaudevillian-like. I thought, "What the hell does that mean?" But his wife was there and explained that a lot of artists if they're from out of town will have a friend who has a loft. They set up their work in the place. You can't expect them to make a decision without seeing the actual work. Fortunately I did meet a friend of a friend I knew out here that had a one room loft that was a big space with white walls. I showed about eight or nine pieces. It was a gamble but he seemed positive about the work. It was expensive, but it was exciting and fun to do. You know, it was scary.

I think it's a waste of time and energy to be cynical. Whenever I felt cynical, I knew that there was something I wasn't doing that I was afraid to do. How could I be angry about not being accepted in New York if I'd never been there and tried it? So I tried it and was fortunate enough to have it work for me pretty soon. It's tough being an artist, and you can't help being down sometimes, but being cynical is not a solution.

SELECTED BIOGRAPHY

BIRTHPLACE

Alamosa, Colorado, 1948

EDUCATION

Orange Coast College, Costa Mesa, 1968 to 1969

SOLO EXHIBITIONS

Orange Coast College, 1972
A Place, New York, 1983
O.K. Harris, Scottsdale, Arizona, 1983
Hunsaker/Schlesinger Gallery, Los Angeles, 1986
O.K. Harris, New York, 1987

GROUP EXHIBITIONS

Quint Gallery, San Diego, 1984
"A San Diego Exhibition," La Jolla Museum of Contemporary Art, 1985
"Faux Art: Illusions in Contemporary Art and Design," La Jolla Museum of Contemporary Art, 1987

COLLECTIONS

Federal Reserve Bank, Los Angeles
American Title Insurance
La Jolla Museum of Contemporary Art
Marilyn and Ivan Karp, New York
Robert Venturi

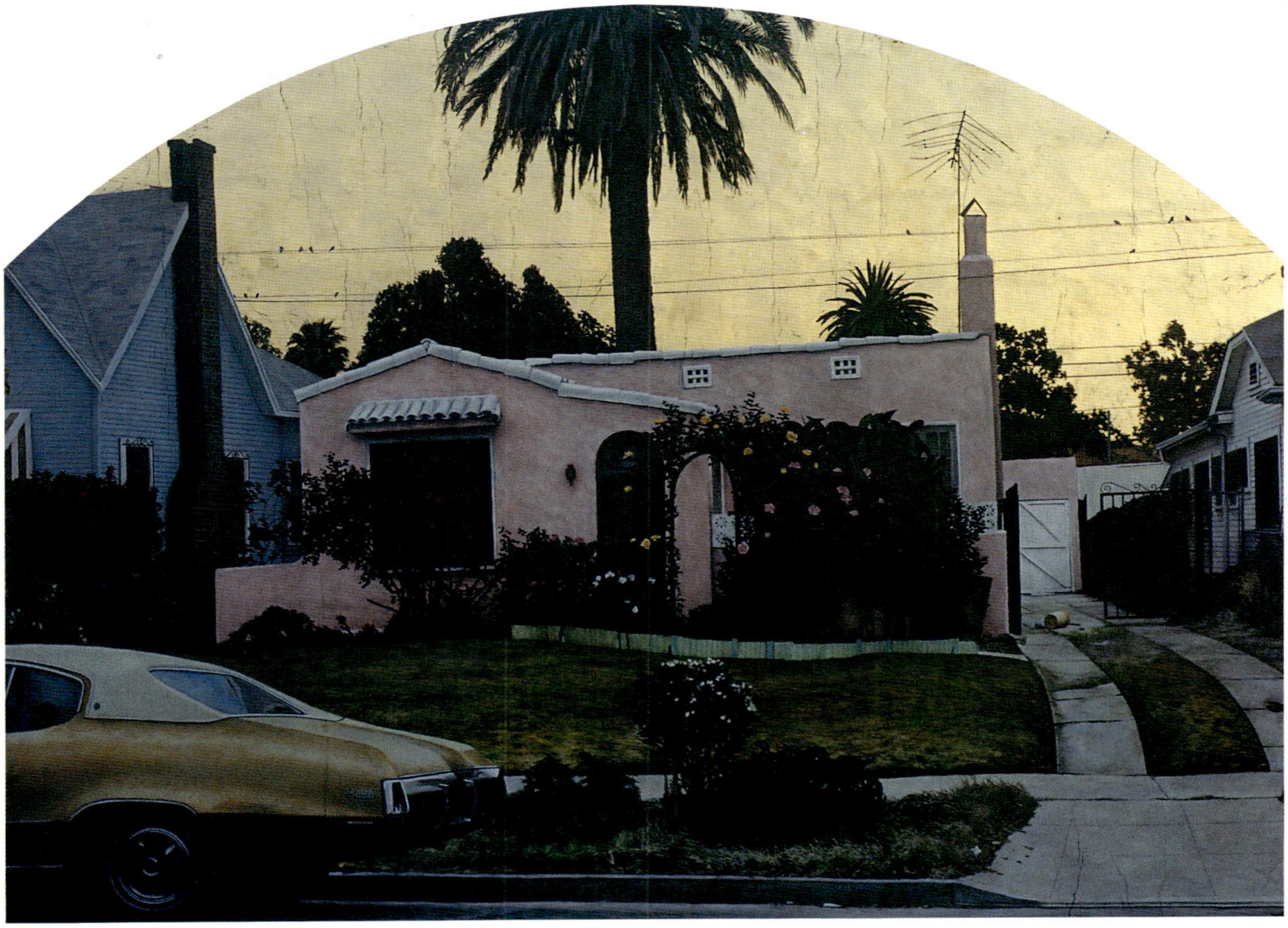

Home, oil and gold leaf on wooden panel, 54″ × 40″, 1987

Collection of Ivan Karp

Ethel Greene

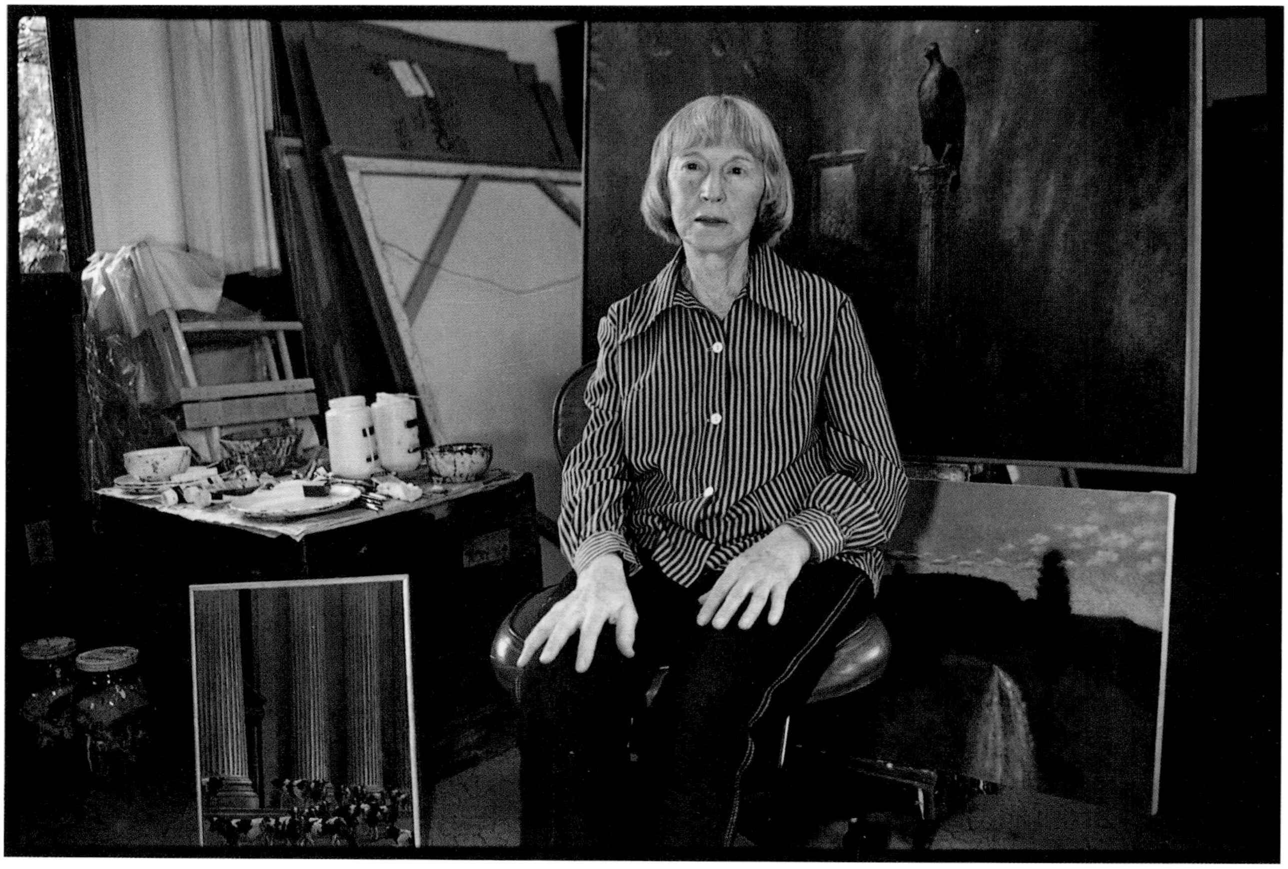

If you live long enough and keep showing constantly you get kind of venerated. Just sheer age and sticking in there counts quite a bit.

In the company of a large orange cat, Ethel Greene works in a canvas-filled studio overlooking the native vegetation indigenous to her property in Spring Valley. She lives and speaks with a directness and simplicity that are in contrast with the undercurrent of mystery and irony that have long been a striking element in her work.

Greene's sources are primarily from the contemporary life around her, with an unusual twist of detail from antiquity or from the unconscious. This makes her images powerful and at times disquieting. An admirer of artist Cliff McReynolds, Greene aspires to create visionary works while humbly discounting the magic of an ongoing series of paintings showing a large translucent egg stuck in unlikely places, such as a lone shopping cart in a parking lot, or water gushing in or out of the earth as if controlled by supernatural forces.

She grew up in Massachusetts with one brother, a quiet father, and a strong mother. She lives alone in her wood and glass home with several paintings by the late artist Dan Dickey, to whom she was once married. She has long been active in the San Diego Artists Guild and is the champion of many women artists.

On her studio doorframe hangs the following warning:

If once a man indulges himself in murder
very soon he comes to think very little of robbing;
And then he comes to drinking, and
Sabbath-breaking
and from that to incivility and procrastination.

Thomas DeQuincey, 1785-1859

I first saw surrealism when the Boston Contemporary Museum opened. I was enthralled by it. But it faded from my mind and surrealism wasn't really popular for quite a number of years, and I didn't really see much of it. I don't know exactly what got me into it for the first time. Along about the 60s I launched into it and stayed with it about as long as I've stayed with anything, except the kind of realism that I've been doing since I was four years old.

People like surprises and I like trying to think of them. I like work that reflects our times, like highways and supermarkets and the way we dress. I don't read anything else into it. That's for the critics.

By the time I was in high school I knew I wanted to go to art school. I relied on my mother to guide me through life at that stage; it was quite brave of her to let me go because that was almost the depths of the depression, 1932. It was pretty well known even to naive and unsophisticated people like my mother and me that people don't make a lot of money on art, which was one of the reasons why there were so few male artists in the art classes at the Massachusetts School for the Arts.

I didn't have to go into the WPA, although those were the golden years. I did fashion illustration and then worked for greeting card companies doing sales samples. Sometimes I worked day and night at two different jobs and after several years I changed to the Metropolitan Engraving Company where I was allowed to create, made twenty dollars a week and didn't have to work Saturdays. I was a Sunday painter through all of this.

By 1943 people were leaving, feeling that it was a frivolous business. I thought, if this job isn't going to last, I might as well go away as far as I can. I looked at a map and saw that the farthest place from Boston was San Diego. So I bought a San Diego newspaper in Boston and learned there was a place called Consolidated Vultee, now General Dynamics. They gave me two weeks to get there. They hired anybody in those days. I was to do mechanical drawing.

I arrived in San Diego by bus on Valentine's Day, 1943, at one or two in the morning. I took my first taxi and rented a ramshackle little place with as many girls as the landlady could squeeze in. I shared the living room with a Louisiana girl named Lulu Saturday while I worked the nightshift drawing airplane parts from 4 p.m. to 1 a.m. It was easy to make friends who had the same hours. Downtown was jumping. We'd go to Tijuana at 1 a.m. You couldn't get fired. I worked there in different departments until 1945 and made some lifetime friends.

Then I worked at the University of California Division of War Research that was located at the Timken family mansion in Point Loma. The department was comprised of artists and writers, my first taste of culture in San Diego. I was so impressed by some of the people I worked with. Among them were Harry Bertoia who had designed the Eames Chair while working with Charles Eames and later became a noted sculptor, the printmaker Barney Reid, Bill Kelly who runs Brighton Press now, and many teachers who were working for the war effort. When the war ended John Theobald went back to San Diego State and Sam Hinton went back to Scripps Institution of Oceanography. Many of us went to the Navy Electronics Lab, where once in a while we would be able to paint a picture. I stayed until 1955.

All the while I saved money so I could retire at the age of forty-three. How could I ever be a real artist if I had to wait until I was sixty-five? So to augment my savings I bought a piece of land in Point Loma, which I sold. Then the artist Jean Swiggett told me about some houses that were to be moved for highways, one of which was designed by Lloyd Ruocco. I was the highest bidder. I'd become a real estate mogul!

It never occurred to me to sell a painting. After several years of exhibiting, a man bought a painting at an Artists Guild show at the San Diego Museum of Art. I hadn't signed it; I didn't see any point. Nobody was going to buy my work. But he wanted it signed. After that I thought I'd better sign my paintings.

During this time the best galleries, like Leo Castelli in New York, had hardly any women artists. The second rate galleries would have some women. I suppose we women didn't expect much; we knew it was a man's world. Then the women's movement began.

I don't have any grand notions that everybody has to have art in their lives. I don't have any grand ideas about my art. You know, it's just paint on canvas. But I guess Shakespeare is just words on paper.

If you live long enough and keep showing constantly you get kind of venerated. Just sheer age and sticking in there counts quite a bit.

SELECTED BIOGRAPHY

BIRTHPLACE

Malden, Massachusetts

EDUCATION

Boston University School of Art
School of the Boston Museum
Massachusetts College of Art, graduated

SOLO EXHIBITIONS

La Jolla Museum of Contemporary Art, 1956
Arizona State University, 1972
Women's Building, Los Angeles, 1975
Taylor Gallery, Taos, New Mexico, 1980
(Two person), Maple Gallery, San Diego, 1984

GROUP EXHIBITIONS

Long Beach Museum of Art, Long Beach, 1963
Gump's Gallery, San Francisco, 1964
Bertha Schaefer Gallery, New York, 1966
Newspace Gallery, Los Angeles, 1978
San Diego Natural History Museum, 1986 (Two person)

COLLECTIONS

San Diego Museum of Art
Walbridge Collection, San Diego
Elizabeth Taylor
Danah Fayman, San Diego
Larry Bell, Taos

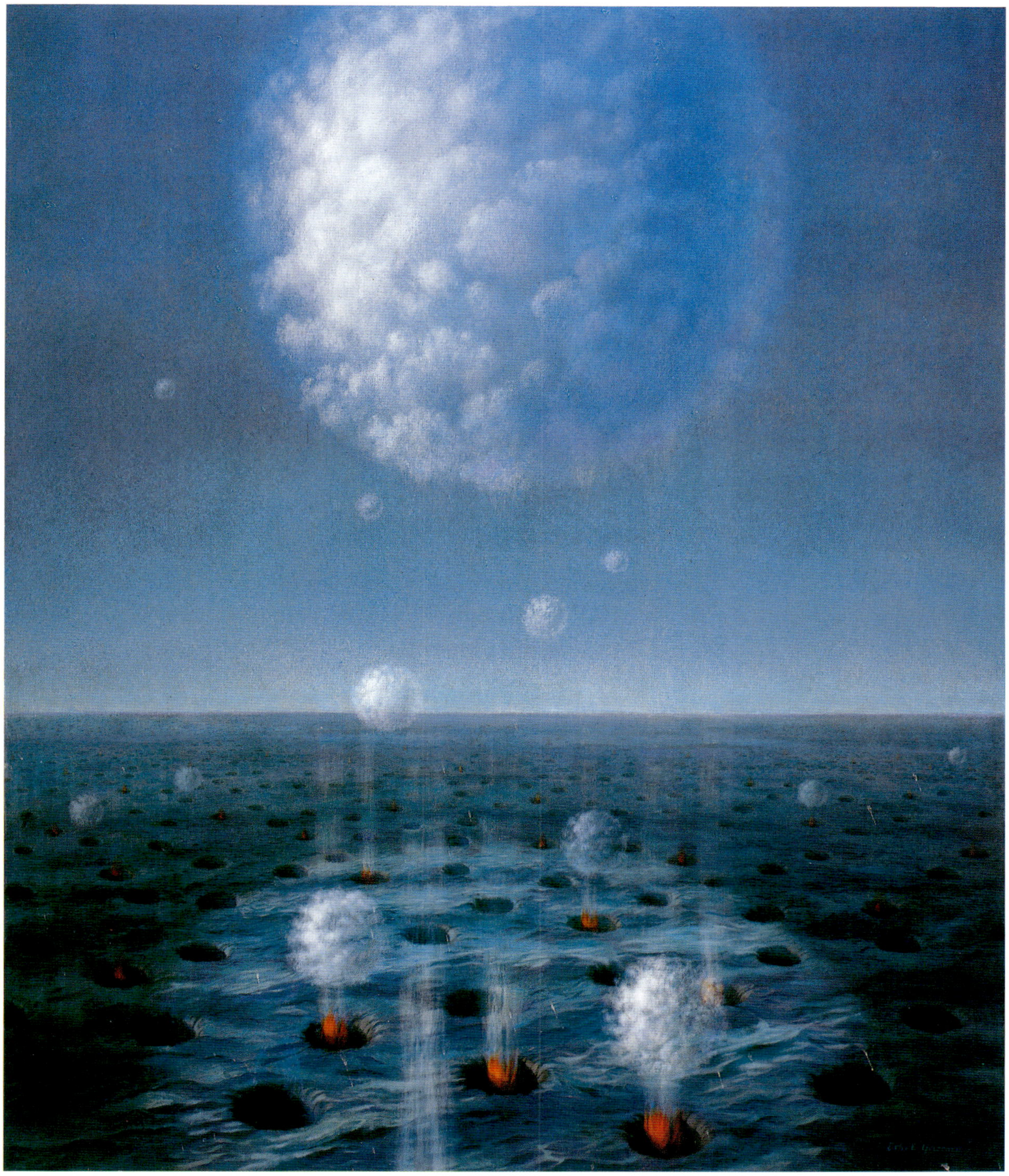

Phenomenon at Sea, acrylic/canvas, 56"×48", 1981

Collection of Larry Bell

Erik Gronborg

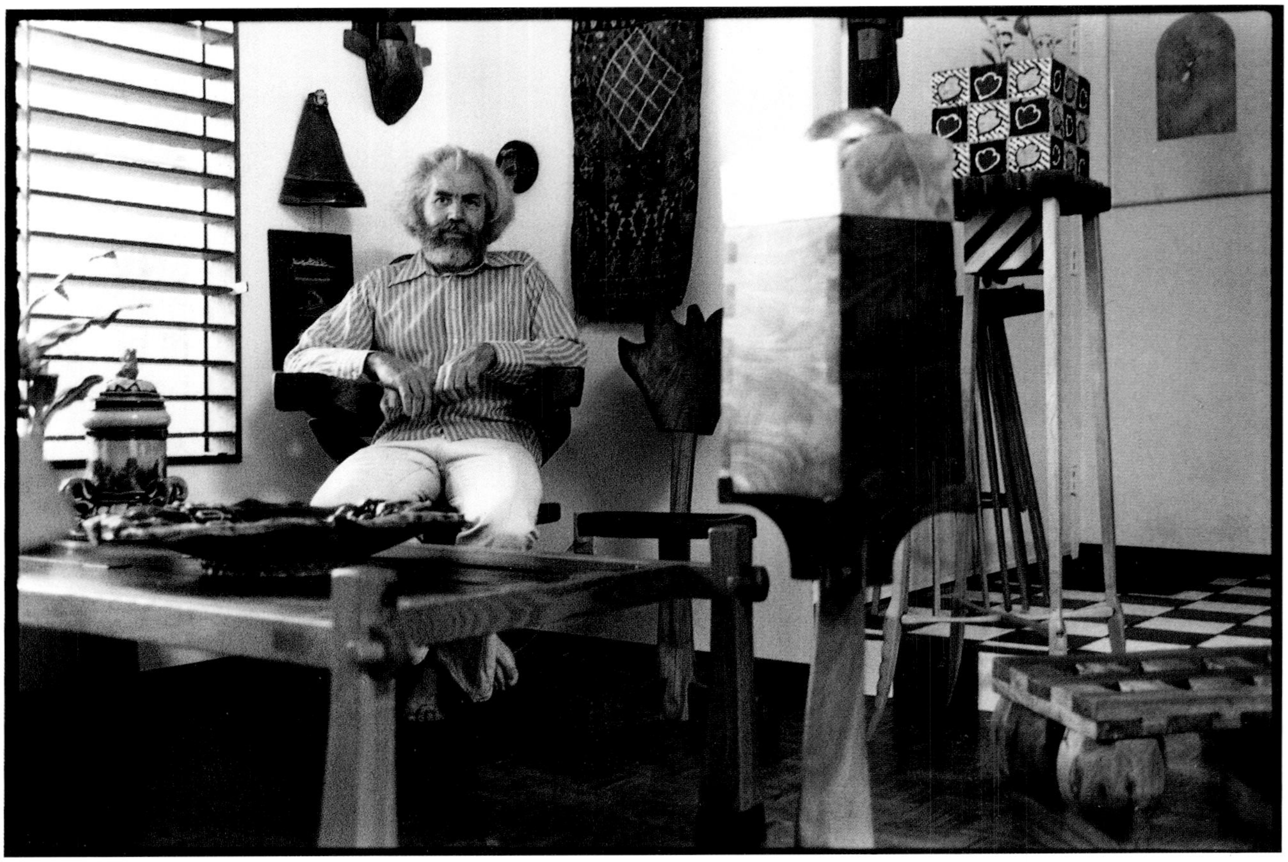

The band saw is my main tool. You can draw with it, you can cut fast. . . . as in abstract expressionist painting, the process is a significant part of the subject matter.

With long silver hair, a full beard, and clothed in his usual colorful manner, Erik Gronborg is as strikingly individual as his art. He has, in fact, stressed in his teaching and living that what one does as an artist can integrate perfectly with how one lives. He is therefore at home amidst the strong primary colors of his Solana Beach home and the lush gardens he has cultivated with his wife, Rina.

Gronborg's interests combine wood, ceramic, and metal. His early sculptures had a strong, massive feel that has been carried into his sculptural vases and teapots, for which he has become best known. His ceramic works retain the feel of the human hand, yet there is a deliberate decorative irony of political and social commentary embedded discreetly in the photodecal designs and sculptural details.

He grew up in Copenhagen without family encouragement or a tradition in art, though he had a younger brother who showed an interest in music. He is the first person in an extended family of more than fifty cousins to pursue a college education. Rina Gronborg teaches drawing to theater design students at UCSD and is known for her sensitive botanical illustrations. They have a daughter studying medical anthroplogy and a son in college.

Lately I've been interested in doing tables, cabinets, and desks, so that both wood and ceramics are incorporated, not just as a minor accent to each other. Combining the two involves a purely mechanical problem I have to deal with if I want it to last. That complicates it on top of the aesthetics. Most artists and certainly most people involved with crafts seem to have competence in one area – ceramics or wood or metal. I happen to have an interest and knowledge in metal work, wood work, and ceramics so that I can make use of all of those different things.

My inclination has always been sculpture. I was doing that from the time I was a teenager, mostly woodcarving. I really wanted to become an artist and felt that the conditions in Denmark were just too restrictive. The Royal Academy is the only art school in the whole country. It's assumed that nobody can do any work of significance until the age of fifty or sixty years old. You grow into a position of prominence. I felt that in the U. S., whatever the age, if you did something good you would get the recognition, which I think is the case. I worked in the electronics industry in Denmark almost ten years before I decided to emigrate.

The University of California at Berkeley was really an interesting place from 1960 to 1965. At the same time that I got there they had hired a couple of new people, Peter Voulkos and Harold Paris. I worked particularly with Harold Paris. He came from New York and was very theatrical and had an intensity about him, about being an artist.

I was very close friends with Paris. I would go to his studio frequently to help him. He had a big warehouse, a huge space. He was living in a corner, a kind of screened off area with a bed and a refrigerator. Even at that time it struck me as strange that a person whose whole existence and purpose in life was to deal with vision could be so oblivious to his surroundings, to work in a dump like that. As a contrast I would sometimes go to help one of the older professors who lived in Marin County. Richard O'Hanlon had integrated his studio into the garden, combined it all into one and it was just an amazing concept. When I got away from there and went to teach in Portland I realized it was nice to have a pleasant surrounding. Rina and I both find the house and garden are very much a part of our art.

I don't see that there is any real difference between my older sculpture and the furniture because it's done the same way, cut on the bandsaw with emphasis on planes. Both my ceramics and woodwork emphasize structure so that it is very obvious how it is put together, even to the point of exaggerating joinery to show that this is put into that. I do the same thing with clay handles. There is no attempt at hiding the fact that it is attached as a separate thing. I think it is one of the key forces of twentieth century society that we assemble things rather than make things out of one piece.

I've been interested to see if I could work with wood in the same spontaneous way as I've done in clay, where you can see every mark when bending, twisting, and cutting. I wanted to do the same kind of thing in wood. Traditionally furniture is a very controlled art form usually made with a plan and exact scale drawings. It doesn't leave much room for spontaneity. I use chunks of wood, mostly avocado because of availability; it's a really nice color and easy to cut. The band saw is my main tool. You can draw with it, you can cut fast and change your mind instantly. The process is very obvious. Just as in abstract expressionist painting, the process is a significant part of the subject matter.

I never used color much until I started ceramics. My use of color was a reaction to the Voulkos aesthetic which tries to make things look as non-pretty as possible. In the ceramics I was showing how I was putting things together in parts. Traditional drawing seemed not to be in keeping with that and so around 1968 I started using photo-decals instead of drawing on leather-hard clay. Photography seemed to be logical since it was a modern mechanical process.

I find it sort of ironic that you can go to a fancy art opening where people admire the expensive paintings on the wall and drink champagne out of plastic glasses. They do not carry that appreciation of art into everything around them. The glass you drink out of should feel good, should be real glass. The furniture you sit on should be well made or even interesting. This is maybe one of my goals, to do work where people can appreciate the quality of craftsmanship in such a way that it's not just a throwback to the past but a viable contemporary art with a sense of quality running through it.

SELECTED BIOGRAPHY

BIRTHPLACE

Copenhagen, Denmark

EDUCATION

University of California, Berkeley, BA, 1962; MA, 1963

SOLO EXHIBITIONS

Musee d'Art Moderne, Paris, 1965
Museum of Contemporary Crafts, New York, 1969
The Egg and the Eye Gallery, Los Angeles, 1973
Silvan Simone Gallery, Los Angeles, 1973
Bonython Gallery, Adelaide, Australia, 1976, 1978, 1983

GROUP EXHIBITIONS

"Objects USA, The Johnson Collection of Contemporary Crafts," travelling exhibit to all major cities in the U.S. and Europe, 1969
"International Ceramics Exhibition," Award, travelling exhibit, Victoria and Albert Museum, London, 1972
"Contemporary Porcelain," travelling exhibition, Renwick Gallery, Smithsonian Institution, Washington, D.C., 1980 to 1983
"Art in Clay: 1950s to 1980s in Southern California," part of the Olympic Arts Festival, Los Angeles Municipal Art Gallery, 1984
"Subtractive Woodworking," Snyderman Gallery, Philadelphia, 1985

GRANTS

Rockefeller Grant in Creative Art
National Endowment for the Arts, Arts Craftsman Grant

COLLECTIONS

Bellerieve Museum, Zurich
Los Angeles County Museum of Art
Museum of American Crafts, New York
Besser Collection, Arkansas Decorative Arts Museum, Little Rock
Oakland Museum, Oakland

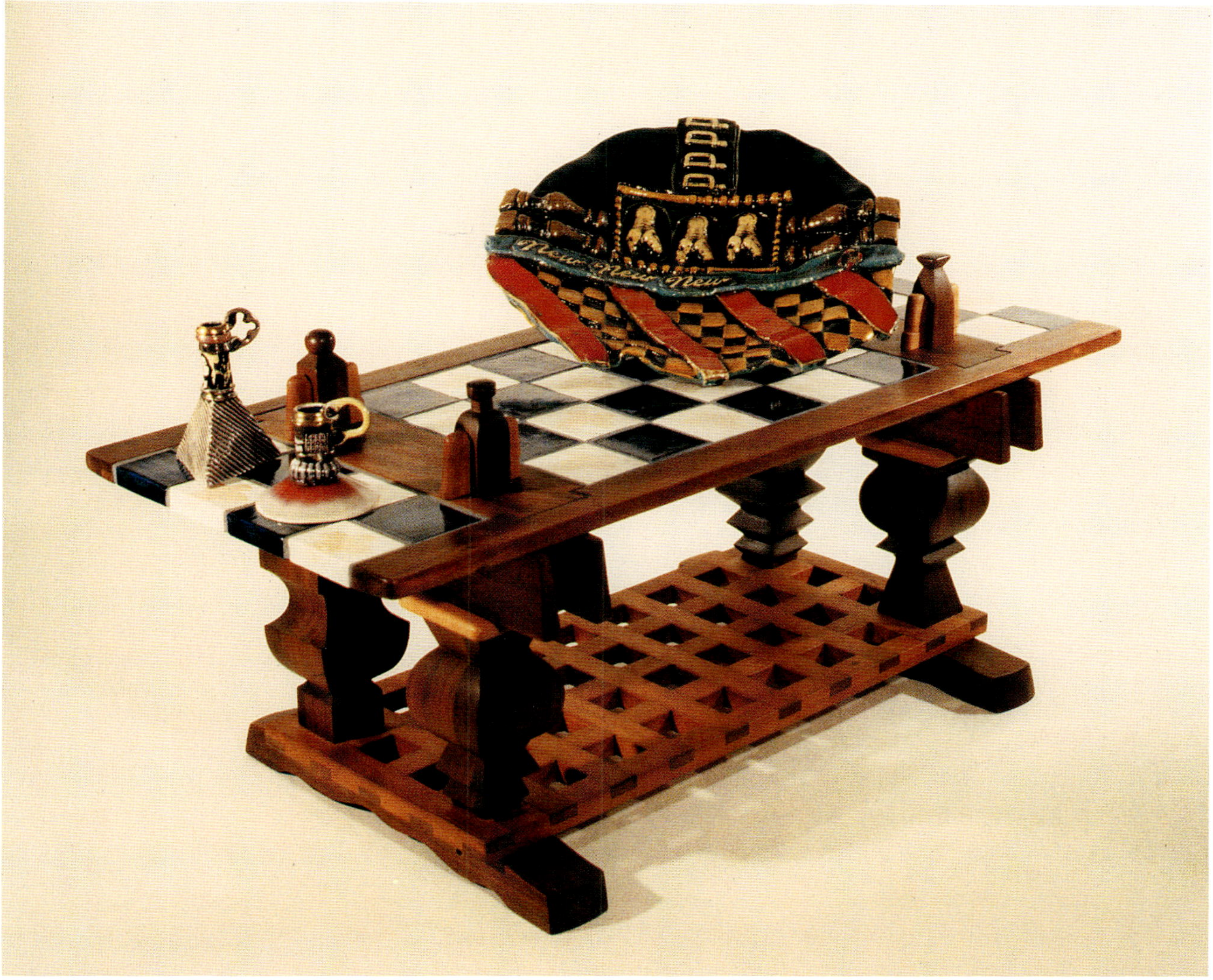

Ceramic table, hardwood and tile, 52″×25″×18″, 1987; Ceramic plate, 22″ diameter, 1987; Two porcelain cups, 6″ high, 1986

Tom Grondona

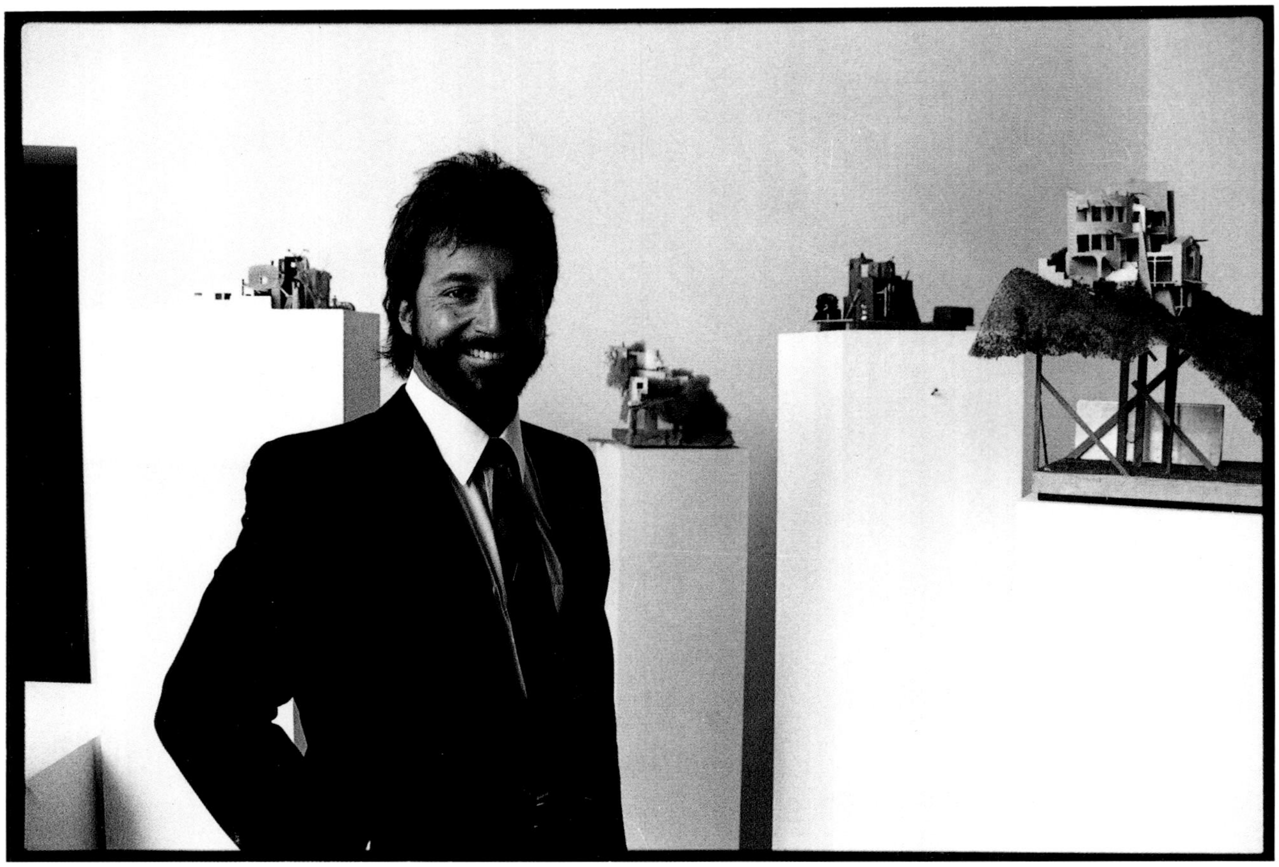

I want to wake people up and let them know there is something more than what they have and that they can have it.

Tom Grondona's playfulness with serious subjects is a survival technique that serves him well as he forges a career in architecture. His style is as volatile and imaginative as that developing career. His enthusiasm helps to integrate these attributes into his designs and make them realities.

For Grondona, each project is a fresh start. To develop his ideas he builds study models before drawing out detailed plans. His popular work on Claudia's and other shops in Horton Plaza have been the subjects of numerous awards and features in Progressive Architecture *(September 1986) and* Architecture Magazine *(May 1987). Critic John Pastier describes his work as "unmistakably an architecture of tangible experience rather than one of theory."*

His early artistic abilities were nourished in elementary school by teachers who let him do art in the coat room while everyone else did history. He and his brother, in computer graphics, were raised in San Diego by their mother, a dean's assistant at United States International University, and their father, an aerospace engineer who occasionally helps him on projects.

While heading his architectural firm in Point Loma, Grondona still surfs with childhood friends and is currently working on his own home in Point Loma. He says it will incorporate "every idea I've ever had in my whole life."

It seems like the critics and artists and architects are all trying to define what art and architecture are. But there is something that happens right in the middle. It's not really when an artist does an architectural piece or when an architect does an artistic piece. It's when you come up with something that was influenced by both disciplines at the same time.

I got into architecture thinking that maybe this is a situation where you can do artistic things in more of a technical way. The more I got into architecture the more I got fascinated with how most of the time architects think with too many preconceived ideas. I thought there were so many boring architects out there – let's call them "businessmen-architects" who have a business to run, bills to collect – that people would want art-influenced architects to do projects for them. I figured that there would still be fewer of us and that the ratio would mean we would still have work.

The sad thing about being an architect is that you have to wait for commissions or develop them yourself. The amount of awards and notoriety you get are not directly proportional to the amount of work you get. I've gotten a lot of great awards, but a real thrill would be to develop a salad dressing that would enable you to eat your awards and eat all your press! (laughter) I want to invent my own *Grondona's Own Salad Dressing*, like Paul Newman did, and market it for artists that are under the eye of the critics but never get a commission.

I don't see myself wanting to lead a sheltered life, wanting to be the artist who has the secluded studio, who isn't in touch with the city, the downtown, the problems. I want to be an architect solving architectural urban problems in an architectural way, kind of like we did with Claudia's. It embodies what we're trying to do. We put in art to solve the architectural problems and to get people to think about what they're doing in an artistic sense. It is really an art gallery. It's a piece of art that everybody gets to use, like a walk through an urban piece of art.

Frank Lloyd Wright's career kind of went up and down, up and down. He was a big hit, then all of a sudden he went ten years without a project, then he got back up again. As he got a bit older he went downhill and right when everybody was thinking of him as the old master, a nice guy, all of a sudden he did the Johnson Wax building and his career skyrocketed again. He would create all his ideas when he didn't have a project and when he did have one he'd just take those ideas and put them on the project.

But when I don't have work it's depressing. For the kind of work I do I need to come up with an idea to have a sense of well-being, to know that I've got a secure project. It is then that my mind is free to think about all these great ideas.

Rob Quigley and Ted Smith are other artists doing architecture. Rob calls Ted "The Philosopher," himself "The Architect," and me "The Artist." I can kind of see how that works. Rob doesn't profess to be an artist. I think it's semantics. The way he looks at a project is with the eyes of an artist. But he wouldn't be as excited as I would about doing a "House of Furniture," like I designed for Robin and Mike Morgan that has an exterior with shapes like drawers, chairs, and a giant bed. I don't think he'd want to do it. He'd want to be more the architect. I think I've got a real battle ahead being an artist/architect.

I went into architecture because of the art. It turned out to be more art than I ever imagined. I never saw myself in three-piece business suits playing the role of architect, but I did see myself having projects. I don't know how I never connected the two.

I go in stages of getting something that is unattainable and making a success of it and then looking back and thinking that was great, that was easy. I wonder what's the next step.

I want to wake people up and let them know there is something more than what they have and that they can have it. If you don't have money, big deal, you can still have a piece of art, you can still do something people want to come and experience. But it doesn't take money, it takes you!

SELECTED BIOGRAPHY

BIRTHPLACE

San Diego

EDUCATION

California State Polytechnic University at Pomona, 1971 to 1972
Southern California Institute of Architecture, Santa Monica, Bachelor of Architecture, 1974
Registered Architect, State of California, 1983

SOLO EXHIBITIONS

Art D'Tevere, Rome
"I am an Architecture," San Diego Museum of Art, 1981

GROUP EXHIBITIONS

"Young Architects Forum," New York Architectural League, New York, 1981
"The California Condition," La Jolla Museum of Contemporary Art, 1985
"New Faces," curated by Robert McDonald, Shoshana Wayne Gallery, Los Angeles, 1986
"Proposed Installations," Museum of Seasonal Change, Imperial Bank Building, San Diego, 1987
"Architects/Designers/Planners for Social Responsibility/New York," Max Protetch Gallery, New York, 1988

HONORS

Citation for "Twenty-first Century Castle," 1984; Award of Honor for "Claudia's" and Citations for "Morgan's House of Furniture," and "Tower to the Stars," 1986 by American Institute of Architects, San Diego
Honor Award for "Claudia's," 1985 by American Institute of Architects, California
Honor Award for "Claudia's," 1987 by American Institute of Architects, National
Citation for "Barstow Dental Office," 1987, Progressive Architecture Magazine

COMMISSIONS

"Rollercoaster," sculpture, National University, San Diego
"Claudia's," A cinnamon roll store; "Boardwalk Fries" and "Wonder Sushi," Horton Plaza, San Diego
"Barstow Dental Office," Jan and Gerald G. Barstow, DDS, San Diego
"Vicolo," private residence of Dr. David A. Schein, San Diego
"Kindig Construction," private residence of Donna and David Kindig, San Diego

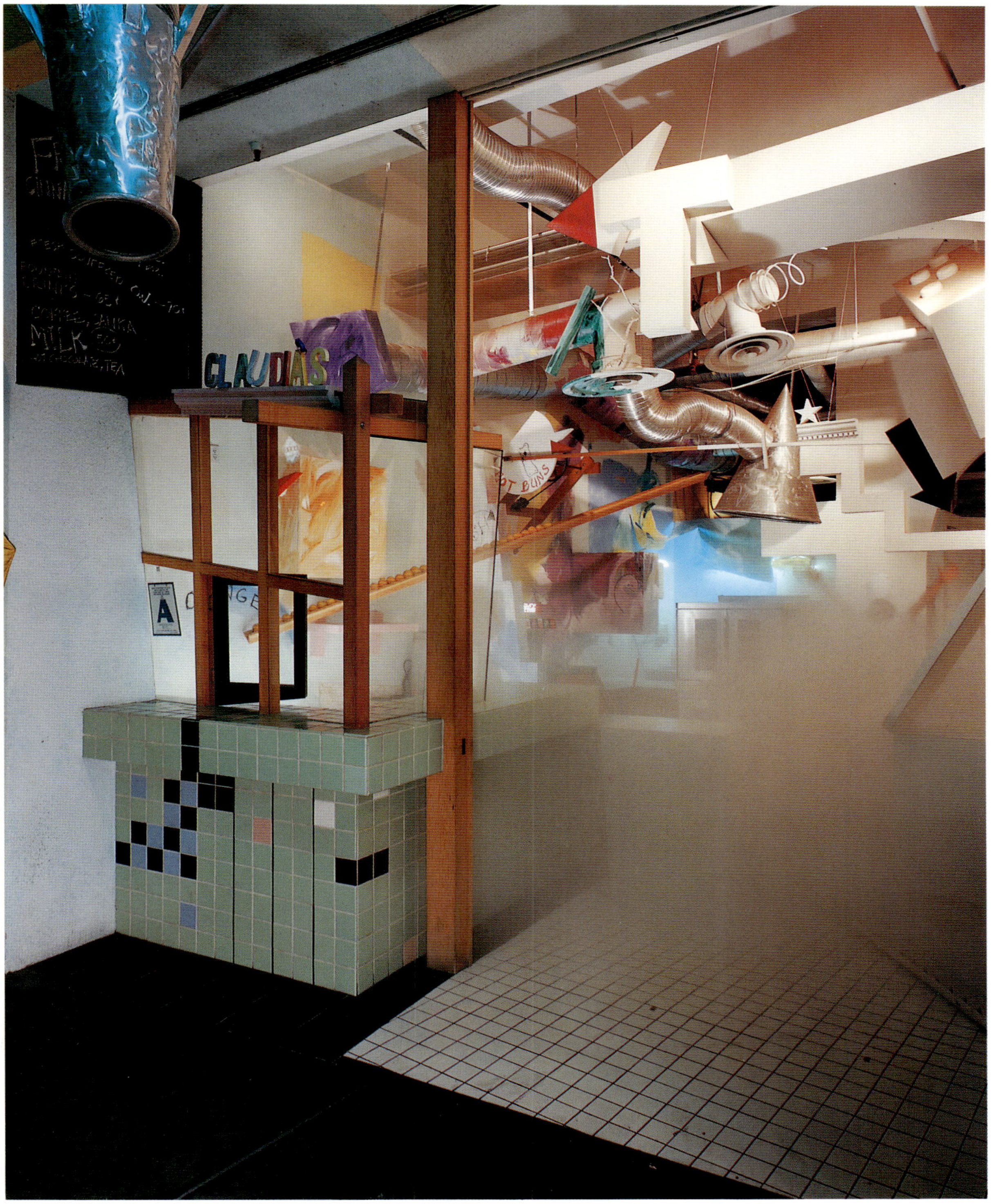

Claudia's – Horton Plaza, architectural installation, mixed media, 15′6″ × 16′ × 33′5″, 1986

Raul Guerrero

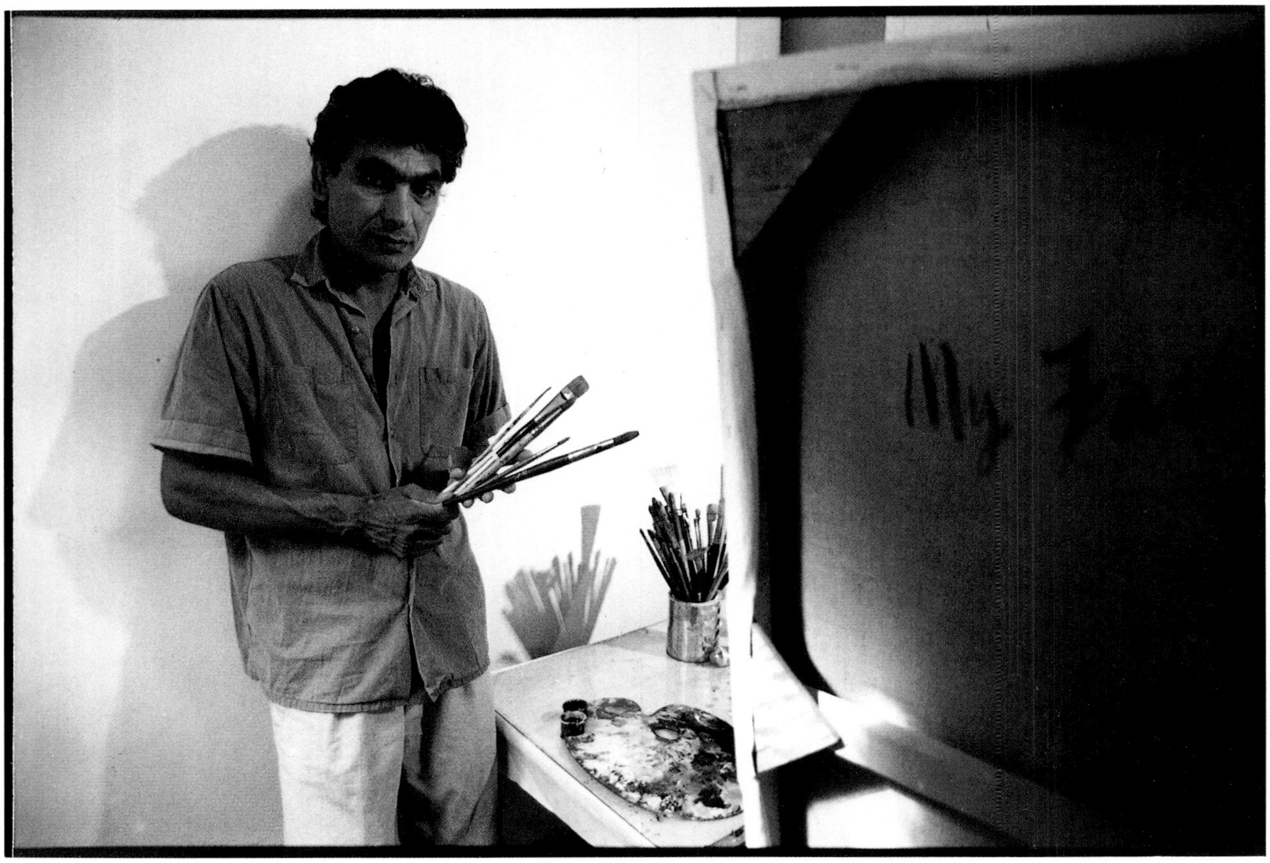

I think it is important in our time to look at what is going on in aesthetics. Aesthetics is a factor in our evolutionary competence.

Recently giving up his downtown studio to work in the more aesthetic surroundings of his home and garden in North Park, Raul Guerrero is a study of self-conscious intensity as he discusses his theories and views of the art world.

His work over the years has slipped between labels, described simultaneously as surrealist, conceptual, kitsch, romantic, primitive, eccentric, and mystical. It is no wonder that ten years ago William Wilson in the Los Angeles Times *(March 17, 1978) called him "a cult figure," for Guerrero manages to infuse into his paintings and installations certain elements of American Indian, East Indian, Mexican, Pre-Columbian, and European culture – both agricultural and cosmopolitan – and still maintain his ties to Los Angeles, whether he is working in New York, Paris, Oaxaca, or San Diego.*

Guerrero was raised with one younger and two older brothers and an adopted sister in Blythe, California. When he was eleven the family moved to National City. His mother, a beautician, and his father, a laborer, were both born in the U.S. of Mexican-East Indian heritage and raised the family in an atmosphere filled with discussions of both poetry and politics.

When his ex-wife died, Guerrero returned from New York and worked at Green Tiger Press while caring for his son, Quinn, then six years old. With Quinn soon in high school, Guerrero's commitment to art is resulting in some solid financial as well as critical recognition. He recently received a large commission from the city of Los Angeles.

From the time I was seven years old I would spend summers with my grandmother and her third husband, a Hindu Indian who managed a grape ranch in Fresno. I would sleep in the living room surrounded with pictures of all the Indian deities that lined the walls. I remember one time when I was about sixteen I was lying under a vineyard there, picking grapes to earn money to buy my clothes. I was thinking, I've got to do something else besides just lie here underneath this vineyard. I thought I'd like to be an architect. The antithesis. Can you imagine? If you've ever done work like that it's pure hell. It's hot and dirty work and your hands swell up.

I knew nothing about the art world. I didn't have any expectations out of school except to get a job. Fortunately there was a ceramist, Mark Fleming, who lived in Chula Vista and he introduced me to Beat poetry. I couldn't relate to the Mexican kids because I liked to play chess and read, stuff like that, effete things. I couldn't relate to the Anglos because they were either surfers or socialites. All that were left were the nerds, the outcasts, and their interests were driving cars. So I was basically alone. I spent the twelfth grade reading Sherlock Holmes and Edgar Rice Burroughs and making these terrible little ceramic pieces. Then I had a teacher – Willis C. Bernard – who had come from Boston and was doing abstract painting. At that point an alternative lifestyle opened up and all of a sudden I found a niche, an area that I could belong to that was more intellectual, about reading. It wasn't just driving around and cruising.

I went to Mexico, attempting to find myself. I felt I didn't have a place to call home. When I was finally admitted to Chouinard Art Institute in Los Angeles it was like I'd found my home. It was like the refuge of all of the weirdos from my generation, the sanctuary. People from moneyed families in Hollywood and strange guys from queenland, and Texans walking around barefoot. The parties were really wild at that point. People would be peeing in the fireplaces; it was just mayhem. You were an artist, so you could do what you wanted. The excitement of going to a school like that was phenomenal for me. I'd get up in the morning and couldn't wait to go to school to draw again. You were free to express yourself and didn't have to be in some stodgy classroom having to answer another stupid question.

Some people feel that they have to explore every aspect of an idea and take it from end to end so that it relates very closely to itself. There is some evolutionary context to that body of work. I don't like that idea so much because it doesn't allow for the input that I'm continually getting from the world. The complexities of the mind vary continually. As a person I change from year to year, at times from day to day, and I need to address that also. In a way I consider myself a medium for society. I am a medium for myself which may be a more appropriate way of saying it. So I need to see what it is that I am about as I continue my relationship to the ideas that are pertinent to my time. I am not exclusively dealing with my ideas for self-gratification, but rather ultimately the pleasure of the viewer. I'm working to have the work viewed by a public. I want that. I think that in many ways art can be a very evocative, erotic, enlightening manifestation of what a human being can do.

I think it is important in our time to look at what is going on in aesthetics. Aesthetics is a factor in our evolutionary competence. In terms of society it affects us. We, as artists, are delving into the inner psyche and figuring out what it is we, as human beings in our time, are about in terms of what art is. It has repercussions later on. If you look at architecture, the Germans figured out the International Style and it's permeated everywhere.

I'm the product of a culture that's very rich, very sophisticated, and there's a sensibility which that culture represents. I don't think it has to do with the political aspects of it. I want to deal with the pure artistic sensibility, which is phenomenal. It hasn't even been seen yet. You have people like Diego Rivera or Ruffino Tamayo, but they deal in a provincial state of aesthetics. I'm interested in the overall function of aesthetics in terms of how it relates to the world and the growth of the world in general.

I think that the Mexican-American heritage – Mexican Indian particularly – is really fascinating. Also, I think that my kind of aesthetics wouldn't have happened if I'd been in Mexico because I am a product of the American cultural influence from the European.

An itinerant immigrant laborer could come to the United States and become a millionaire, if he wanted to. Or the offspring, like me, could become an artist if he desired. That wouldn't happen in Mexico. Because the artist traditionally comes from the upper middle class, I would not happen in many countries.

SELECTED BIOGRAPHY

BIRTHPLACE

Brawley, California

EDUCATION

Chouinard Art Insitute, Los Angeles, BFA, 1970

SOLO EXHIBITIONS

Long Beach Museum of Art, Long Beach 1977
Los Angeles Institute of Contemporary Art, 1982
Richard Kuhlenschmidt Gallery, Los Angeles, 1985
USC Atelier, Santa Monica, 1986
Saxon-Lee Gallery, Los Angeles, 1987

GROUP EXHIBITIONS

"L.A.," San Francisco Art Institute, 1977
Hallwalls, Buffalo, 1978
"A San Diego Exhibition," La Jolla Museum of Contemporary Art, 1985
"To the Astonishing Horizons, L.A.V.A.," curated by Peter Frank, Los Angeles Design Center, 1985
Phoenix Biennale, Phoenix Museum, AZ, 1987

GRANTS

National Endowment for the Arts, Photography Fellow
NEA/COMBO Grant

COLLECTIONS

Long Beach Museum of Art, Long Beach
Security Pacific Bank, Los Angeles
Phoenix Art Museum, Phoenix
Scripps Clinic, La Jolla
Fountain, Grand-Hope Park, landscape cesign by Larry Halprin, Community Redevelopment Agency, Los Angeles

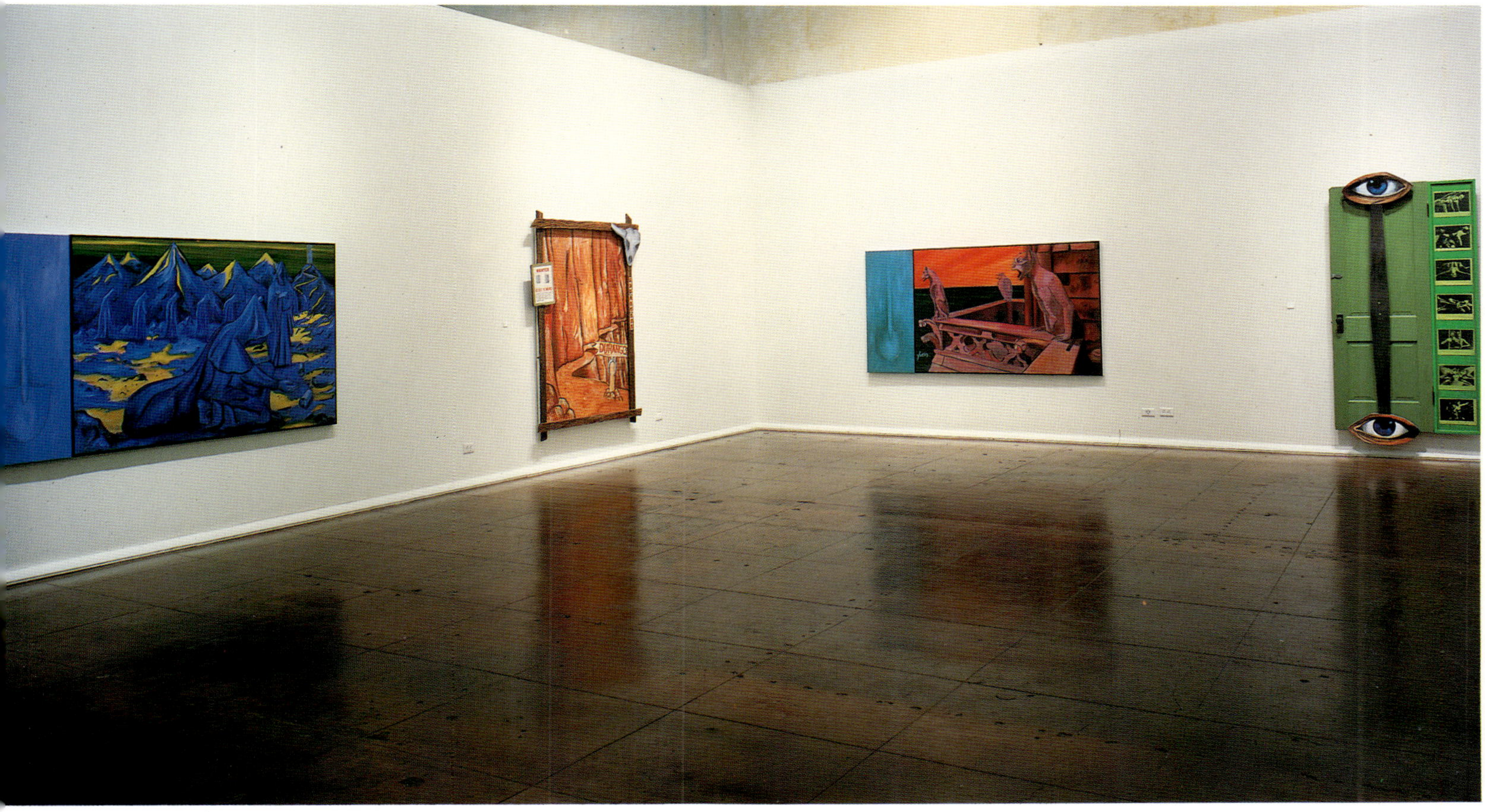

allation, Saxon/Lee Gallery, Los Angeles, oil/canvas with objects, 1987

Helen and Newton Harrison

We've sort of blasted our cities into existence; they've not been created and recreated like the great cities of Europe. –NH

As freeways and other things broke up established patterns, new kinds of social arenas have to be made. It's time now when people are beginning to think about these things. –HH

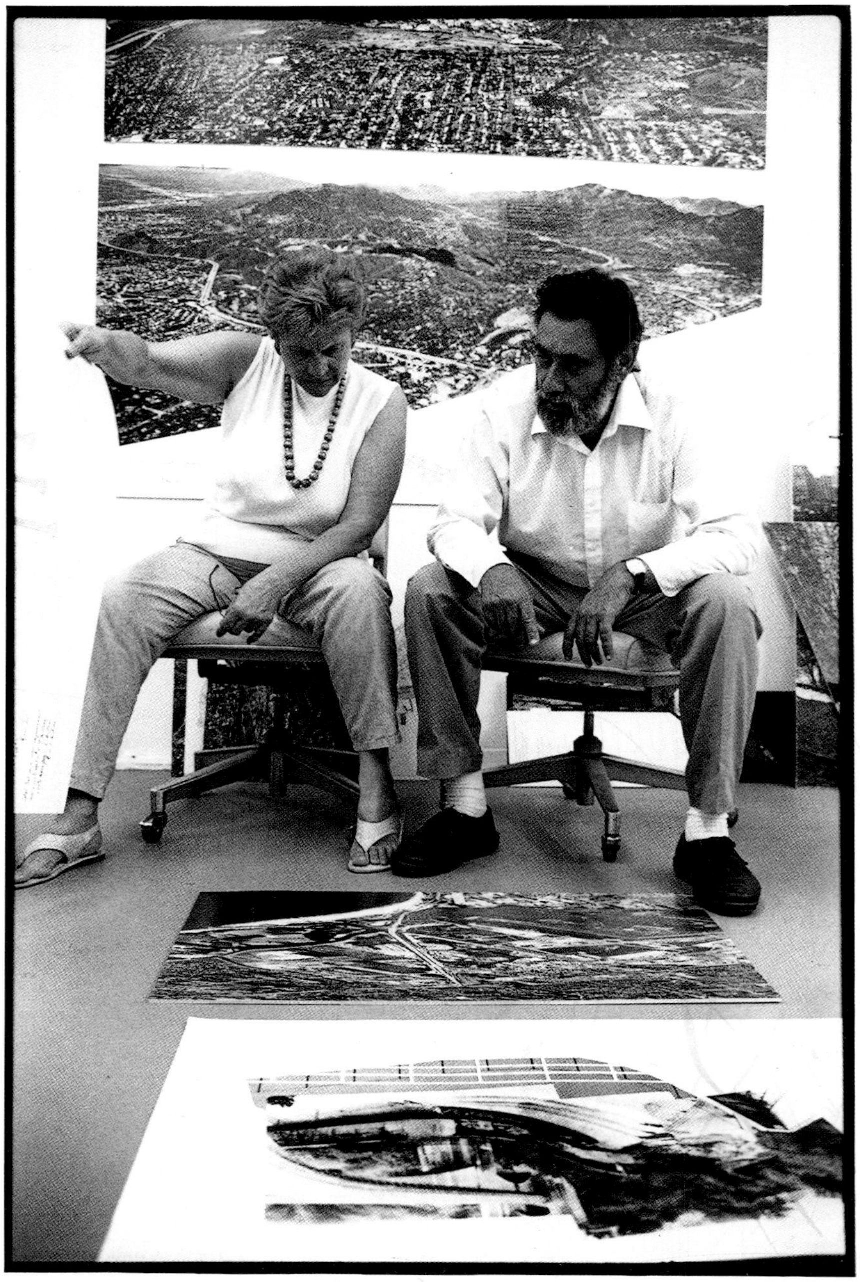

The walls and table tops of their UCSD Water Tank studio are resplendent with tinted aerial photographs and maps which assure the visitor that Helen and Newton Harrison are energetically pursuing their ecologically and sociologically concerned collaborations. Their major body of work is "The Lagoon Cycle," a 350 foot long narrative in which they adopt roles of "The Lagoonmaker" and "The Witness" in a consideration of endangered estuarial lagoons, a metaphor for life itself. This and numerous other site-specific pieces have been described in performances, videotapes, catalogues, and interviews that have received wide national and international attention.

The Harrisons have formally worked on projects together since 1970 and share a professorship on the UCSD faculty. In their life and in their performances they also share a strong voice, allowing time for one to take a breath while the other continues or embellishes the idea. Both have had lifelong interests in education, science, and psychology.

The Harrisons have three sons and one daughter who are grown. With the company of several dogs, the couple continue their appreciation of nature by daily looking through the picture windows of their small comfortable home. Their rural plot of land is one of a few remaining Del Mar properties unmarked by developers.

(From a presentation at the La Jolla Athenaeum, October 21, 1986)

HH: We lived in Italy for a number of years in the late fifties. We're New Yorkers and when we came back to New York we were suddenly shocked. We saw the city with new eyes. I think New York is a great city in many ways, as cities go, but we realized that a city could also be very centered in a way that New York wasn't and we thought about coherency and community.

NH: In the last five years we've been photographing the urban landscape at great heights, treating the photograph as if it were a sort of field painting, looking for discontinuities and proposing new continuities. The reason we're able to do this is that the planning process itself virtually guarantees the dividing up of community. It guarantees it. And above all, the planning process guarantees the destruction of rivers, the breaking up of promenades.

HH: It doesn't have to.

NH: – The American planning process as it operates –

HH: Paris had some wonderful planning done in the eighteenth and nineteenth century. The city of Washington was well planned, initially. What happens is that too much of the planning is done for expediency. People go into city planning, I think, full of good ideas and full of desire to see something happen and something different. And they gradually get worn down by what is possible.

NH: We tend to be invited to cities to come and think.

HH: Primarily by museums or universities or art organizations of some kind, and we don't make any guarantees about this coming and thinking because sometimes we have a good experience and sometimes it's less so. And when it's less so we get very critical.

NH: We were asked to take up the issue of San Diego, actually the issue of the relationship of Balboa Park to the Harbor by Lefty Adler and the San Diego Art Center that is currently closed for rethinking. We came up with the idea of "A Grand Round for San Diego."

HH: Imagine a Grand Canal along Mission Valley that extends from Route 5 on the west to the Stadium on the east. It is simultaneously an urban fantasy, possibly even a flood control measure. Imagine the small canal section necessary to connect Mission Valley to Mission Bay, and thus connect Mission Bay directly to the San Diego Harbor. Imagine a promenade from the Harbor up Sixth Avenue along Balboa Park to University Avenue where an aerial chairlift would run west of Route 163, but roughly parallel to it, extending down the canyon across Route 8 and part of Mission Valley to the Mission Valley Canal.

HH: Imagine a bridge across Route 5 at Sixth Avenue and the corner of Balboa Park turned into a public park by extending the bridge, cantilevering it to the west, thereby making room for extensive planting in a glass wall, while simultaneously offering views to the Harbor west across the freeway and down Sixth Avenue.

NH: Imagine a vaporetto moving from the new harbor at Sixth Avenue with stops along the way through the MCRD Channel to its most easterly terminence, then along the new channel to present parking lots beneath the Mission Valley Canal or through the Canal extension to Mission Bay.

HH: One may begin the Grand Round anywhere. What we're proposing essentially is through San Diego by foot, through the water, through the air, so that the one thing we left out of this plan is the way we normally go into San Diego – by car. We feel that every great city needs features that employ the uniqueness of its site, the economic, aesthetic, and social values all at once. Features that distinguish it from other cities. We feel that the Grand Round employs San Diego's unique terrain and satisfies that need.

NH: Yes, it is expensive, but so was the coliseum and so have been many great works done by human beings. We've sort of blasted our cities into existence; they've not been created and recreated like the great cities of Europe.

HH: And a lot of the development and redevelopment has been done crudely. As freeways and other things broke up established patterns, new kinds of social arenas have to be made. It's time now when people are beginning to think about these things.

NH: In essence, every city has to rebuild itself intermittently because buildings don't last forever, streets don't last forever and intentions for spaces don't last forever. We have to be thinking of entirely humane ways to proceed and new ways to enrich urban life.

SELECTED BIOGRAPHY

BIRTHPLACE

HH: New York City
NH: New York City

EDUCATION

HH: Queens College, BA English literature, 1949
New York University, MA in education, 1953
United States International University, San Diego, Ph.D. coursework in Psychology, 1967
NH: Yale University, New Haven, BFA, 1964; MFA 1965

TEACHING

HH: University of California, San Diego, 1982 to present
NH: University of California, San Diego, 1967 to present

SOLO EXHIBITIONS

"Baltimore Promenade," mural-sized photographs with text and "Baltimore Promenade," performance, Decker Gallery, Maryland Institute, 1981 and (with Steve Pearson, mime) Washington Project for the Arts, Washington, D.C., 1982
"The Fourth Lagoon" and "San Diego as the Center of the World," 1974; "Fifth Lagoon," 1975;
"Gabrielino Meditation," 1978; "The First Lagoon" and "The Sixth Lagoon," 1980; "Barrier Islands Drama and Baltimore Promenade" and "Revolutions per Minute," 1982; Ronald Feldman Fine Arts, New York
"Guadalupe Meander, a Refugia for San Jose," with performance, San Jose Museum of Art, San Jose, 1983
"The Lagoon Cycle," Herbert F. Johnson Museum of Art, Cornell University, Ithaca, 1985

GROUP EXHIBITIONS

"Art World," Whitney Museum of American Art, 1976
Venice Biennale, 1976 and 1980
"Equinox 80," travelling exhibition, Centre Georges Pompidou (Beaubourg), Musee d'Art Moderne, Paris, 1981
"Art and Technology," (NH) 1971; "The Artist as Social Designer: Aspects of Public Urban Art Today," 1985 Los Angeles County Museum of Art
"Museum of Drawers," 1972 and 1977; 1987, Documenta, Kassel, West Germany

GRANTS

Sea Grant
Creative Arts Institute, University of California, San Diego

COMMISSIONS AND COLLECTIONS

"The Lagoon Cycle" commissioned by John Kluge, President, Metromedia, Inc., Los Angeles
"Barrier Islands Drama," commissioned by The John and Mable Ringling Museum of Art, Sarasota, Florida
"Fortress Atlanta: On Rites of Assembly and Rights of Passage," commissioned by Emory University, Atlanta, for year-long Symposium on Human Rights, 1983
Northwest Energy Company
Museum of Contempory Art, Chicago

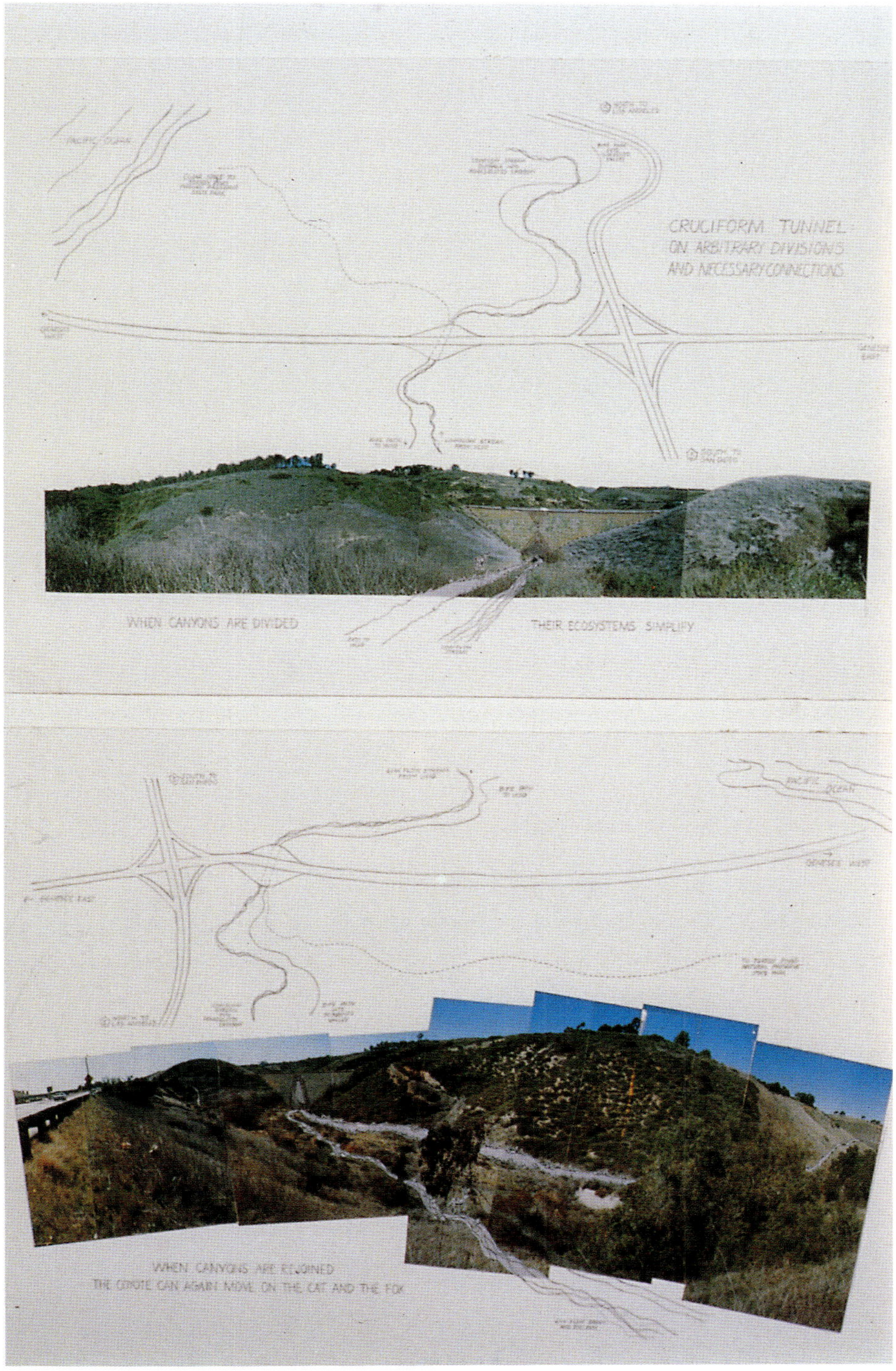

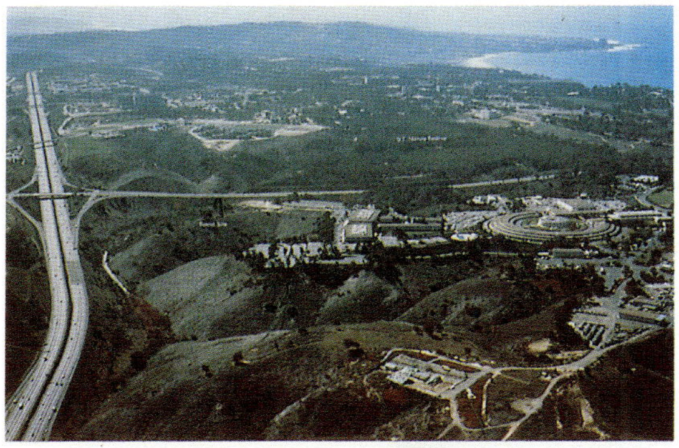

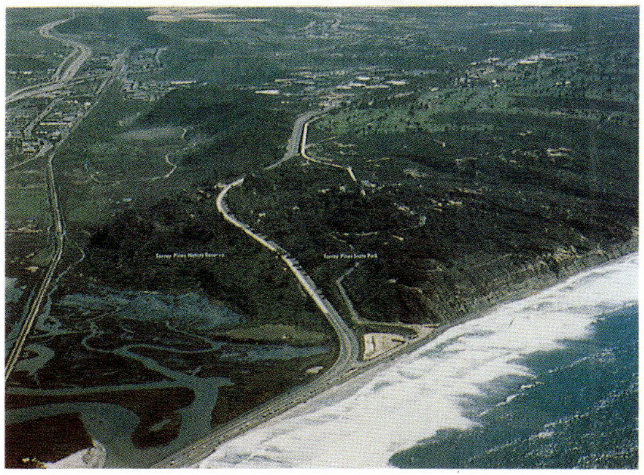

When canyons are divided,
their ecco-systems simplify.
When canyons are re-joined,
the coyote can again move
on the cat and the fox.

Cruciform Tunnel: Arbitrary Divisions and Necessary Connections, color photography and ink on vellum, 14″ × 20″, 1987 (Site: Genessee Ave. at Route 5, San Diego)

Margaret Honda

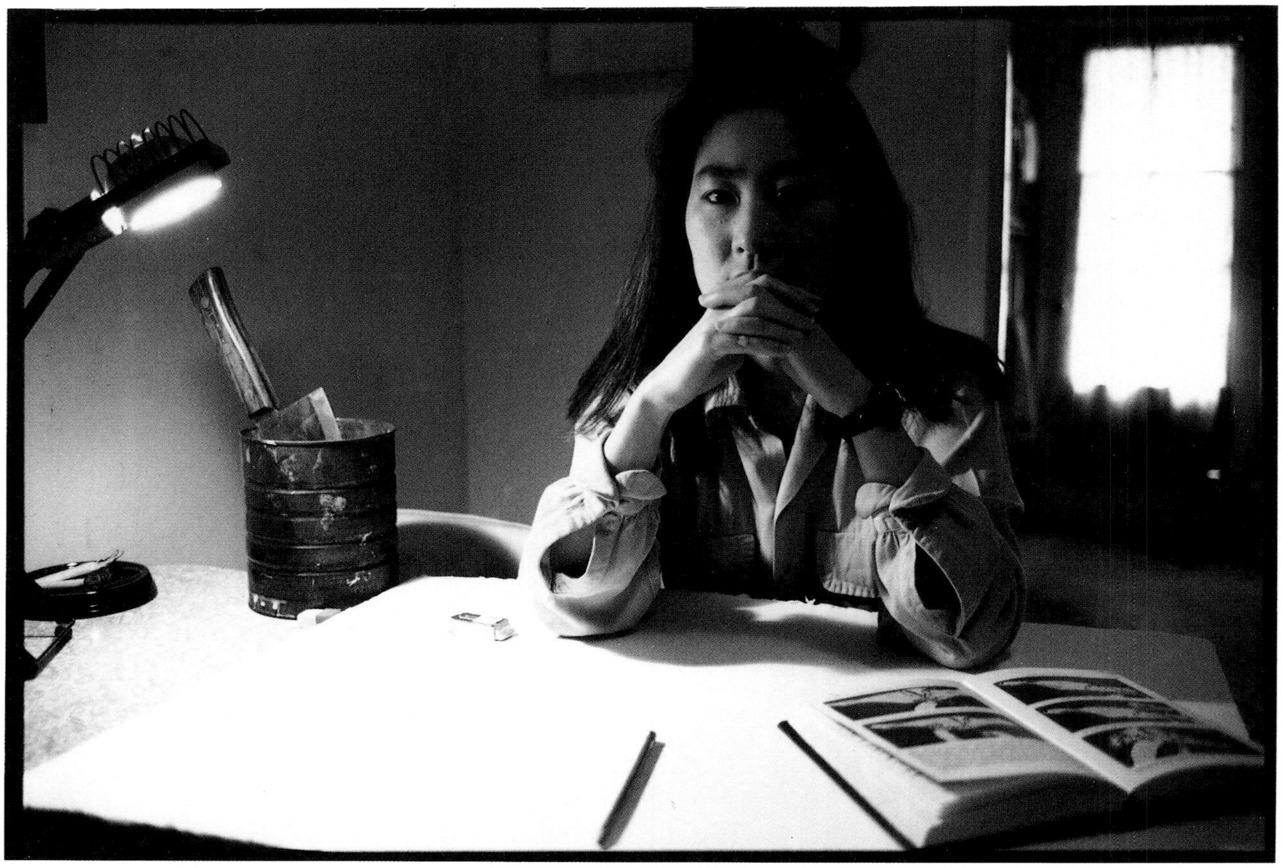

There are certain injustices I was always aware of. . . .that I had to watch everybody deal with. I'm sure it had an impact on my way of thinking and also using barbed wire. . . .

Expressing herself with an incisive, quiet intelligence, Margaret Honda talks about her art, the works which have already influenced other artists, even though she has only been exhibiting for the two short years since her graduation from UCSD.

As she defines the literal and figurative "cutting edge" of her art, coils of barbed wire presented as sculptural garments hang ominously in the background and, as a chilling reminder of the human war against nature, a butcher cleaver at her elbow is half buried in a coffee can of lard. This, she explains, is a re-creation of the old pioneer method of keeping ravenous wolves from attacking sheep; in the wolf's haste to lick up the fat he cuts his tongue to ribbons.

Raised in the North Park area of San Diego, Honda's brother is a Union-Tribune *photographer and her sister a linguist. Her gardener father and her mother are both American-born of Japanese descent. Married to artist Brent Riggs, a Mandeville Gallery curator at UCSD, Honda is currently in a two-year American Studies program at the University of Delaware. In 1986 she and Riggs went to Japan where he curated the art for "Japanese Art Today" and together they wrote the catalogue for this UCSD exhibition.*

I always made clothing when I was growing up. I had been thinking about making clothing in a formal sense that was much more economical to make, that wouldn't waste any fabric, that would address what clothing was really all about as a protective device, as every day ritual or ritual on a grander scale. So I did a series of clothes based on armor and clerical robes. My performance at the La Jolla Museum that was called "Just Clothes" – which was sort of a pun – wasn't just about clothing, but was also about clothing that is generally regarded as being used for just purposes like battle or religious ceremony.

After this, I wanted to do a series on armor, so I decided to do something in metal. Flat wire didn't feel right. Barbed wire has had a very long history of being involved with a lot of battles, legal battles and physical battles. It was used in both world wars quite extensively and in patent wars. It marks where your territory ends and everybody else's starts. That's how the West was won. People would go out with their barbed wire and fence off however much land they wanted. Not only is it really mean material, but it has a mean past, which interested me because there are all types of barbed wire too. The primary and original purpose was to detain cattle and keep them out of the grazing land and in the farm land. Then it sort of changed over a period of time when farmers were putting it up to contain their farm land, so it worked from both sides.

I started making barbed wire body armor shown at the level it would have been worn. The helmet was at head height, the boots were on the floor, the thigh guards were at thigh height. The effect was often dismemberment, which I wanted to achieve. The shadows formed illusions.

I grew up in a very passive household. During the war, everybody in my family from my parent's generation was interned. This is essentially part of the family's history, because it was a chapter in everybody's lives. I guess I was always aware of it. There are certain injustices I was always aware of throughout my whole life that I sort of had to grow up with and had to watch everybody deal with. My parents were my age and younger at that time. I'm sure it had an impact on my way of thinking and also using barbed wire in that sense. I'm sure a lot of that was real personal.

Both of my parents were Buddhists. My grandfather started the Orange County Buddhist Church. I stopped going in the sixth grade. It's not like I really turned my back on it. It's more like a philosophy. It gives me a sense of what ritual is all about: how certain things can mean certain things, how if you use things in a certain way and you use it in a different way it means something else. That's been important in my work, to see ritual in action.

I think my art also addresses the sensibility to try to rebuild things to see what they were like for yourself. The barbed wire is dangerous stuff. I could appreciate it while I was putting it together from a crafts sense as I was making it myself. But then I had to ask why I would want to work with a material I was so repelled by.

We are repelled by gore movies and yet people flock to them by the millions; they love to see bodies blown up. I was trying to find both the material and the form that would serve as the thrust behind contemporary society.

SELECTED BIOGRAPHY

BIRTHPLACE

San Diego

EDUCATION

University of California, San Diego, BA in Art History, 1984
University of Delaware, Winterthur Program in Early American Culture, MA in progress

SOLO EXHIBITIONS

Fine Arts Building, Los Angeles, 1985
Installation, Grossmont College, San Diego, 1986
Anuska Gallery, San Diego, 1986 and 1988

GROUP EXHIBITIONS

"San Diego Exhibition," La Jolla Museum of Contemporary Art, 1985
Biennial, Installation Gallery, San Diego, 1987
"Sculpture Arenas," Mandeville Gallery, University of California, San Diego, 1987
"Newcomers 1987," Los Angeles Municipal Art Gallery, 1987
"Works from the Collection," J. Patrick Lannan Foundation Museum, Fort Worth, 1987

GRANTS

NEA/COMBO grant

COLLECTIONS

Carol and Saul Rosensweig, Beverly Hills
Oliver McMillan, Inc., La Jolla
Jeri and Bert Stoddard, La Jolla
Faiya and Milton Fredman, La Jolla
Marne and James DeSilva Collection, La Jolla

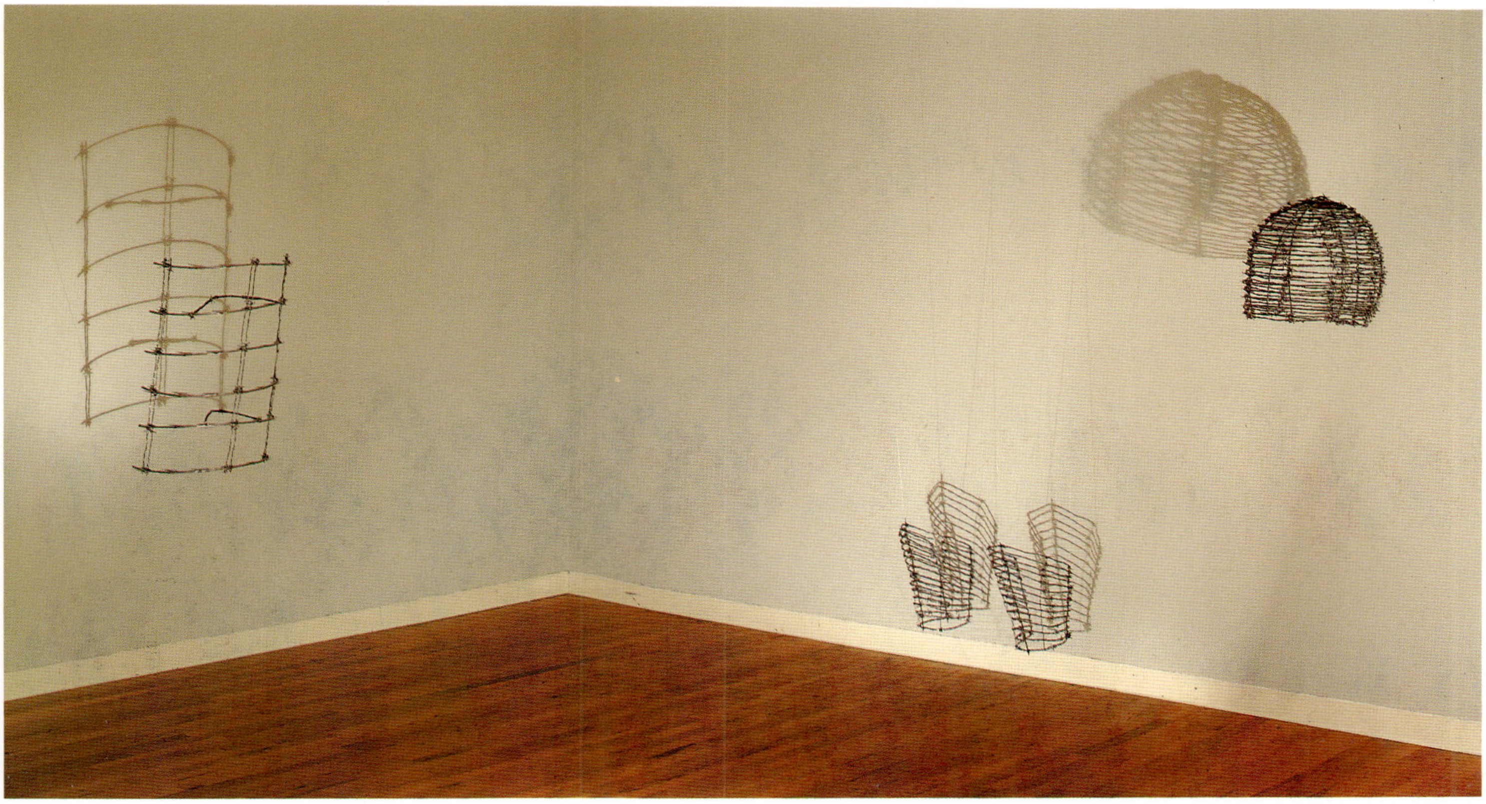

Photo by Kimball/Nanesscence

Installation view, barbed wire and razor ribbon, 1987

Courtesy Lannan Foundation Collection, Los Angeles

Suda House

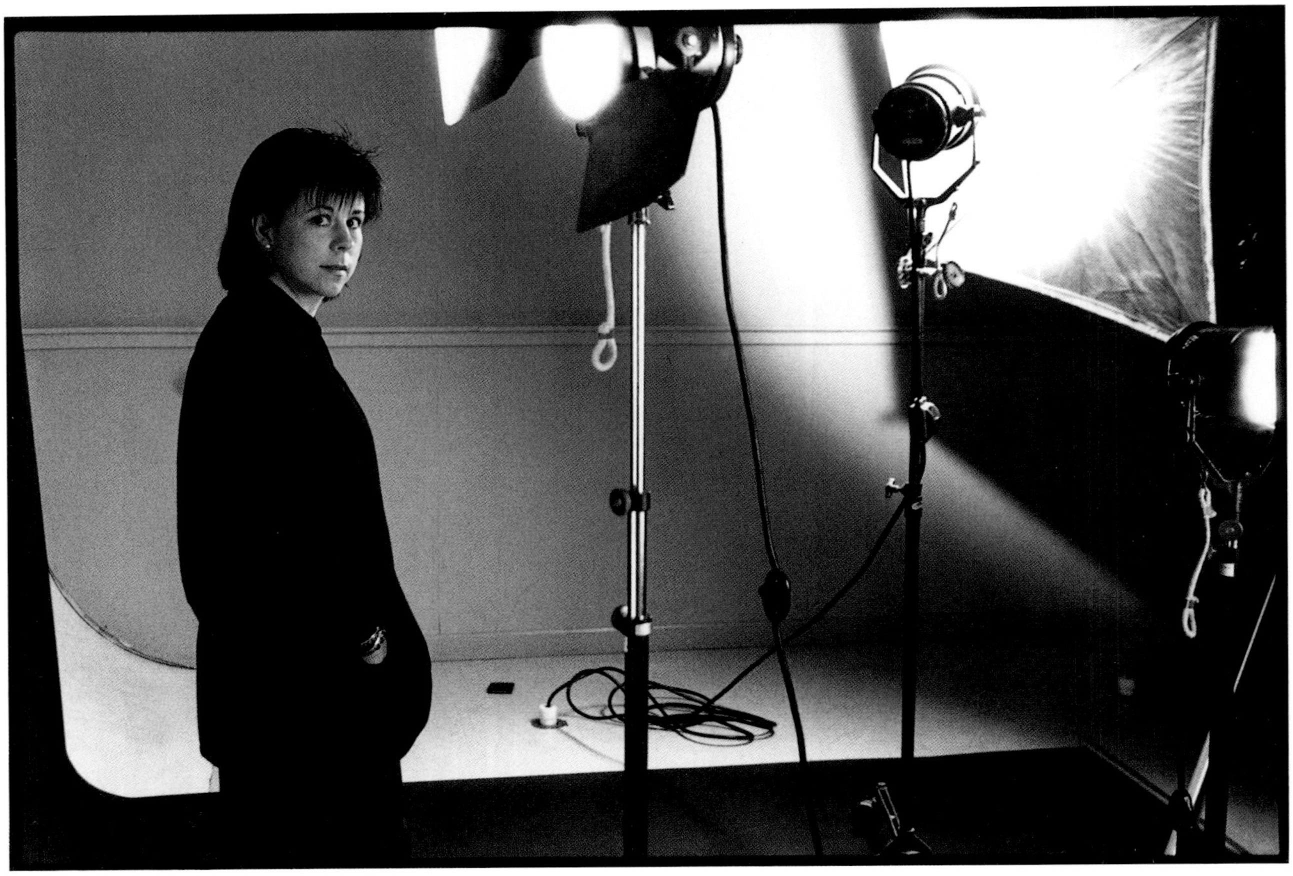

When you're really into making your work, that's about the only place in your whole self where you can be who you are and you can't kid yourself.

It is her singlemindedness, control, and sense of detail that are salient features in each of Suda House's dramatic, unique photographs. Whether she is rough water swimming, teaching, or creating her evocative images, House is tenacious in her concentration on excellence, on perfecting and realizing her inner vision.

During the 1970's, House employed a new 3M color process which generated dye transfer color prints and which soon led to experiments with other photographic processes. When only in her mid-twenties she had already gathered enough material to publish her own book, Artistic Photographic Processes.

Throughout her body of work are subjects expressing feminine strength, photos both sensual and thought-provoking. Her latest works, the "Aqueous Myth" series, are underwater creations sparked by various "goddess" legends in which her friend and artist, Alexia Markarian, becomes the make-up expert, creating formulas that survive beneath the waves.

House was raised in Los Angeles with two art-oriented younger sisters by her father, an advertising man, and her mother, both of whom share her interest in the arts. When not out bicycling or swimming with her friend Tom Lazzara, House relaxes in her La Mesa hillside home with her friendly sheepdog.

I came here from Los Angeles to teach at Grossmont College and after a year I basically declared this as home. I got a studio all in shape and I said, what am I going to do here? I looked the part: I had a full time teaching job, some money, some time to work, a dark room, two rooms to shoot in, equipment at school. I made a series of autobiographical images that dealt with separation from home and roots and I actually put myself in images that projected slides. I kind of did what I would call a catharsis, but I've only shown them once and never again. I used my art to cleanse myself and make a break with a lot of things in the past. I really hate people who use their art for therapy but I guess I did.

Then I started swimming out of a need. I became a San Diegan at that point. It was either fight or switch, so I became a swimmer, swimming away, learning how to do it right. I really had this kind of – not a void in my head exactly – but just the feeling like, well, something is going to happen; you're going to see something and it's going to be pure Suda because you leave nothing in the closets.

Some people become obsessed with souffles or omelettes; I became obsessed with swimming, with strokes, everything about it. I've talked about this with my friend Louise Kirtland, director of the Boehm Gallery at Palomar College with whom I swim occasionally, about how athletics is the closest thing to art in discipline, a self-imposed discipline. There's this arena of training and pushing. I think there might be potentially the same thing chemically in your body, because you know your limits when you swim and I think the same thing happens when you work. You're in tune with yourself. The creative juices have got to be similar. When you're really into making your work, that's about the only place in your whole self when you can be who you are and you can't kid yourself. I like doing art work because there's a feeling of being who I am and nobody's telling me what to do. I can open up.

It was Fate, or whatever, when Arthur Ollman asked me to come into the Museum of Photographic Arts to work with a special, huge Polaroid camera that made 20 by 24 inch prints. At the time I was just treading water, to use the pun. I was just a San Diegan swimming, teaching, and struggling to find a handle on what I was going to do for the rest of my artistic career.

In preaching to my students, I would tell them to photograph what you know. I asked myself, "What do you really know?" and I said "I know a lot about swimming." Using a specially constructed plastic tank, I set up simulations of the underwater swimming experience. The sixty unique prints remain part of the Polaroid travelling exhibition.

After that, I swam a race in Del Mar and I went looking for other races. I found a five-miler in Hawaii in December and I took second place in the rough water swim in my division. There was something about being on an island and being around volcanos and the museums had Hawaiian gods that come from the sun. I went to a tropical paradise and I found a perception of the water different from the La Jolla Cove.

In February I came back and decided to make my own water realities at home in my studio with a tank. I'd been under the water long enough to attempt to describe what it was like. I started reading books on swimming and one was talking about the mythological, mysterious, therapeutic qualities of the water.

I started putting images in water and looking in art history books that had water images and reading Barbara Walker's *The Woman's Encyclopedia of Myths and Secrets*. I started gathering data and the first image I made was with a friend in the tank with shells – probably over-propped – and with a dead octopus.

My work happens in the planning stages. Once I start to make a picture, I've got all these other people helping me. I have to keep focused on the intent of the image and not be influenced should they interject an idea other than an issue of safety or technology. My work does alter a little bit when I start to involve makeup people, models, but the real creativity has to come in the thought process, in the idea. I use the hand-held camera to gather data, but basically everything I've done has been pre-meditated. I systematically work through what I'm going to do and then I let chance have a little room in there.

I think that if you're going to go through all of this you have to be in a position where you're pushing yourself. My students complain that I work them too hard, that I make them do too much. I do the same thing to myself. I push them as hard as I do myself.

SELECTED BIOGRAPHY

BIRTHPLACE

DuQuoin, Illinois

EDUCATION

University of Southern California, BFA, 1973
California State University, Fullerton, MA, 1976

SOLO EXHIBITIONS

BC Space, Laguna Beach, California 1984
Quint Gallery, San Diego, 1986
The Photospace Gallery, Northern Illinois University, 1987

GROUP EXHIBITIONS

"LA ISSUE," Twenty-one photographers from Los Angeles; limited edition portfolio, travelling exhibition, Los Angeles Center for Photographic Studies, 1979 to 1981
"Electroworks," travelling exhibition, George Eastman House/International Museum of Photography, Rochester, 1979 to 1981
"Photographer as Printmaker: 140 Years of Photographic Printmaking," travelling exhibition, Arts Council of Great Britain, London, 1981 to 1982
"Polaroid: The Big Picture," travelling exhibition, Museum of Photographic Arts, San Diego, 1983 to present
"A San Diego Exhibition," La Jolla Museum of Contemporary Art, 1985

PUBLICATIONS

Artistic Photographic Processes, Amphoto, Watson-Guptill Publications, New York, 1981

GRANTS

National Endowment for the Arts, Emerging Photographer Fellowship

COLLECTIONS

Los Angeles County Museum
Santa Barbara Museum of Art, Santa Barbara
Polaroid Corporation, Cambridge, Massachusetts
Museum of Photographic Arts, San Diego
Frederick S. Wight Gallery, University of California, Los Angeles

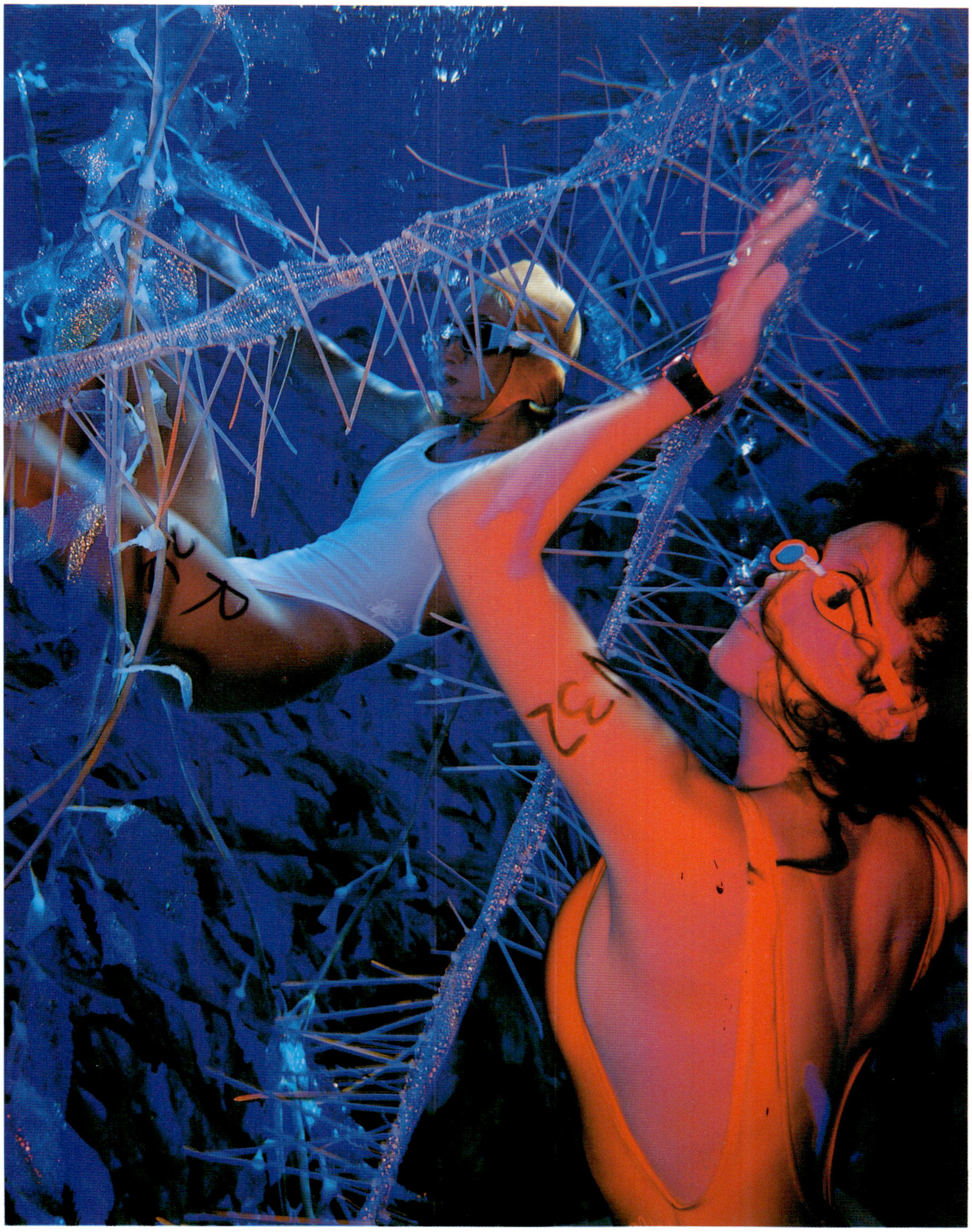

Damia and Anxesia, from the Aqueous Myths, cibachrome photograph, 40″×30″, 1987

James Hubbell

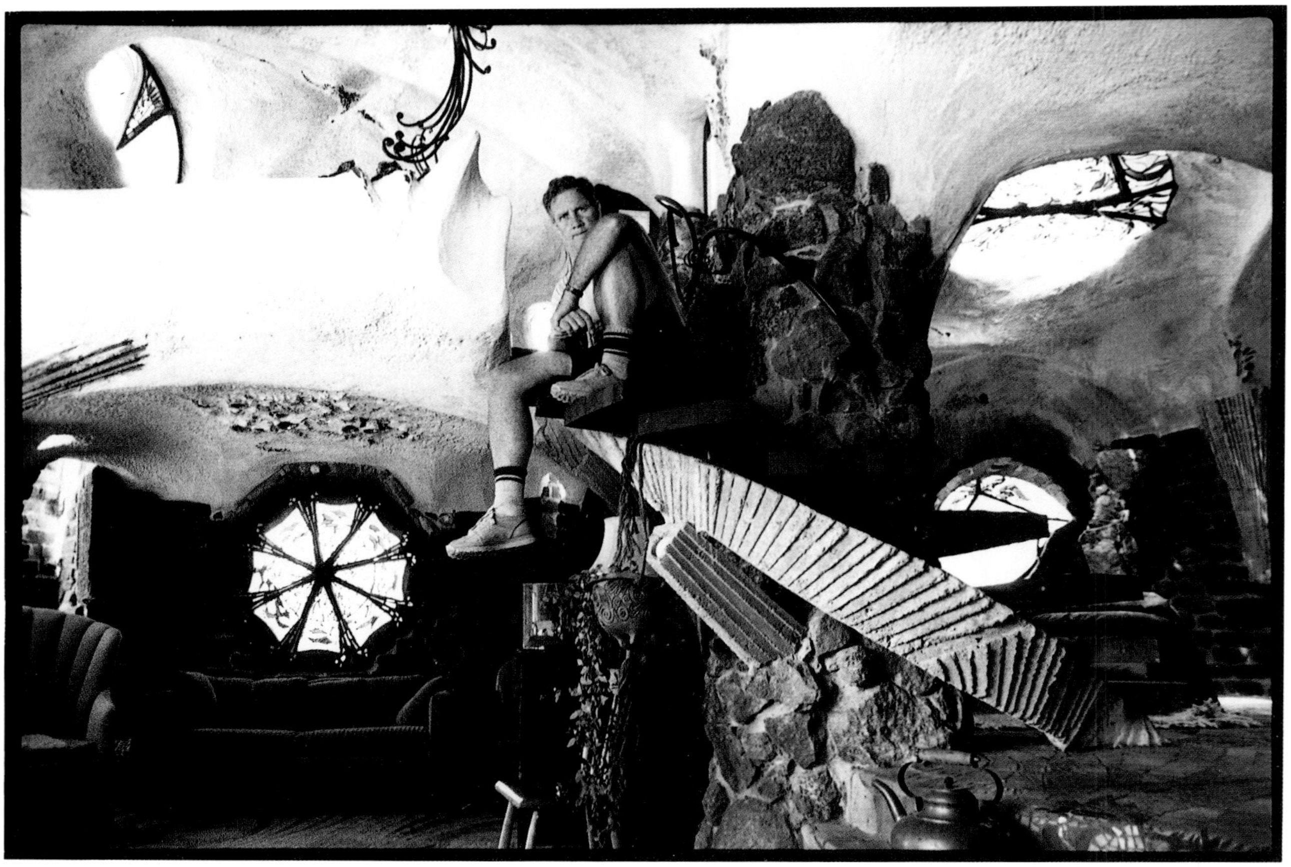

The problem is that most of the culture doesn't know how to deal with an eclectic, or a synthesizer. . . . As a culture, we've tried to understand what life's about by separating things.

Nestled in the sage-covered rolling hills near Julian, an hour's drive from San Diego, is the cluster of structures that comprise James Hubbell's living and working spaces. Designed and built by him, they are marked by eccentrically curved roofs and a rich use of tile, stained glass, and unpainted building materials. Vaguely reminiscent of Arcosanti, Hubbell's largest two-story studio shelters a handful of assistants who daily help with various aspects of his projects.

He overcomes his natural introversion with a boy-like shyness as he begins to talk about his work and interest in art. The Ilan Lael Foundation, founded and spearheaded by him, is one of his ongoing concerns. The foundation sponsors art exhibits, arts programs, and a regional publication called Hidden Leaves.

His early carved doors and stained glass works were enthusiastically accepted and freely incorporated into the architecture of Sim Bruce Richards and Kendrick Bangs Kellogg, who consistently lent admiring support. Books about Hubbell by Otto Rigan richly illustrate and describe his artworks in From the Earth Up *(McGraw Hill, 1979) and* The Palace Doors of Abu Dhabi *(Hidden House Publications, Palo Alto, 1982).*

Though Hubbell's parents were separated when he was young, his mother had an early interest in the theater and gave him encouragement in the arts; his sister, as well, became a jazz dancer and his brother a sculptor. This brother has lived in Japan for over twenty years. After high school, Hubbell travelled with a photographer through Africa and Japan before enlisting in the Army. Stationed in Germany for a while, he found his niche painting large semi-abstract murals in Army mess halls.

His wife, Ann, has been an integral part of his career since they began work on the family buildings in Santa Ysabel in 1958. Their four sons are pursuing various paths in the arts.

I design very much from the feel of things. People call my work organic, which I hope it is, but I have a peculiar way of defining organic. It doesn't mean wiggles to me. It means that the solution comes from a problem, so that if you had people whose psyche was very square, then it would be appropriate to do that type of a building. When I began buildings here in Santa Ysabel, my life had been so erratic that I needed something solid. The thing that upset me the most was plastic stuff, which I still think is terrible because it makes you not sure what's real and what isn't. I needed a very solid place. I find now when I design, I'm interested in things that are very light, so that reflects a transition in my own life. Each one of the buildings here I used both physically and aesthetically in the training process.

Most of all I'm interested in light, particularly glass, which to me is really light. I'm interested in the color, because emotionally and physically I like it and so I try to talk owners into doing certain things because I just want to see a lot of color. I use color either to accent edges or to try to pull the sky down into the earth. I use it as another thread in a coverlet, a weaving, or a piece of music.

I really design through the senses. I plan a bench because I want to sit on it, or an arbor because I want to walk under it. And so when I'm drawing something I'm actually kind of walking through it myself. It's not a kind of theory.

When I began I was very bad at school and a lot of things were going on in my life that were quite hectic, chaotic, so I kind of disappeared into nature. For a long time I hardly talked to people. After I married Ann the world got a little bigger. That period was one of learning how to relate to other people, having a studio, having clients, dealing with architects, having people work here. I began to get jobs that were bigger, jobs outside of San Diego, and I began to be interested in the cities. My life has been divided into periods of a pretty introverted family time and now my concerns are pretty broad.

I've always liked Don Quixote very much, but I find I can't defend him the way I used to. Those ways of relating to the world aren't working. They don't fit the way I am now. I'm trying to learn how to deal with a world which is really different from what I had been trained to deal with.

I've realized that my real skill is putting a great diversity of things together and if I tried to say I was only one thing, it would be very unreal. The problem is that most of the culture doesn't know how to deal with an eclectic, or a synthesizer. I think that as a culture, we've really tried to understand what life's about by separating things.

What I think the artist does is to discover something that everybody else knows but doesn't know how to say. Whatever is happening is already there. If somebody gives a great speech and everybody says he's amazing, the reason he's amazing to them is that he's saying something that they wanted to say but didn't know how to. He's put it into words.

I think the artist's work is to make material what is felt inside. The problem is that we, as artists, have sort of distracted ourselves with things like economics and shows and criticisms and all these things. It's not only the artists and the clients. We talk about science for science's sake and build whole systems on ideas that have no relation to the way the world is and the way people are.

Somehow, I have to make a pattern with my life that says the world is still livable even though there is the atomic bomb, the nuclear age, overpopulation, and AIDS, even though all this is happening. What I do is I make a home, or whatever an artist does. Now, sometimes that pattern helps the rest of the people and that's when we start calling it art.

For a long time I've been interested in cities and education. Ilan Lael Foundation – which in Hebrew means "tree that belongs to God" – started as a school with top craftsmen for people to come to study under and learn from. After we published the first *Hidden Leaves* Kay Kaiser, the architecture critic for *The San Diego Union,* got involved. It may still become a school; a lot of things happen not because you want them to happen but because they won't go away.

Some of my friends discuss political art, which is one way of changing the pattern, but I think there's also another way of changing and that is the actual living of it, which might have to do with whether a culture is using circles instead of using squares. A different rhythm that comes through the forms we use, the sound or the rhythm of the music. I don't think it's always in the literal sense that you change things.

SELECTED BIOGRAPHY

BIRTHPLACE

Long Island, New York

EDUCATION

Whitney Art School, New Haven, 1952
Cranbrook Academy of Art, Bloomfield Hills, Michigan, 1955 to 1956

COMMISSIONS

Buildings:
- Triton Restaurants, San Diego and Cardiff
- Sea Ranch Chapel, Sea Ranch, California
- Five private handcrafted homes

Stained Glass Windows and Doors:
- Palace Doors in Abu Dhabi, U.A.E.
- Findhorn Community Hall, Scotland
- Piedmont Community Church, Piedmont, California
- All Souls Episcopal Church, San Diego

Sculpture and Mosaic:
- San Diego County Courthouse, Vista
- Benches, lights, gates, railings, City of Carlsbad, California
- Trinity Episcopal Church, Escondido, California
- First Unitarian Church, San Diego

HONORS

"James T. Hubbell Day," San Diego County Board of Supervisors/Public Arts Advisory Board, 1980
Award for Excellence in Landscape Design, American Society for Landscape Architects, San Diego, 1982
Special award with Kay Kaiser for promoting better design and planning through "Hidden Leaves," an Ilan-Lael publication, American Institute of Architects, 1984
Excellence in Craftsmanship Award for Sea Ranch Chapel, California State, American Institute of Architects, 1985
Gold Nugget Award, for Sea Ranch Chapel, Pacific Coast Builders Conference, 1986

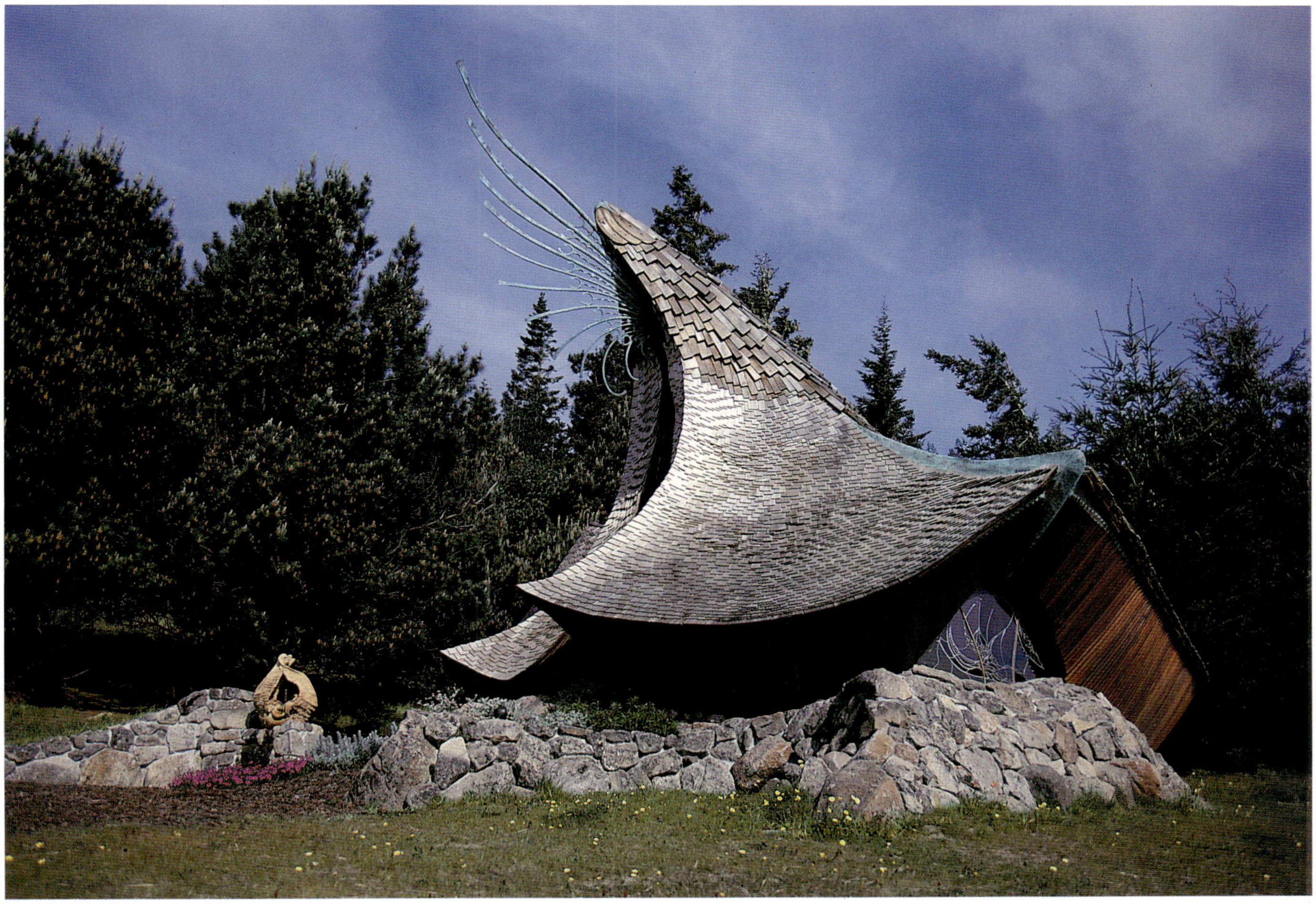

Sea Ranch Chapel, Sea Ranch, California. Thamby Kumaran, contractor; Dr. and Mrs. Robert Buffum, clients, 1985

Jay Johnson

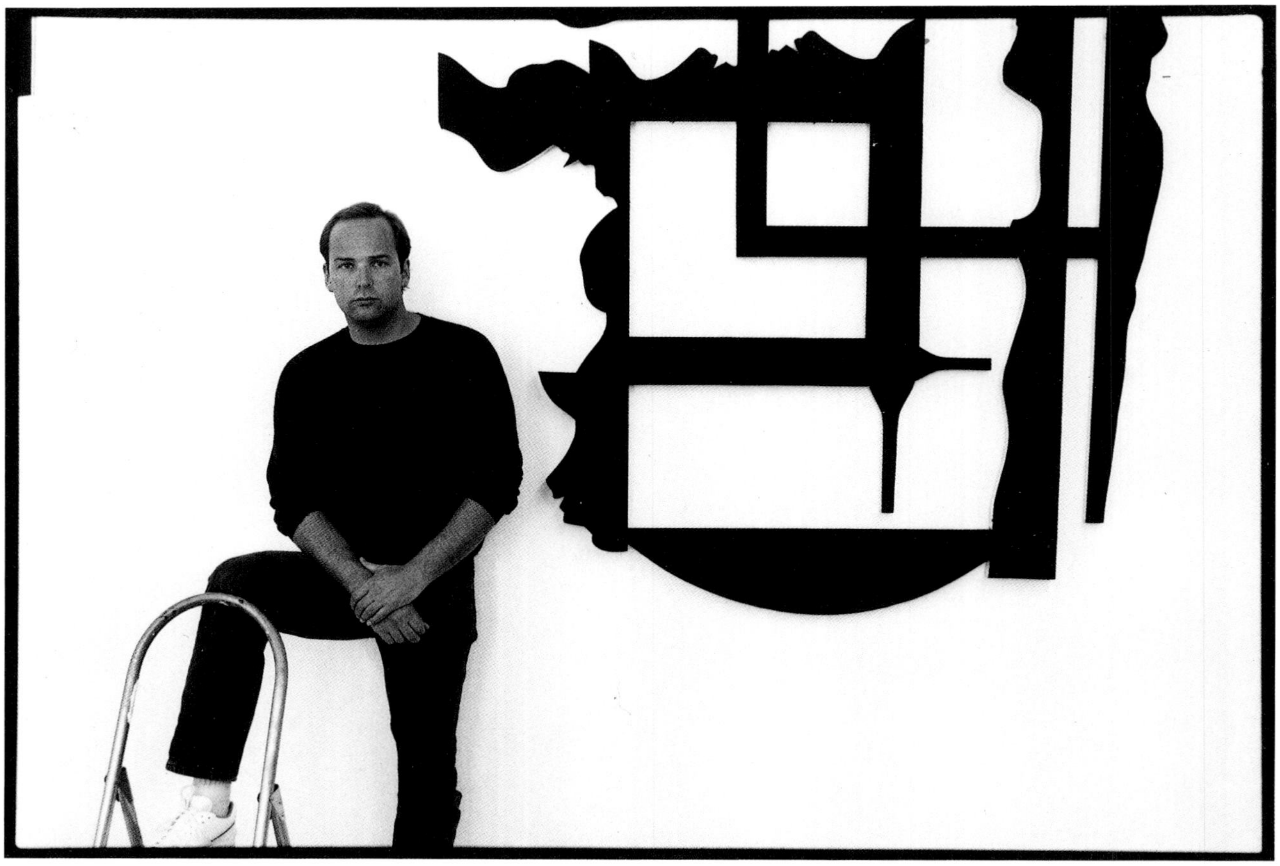

If you want to go for meaning. . . . fine, but I think the things in life that are most interesting and hold my attention longest have always been ambiguous, elegant, and mysterious.

Jay Johnson's "G" Street studio downtown could be a well-equipped woodworker's shop, with high ceilings, sawdust mounds, and ready access to a pack of cigarettes, can of beer, or cup of coffee. His deliberately casual manner barely masks an obvious commitment to his sculpture.

Following his interest in crafts, Johnson became an assistant to Erik Gronborg during Gronborg's teaching stint at SDSU. Since then, he has become a mainstay in the downtown art community where he seeks to create a family of artists. When in his twenties he established both the Pawn Shop Gallery and, later, Pawn Shop Two. These were among the forces generating a downtown art scene early in the decade.

His work has developed in sophistication through several phases, from installations to the current wall pieces that explore shape and scale. Achieving a maturity in both concept and execution, Johnson has continually focused on creating an elegant and architecturally-scaled body of work.

He was raised – along with two older sisters who were art majors in school – by a mother who worked at the San Francisco Museum of Modern Art and a commercial artist father. Johnson occasionally surfs with art dealer Mark Quint and exchanges ideas with his friend, Gary Ghirardi and, for short periods, lives alone in his studio.

About 1979 or 1980 I got kind of involved with the Punk scene through a girlfriend. For a year I laid off making art, cut my hair, felt like a tough guy. I'd given up being a waiter and so she hired me to fix up her club on Market Street called the Skeleton Club. I started looking around downtown, spent more time there, and realized that you could rent a big space for cheap. I was kind of fed up with surfing and living at the beach. I got this thing in my mind that I wanted to be a serious artist. It took me a long time to try to find a space because I didn't know any artists at that time.

Finally I found a space on Fifth Avenue, an old pawn shop. That became a big project. It was an adventure to clean the place out. I got infatuated with the idea of having a loft. I don't know where I got the idea because I don't think I'd ever been in a loft or a big studio.

One night I was coming back from a show and walked by a store front. It was late at night and I looked in the window and there were all these people setting up a show, an art exhibit. I stood there in the window. They thought I was a street person, which I probably looked like at the time. I kept knocking and saying, "Hey, I'm an artist! I'm an artist!" If anyone did that to me now, I'd probably treat them the same way. They were Richard Sigmund, Richard Allen Morris, Tom Driscoll, Gary Ghirardi, and a couple of others. Finally Richard Sigmund came to the door. I thought he was going to punch me. We ended up walking to his studio.

A few weeks later Gary Ghirardi came by and we started talking and we've been friends ever since. He was starting Installation Gallery at about the same time. After talking to Gary I decided to show other people's work, not just my own. I didn't want to sell anything, I just wanted to be around other artists. Patty Aande was my girlfriend about the time Pawn Shop Gallery started and we were really poor. I sold my truck to get the water heater and plumbing and she got a job down the street. It was the typical romantic art deal the way it started out. We were in love. She wrote really good poetry.

In 1982 the Pawn Shop space was for sale and we saw this space on Ninth Avenue that looked too expensive. But we got Bob McDonald, who was then curator at the La Jolla Museum, to write a letter of recommendation to the landlady who thought we were crazy. That became Pawn Shop Two (P.S. 2). Patty ran the business end of it and in 1984 it became Patty Aande Gallery. Meanwhile,

Mark Quint had moved his gallery upstairs.

We were just totally immersed in the art world. We had no social life other than the openings. Everything we had we'd put into having shows every month. We started to sell a little bit, just enough to pay for the next show, but I was getting more and more into my art and less and less into other people's.

For the last three years I've been in the biggest studio I've had. When I have a big space it makes me want to work. My art is like an addiction, I think. If I stop doing it for a month I start to go kind of crazy. Especially if I see some good art, or hear a good band, or go to a good play, or do anything that's got some soul, or some creativity, or some spark to it, I just want to get back into my own work. Or if I'm around a bunch of square people for a while I go crazy. That can take an hour. Whereas if I cruise along day to day, go to the library, and work for my rent, it takes about a month.

Patty and I went our separate ways after six years and last summer I couldn't get myself to work. So for a while when I saw a striking image in a magazine, I wouldn't question, I'd cut that page out and put it in a box. I got my hands on a lot of women's fashion magazines. Not that I wanted to design fashion, but I kept those for forms. Another image I kept cutting out was different shapes of bottles. I guess that comes from my interest in ceramics. I've always loved a flaring bowl if it was done right. I started to think about metaphors for the bottle. My cut-outs became faces, the bottles took on a figurative shape, silhouettes. People stop and look at them more. I feel that my art is more accessible now and that makes me happy.

My art's not about preaching to you. It's mysterious and kind of elegant. That's what I'm shooting for the viewer to feel. If you want to go for meaning from there, fine, but I think the things in life that are most interesting and hold my attention longest have always been ambiguous, elegant and mysterious, almost on the edge of being identifiable. I've always shied away from art that tells you right away what the artist is trying to say.

SELECTED BIOGRAPHY

BIRTHPLACE

Berkeley, California

EDUCATION

San Diego State University, 1972 to 1977

SOLO EXHIBITIONS

Thomas Neumaier Gallery, San Diego 1982
Installation Gallery, San Diego, 1982
Jewish Community Center Gallery, San Diego, 1983
Thomas Babeor Gallery, La Jolla, 1986

GROUP EXHIBITIONS

Saxon-Lee Gallery, Los Angeles, 1986
Quint Gallery, San Diego, 1984 to 1987
The Works Gallery, Los Angeles, 1986 and 1987
"A San Diego Exhibition," 1985; "Faux Arts: Illusions in Contemporary Art and Design," 1987, and "Selections from the permanent Collection," 1988, La Jolla Museum of Contemporary Art
"Phoenix Biennial," Phoenix Museum of Art, Phoenix, 1987

COLLECTIONS

Marshall Fields Stores, Chicago and San Antonio
Federal Reserve Bank, Los Angeles
La Jolla Museum of Contemporary Art
Elizabeth and Mason Phelps, La Jolla
Mark Quint, La Jolla

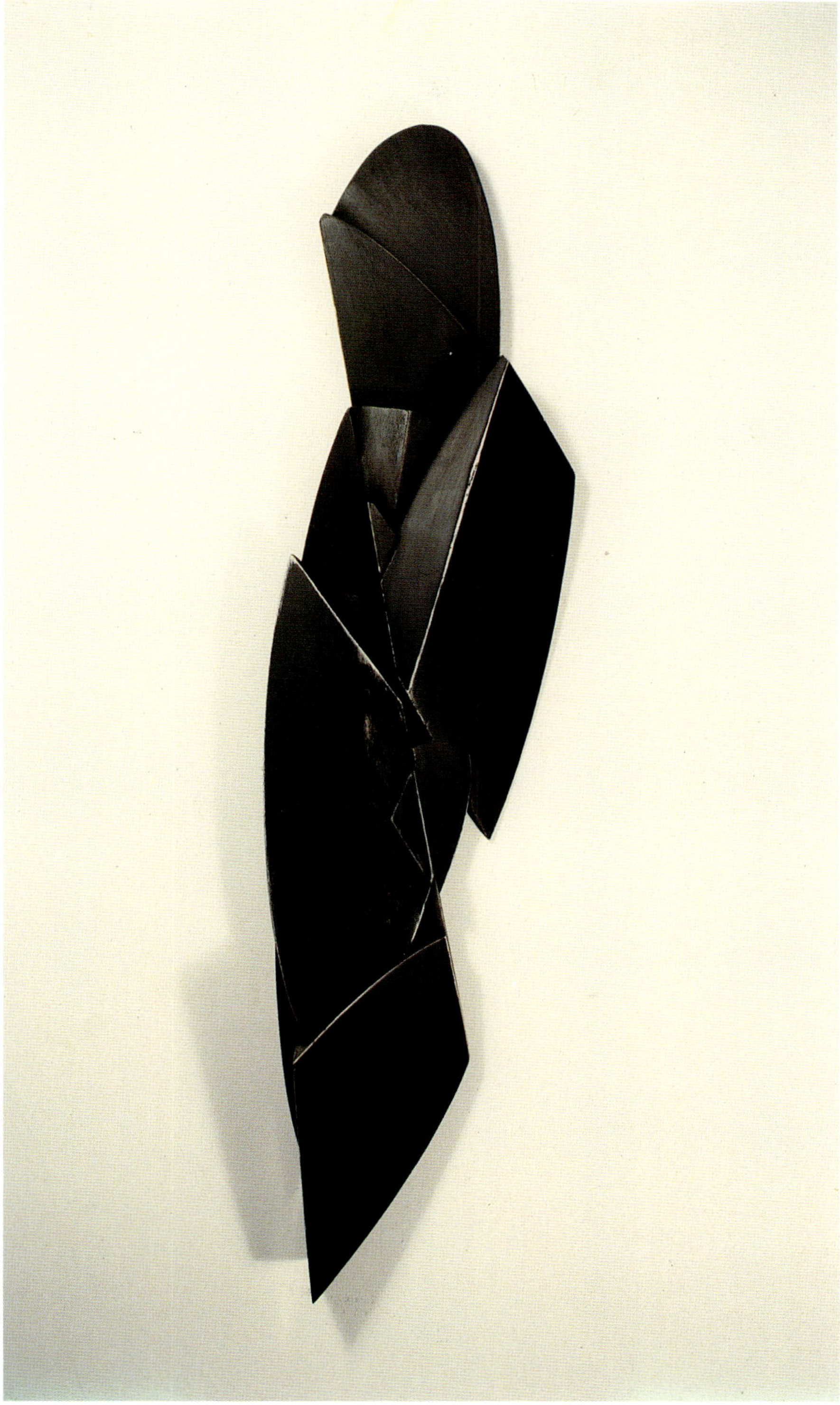

All Black, enamel and casein on wood, 28″×7″×3¼″, 1986   Collection of Mason and Liz Phelps

Philip Kirkland

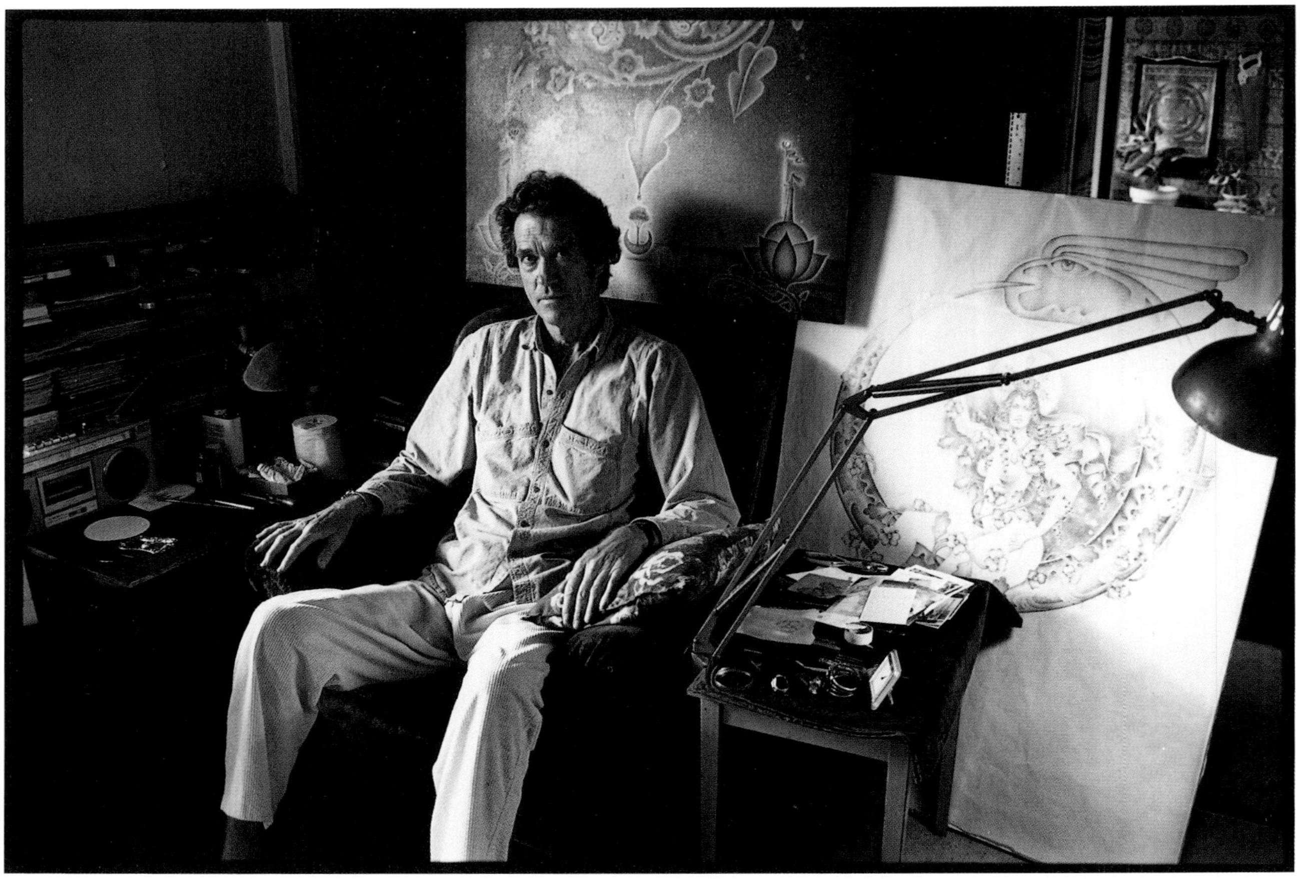

It's visual, not audial. It's beyond language.... It's almost impossible for me to tell you what my work really means.

Reclusive, living in a ramshackle Encinitas cottage overgrown with native plants, Philip Kirkland seems content being one of the area's best kept secrets. His works are masterpieces of a slick and overtly sensual style that celebrates erotic spirituality, a blend of the surreal and esoteric.

With an accomplished background in advertising and as a cover illustrator for Psychology Today, *Kirkland left the successes that established him as a top textbook illustrator of psychological themes. Once a close friend of artist Cliff McReynolds, Kirkland's shared interest in a spiritual path suddenly turned towards the metaphysical. In the mid-1970s he began work on a series of paintings which he expects to complete in the late 1990s. Hidden among other images which personally delight him, these works contain Sanskrit messages by Sai Baba which Kirkland has transformed into scouting codes.*

Kirkland, a native of San Diego, grew up in the North Park area where he and an older sister, now a librarian, were raised by their mother, a nurse. His father died before he was born. Twice-married, Kirkland's companion of ten years, Lilli Hill, is a cloisonn jeweler. He lives alone and does mantras as he swims four times a week at the neighborhood YMCA. He has one daughter in college.

When I moved out from New York I left a top advertising company on Madison Avenue, three-piece suits, and three martini lunches. I'd have my little glass of champagne and my lobster for breakfast and I'd go down to the La Jolla Cove with my little blanket and lie down in the sun all day long. I'd have my friends down there and in the evening have a few martinis. I never got a chance to do any painting because of my lifestyle. When my lifestyle slowed down I started painting. There was nothing else to do to fight the boredom. Like Alan Watts says, living is hazardous to your health. It'll kill you in the end. Once you realize that you're not going to get any better, then everything's all right and you start feeling better.

When I started doing art for *Psychology Today* I had to do so much that it started giving me discipline. For all of my work in the last ten years or longer I've made very careful drawings.

About ten years ago I was doing a painting of St. Augustine and I started painting these lights emanating from his head and I got the feeling that it was fun trying to depict energy on canvas. So I kind of shifted into mysticism as a way to really use it. I met Lilli, who was interested in that sort of thing, and she had a lot of books around. My mother was not really into mysticism but on the fringes of metaphysics. She went to Unity Church and was always trying to get us kids into line. Of course we weren't interested in that kind of stuff, but that was really valuable spade work.

I haven't had any mystical experiences. If I did I'd be a mystic. The only thing I have in mind is trying to make a beautiful picture. I realized a long time ago that I'm talking to myself ninety-nine percent of the time. I'm not really doing it for anybody else. I found out that's the way a Taoist would do it.

I've always liked to paint nudes, so this gives me a chance to do it legitimately. It's visual, not audial. It's beyond language. People ask, "Oh yes, but what does it mean?" It's almost impossible for me to tell you what my work really means. When I lived in La Jolla, I discovered that the drawings I did on the wall when I was talking on the phone were more interesting than when I sat down and did drawings. I do drawings when I watch TV. The intellect isn't filtering out all this stuff and the creative process is shooting right through you.

The white of the canvas is my white pigment. I don't mix white with any of my colors. I do make a lot of little dots with white, but then I glaze over it. Maxfield Parrish painted that way. He'd paint the whole painting in blue, let it sit for six months, varnish it, let it sit another six months or so. I don't have to let mine sit that long. I don't paint exactly the way he did. I'll paint in a neutral color and then I may go ahead and start glazing over it with another transparent color like alizarin crimson, thalo blue, and thalo green. I use copal medium, a mixture of linseed oil and varnish. I got to the point where I would glaze and I finally cut out the white altogether. Now it would be ridiculous to mix white and get the whole gooey mess going.

Looking at art magazines it seems like nothing really changes that much except for people throwing canvases over the Grand Canyon. For many years I've seen a lot of stuff I could go home and create in half an hour and save $5000. These people can whip out five or six paintings a day and the works look that way. They say they're being expressive. But it's not what I like. It's over too fast. I can't sit there and look at it for any length of time. I would much rather see something by Monet or Picasso or Botticelli.

I'm not really concerned with politics and intellectual crap. All I'm interested in is to get to the point where there is this really joyous feeling, the joy of getting a color right. Looking at it is a lot of fun. That's a role I think the artist has, to have some fun. It's kind of like a by-product to have someone look at your painting and to be amazed. Like one man said, "This is such an uplifting experience!" and a woman once told me, "I've been looking at your paintings over the years and they've improved my sex life." Now that's something good; an uplifting experience and an improved sex life. That's the role of an artist, isn't it?

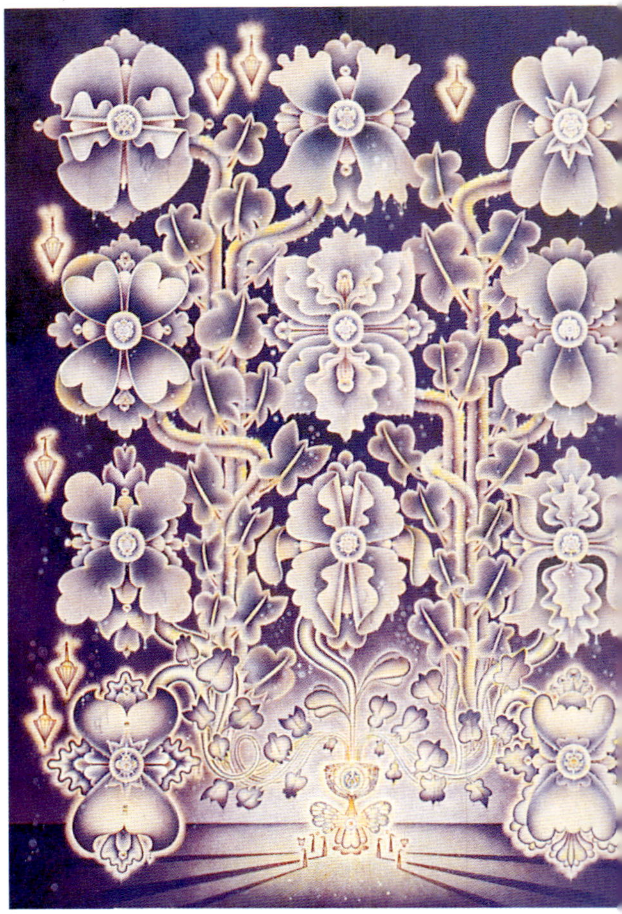

SELECTED BIOGRAPHY

BIRTHPLACE

San Diego

EDUCATION

Chouinard Art Institute, 1947 to 1949; 1952 to 1953

SOLO EXHIBITIONS

Art Collector, San Diego, 1975 and 1979

GROUP EXHIBITIONS

La Jolla Museum of Contemporary Art, 1965

COLLECTIONS

Southwestern College, Chula Vista, California
Barbara Walbridge, La Jolla
Mr. and Mrs. Joseph Manno, La Jolla
Mr. and Mrs. Robert Matheny, San Diego
Lilli Hill, San Diego

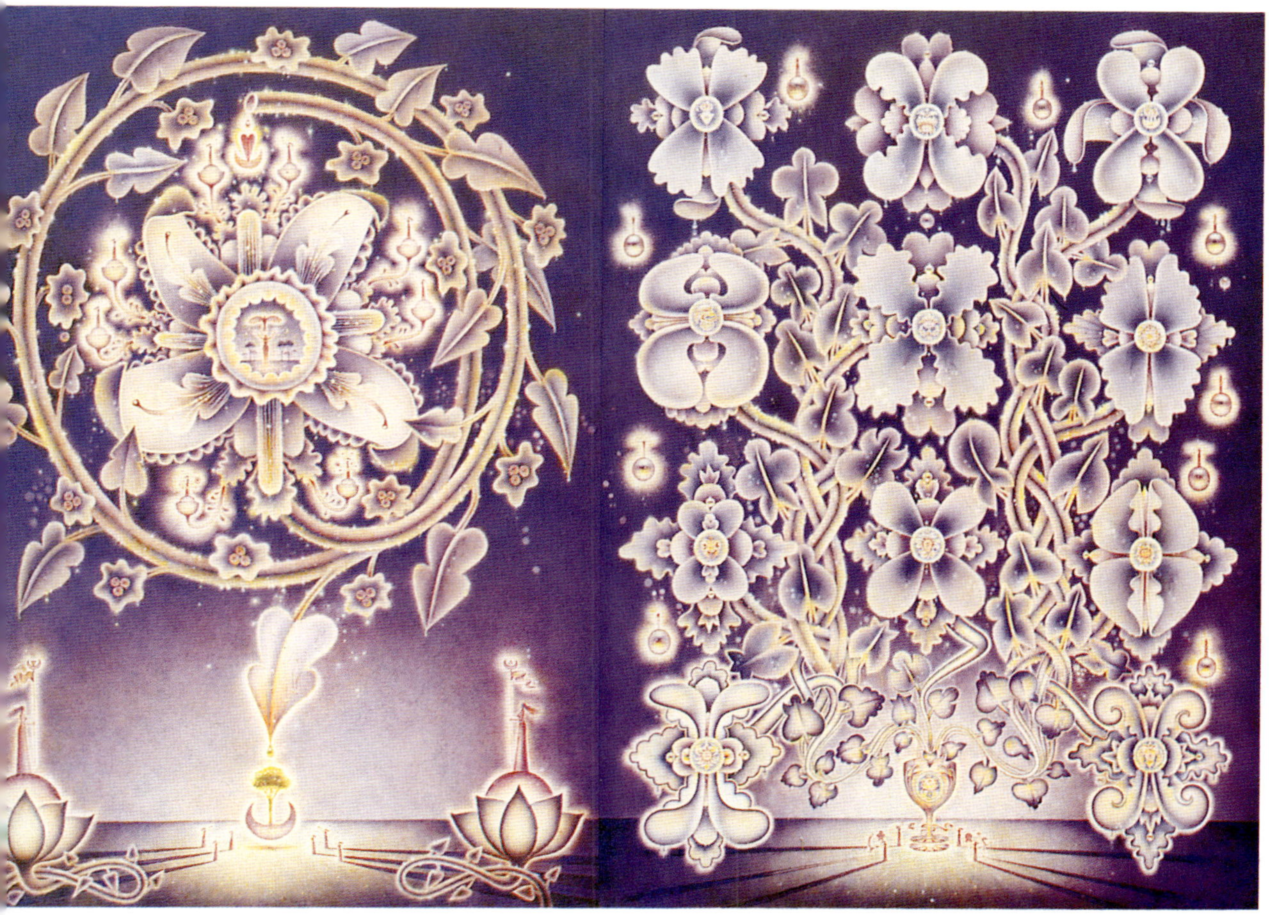

Photo by Robert Perine

Does Matter Create the Space It Occupies?, oil/canvas, 108″ × 48″, 1986

Collection of the artist

Nancy Kittredge

My symbolism is related to my religious thinking. . . . my belief in an afterlife is just as much a reality to me as talking to you.

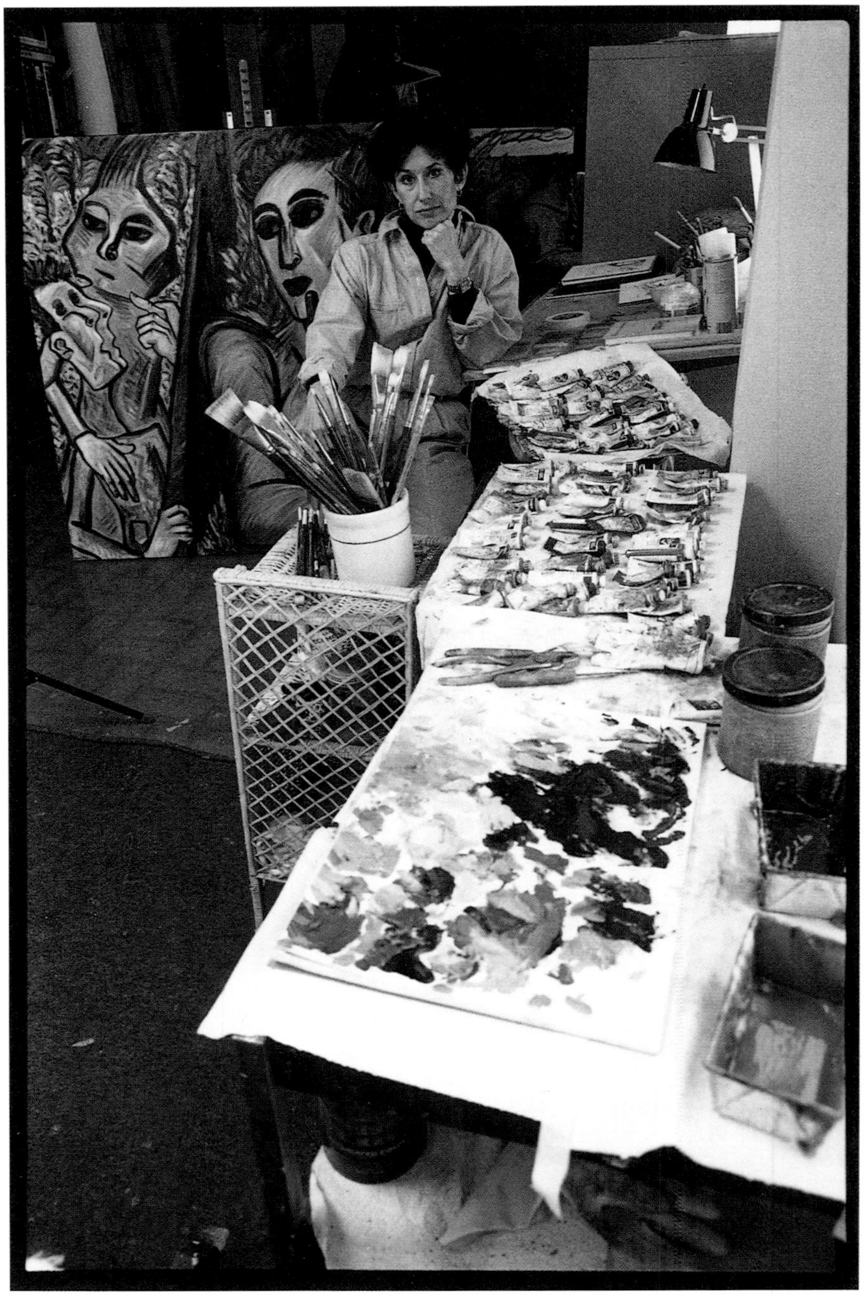

Nancy Kittredge seems most comfortable when she is in her private working space, a sunlit room tucked away in a corner of her Del Mar home. Her own fragile features and soft voice are in striking contrast to the vital, strongly expressionist figures which colorfully activate several large canvases ringing the room.

Through painting, Kittredge has long been communicating her fascination with the duality in human nature, with the different levels of reality in which she believes human beings and spiritual entities co-exist and interact. While her works in the 1970's were smooth, richly colored figures from some dim 1940's nightclub, the recent work seems to evoke pre-World War II cabaret images, people who wear mask-like expressions of the anxious, wide-eyed, perhaps tormented soul.

Kittredge grew up in Maine with an older sister in a house built by their father. She was very close to her teacher mother who died when Kittredge was twenty. She was active in summer stock and taught theater as well as art. She lives in Del Mar with her husband Robert Jellison, a retired Navy pilot. Jellison's high school-age daughter lives with them.

People have always said that my experience in the theater affected my color. I'm not sure that's true anymore. Color just comes natural to me. I was always aware of it. I can remember the first time I discovered color; there was a bright red wagon against green grass and I thought that was the most wonderful thing I ever saw in the world. Red and green always seemed to be in my memory.

My mother wrote and had a very creative mind and my grandfather was an artist. I lived in Maine until I was twenty, when my mother died. Two weeks before she died she was teaching school. Her death devastated me. I never quite got over it. After she died I picked out five names of cities and put them in my Bible. I said that the last one I pick will be where I go. The last one I picked was Jacksonville, Florida. Imagine! So I went to Jacksonville and started teaching and then doing summer stock there. Then a friend told me if I wanted to paint I should go to New Orleans, so I went to New Orleans. I arrived on Halloween night in the French Quarter. I lived there for five years as a street artist. They were very good times. I was able to devote ten or twelve hours a day to my art and I met people from all over the world.

My work depends not only on my inner thoughts, inner resources, but on what happens in my life. I'm very much affected by my environment. I don't like so much television. I need to close the door and it makes my little world complete. The minute I open the door there's an infringement there. Even without anyone around or in other places in the house, I need that privacy, that separation.

I don't think I'm one of those artists who could work with other artists. I need peace and quiet. I also rarely work with music. I open to the sound of the birds and that's fine. Sometimes at the very beginning when I'm trying to get the thing going or at the end when I'm jubilant because I'm getting it, then I will turn on the music. But otherwise I don't want it. I suppose that's from years of living by myself.

The paintings I'm doing now really interest me because they're not cut-and-dried. I really don't know what's going to happen with them until they're done. I don't entirely understand them until maybe two-thirds of the way through because they change so much. I sketch beforehand just to get my ideas flowing but the sketch never resembles the final project. I draw on the canvas with charcoal and cattlemarkers. Martha Matthews, who does wonderfully imaginative artwork in many media, introduced them to me. They are really fun to use with big drawings as they have an oil base and are bigger and much more fluid than oil pastels.

I don't want to be labeled a religious painter but nevertheless my faith plays a stong part in what I do. It's part of my thinking. My faith has seen me through a lot of things. "Door to the Wind" is one of my paintings where the wind represents the spirit of Christ and the figure is not sure whether or not she is going to go through that door and a conflict is set up. My symbolism is related to my religious thinking. It all ties in. My belief in an afterlife is just as much a reality to me as talking to you. It doesn't seem strange to me at all. So I don't find anything astonishing about it. I accept the fact that we live on two different spheres and that we are going on to something different and have been somewhere else.

I'm interested in the relationship between scientific reality and real reality and the fact that there is a known world – a physical world – and a world that is visible only through a microscope. Then there is a third plateau where there is a world that we cannot see. We can't see the wind, for example, and yet it's there. All of that is fascinating to me. We know so little here. There's a vast expanse of knowledge that we haven't even tapped into yet. And that's why creativity is so exciting, becuse you can at least tap into your imagination and see what comes out. And what comes out, you sometimes wonder where that comes from.

SELECTED BIOGRAPHY

BIRTHPLACE

Ellsworth, Maine

EDUCATION

University of Maine, Orono, BA in Theater
University of Miami, Coral Gables, MA in Theater

SOLO EXHIBITIONS

San Diego Museum of Art, 1981
John Douglas Cline Gallery, Phoenix, 1982
Suzanne Brown Gallery, Scottsdale, 1983
Joy Horwich Gallery, Chicago, 1984
San Francisco Art Exchange Gallery, 1986

GROUP EXHIBITIONS

La Jolla Museum of Contemporary Art, 1975
Ankrum Gallery, Los Angeles, 1982
"Women in Art" United Nations Conference, Nairobi, Africa, 1985
Alexandria Museum of Art, Los Angeles, 1986
"California Women Artists," Riverside Museum of Art, Riverside, California, 1987

COLLECTIONS

Industrial Metals of the South, New Orleans
Capitol Intermediaries, Des Moines
University of Maine
Erma Bombeck, Scottsdale
Steven Brezzo, La Jolla

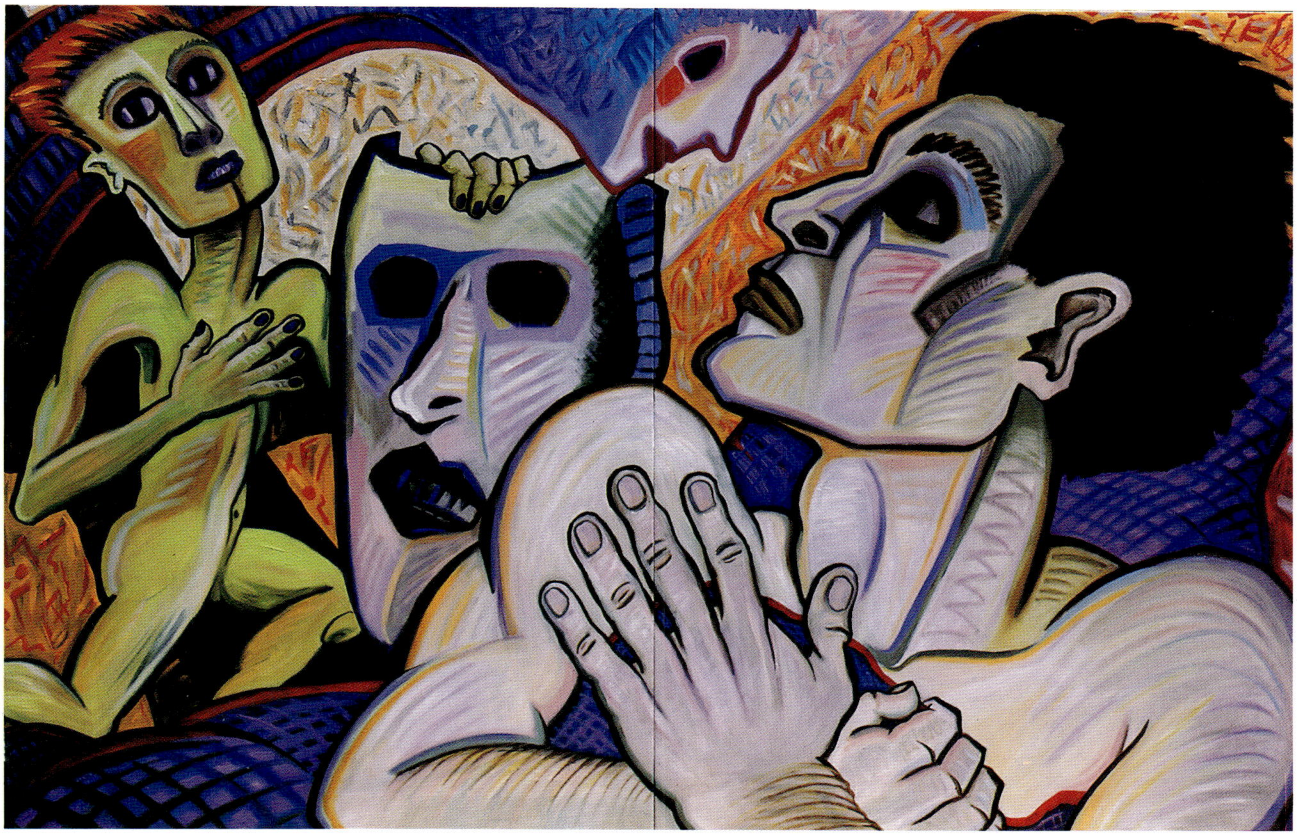

Photo by Leonard Tobey

The Calling, oil/canvas, 96″×60″, 1986

Courtesy J. J. Brookings Gallery, San Jose

Mario Lara

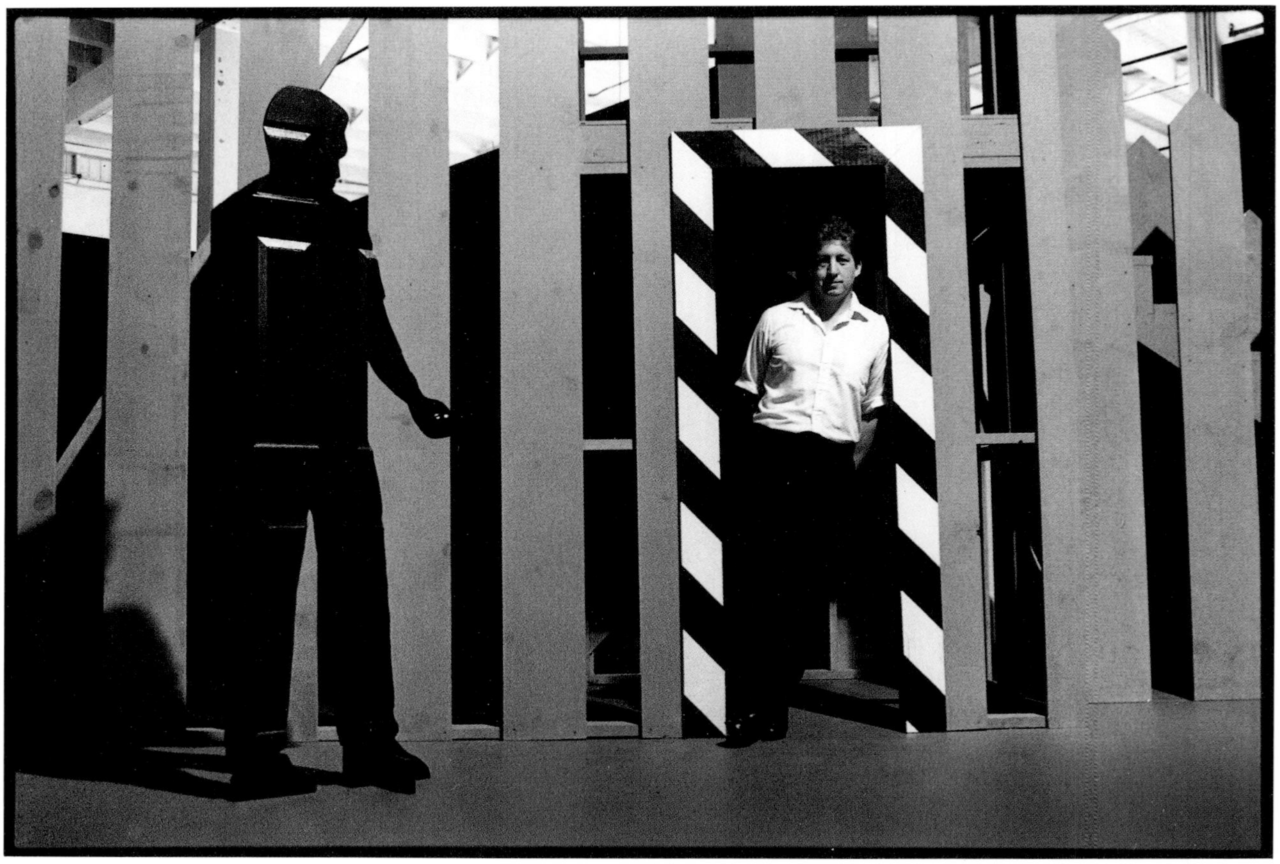

I like the commonality of the two-by-four, corrugated metal, plywood, latex paint. These are all elements that are used day in and day out that the common man can relate to.

Mario Lara's studio is just off the entrance hall of Installation Gallery, downtown. It houses ladder-like structures and kiosks which are parts of site-specific works the artist has been showing around the city. He is direct and articulate in his reasoning, explaining his interest in site works and why he shows primarily outside of traditional art spaces.

While at San Diego State University, Lara assisted environmental design professor Eugene Ray in creating Ray's unique vaulted-ceiling La Jolla home. Continuing in construction work after college for architect Kendrick Bangs Kellog and others, Lara primarily focused on the exploration of correspondence art with the encouragement of SDSU sculpture professor John Rogers.

Through this mail art – and a related interest in hand-made art books – Lara found himself in contact with a broader art world, a global community of artists. He has maintained this thrust by creating public works – graffiti – which are deliberately placed where people do not expect them or in situations where separate communities are stimulated to communicate with each other.

As a Navy brat, Lara grew up in several areas of the U.S. He was the oldest of nine children of a Mexican-born father. Never married, Lara himself has served in the Navy, during which time he acquired a dramatic sea dragon-and-anchor tattoo.

Nobody else in the family has an artistic inclination at all. When I was in kindergarten in Mexico City I took a bunch of wood that was there for the kids to play with and I took a hammer and nailed the pieces onto each other and onto the floor. The teacher had a fit, but I remember how excited I was that I was connecting the things and building them up, making my first sculpture.

I was in Mexico City just one year. We moved almost every year. To grow up in different environments gives you a different attitude about what the country's about, but it doesn't give you the opportunity to put roots down anywhere and establish friendships. I got tired of having to learn and unlearn a new system. I was getting terrible grades because I lost the desire to learn, was frustrated with having to keep on top of it. My parents were divorced when I was in the third grade but my mother didn't bother to tell me until the fifth grade, we were so used to Dad being gone so long. She had to tell us because she had to give us to him.

I ended up spending a lot of time by myself. I created my own little world, my own fantasy land, and I entertained myself a lot. A lot of the bigger issues I'm dealing with are to get closer to some sort of resolution to alienation, to fears, and to my frustration growing up in a society that basically had no real sense of itself. Everybody was in constant motion. America was a new country looking for its identity and I felt that I was doing the same thing, establishing an identity for myself because I didn't really have a home. A nurturing environment was not really available to me so I had to go much deeper than that and look into myself for nurturing. I became very introspective.

My commitment is to try to enhance the urban environment, to develop appropriate public art, to give something that people can relate to, that stimulates and develops dialogue. European cities have a long history of public places being very vital for political discussions, whereas American streets and plazas are quite the opposite of that.

I don't really think of myself as a sculptor, if I was to put a tag on myself, because I'm not a form-giver, per se. A lot of poeple who look at my work are impressed with the form of it. That, for me, is just a secondary item. It's the experience that I'm more interested in, not the finished object. I don't like people to just stand back and admire a piece of mine. In traditional sculpture, like a Henry Moore, you stand back and do your admiring and you're not really encouraged to climb on it.

If you have to pick a term, I'm an environmental artist. It is the environment itself that I'm concerned about, indoors as well as outdoors. The building is not the only complete thing; it's what happens in the buildings.

A lot of things I've done up to now are with materials I've been able to afford to purchase on my own. They don't cost much money because I don't usually get fat budgets. I like the commonality of the two-by-four, corrugated metal, plywood, latex paint. These are all elements that are used day in and day out that the common man can relate to. I like the idea of elevating materials to another level, as opposed to working with marble and bronze. I prefer concrete, raw steel.

I began using lingerie material on pieces because it provided a surface of color and you could see through it. I like taking it completely out of context. It made pieces very touchable. It's cheap, comes in colors, and is easy to work with. I've never found other materials that could work better than this stuff. When something is very vulnerable and yet very sensual and the whole piece is temporary, that borders on being an event in itself.

I have a lot of heroes, which is very unpopular these days. People like Alice Aycock, Mary Miss, Robert Irwin, and James Terrell. The more I learned about them, and others pursuing similar interests, the more I began to feel I was part of a group of people doing things that weren't widely accepted but were being acknowledged.

I can't picture a time I wouldn't be doing a project. It's what makes me want to get up in the morning. If I just wanted to make a dollar, that would not be enough to put up with all the nonsense. The ability to do creative investigation makes my life meaningful and enriched. I feel sorry for people you haven't found something they can sink their teeth into, that can feed back into them and make their life significant. Not that everyone needs to draw or do music, but to find a creative lifestyle that is nurturing and specific to themselves to help them to identify who they are. There are a lot of people running around out there that don't have the tools. They're grabbing at random lifestyles and trying them on like clothing, but it doesn't get them any closer to understanding themselves.

SELECTED EXHIBITIONS

BIRTHPLACE

Milwaukee

EDUCATION

San Diego State University, BA, 1978

SOLO EXHIBITIONS

"Construc," installation, Patty Aande Gallery, San Diego, 1983
"Scenarios for a Song," public art project sponsored by COMBO/SLPP, Quint Gallery, San Diego
"Neofest," 1984; "Streetworks," site installation, 1986; "Artists By Themselves," 1986, Sushi, San Diego
"Denominator," installation in Horton Plaza Mall, produced by David Lewinson, ART/WORD, San Diego, 1986
"Big World, Little House," Centro Cultural de la Raza, San Diego, 1987

GROUP EXHIBITIONS

"California Bookworks: The Last Five Years," Otis Art Institute of Parsons School of Design, Los Angeles, 1984
"A San Diego Exhibition," La Jolla Museum of Contemporary Art, 1985
"New Faces," curated by Robert McDonald. Shoshona Wayne Gallery, Los Angeles, 1986
"Interior: The Home; Exterior: The Landscape," installation, Wita Gardiner Gallery, San Diego, 1987
NEA National Site Artist, Atlanta Arts Festival, 1987

GRANTS AND AWARDS

Reginald A. Fessenden Educational Fund grant
COMBO/State-Local Partnership Program grant
National Endowment for the Arts/City of San Diego
Finalist, Harbor Island Sculpture Competition, San Diego Unified Port District

PUBLICATIONS

Things To Think About in Space, a mail-art project, limited edition, Commonpress #37, 1980
IN-SIDE-OUT, limited edition hand-made bookwork, 1983

COLLECTIONS

Other Books and So Archives, Amsterdam, Holland
Art Pool, Budapest
Franklin Furnace, New York
Jean Brown Archive, Tyringham, Mississippi
Ruth and Marvin Sackner Archive of Concrete Visual Poetry, Miami Beach

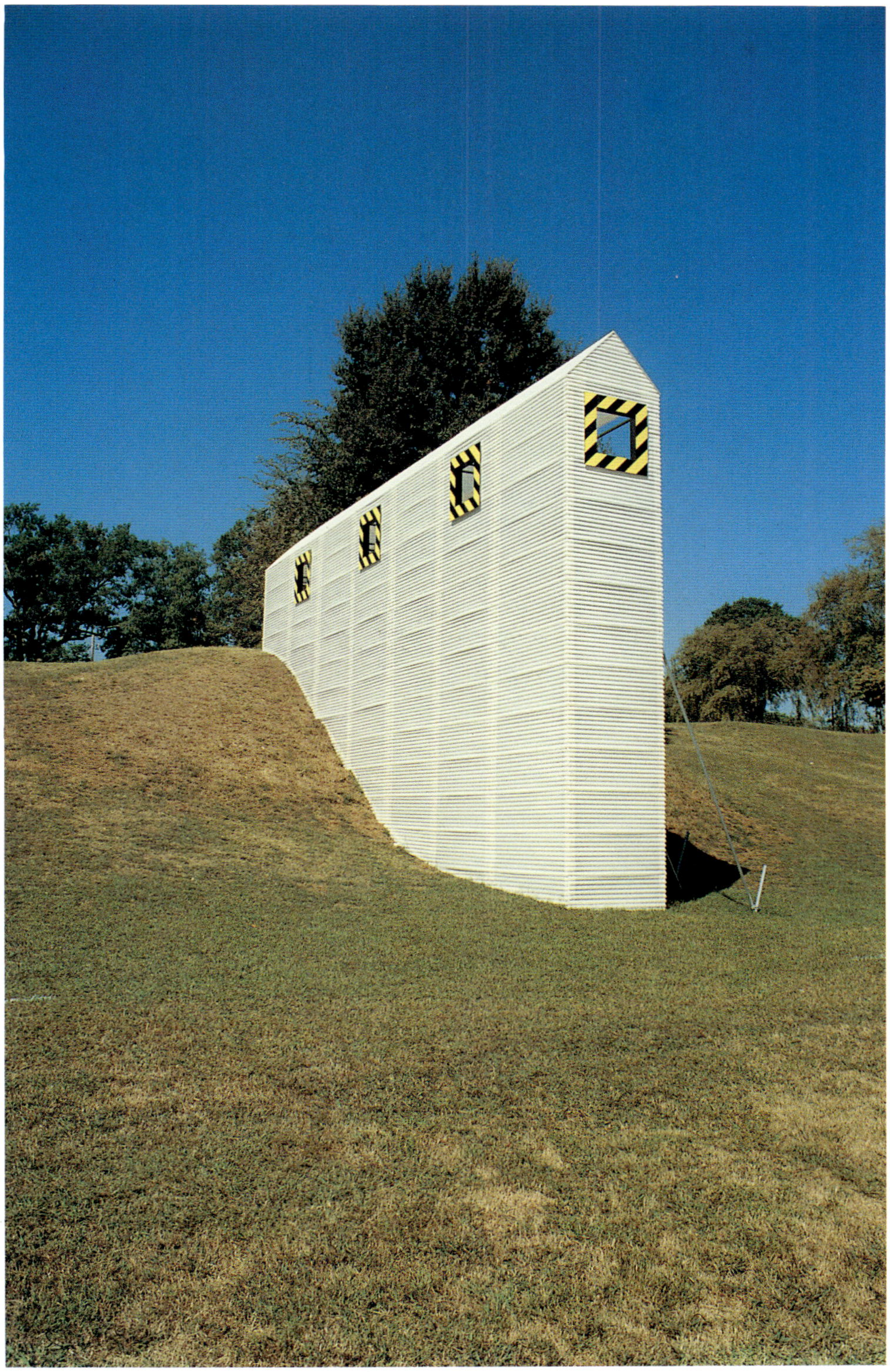

E-Six Lab, Atlanta 33, architectural site work, scaffolding covered with corregated fiberglass, 50′×30′×5′, 1987

Christopher Lee

I try to figure out where we lie on that line between good and bad, violent and passive, and male and female. It's like we're all treading that line all the time.

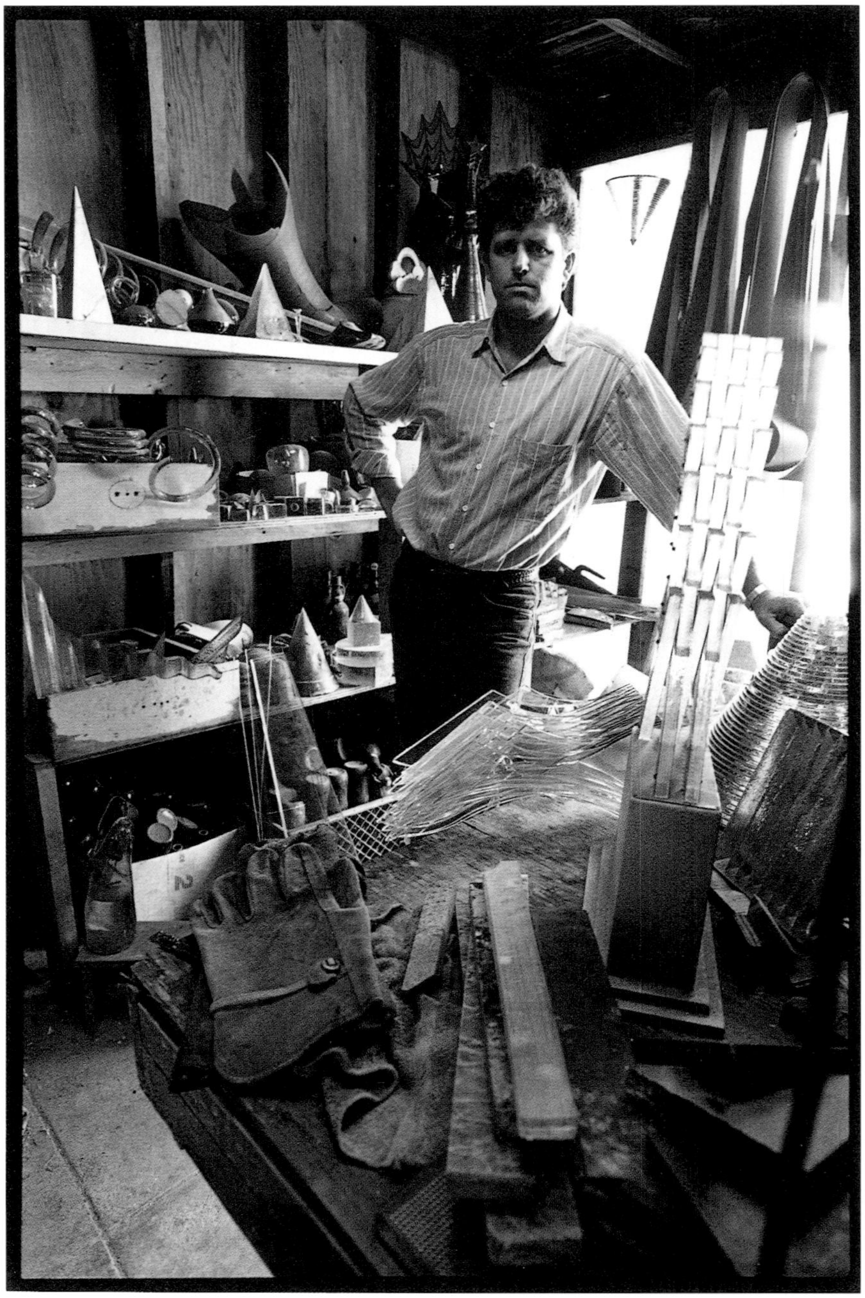

Just over the bridge on Coronado Island is Christopher Lee's corner lot home and studio where he breaks and laminates glass to form dynamic and seductive sculptures. His tall, petulant good looks seem a natural complement to these contemporary works that combine danger and beauty, anger and classical design.

Supporting himself through San Diego State University by doing stained glass commissions with his brother, Lee gained attention by focusing his fresh artistic vision on the natural reflective qualities of thick plate glass. He has since built tall towers with jagged edges, wall reliefs, and free-standing sculpture installations. He uses the glass in combination with various metals, marbles, and paint colors.

When he wasn't drawing, Lee says, he and his older brother carried on their sibling rivalry in the back seat of the family car. Later they shared a stint in the Navy together and subsequently began the architectural stained glass work together. His brother now works with their father selling cranes and tailgates. Living alone, Lee has gone with executive secretary Arlene Jaekel since 1976. He works out with weights in his backyard while listening to his favorite music – the classics and jazz.

The first installation of weapons I did was in San Francisco at the Bank of America headquarters. I had been working with wall weapons, very undefinable bludgeons or guns or knives. They could even almost be crucifixes. I took them off the wall and made them columns that stood up like lances or swords. The newest pieces, the bomb clusters, carry it even one step further. The free-standing weapons were very specific; some of them even had the specific names of some of the medieval weapons, like Snicker-snee or Scramsax, from King Arthur legends and sorcery names.

I think I started making weapons because the work I was doing had a violent aspect to it. I was intrigued that people were attracted and repelled by it at the same time. It had to do with our perverse attraction to violence, in general, and I just took it one step further to make it very literal and undefinable at the same time.

When I was in school I struggled with a lot of different materials; I did a lot of stained glass, ceramics, metal work, welded steel, cast bronze, intaglio, and painting. Eventually I started working in glass, just being enamored. It's wonderful stuff in and of itself. It does so many things. It reflects, refracts, holds, contains, repels. I wanted to use it sculpturally. Years of using glass, seeing what it could do and understanding its innate properties, guided the vision I had. What came out is a reflection of the process of drawing on emotions of power and fear and strength.

I always knew I'd do art. I was always sitting in the back seat drawing barns and silos as we were driving across the Midwest when I was growing up. My dad sold heavy equipment and the company kept moving him around, which was good in a way. It was bad because we hated moving. All I wanted to do was draw. I remember in the fourth grade the teacher asked us to write about what we wanted to do when we grew up. Everybody was madly writing away. I was sitting there with my head in my hands. The teacher came around and she grabbed me by the ear and took me out in the hall. I was in tears by that time. She said, "You've got to write something." I said I wanted to be an artist but my parents told me I couldn't do that because there's no money in it. She said, "Well, just write that. Write that you don't know what you want to do, but you want to be an artist for a hobby." It was just traumatic at the time to feel that amount of pressure at that age, not to be able to do what was most natural to me.

So it was out of spite, I guess, I decided to be

an artist. That's what I've always wanted to do. My parents are real supportive now, and they come to every one of my openings.

People wonder when they look at this stuff, am I angry or frustrated or something. I don't think so. I think it comes from the material, the process, and a fascination with the feelings that people have. It's not so much a comment on my inner feelings as much as a comment on the rest of society. I try to figure out where we lie on that line between good and bad, violent and passive, and male and female. It's like we're all treading that line all the time. The work is not defining it, it's just making you think about it a little more. I'm very commited in my feelings, in my ideals, in my dreams. I love strong, I hate strong. You've got to have that. I think people who deny those feeling and keep saying it's bad to hate would have to say that it's bad to love too. You've got to have both parts. Otherwise you're nothing.

The most important thing to me is work. My studio is ten paces from my living space and I have my TV and my stereo out there. I'll work maybe fourteen, sixteen hours a day and I do that kind of normally all the time. I don't think I'm working hard or I'm overworking myself. It's just what I do. I know other artists who say they can't stay in the studio for more than four or six hours a day. I can't imagine what I would do with the rest of my time if I wasn't working.

Someone asked Salvador Dali once what was the best thing about being an artist and he said, "Getting checks in the mail." I'm happiest when I'm working, but also when I'm working and have money in the bank. If I'm working and broke, I'm miserable. You've got to have money to get by. You've got to sell the stuff.

It's pretty presumptuous to call yourself an artist. If you've got a job, you dig a ditch, sell some stocks, sell some shoes. It's really straight forward, you have a function and you do it. But to elevate mankind? It has always bothered me about "artist, art." I make objects. I think some of them are pretty good and have some content, but who are the people who decide who artists are?

SELECTED BIOGRAPHY

BIRTHPLACE

Seattle, Washington

EDUCATION

San Diego State University, BA, 1978; MA, 1981

SOLO EXHIBITIONS

Matrix Gallery, Austin, Texas, 1984
Ivory/Kimpton Gallery, San Francisco, 1985
Bank of America World Headquarters, San Francisco, 1986
Kurland/Summers Gallery, Los Angeles, 1984 and 1987
Thomas Babeor Gallery, La Jolla, 1981, 1983, 1985, 1987

GROUP EXHIBITIONS

"Six from San Diego," Newport Harbor Art Museum, Newport Beach, California, 1981
Collaborative installation with John Luebtow, Brand Library Art Gallery, Glendale, California, 1986
New Art Forms Exposition, Navy Pier, Chicago, 1987
George Saxe Collection, American Craft Museum, New York, 1987
"Another State of Mind: Southern California Crafts," California Crafts Museum, San Francisco, 1987

COLLECTIONS

Forty works, Saks Fifth Avenue
First Interstate Plaza, San Diego
Dramatic Arts Theater, San Diego State University
Elizabeth and Mason Phelps, La Jolla
Danah Fayman, San Diego

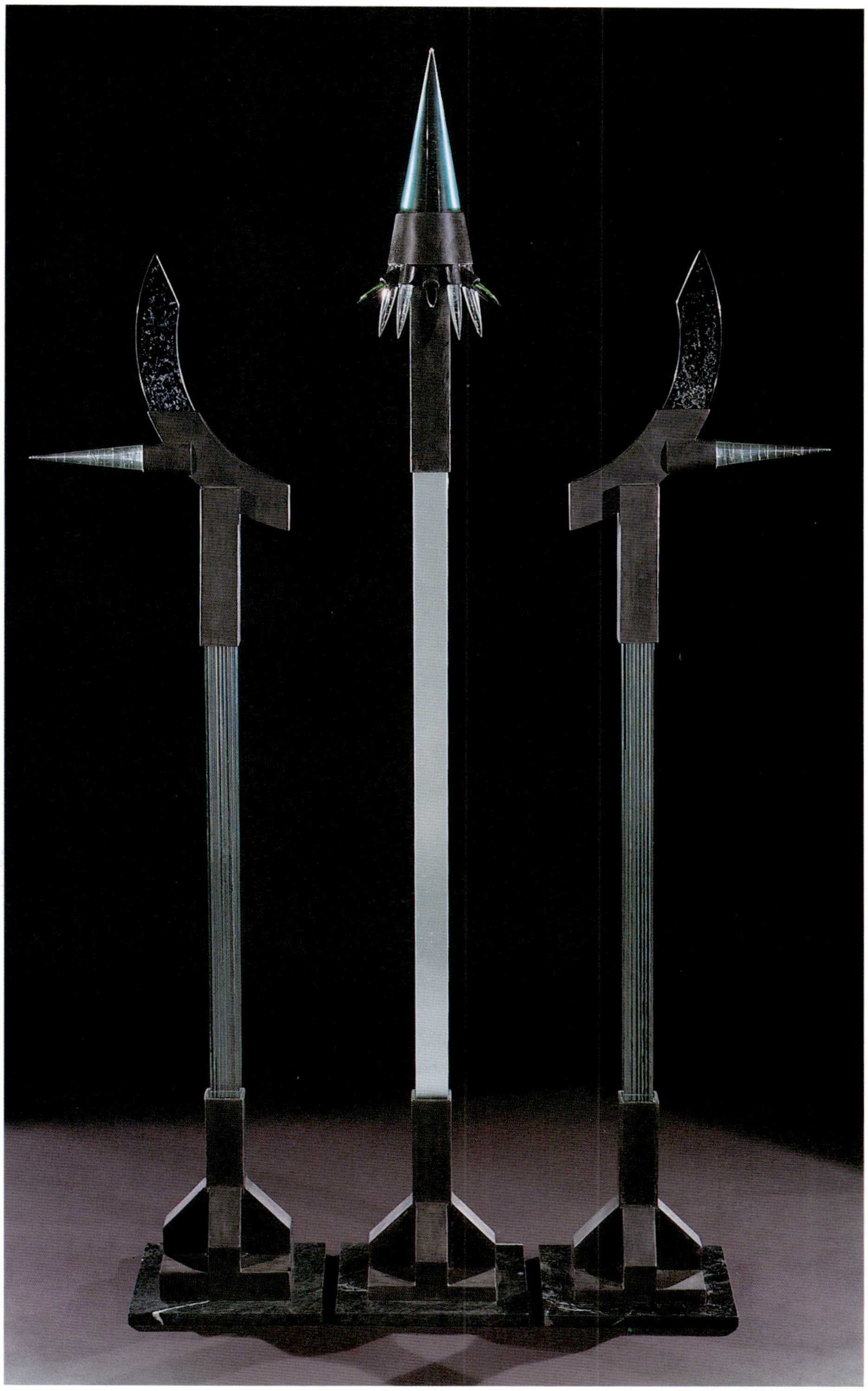

Weapon Formation #2, glass, lead, marble, 60″×48″×12″, 1987 Photo by Leonard Tobey

Kim MacConnel

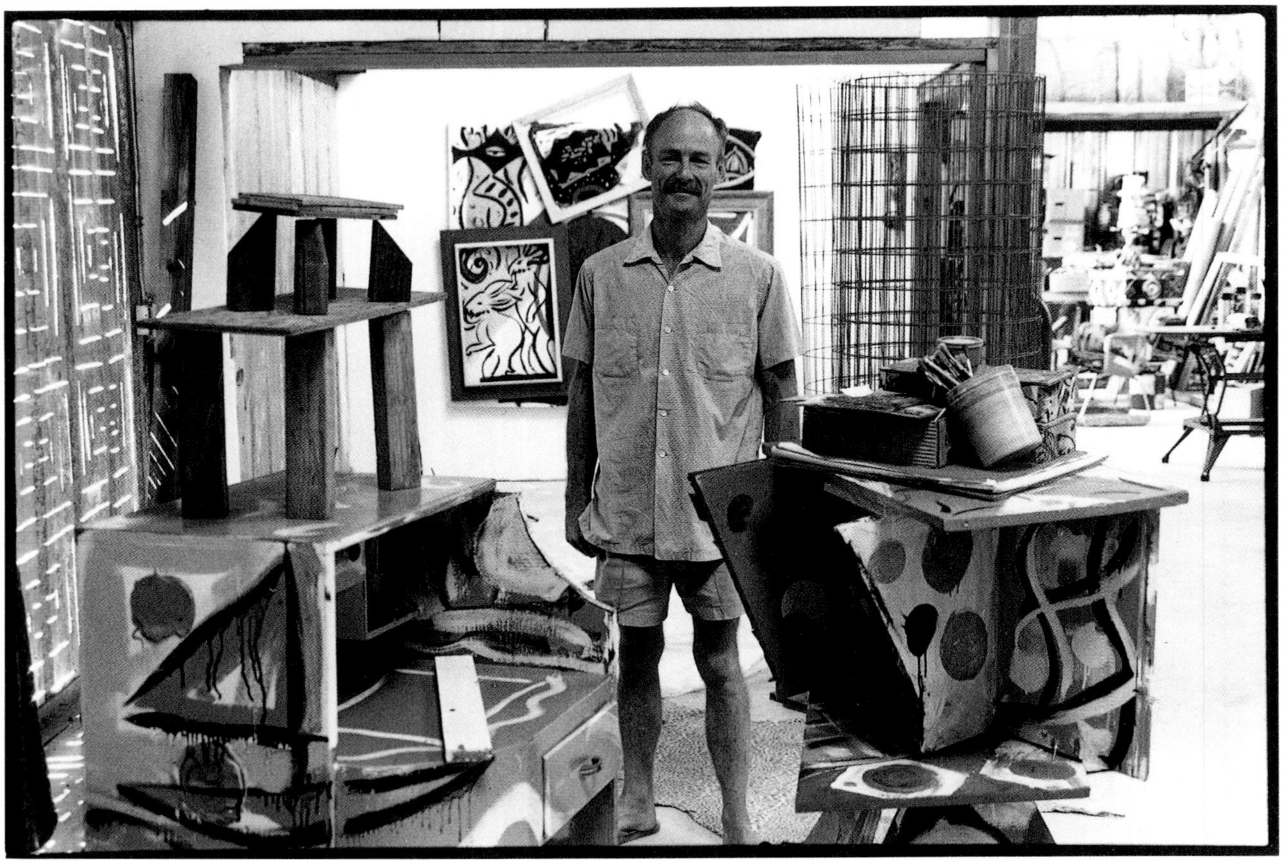

If you don't track yourself, or give yourself free license, or put yourself in a position to tax yourself financially, economically, artistically, then there's no way to know what you're throwing away and what you're saving.

Kim MacConnel comes up from the field in front of his large warehouse-like studio near the San Elijo Lagoon in east Encinitas. He wears a triangular straw hat that from a distance makes him look more like a Chinese peasant than an artist whose work is shown in some of the most significant exhibitions and galleries worldwide.

While his manner is unassuming, his art is profoundly innovative, forcing the viewer to consider time, place, materials, and culture in a way that is oblique to the usual. He paints with bold colors and moves his forms across walls, desks, chairs, and rugs with a deft intuition for the decorative. At the same time his sensibility combines abandoned furniture styles and kitsch artifacts which most of us would have tossed away long ago.

MacConnel and his younger sister, a bilingual teacher and video artist in San Diego, were raised by their mother in Texas and Mexico City. With his wife, Nina MacConnel, from whom he is now separated, he lived more than a year in Mysore in southern India. They travelled throughout India, Africa, and Europe while she conducted interviews for her forthcoming book about women in power.

All of the things I've been working on come pretty much out of an interest in non-western aesthetics. Western aesthetics are not universal. What we consider art or beautiful or of interest or important is not universal. It is based on this one asethetic concept of the adoration of the Greeks that has been beaten into our heads since the sixteenth century. Everything I've been involved in since school has been to undertand what that aesthetic is by looking at non-western values and aesthetics.

I have a strong affinity for loose cloth. I began painting on furniture as simply an economic problem, not having money. The house we moved into had an old greasy wingbacked chair too nice to throw away because of the way it looked and I needed a studio chair. So I just painted it white and sealed the grease in and then painted something over it. But where that immediately led was to the realization that you could bring painting off the wall. I don't want to say "free it from its confines," because that's a little too dramatic, but it's pretty true. I wanted to get painting into the room, literally get it out of its box, off the stretcher bars, and onto something else. I wanted to combine it with other kinds of paintings to create an environment not dissimilar from the French salons – or the idea of a salon.

There are a limited number of responses when you decide you're not going to paint on canvas. What you're able to do if you want to be a painter is somewhat limited. You've got to paint on some kind of surface and it'll either be wood, cloth, or canvas, and you're going to stretch or mount it, and you're bound to cross some other culture's production at some point.

When I was seven my mother, younger sister, and I moved from suburban Houston to the heart of Mexico City. I went to a lot of schools, partially because I didn't do very well in school and partially because I was very introverted as a kid and I really liked to wander around Mexico City. Anywhere probably would be fascinating to a kid, but Mexico City was particularly fascinating to me. I spent my allowance on bus rides to the center of town, to the Zocalo, the Merced, the other markets. I just wandered around in the old area of town and whatever money I had left over I used to spend at the thieve's market on fake artifacts. I think it's very funny when I look back on it.

I was sent away, went to boarding school in New England when I was twelve. Candidly, I had this great fear of going to the American High

School. It was to me Gangland, the other side of the 1950's that no one wants to remember. Gang fights, knifings, rumbles, stuff like that. It was real mean and it was mostly American students versus Mexicans and I had an identity as a Mexican – even though I was a blond and blue-eyed MacConnel kid. To some degree I still have that identity. You hear jokes, or people rib you and you have a defensiveness which doesn't fit. It tends to screw you up.

Any sort of expatriate culture enclave breeds the same sort of wagon train mentality. Approaching high school you start being incorporated into your society. Prior to that you're just a kid. If I got anything out of my youth it was the appreciation of free license, which is why I like being an artist. It's about the only thing you can do and have free license. I'm not afraid to do X, Y, or Z, so there's nothing stopping me if I want to do it.

All these things, tracking yourself, analyzing, all have to do with an ecological frame of mind, I suppose. If you don't track yourself, or give yourself free license, or put yourself in a position to tax yourself financially, economically, artistically, then there's no way to know what you're throwing away and what you're saving. There are so many good ideas and things that are just thrown out constantly. The only way you see them saved is through artists. You see artists constantly dragging this stuff back and sticking it in front of our faces. To me this is what artists do. We're out there mining stuff while the rest of society is going about its business, looking at the status quo, and being very self-satisfied, forgetting where we were ten, twenty, thirty, one hundred, two hundred years ago. This is what I earlier meant by this "box," this aesthetic trap that quite actually we're all in.

Americans are just awful, totally wasteful, wasteful with everything. In Tijuana, Bombay, or Accra, where people are really poor, they are really inventive. And by and large their culture in some sense is visually much richer than what we have to show in North City West or the Golden Triangle, or any enclave housing development. There is no decoration, no one is trying to invent, you're not allowed to. You can't be eccentric. That is pure poverty. What it breeds in terms of culture is a dependence on specialists such as artists to do things for them. People just don't know this. They watch TV. TV invents your spare time for you. Ecologically speaking, I go for poverty.

SELECTED BIOGRAPHY

BIRTHPLACE

Oklahoma City

EDUCATION

University of California, San Diego, BA with honors, 1969 (Special Pre-Doctorate Fellowship); MFA with honors, 1972

TEACHING

University of California, San Diego, 1987 to present

SOLO EXHIBITIONS

"Kim MacConnel Salon," installation, The Ackland Art Museum, University of North Carolina, Chapel Hill, 1980
Studio Marconi, Milan, 1984
James Corcoran Gallery, Los Angeles, 1982 and 1986
Quint Gallery, San Diego, 1986
"Collection Applied Design," travelling exhibition, 1975 through 1976; "Furnishings," 1977; "Third World Series," 1978; "Flies," 1979; "Cutups," 1980; "Luft Geschaften," 1982; 1984; "Western Painting," 1986, "Flower Vases," 1987, Holly Solomon Gallery, New York

GROUP EXHIBITIONS

Forty-first Venice Biennale, Italy, 1984
Biennial, Whitney Museum of American Art, New York, 1985
"After Matisse," travelling exhibition, Independent Curators Incorporated, 1986 through 1988
"Focus on the Image, Selections from the Rivendell Collection," travelling exhibition, Phoenix Museum of Art, Phoenix, 1986 through 1990
"Living Spaces," The Los Angeles Institute of Contemporary Art, 1987

COLLECTIONS

Whitney Museum of American Art, New York
Morton G. Neumann Family Collection, National Gallery of Art, Washington, D.C.
Albright-Knox Gallery, Buffalo
Chicago Art Institute
Rothchild Collection on loan to the La Jolla Museum of Contemporary Art

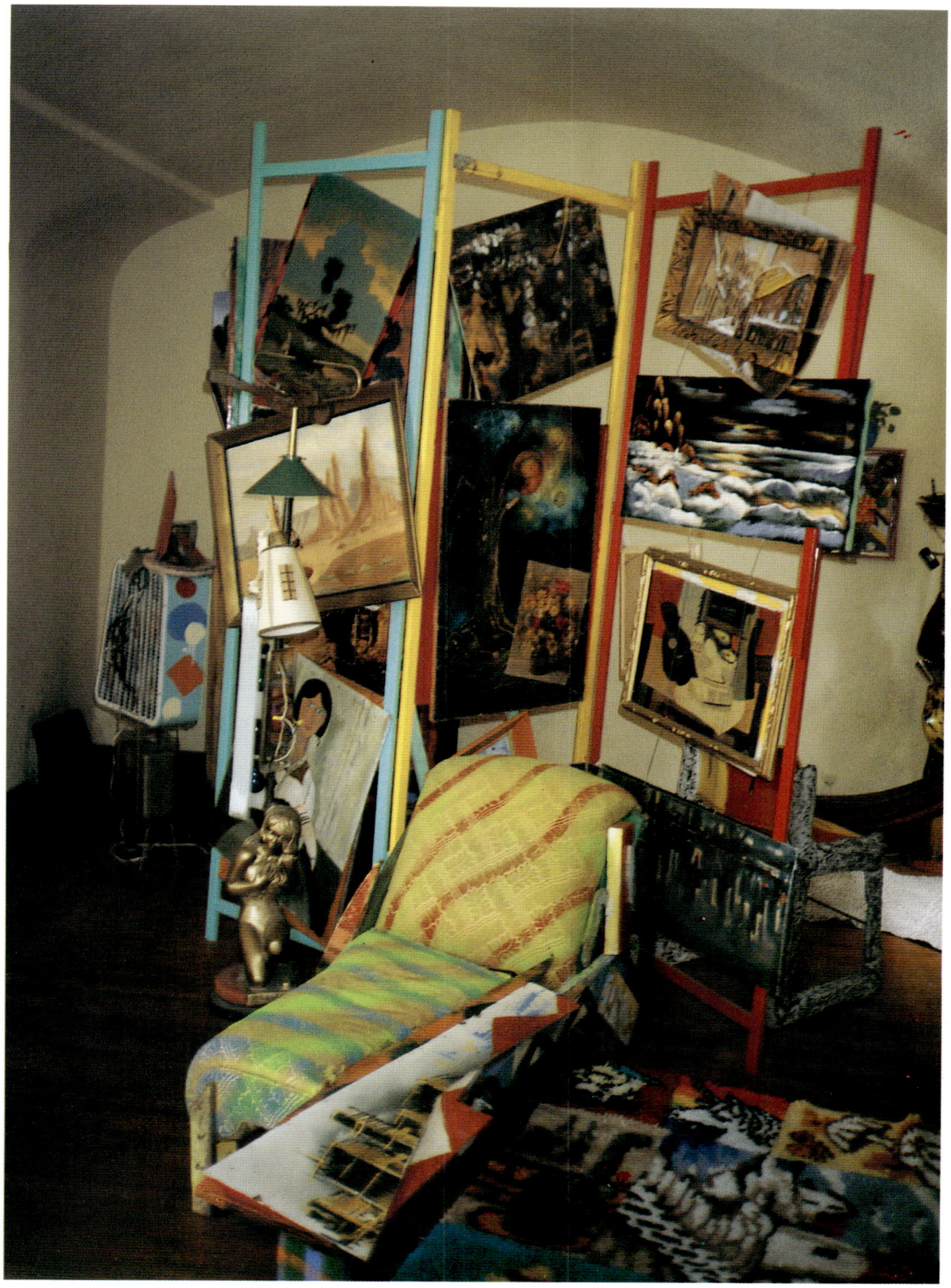

Living room in "Living Spaces," LAICA Exhibition, 1987

Deloss McGraw

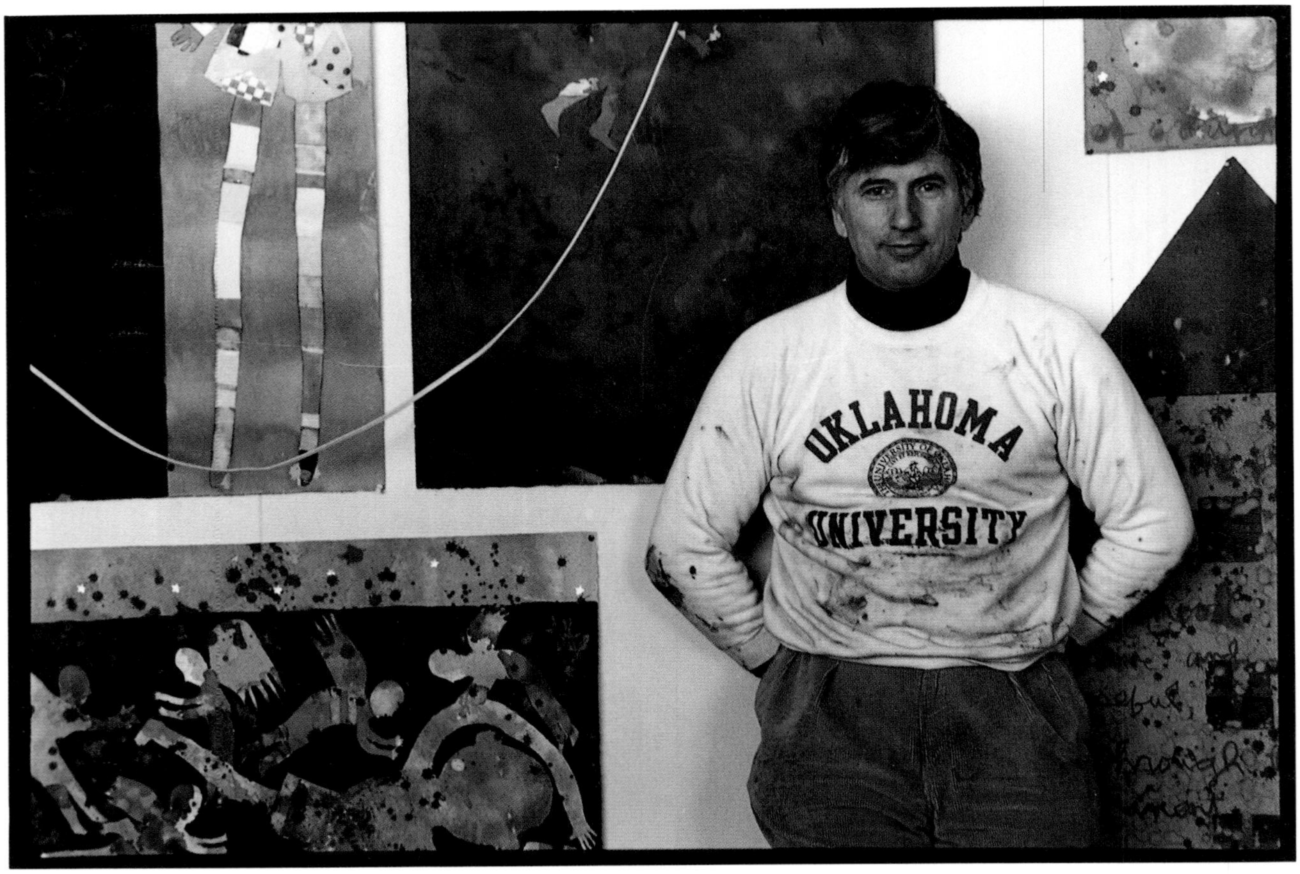

I really think that the poets today in our country are doing a much finer job than the visual artist. I think they are closer to the heartbeat, probably because artists have the opportunity to be corrupted.

Working in the upstairs studio of an industrial complex in San Marcos, Deloss McGraw is surrounded by the ungrounded, naively flexible figures that flow unendingly from his imagination. This painter retains his own boy-like wonder of himself in the world, constantly questioning and examining exterior sources such as literature and poetry, the basic references which stimulate his prolific creativity.

He maintained a figurative style through the Minimalism of the early 1970s and has found sudden critical acclaim since responding to W. D. Snodgrass's poem, "Who Killed Cock Robin?" in 1983. The artist and poet now have a symbiotic relationship which has stimulated several collaborations; Snodgrass writes, then McGraw paints or, occasionally, they work in reverse order.

McGraw has also produced several art books with Bill Kelly of the San Diego-based Brighton Press, and has created set designs for Barton Thurber's jazz opera, "Monstrum." Among the other writers and poets who have inspired his work are Mary Shelley, William Butler Yeats, Lewis Carroll, Dante, and Mother Goose.

McGraw's parents divorced when he was a year old and he was raised by his mother, a professor of literature at a small college. He lives in Encinitas with his wife, Shannon, and plays when he can with his four toddler-to-teenage children.

The child has that wonderful mental state where regardless of what the experience is, he doesn't judge. Judging someone else isn't going to correct things, it just makes the problem worse. Condemnation and judgement kill a person. Childhood is of tremendous interest to me. To me the innocent childlike view of things holds the essence of happiness. I think that's what we all want, that's the bottom line. I've always been drawn to childlike work. I collect a lot of folk art. Painting in a childlike manner gives me the opportunity to deal with serious issues and not become maudlin or sentimental.

My mother was a literature professor at a small college in Oklahoma. I was raised in academia while she worked at all of her degrees. The first art exhibition I went to was when I was about five or six. It was a reconstruction of Leonardo DaVinci's tools and inventions at the University of Oklahoma. When I was a senior in high school I can still remember being impressed by the color in a Bonnard exhibition. I think I also responded to the bathtub painting.

All my paintings are concerned with my own experience. I developed this form of a man, he became a balded figure. The works are narrative statements on things that are happening to this individual. That's the issue of the painting. Not that the person looks different from the other ones. I give a lot of written titles and I'm trying to explain as much as possible what's going on. To me that's an obligation I have as an artist. But I think this bald-headed person has come about because it calls for a greater sense of innocence. If I work on a particular aspect of him it's to make sure that there is a certain softness, a receptivity. I don't want the women to be sensuous. I'm not interested in that. I'm interested in their dealings with the issues in life that are important, not for sensuality.

Painting the figure is just another statement identifying ourselves. Not myself, it's man in general. I feel like I paint the human condition, but I don't look at the world through rose colored glasses. I think that's of little use; you can find that in the parks on Sundays, it lacks sincerity.

When I was first doing this work it wasn't accepted. No one was interested in this in 1971. Minimalism was going on then. If I ever change because the styles change then I'm subject to question, I think. I feel a commitment to the audience, to the gallery; there's nothing wrong with that. You know, you have such a different perspective being an artist who is employed by his work than you do from the ivory tower. People who write about artists are art historians who themselves never support themselves from their art. Those who teach it have read what those who write say. So much is lost. They have no idea.

I work all the time. Last week I worked until one every morning. It's not that I'm prolific; I work my ass off! You can't ski in the alps and do it. I approach it as a refuge.

Basically what I do is find a concept and saturate it with a lot of reading. I really think that the poets today in our country are doing a much finer job than the visual artist. I think they are closer to the heartbeat, probably because artists have the opportunity to be corrupted. I really do think that the writing being done is almost unread.

I recently did a show in Los Angeles based on the writings of Daniel Halpern and Robert Hass. I wanted to find two poets my own age, because they had the same experience as I have. Our experience would have been similar, the experience of rebellion in the 1960s and, I think, the experience of loneliness. Our generation has gone through difficulty in the ability to find someone to share life with, life forces. I've been married three times. This is tough; I think we're in a generation that involves a real sense of revolution, or ideals about marriage.

Working thematically in a series enables me to be productive. It keeps the enthusiasm. I can remember a time when I didn't feel like painting that day. It happens lots of days. Nothing. Nothing. It was terrible. This happened two times this year. I thought, God, if there was another color. I had red, yellow, blue. I thought, if there was just another color! I had to laugh at that because I realized that it wouldn't help because it's only in relationship. Painting is in relationship. Like there's no such thing as a muddy color. There isn't. It's within the context of the painting that it appears to be ugly.

SELECTED BIOGRAPHY

BIRTHPLACE

Okemah, Oklahoma

EDUCATION

Otis Art Institute, Los Angeles, 1966
Art Institute of San Miguel Allende, Mexico, 1968
California State University, Long Beach, BA, 1969
Cranbrook Academy of Art, Bloomfield Hills, Michigan, MFA, 1972

SOLO EXHIBITIONS

"In Response to the World of W.D. Snodgrass," Adrianne Simard Gallery, Los Angeles, 1983
"Frankenstein and Mary Shelley: Monstrum," Koplin Gallery, Los Angeles, 1984 and the Laguna Art Museum, Laguna Beach, 1985
"Secret Response to the Writings of Emily Dickenson and Franz Kafka," Moss & Chumley Gallery, Dallas, 1987
"Wings," ASB Gallery, London and Munich, 1987
Harcourts Contemporary, San Francisco, 1984, 1985, 1987

GROUP EXHIBITIONS

"Drawing Invitational," San Diego Museum of Art, 1977
Newspace Gallery, Los Angeles, 1978
"Acquisitions," Cranbrook Museum of Art, 1982
"Newcomers 1981," and "Magical Mystery Tour," 1984, Los Angeles Municipal Art Gallery
"The House in Contemporary Art," California State University, Stanislaus, 1987

PUBLICATIONS

Art Books, Brighton Press, San Diego:
The House the Poet Built, with W.D. Snodgrass, 1984
A Colored Poem, with W.D. Snodgrass, 1984
Father William, Poem by Lewis Carroll, 1985
The Wounded Angel, with Robert Phillips, 1987
Kinder Capers, with W.D. Snodgrass, Nadja Press, New York, 1986
The Death of Cock Robin, Poems by W.D. Snodgrass and 34 illustrations and color plates by DeLoss McGraw, University of Delaware Press, 1988

COLLECTIONS

Houghton Collection, Harvard University
Bodleian Collection, Oxford University, England
Library of Congress, Washington, D.C.
Whitney Museum of American Art, New York
Cincinnati Art Museum

Private collection, Vermont

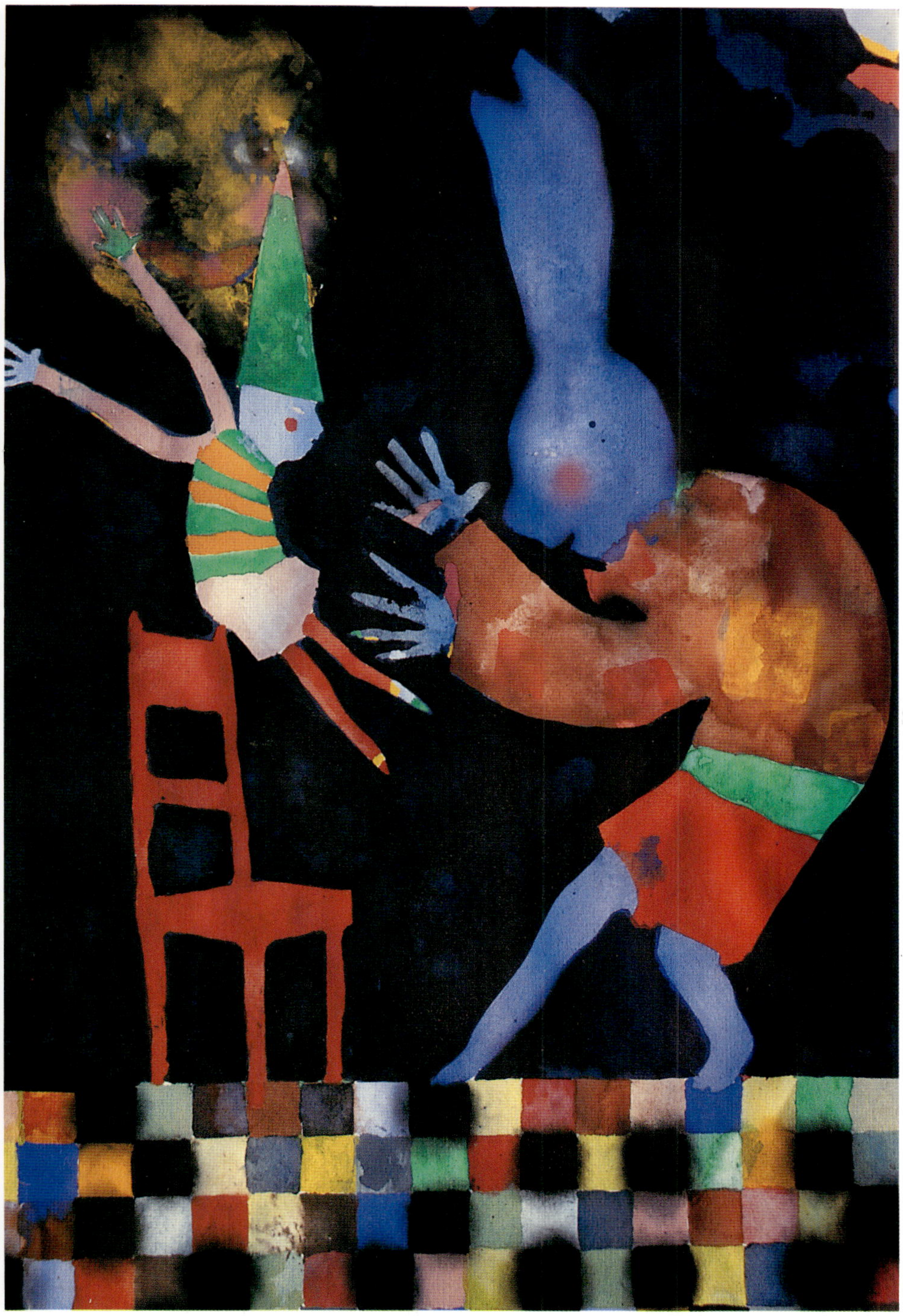

DOSTOIEVSKY WARNS W.D. ABOUT WEARING RASKOLNIKOV'S HAT

(Dostoievsky, a large blue rabbit,
addresses a startled child)

To step out sporting such a topper
Seems highfalutin' and improper
To men of average ability;
You catch their eyes, then their hostility.
They'll brand you uppity and vain,
Acting as if you had more brain
To cover up. It may be said,
There's more inside this than his head –
What if he's smuggling contraband,
Cocaine or concealed weapons? *And*
There's room in such a tall hatband
For worse: a pair of rabbit ears!
He could be one of those who hears
Lost voices, taps top-secret thought
Whose meaning even we forgot,
Who scans, like supersonic bats,
The blips we keep beneath our hats,
Decodes brain waves, bugs dreams of ours,
Broadcasting them to foreign powers!
Why else would he need such antennae?
Good honest folks sure don't have any.
Let's get rid, quick, of this high-hatted dude;
Besides, we just don't like his attitude.

Dostoievsky Warns W.D. About Wearing Raskolnikov's Hat, gouache, 29¾" × 22", 1986

Cliff McReynolds

As I see it there is a vast order, a great many everlasting principles by which the universe is ordered and art is really just the aesthetic version of that order.

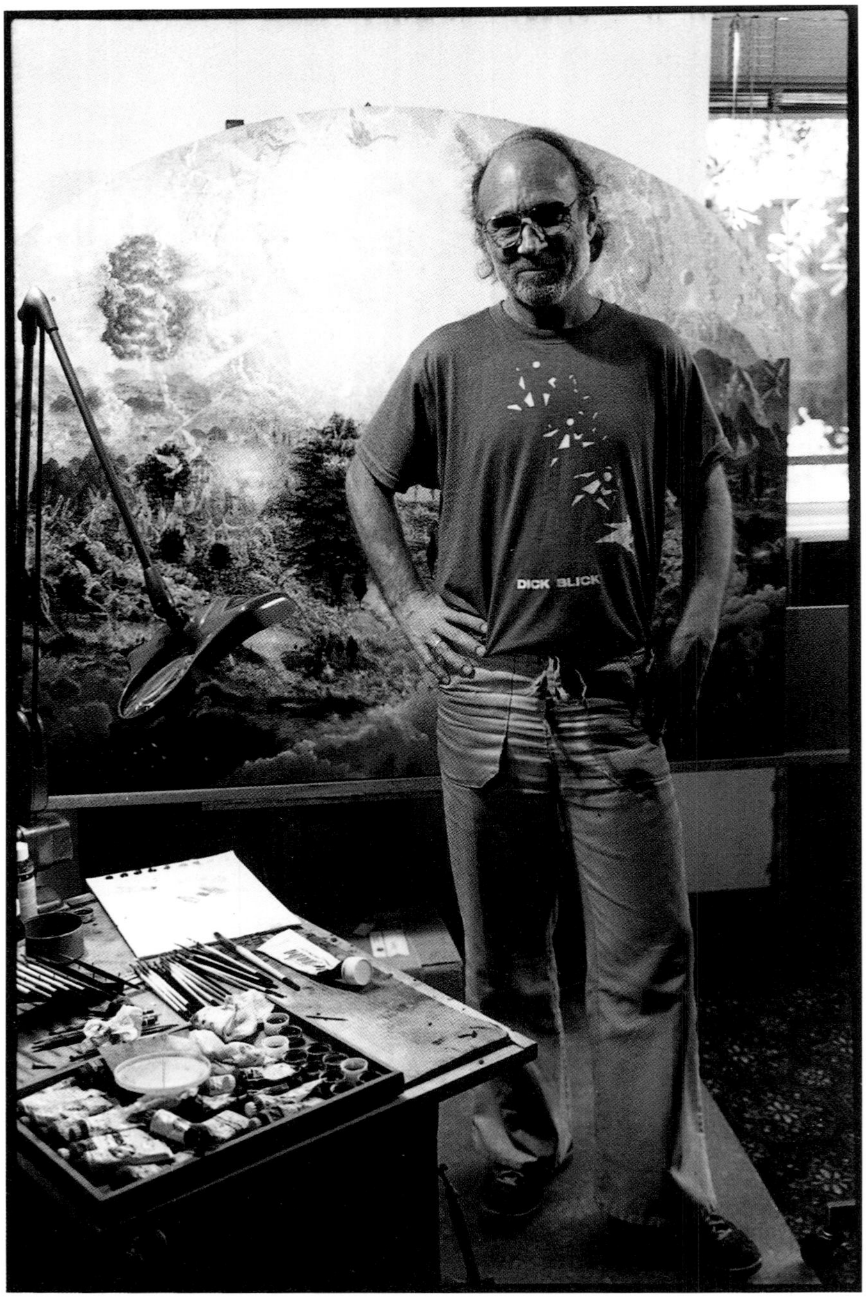

Cliff McReynolds paints in a darkened studio in the back of his house. To his left is a wall of art books and on his right a tabaret sporting a Dazor lamp with magnifying glass. His hair pulled back in a knot, wearing wire-rimmed glasses and a mischievous smile, he seems more comfortable asking questions than answering them, especially about himself and his art.

Replete with solid draftsmanship, the content of McReynold's early iconoclastic work underwent a transformation in 1970 when he became a Christian and dedicated himself to creating celebrations of earthly and paradisiacal delights. His paintings are expertly crafted with highly rendered, glistening waters and lush foliage. Even the minutest elements in nature are treated with loving care.

McReynolds and his slightly younger brother spent much of their youth in and out of institutions when their mother was having difficulty caring for them; their photographer father had left when the boys were small. His artistic talents were nevertheless encouraged by his mother and by his teachers during childhood.

With his wife Patricia, an art historian whose loom and piano are warm additions to the dining room, McReynolds lives in a small La Jolla home that is often visited by Patricia's four grown children and by his own son Stephen, who has realized a lifelong dream of becoming a pilot.

I've spent four and a half years on the five panels of the *La Jolla Diptych*. It was something I knew I had ahead of me. I'd get these flashes. Beyond the physical labor there is a kind of inner drive that keeps you going. The creative process is such that it's very much start and stop. You get discouraged, depressed. Ideally you rebound, but that can be exhausting if it goes on too long.

Our culture at this time communicates against this very thing that I'm describing. The attitude is, oh my goodness, if it takes longer than five or ten minutes then let's move on to something else. Instant gratification has become an aspect of our national character, it seems to me.

The classic definition of surrealism as painted from dreams has nothing to do with the motive, the source from which I derive my imagery. Another definition of surrealism is putting real things in an unreal situation, or vice versa, and to some degree I do that. But the motive is the big thing. I think the surrealists were trying to handle their psyches, dig and dig and scratch and burrow into it and I am not interested in working like that.

I call my work Revelation Art. As I see it there is a vast order, a great everlasting principle by which the universe is ordered and art is really just the aesthetic version of that order. I happen to define art as the creative expression of truth, God's truth. I'm not interested in any sort of rebellion against things as they are or as they've been or making anything original or expressing myself or any of that bat guano. That's a lot of irrelevant nonsense as far as I'm concerned. I'm focused on getting in touch and in tune with this order that I sense. Anyone who paints in that way is subject to inspired insight. You know, when you look for the truth you tend to find it.

For years I thought that my tenacity was probably my only virtue. You know if you chop an eel's head off when it bites into you it still won't let go? That's sort of how I am. I really get into things, whatever it is. But the problem with that is I have had a lot of trouble distinguishing between willfulness and tenacity. There could be a very fine line and I've often gone over it, not knowing I had.

I get up in the morning and I pray before I work. Essentially my prayer is "God, lead me. Lead me in what I paint." But for many years I already had it pretty well figured out exactly what I was going to do and God help anybody who got in my way. During those years if something went wrong I would conform to pattern and whine and say painting was just all rolling boulders up hill.

Well, one day about four years ago, an event happened when I was working on a painting I'd been struggling with, on and off, for about three years. It was one of the toughest paintings I ever did. I prayed, "Lord, help me with this painting. It's going all to hell, it's all screwed up." I got very angry, the way I usually did, real upset and distressed and started bouncing off the wall, which was my custom, just a normal aspect of the creative process as I practiced it. But there was this difference; I was so upset that I prayed then again. I did that occasionally at times like that, but usually kind of testing a little prayer, "God, godammit, would you please work this out!" But this time it was different. It was, "Okay, I don't know what's going on here." I got on my knees and said, "I'm not getting up until I *know* what I'm supposed to do." I was doing some pretty serious praying there for a while. And pretty soon the message I got was to go out to the garage and get another painting, "The Rapture" I had put away months ago, my Bete Noir. And I said, "Oh no, that can't be right. I'm having enough trouble with this one, who needs more anguish?" So I prayed some more for another reading because this was obviously wrong. But I kept getting that message so, with a lot of fear and trepidation, I went out and got it. I put it on the easel and I was looking at it and it kind of fell into place. It was real amazing. In the next two weeks I finished it. It's a painting I don't think I've ever surpassed.

I can still have trouble, but since then painting has been a different experience for me. It's still one step forward and two back, two forward and one back, but not only does it not bother me as much but the highs are more frequent and higher. To just sort of align oneself with the whole experience of the Holy Spirit is to receive the blessings of creativity as we're meant to, I do believe.

From the time I became a Christian the message I got was, "Paint what I give you to paint and I'll take care of the rest." It just never worked for me to try to promote myself. Conversely, just sitting here painting all these years I have been provided for amply. I have just everything I need and more.

SELECTED BIOGRAPHY

BIRTHPLACE

Amarillo, Texas

EDUCATION

San Diego State University, BA, 1959; MA, 1960

TEACHING

Mesa College, San Diego, 1969 to present

SOLO SHOWS

La Jolla Museum, 1959 and 1967
Rebecca Cooper Gallery, Washington, D.C., 1976; New York, 1981
San Jose Museum of Art, 1983

GROUP EXHIBITIONS

"Drawing U.S.A.," travelling exhibition, Minnesota Museum of Art, 1975 to 1977
"Alternative Realities," Museum of Contemporary Art, Chicago, 1976
"California Painting and Sculpture – The Modern Era," San Francisco Museum of Modern Art, 1976
"The Fourth Triennial – India," travelling exhibition, New Delhi, Tokyo, Oakland Museum, 1978-1979
"The Illuminarium," Mill Valley, California, 1982

PUBLICATIONS

Revelation Art: All Things New, Pomegranate Artbooks, Corte Madera, California, 1980

COLLECTIONS

Chicago Art Institute
Edwin A. Bergman Collection, Chicago
Jean Van den Heuvel, New York
Warner Brothers Studios, Burbank
Stroud Connor, M.D., Santa Clara, California

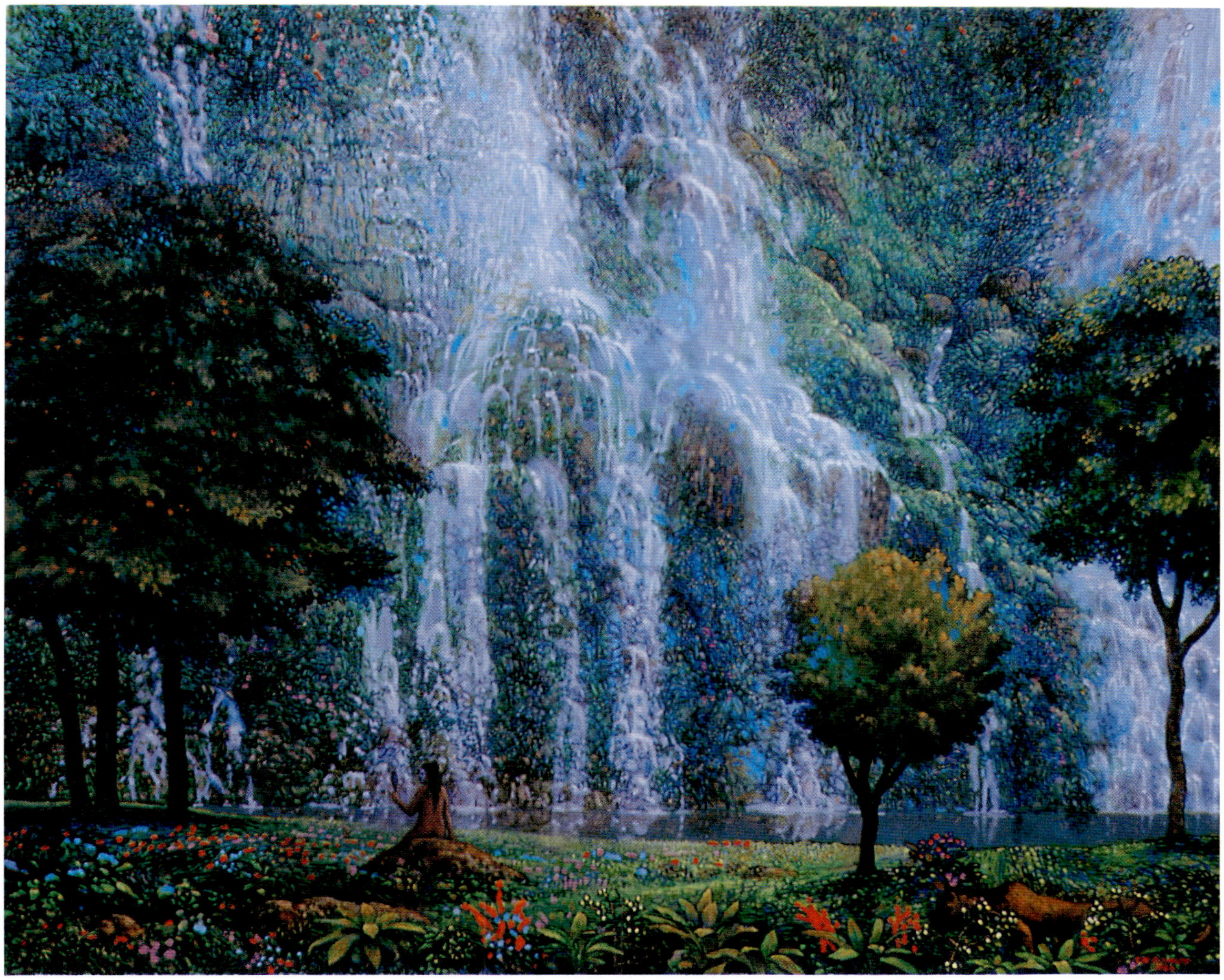

The Garden II, oil/panel, 12½″×16″, 1986

Collection of the artist

Peter Mitten

I am looking at what's happening to the space between objects. I think that the space.... is powerful as the physical stuff that demarcates that space.

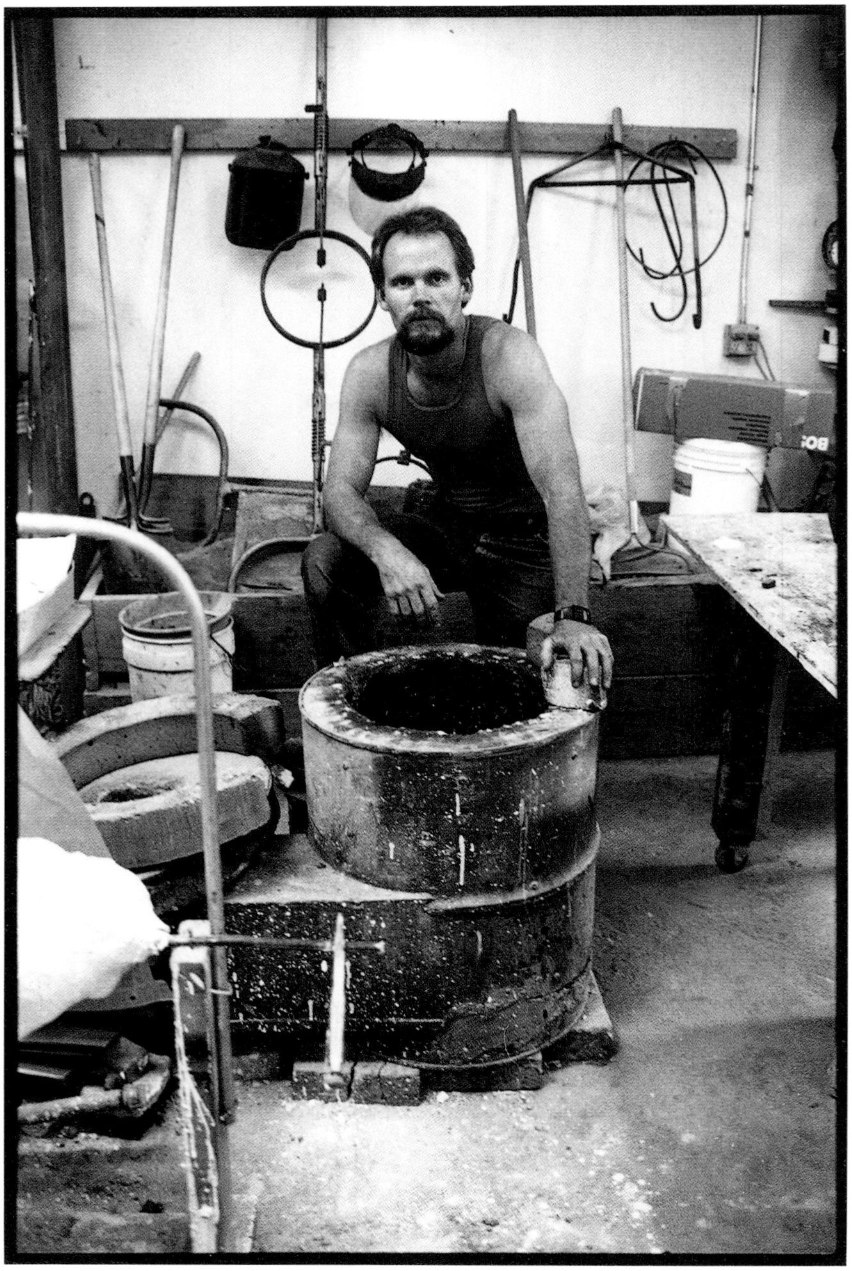

Dedicated to his fascination with all aspects of casting, Peter Mitten sets up his foundry where he teaches. His real home is less where he sleeps than where he makes his forms and pours molten bronze or aluminum.

Invited to be artist-in-residence in several U. S. colleges, he has been tenacious in his conviction that his sculptures are worth the struggle in a time when process and classical materials are little understood and appreciated. Castings with rough seams, bent paper, wire mesh, or embedded symbols juxtaposed against body cast fragments are Mitten's personal language and he uses this in richly patinated monolithic works, shelter pieces, or high reliefs.

He and his three brothers and one sister were raised in Illinois by their mother and father, an Economics and Business Law professor. With the help of his wife, writer and publisher Kristin Buckmaster, he cares for his two grade school sons, Jedediah and Jonathan, who have helped in the studio since they were small.

I feel real comfortable with things that are liquid that turn hard but retain their liquid look. I like chops in the earth that you see when construction crews are blasting through a mountain to make a road. You see the history of all these layers. Even if it happens to be in an igneous rock form, you're getting some history of how liquids have come together and made something really beautiful in nature. I take a lot of clues from that. I don't want to imitate the look of nature, but to accept it as stimulus in terms of color, form, and surface structure – especially structure.

Work that tends to look manufactured and crisp at the edges and more generic and less individualized might be more readily acceptable to a broad audience, but having the process obvious in the work seems to be real natural to the work itself. I mean, if that is a part of how the work got there, why not leave it?

A lot of my experimenting is aimed at either directly or indirectly having more control of the materials I'm using, although lately the experiments haven't been about materials, they've been about proximity – how far apart can things be and how close together before their presences start to impose on each other. I'm looking at what is happening to the space between objects. I think that the space between them is as powerful as the physical stuff that demarcates that space.

My spaces have become more artistic, more theoretical; they're not so literal. You take what you see around you and you deal with certain issues and then it starts to take on its own perspective. You imitate what's around you to grasp an idea, use common examples and say now here's what I can do with that.

I'd be real surprised if any artist said that at some point the work wasn't just real laborious. Work. You have to finish the piece. Like any other job, when you start it you have to finish it, even if you don't know whether it's going to be good or not. That's getting less frequent now and it's seldom that I feel ambivalent towards a work in process. It's an idea that had to develop and you just have to carry on through and take vitamins to keep doing it. You just keep going until it's finished, sometimes feverishly. Something keeps wanting to see that thing finished and it is like a central driving force inside and you don't sleep until it's finished and if you do you dream about it. You may not have a clue how it's going to be accepted; you just know that this is real central, this is me and I want to get this done.

It's getting easier to have my kids in the studio and to share ideas with them, objectives with them, still pretty much on a process level. They know how to use a tape measure now, and a pencil and a drill. It gets done. I had a real neat experience with them last Easter break. Every day we spent in the studio working on a piece together. It went easier than I thought it would. There were days when we were tired but by the end of the week it worked out.

I'd like to feel more integrated into society. There's always this distance, different value systems. Although I want to be successful as an artist in a monetary way, it certainly can't be money that we're working for. How could it be? And we're not stupid. There's a whole different value system we're working for and I don't know if I can put my finger on it. If I was honest, family is real important most of the time...when they're all asleep.

Work time at its best is like being really alone and becoming fulfilled in that, learning to know yourself, like being alone long enough to find out who you are and being fulfilled through exercising who you are in the resulting forms. And when it starts to turn on it's the greatest high, if you can just get that time alone. I think that's a tremendous struggle. I work nights on my sculpture, work sixteen, eighteen, sometimes twenty-four hours.

Deadlines really have this great working pressure. They're great. If it weren't for deadlines nothing would ever happen. I didn't have to work up to deadline for the last show. A crew of people helped me load stuff and get it to the gallery at one or two in the morning and the show opened that night. It feels like I'm getting it together, planning a little better, at least ten hours ahead.

I don't have anything to do with figurative sculpture necessarily, but I'm interested in the figure, particularly sections of the female figure as a metaphor for the land we live on. I use the figure as a metaphor for Mother Earth. Earth is our shelter, environment, safety zone.

SELECTED BIOGRAPHY

BIRTHPLACE

Kankakee, Illinois

EDUCATION

Southern Illinois University, Carbondale, BA, 1973; MFA, 1976

TEACHING

Mesa College, San Diego, 1983 to present
Grossmont College, El Cajon, 1985 to present

SOLO EXHIBITIONS

Point Loma College, San Diego, 1978
Bridge Gallery, Los Angeles City Hall, 1982
Grossmont College, El Cajon, California, 1985
University Gallery, Biola University, La Mirada, California, 1980 and 1986

GROUP EXHIBITIONS

San Diego Museum of Art, 1978
Maple Gallery, San Diego, 1982, 1983, 1984
Thomas Babeor Gallery, San Diego, 1985
Moreau Gallery, St. Mary's College, Notre Dame, 1986
Wita Gardiner Gallery, San Diego, 1987

COLLECTIONS

Santa Rapparata Graphic Arts Center, Florence
Kathryn Scarboro-Kugel, Paris
Guardian Development Corporation, San Diego
Marshall Brown, San Diego
Elizabeth and Mason Phelps, La Jolla

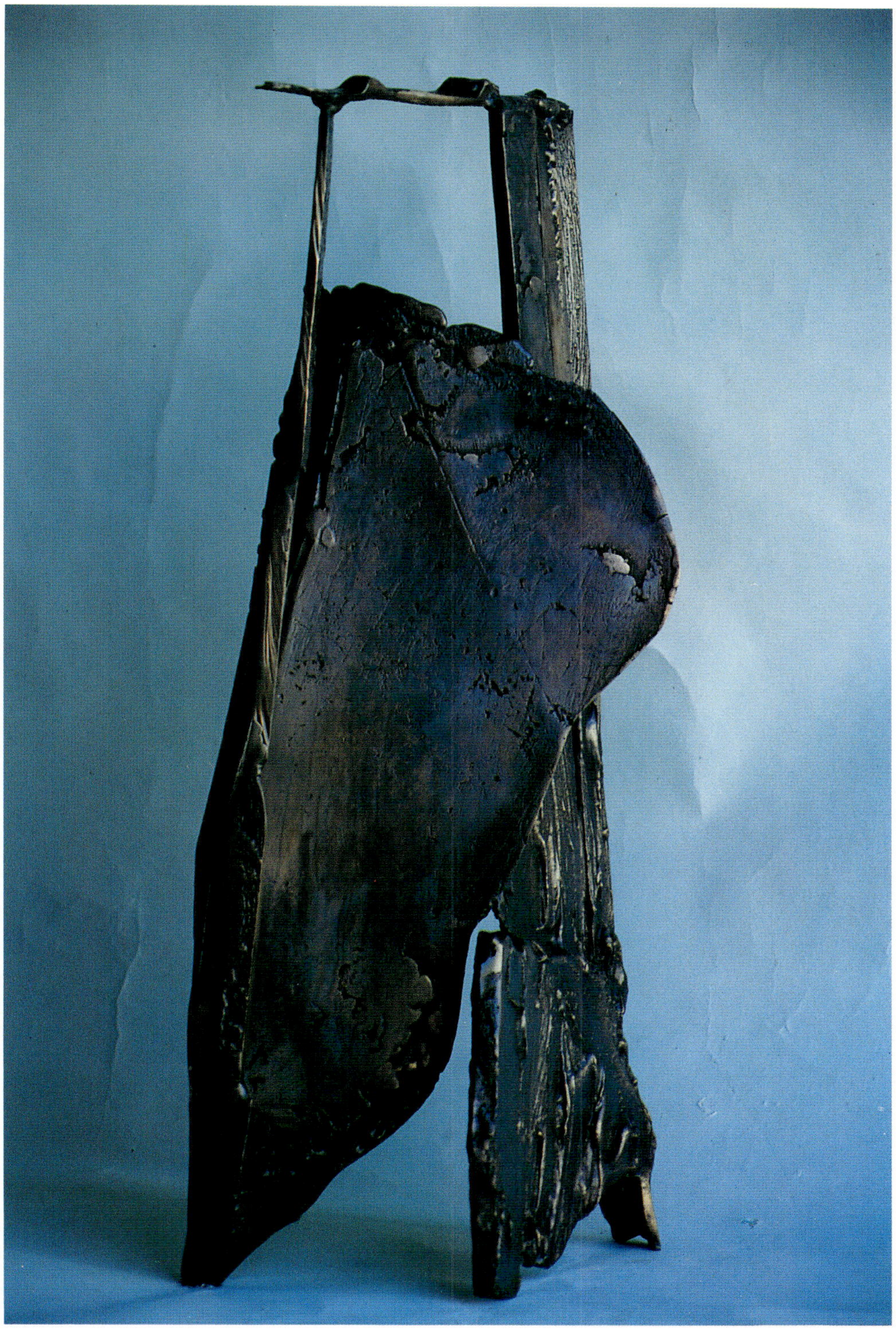

Anthem, bronze, 29" × 15" × 8", 1986 Laris/Cohen

Richard Allen Morris

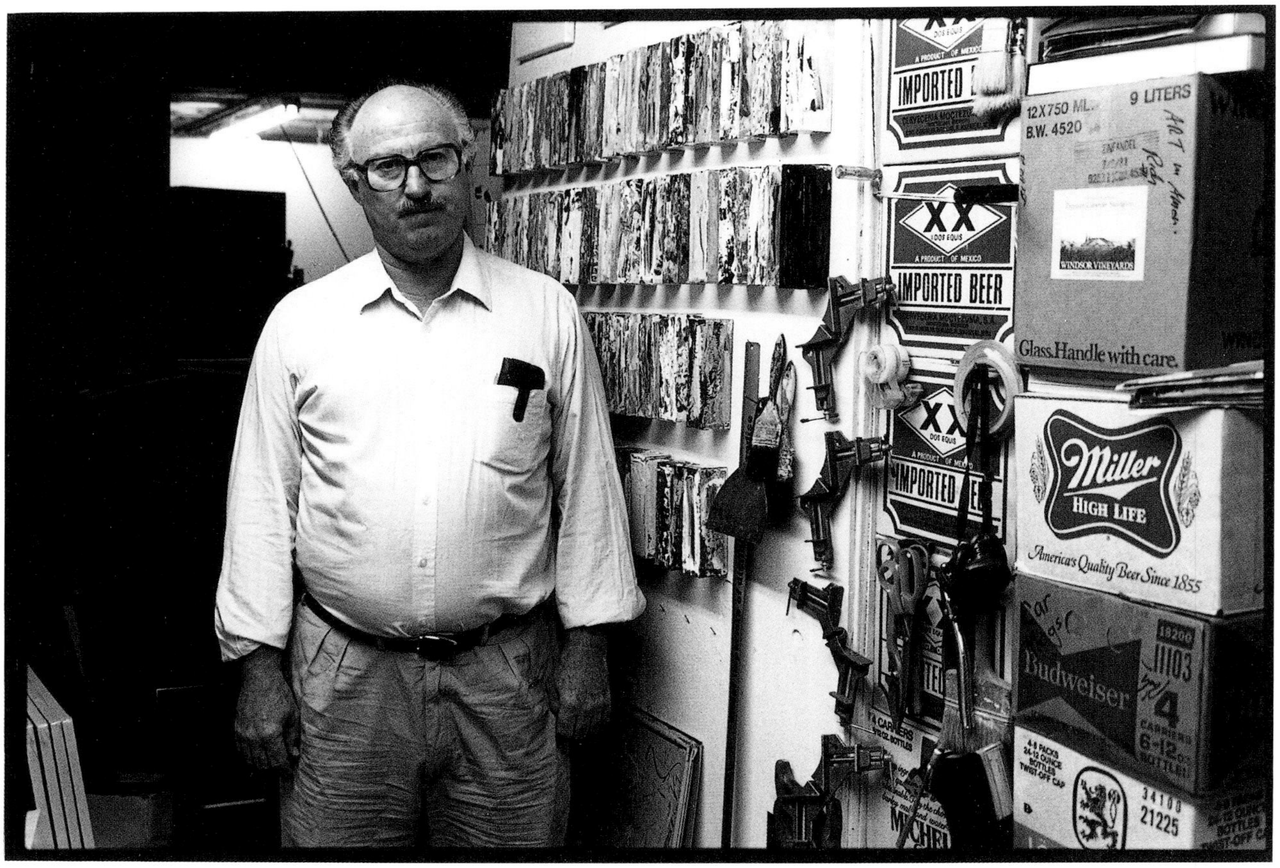

I'm constantly saying here's another border town, here we are deader than a doornail. There's no commitment with the collectors. . . .they've gotta be told what to do.

Richard Allen Morris is an artist's artist. Described as "an articulate recluse," he has struggled, received critical attention, and been totally dedicated to the exploration of his art. His work space is humble, the first floor of a non-descript apartment house in a bland downtown neighborhood. With barely enough room to draw, the studio is so filled with boxes of rare books and old records that no wall space remains for showing his work.

Thick painterly canvases, exuberant and provocative multimedia collages, and sensuous sculptural forms make up a huge body of work whose background may be found in the disheveled stacks of reference materials he searches through to express his current thought on the state of art. If he is critical of the grants process, museums, art galleries, collectors, and public art, it is with a voice echoed by many of his fellow artists. Beyond trends and social polish, he has been independent and fiercely honest in his work.

Morris and his brother, an electrician ten years his junior, moved a great deal with their church-organist mother and stone mason father, neither of whom expressed an interest in art. Living alone, Morris came to San Diego in 1956 and became a book clerk. Mentored by the late Lafayette Young, he was soon immersed in books and as a consequence has joined the ranks of the well-read artist. Sculptor Tom Driscoll and painter Walter Wojtyla work in adjacent studios.

Abstract expressionism was my real foundation. It had great meaning for me. I can remember very clearly picking up *Life* magazine with Clement Greenberg's early responses to Jackson Pollock, Franz Kline, and Mark Rothko. The first one, of course, had Pollock, a double page. *Life*, a very square magazine, opened it up. Here's Jackson Pollock and a passionate writer talking about him, a forerunner. I got abstract real quick.

I saw that when I was in the service, stationed in the Mediterranean, and when I got back to the States I got some books. On the basis that you learn by doing, I did a lot. Luckily I read some good books. Later on when I started meeting other artists, I luckily met good artists. Guy Williams was one of my first friends, Don Dudley was, Malcolm McClain. John Baldessari and I used to go up to shows in Los Angeles together. Baldessari saw immediately that the essential thing to do was do some good planning, some soul searching. If he had a room full of sculpture and paintings that were not selling, he'd do something about it. He's been at Cal Arts for years.

Once I learned that Vincent Van Gogh would scoop the paint off the palette and put it directly on the canvas, I didn't want to stand around. I wanted it fast. I wanted it immediate. And I like the abstract expressionists for that, that direct whip or whatever. Since the first time that I got a tube of white paint I've been painting on boxes. They're all over the place. When I hang them they all become one in a big grid. Not that one of them can't be a little painting by itself.

No matter where you are there's always somebody that's well read or who's got a good head on his shoulders or loves whatever he does – the writing, painting, sculpture – passionately. I wish I would have already gone to New York, even if it was just to stay a few months and see some of the great collections. I'm buried here. I've got to figure out some way to do it before I die, that's all there is to it. It's precious; every damned minute.

In the daytime, when I'm running catalogues at the book store, I dream of painting. That's bad because I'm burnt out by the time I get home. Sometimes I get up in the morning and I'm so damned hungry to paint I'm tempted to call up and say I'm not coming in, but I never do that. I honor the job. I feel I'm so damned lucky to have the job. All book clerks have to do is not insult the public. The onslaught of the public is relentless. I mean there are so many dumb idiots out there who are almost incompetent, incapable of functioning as anything even close to something civilized. You have to bite your tongue sometimes. That's good training. I really think it's good training.

I make the art because I think I'm being civilized. I think it's a civilized act; wonderful people do it. Horrible ones do it too, but I think more wonderful people do it than the terribles. I think artists are so essential. I think they'll help keep things ethical and civilized, though there's an edge to artists now like there never has been before as to ambition and succeeding. I think it's probably essential now that you have that kind of drive.

In a *Paris Review* interview Hemingway said, "The most essential gift for a good writer is a built-in, shock-proof shit detector. This is the writer's radar and all great writers have had it." This goes for artists too. They need to get one as soon as possible. Not only for other works they're looking at, but their own work. Get the crap out of it! These kids around here haven't acquired that. Not even the curators have acquired it. What a privilege to be able to do that. To have a healthy one.

You've got to fight to do the best paintings you can do. Doing art keeps me sane, it keeps me pretty sane. I wanted to open up a book store because I failed at the art. To move as fast as I'd want to move with it, I'd be doing fifteen, twenty-five foot paintings at least, but this is better than nothing. I haven't been cunning enough.

Humor helps a lot, it's essential. And there are funny, strange, horrific things going on. Sometimes you can laugh at them. Luckily I do more laughing than crying, though I'm a griper. I'm always bitching and griping and the only thing you do is get up and go out there and go do it and stop griping. I'm constantly saying here's another border town, here we are deader than a door nail, there's no commitment with the collectors, they're babies, they've gotta be told what to do. Most of the gallery dealers are all fashion moda, they're riding the rails, riding the bandwagon.

But some things excite me immensely. There's always another book to read. I enjoy the painting. The last few nights I've been drawing; it's really going well. I've got a lot of energy. Yeah, I'm still hungry. I think if I were a boxer my face would be really beat up, but I'd still be in there swinging. But it would really show.

SELECTED BIOGRAPHY

BIRTHPLACE

Long Beach, California

SOLO EXHIBITIONS

University of California, Santa Barbara, 1978
La Jolla Museum of Contemporary Art, 1960 and 1965
Santa Barbara Contemporary Art Forum, Santa Barbara, CA, 1984
Quint Gallery, San Diego, 1983 and 1984
Retrospective and New Work, Mandeville Gallery, UCSD and La Jolla Museum of Contemporary Art Downtown, 1988

GROUP EXHIIBITIONS

Los Angeles County Museum of Art, 1960
San Francisco Museum of Art, 1961 and 1962
Los Angeles Institute of Contemporary Art, 1975
Newspace Gallery, Los Angeles, 1978
University of California, Santa Barbara, 1986

COLLECTIONS

La Jolla Museum of Contemporary Art
Southwestern College, Chula Vista, California
Palomar College, San Marcos, California
Robert McDonald, Santa Clara, California
John Baldessari, Los Angeles

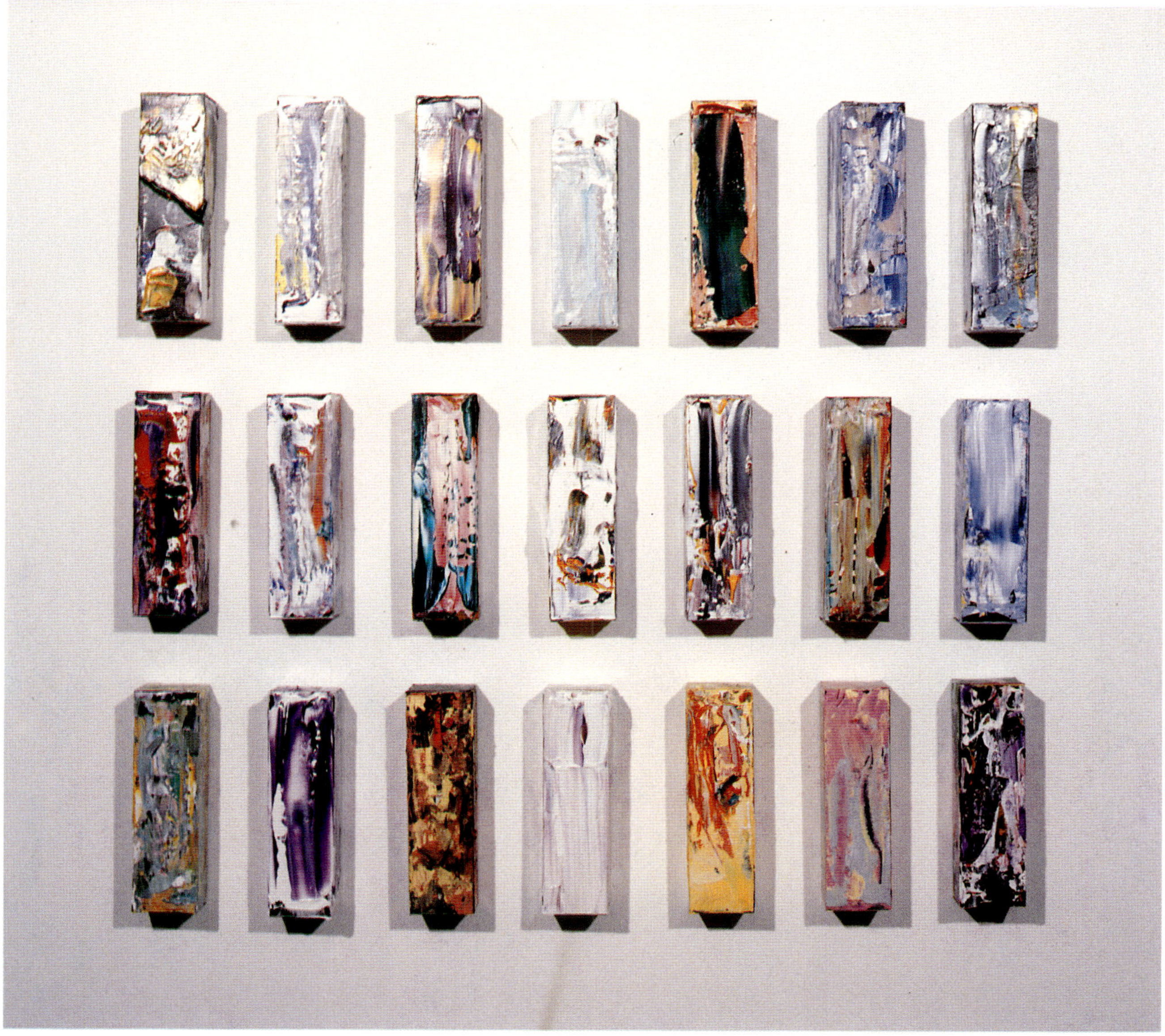

Aggregation, each unit 6½″×2″×2″, 1986

Ming Murray

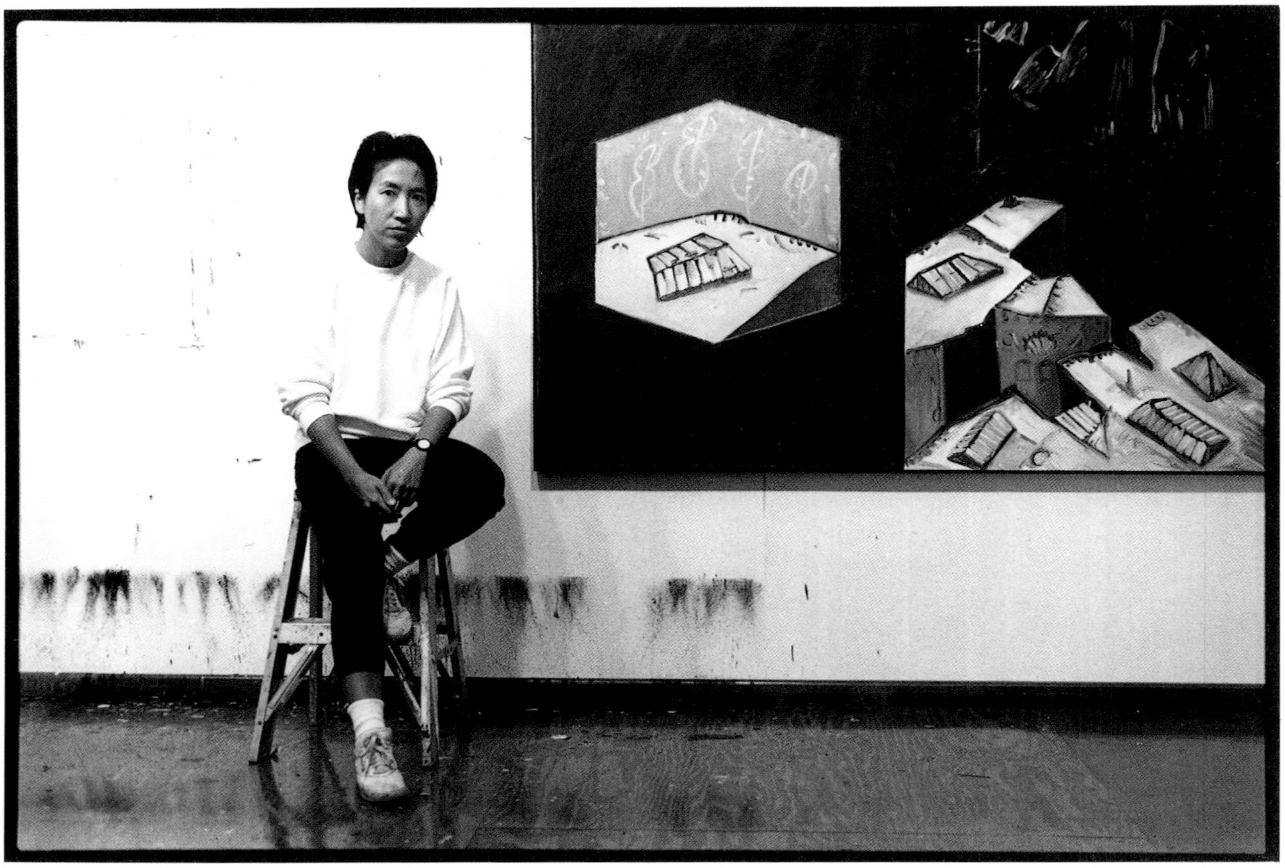

Sometimes I won't be working and suddenly I see in front of me a whole new theme for my work. . . . I take a theme all the way till I exhaust it.

Dark umber papers and canvases delineate Ming Murray's studio as private territory in a life that is otherwise richly filled with people and things. With a thrust that is direct and focused, she has maintained an individual artistic style through personal crises, radical change, and a mix of cultures. Growing through these changes and transitions in her art has meant the kind of adjustments that are both internal and external.

The mood of her paintings ranges from anxious to somber, reflecting a certain angst and alienation. Whether she is painting rooftop scenes or great splits between mountains, she sees life from an unusual perspective, offering up a world of strong colors and contrasts in her unique observance of the human's place in our environment.

Murray is one of four girls and a boy raised by her mother, her father who was a government engineer, and by a lifelong servant named King Goo. To balance the child's Catholic education, King Goo introduced Murray to Buddhist temples and taught her about Gautama and enlightenment.

After the sudden accidental death of her first husband, Murray moved with her small daughter Nicole to New York where she would be near a community of her friends from Hong Kong. She eventually met and married J. Robert Orton, Jr., a social psychologist, international businessman, and art collector. They live in their La Jolla estate and Murray often commutes to her Greene Street studio in New York.

I always loved New York. I moved there with my daughter and I had many friends from Hong Kong who had gone there after graduate school. The first place we lived was a storefront on the ground floor around Chinatown and Little Italy. I had to look up to see everything. The second space was on the eighth story, then the sixth story. I saw all the rooftops around me. One day I pulled a table over and started sketching.

Living in New York is different from visiting. There's a certain grimness about Lower Manhattan. You really feel a certain desperation and that's what I began to portray, the struggle between man and his environment, the color of things – grey, shocking green, purple. Then the work evolved, became more subtle and relaxed, more like observing the image. I did a series of studies on rooftops, antennas, smokestacks, the water tower, all in jagged edges, without people. Those things took the place of people. They became animated, they moved in certain ways.

I visit a lot of rooftops with my friend Ching Ming who is a photographer. We will walk past Chinatown and we'll feel which door is open and if it happens to be open we'll go all the way to the top. She accompanies me. I need someone to go with me. Of course in the Chinatown area you have ducks hanging to dry, rows of these things, and vegetables drying in lines, but then you get a feel of these places which are really bizarre. You start observing from one point to other places. I go to friends. They have a space they can use on the roof, to have dinner there, or a cook out or something. But just the feeling is absolutely different versus looking at it. It's so quiet. They could be raising hell down there but there is something so quiet about being on top. Ching Ming will shoot some pictures of me and I will shoot some pictures of her and we'll shoot around the environment and just go on and on, gather so much material. It's a different feeling when you're on it.

I start thinking of the secrecy and privacy of one's life within these areas above the city, the hustle and violence. It's like a mountain over everything that's going on, this little peaceful area that exists. I will paint the roof top cityscape with nobody, but with a more harmonious feeling; the color is warmer, still there's sort of that animation of things that are going on, the antennas, yet it's quite peaceful.

After that series of work, I was going home. I went to Japan first, then Hong Kong for four weeks. My mother and father had been to China several times but I never had. We have no family left there and I wanted to go, so my parents, my daughter, and other family members made the trip.

We went to Kweilin which is where the Chinese painting influence mainly came from. Straight up and down mountains, just stunning. I never felt just so overwhelmed. I could not take photographs. I felt a certain silence with my father that I've never experienced before. There was some kind of departure. We came back to Hong Kong on a Thursday and on Monday in a shopping center he died. Something very symbolic happened in Kweilin. This was last summer. It really made a big impact on me.

I knew Kweilin was going to affect my work. I was putting the mountains and urban scene together. Even in a place like Kweilin there are certain environmental changes because of the people spreading. There are new buildings in the middle of this. It is so awful to see such solid geometric shapes and in the background is this fluid, beautiful scene.

Urban relics are my latest theme. Subconsciously a theme develops. Sometimes I won't be working and suddenly I see in front of me a whole new theme for my work. I'm now zooming down to one image at a time. I take a theme all the way till I exhaust it.

Bob collects art and it has enriched my life as an artist seeing his interest through his eyes. I guess vice versa in a way too, the myth of the artist and then the reality sinks in. I think the part he didn't know is the roller coaster emotions that one can get involved in going through the struggling stage. He says it's impossible to live with. And he had to also learn that there's a certain privacy and a distance that he has to keep from one's working place.

I do the work in New York as well as La Jolla. I gather information there, draw instead of paint. The work in New York is on a whole different energy level, you're zapped by all these things. It's like running into the wall – sock – and you get this zap of electricity running through you.

SELECTED EXHIBITIONS

BIRTHPLACE

Hong Kong

EDUCATION

Columbus College of Art and Design, Ohio, BFA, 1976
University of Cincinnati, MFA, 1979

SOLO EXHIBITIONS

The Contemporary Arts Center, Cincinnati, 1981
Zolla/Lieberman Gallery, Chicago, 1983
Turnbull Lutjeans Kogan Gallery, Costa Mesa, California, 1985
Alliance Francaise de Hong Kong, 1987
Quint Gallery, San Diego, 1987

GROUP EXHIBITIONS

"Ohio Selections II," New Gallery of Contemporary Arts, Cleveland, 1982
Barbara Toll Fine Arts, New York, 1984
"Recent Acquisitions," Guggenheim Museum, New York, 1985
Cincinnati Art Museum, OH, 1984 and 1986
"New Faces," curated by Robert McDonald, Shoshana Wayne Gallery, Los Angeles, 1986

COLLECTIONS

Solomon R. Guggenheim Museum, New York
Chicago Art Institute
Cincinnati Art Museum
Laguna Art Museum, Laguna Beach
Chemical Bank, New York

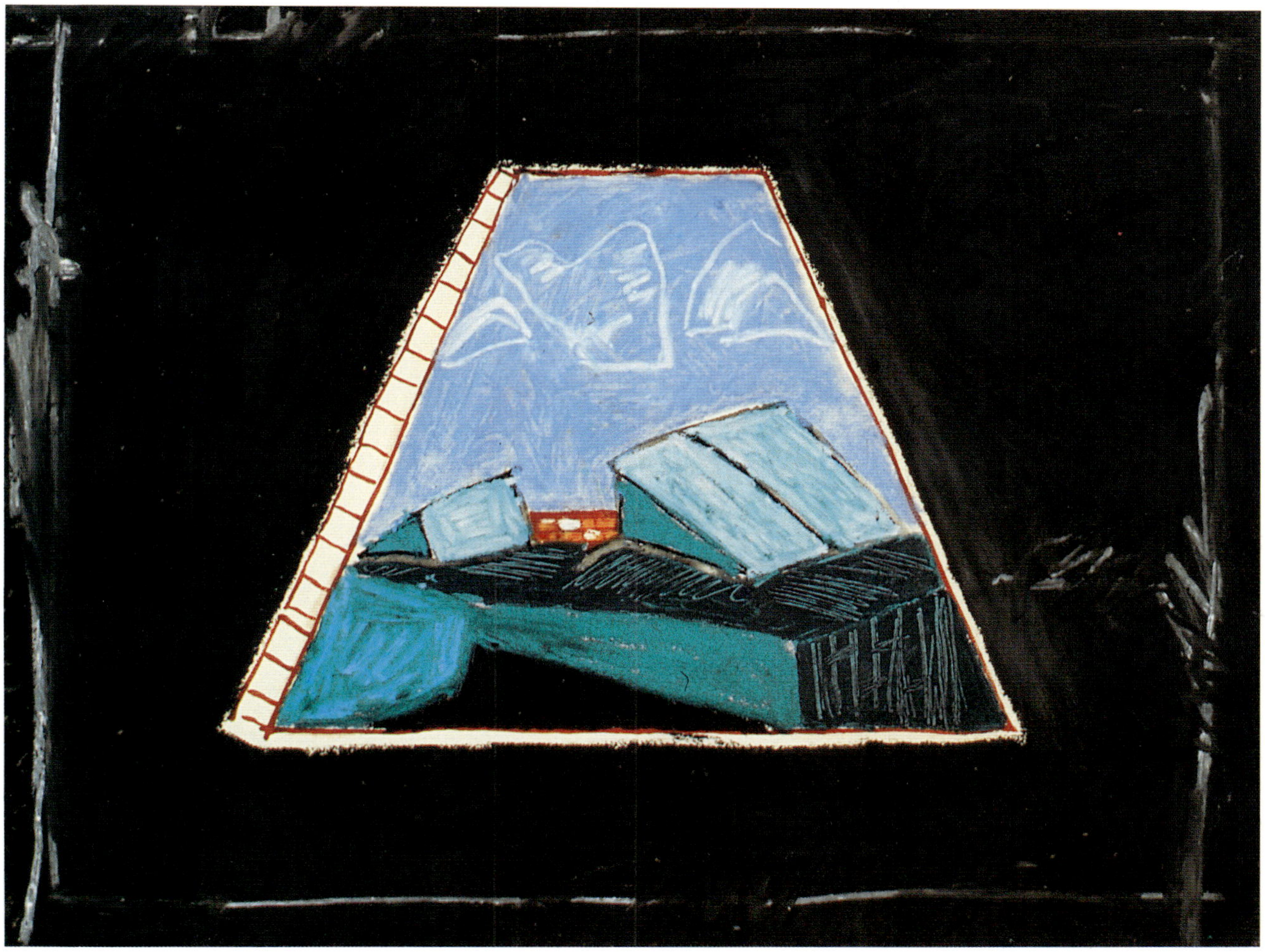

Passing Thought, oil stick and pastel on paper, 39.5×52 cm., 1987

Marjorie Nodelman

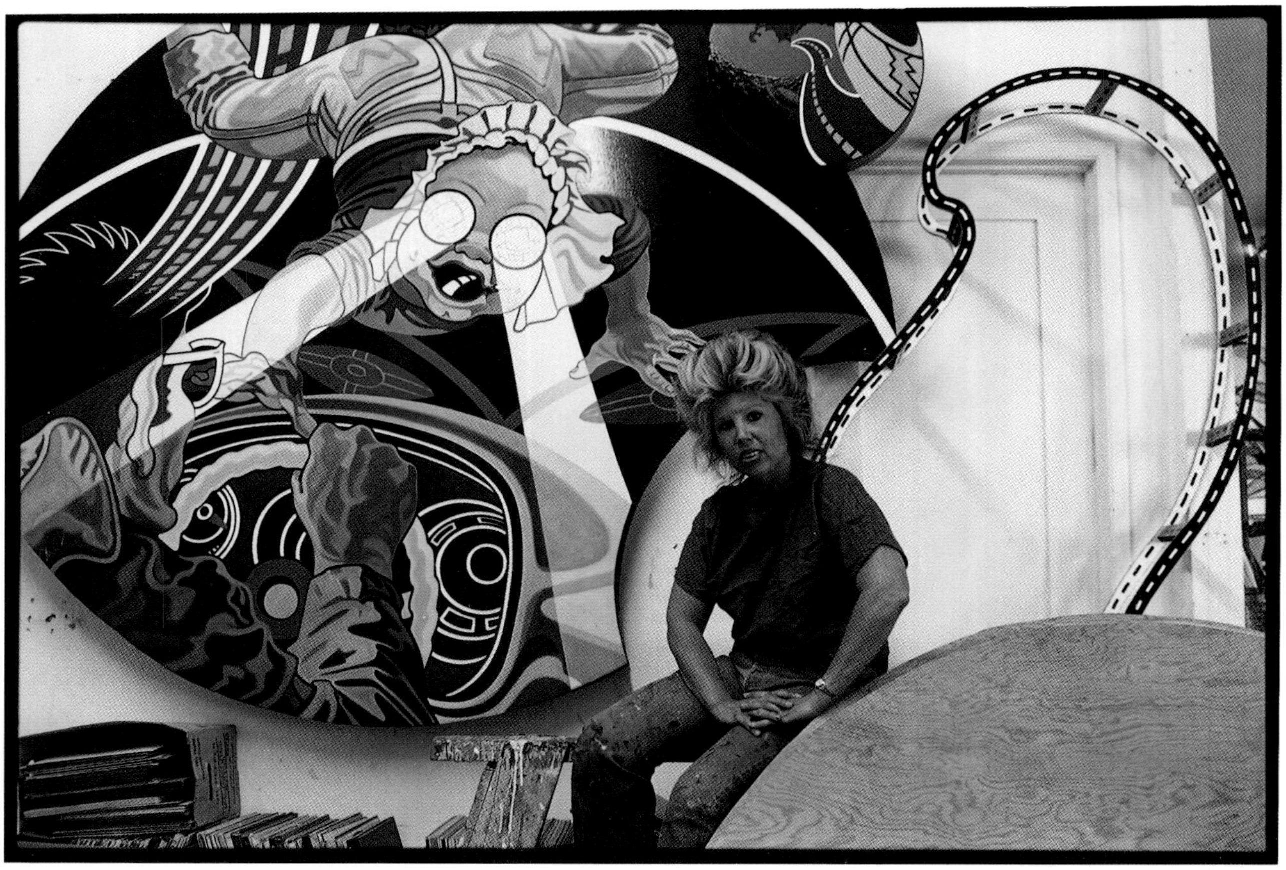

. . . there are moments where there's nothing that's more satisfying and orgasmic than having an image just come alive and nothing else matters.

In a sprawling art studio over a drug store in Ocean Beach, Marjorie Nodelman's eight foot diameter canvases lean against walls and windows. With her waist-length blond hair piled on top of her head, wearing snuggly-fitting jeans, she is at once articulate and expressive. The words flow rapidly as she describes her work with a mixture of humor, intensity, and bravado.

Since she arrived here from Yale University in 1975, Nodelman has been a voice in the San Diego art community, helping organize and house alternative space exhibitions, the kind that jar art world traditionalists and heighten public awareness of new art.

While Nodelman's past themes were done in a unique blend of Mannerism and Captain-Marvel-comic-book linearity, she is currently exploring a combination of Cubist and Futurist elements. Portraits and paintings of highways, military settings, and cockpits are all painted with a sense of centrifugal and centripetal force that moves the images in and out of their circular confines.

Nodelman was raised in an artistic environment with a younger sister – a designer – by a mother who taught art in the public schools and a professor father who taught French Literature at Villanova University. Nodelman continues to be nourished artistically by an enduring friendship with former husband, and UCSD art historian, Sheldon Nodelman, whom she met at Yale.

Wanderlust keeps coming up for me as an underlying theme. The road is my iconography for the desire to be somewhere else, the desire to look just around the corner or that expectation that there's something just waiting right over the hill if you can only get to it. My fascination with the car and maybe even my inertia about learning to drive had to do with this. The car is the metaphor you use to go after things. When I started driving last year, I was trying to memorize the landscape. You know when you're riding shotgun you get to look at everything, but when you drive and enjoy the scenery too much you're in trouble. I was recently driving to Julian through the nearby mountains and I was looking out of all my mirrors at once. The sideview mirror, the rear view mirror, out the window, constantly looking around and all these wonderful vistas were curling like film strips in different directions. I know this sounds dangerous. It was, particularly because I'm not such a great driver yet. It was very exciting like a fourth dimensional take on landscape where various spaces are all appearing at the same time, so you can experience over there and over there all at once. I think it has a lot to do with my use of the circle. So far my paintings have had a single point of view, but driving instead of riding will definitely change this.

Wanderlust is also the desire to be fulfilled, satisfied, happy. To have something new, something just around the bend. It fits in with my three divorces, new studios, new adventures. I use machines, pre-electronic machinery, in my work. I did some paintings about acceleration and speed, about life flying by and you're sort of hit with all these events that go by before you can decide what they mean. This kind of acceleration on life as you get older was what I wanted to get across in my latest paintings. This is why they had these melting lozenge-shaped bits, almost like the visual equivalent of the Doppler effect.

I first started using circular canvases, tondos, when I was at Yale in grad school in 1974. I found a window frame. It was big. I was in New York City and I saw this thing in the street in four sections. It was the coolest thing, this wooden inset of a window that somebody had thrown away. I took it all the way back to New Haven. I literally shlepped it, dragging it, and I thought it would make a great stretcher. I put it together, put canvas on it, and it became the most exciting thing to design in a circle. I always used curvilinear lines anyway and it just felt great. There was always something a little upsetting about a rectangle. I couldn't design around the corners. It had too many straight edges. The circle has a certain stability to it, a certain grace.

I will always use the circle. I broke away from it for a while. I used ovals, ellipses, commas, all kinds of subcircular or curvilinear shapes. I think those work best when they're in between pieces. They function as punctuations. But the circle itself draws you in, you can fixate on it. I've never painted a mandala, but I would say that all paintings are mandalas in a way.

Everybody tells me art is a profession for rich people and yet I'm still insisting on this. It's obviously very crazy on my part. But there are moments where there's nothing that's more satisfying and orgasmic than having an image just come alive and nothing else matters.

It's asking a lot to ask other people to look at your particular neurosis or your vision of the world. It's also presumptuous to think that what you have to show them is interesting. At the same time you almost have to do it. It's not that I don't think every three months that it's time to stop and apply to law school. I think about that too. But if I couldn't even do research in art history, I can imagine just how long I'd sit in a law library.

SELECTED BIOGRAPHY

BIRTHPLACE

Philadelphia

EDUCATION

Philadelphia College of Art, PA, BFA, 1973
Yale University, New Haven, MFA, 1975

SOLO EXHIBITIONS

Floating Wall Gallery, Santa Ana, California, 1977
"Military Industrial Complex," 1979; "Solo," 1980; "Night Train," 1982, Newspace, Los Angeles
"Soldier of Fortune," 552 Gallery, San Diego, 1983
Anuska Gallery, San Diego, 1987

GROUP EXHIBITIONS

"Artists as Social Critics," curated by Josine Ianco Starrels, Los Angeles Municipal Art Gallery, 1979
Los Angeles Institute of Contemporary Art, 1982
"LAVA," (Los Angeles Visual Artists) Stella Polaris, Los Angeles, 1985
"16 x 26," Quint Gallery, San Diego, 1985
"Allegory and Symbolism," curated by Brent Riggs, Mandeville Gallery, University of California, San Diego, 1986

GRANTS

California Arts Council, Individual Artist grant

COLLECTIONS

J. Patrick Lannan Foundation Museum, Fort Worth
Harcourt Brace Jovanovich, San Diego
Oliver McMillan, Inc., La Jolla
Douglas Simay, M.D., San Diego
Marie and Merrel Olesen, M.D., La Jolla

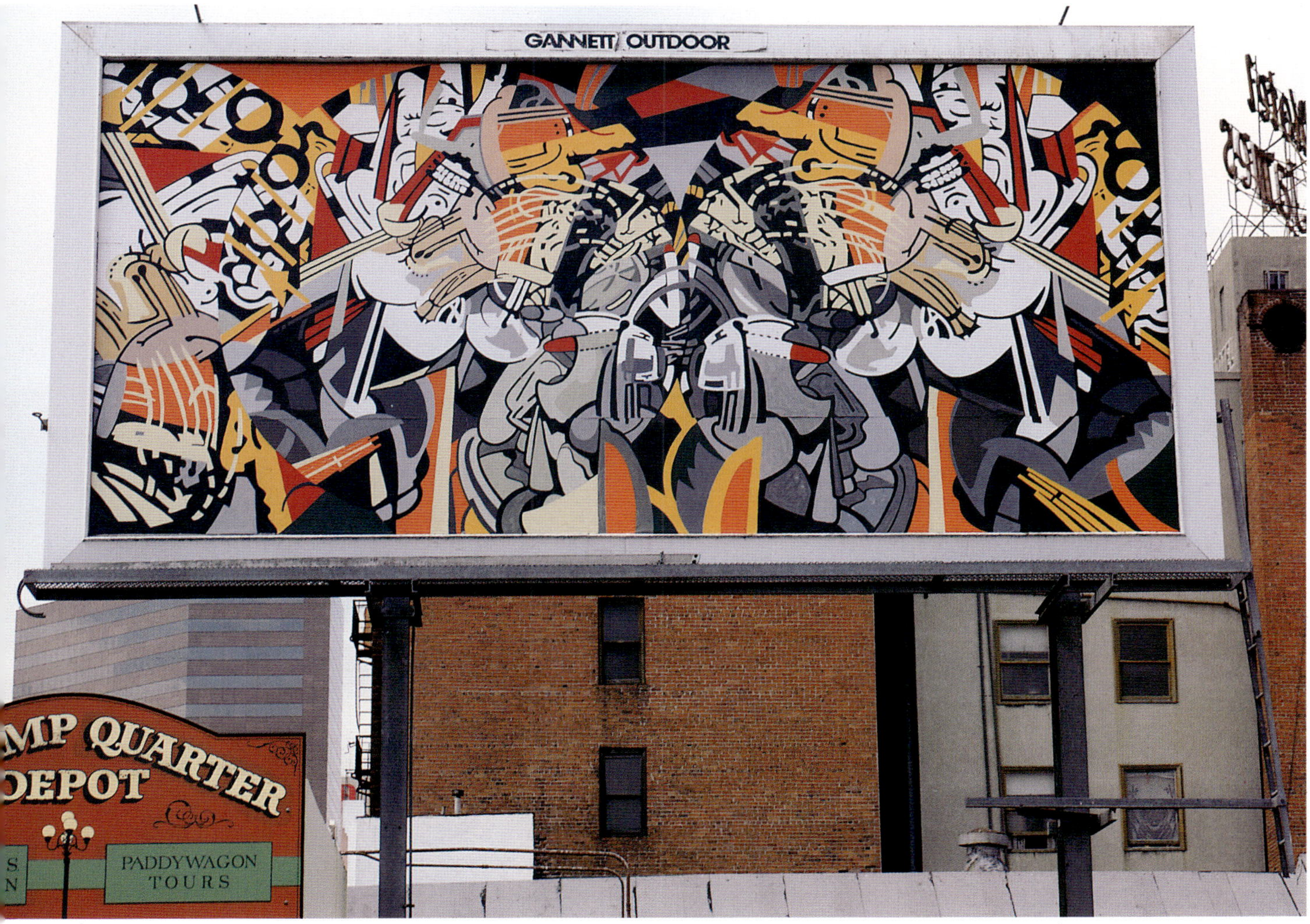

Cubist Pepboys Billboard, oil/paper billboard, 10′×24′, 1987

Photo by Robert Perine

Arthur Ollman

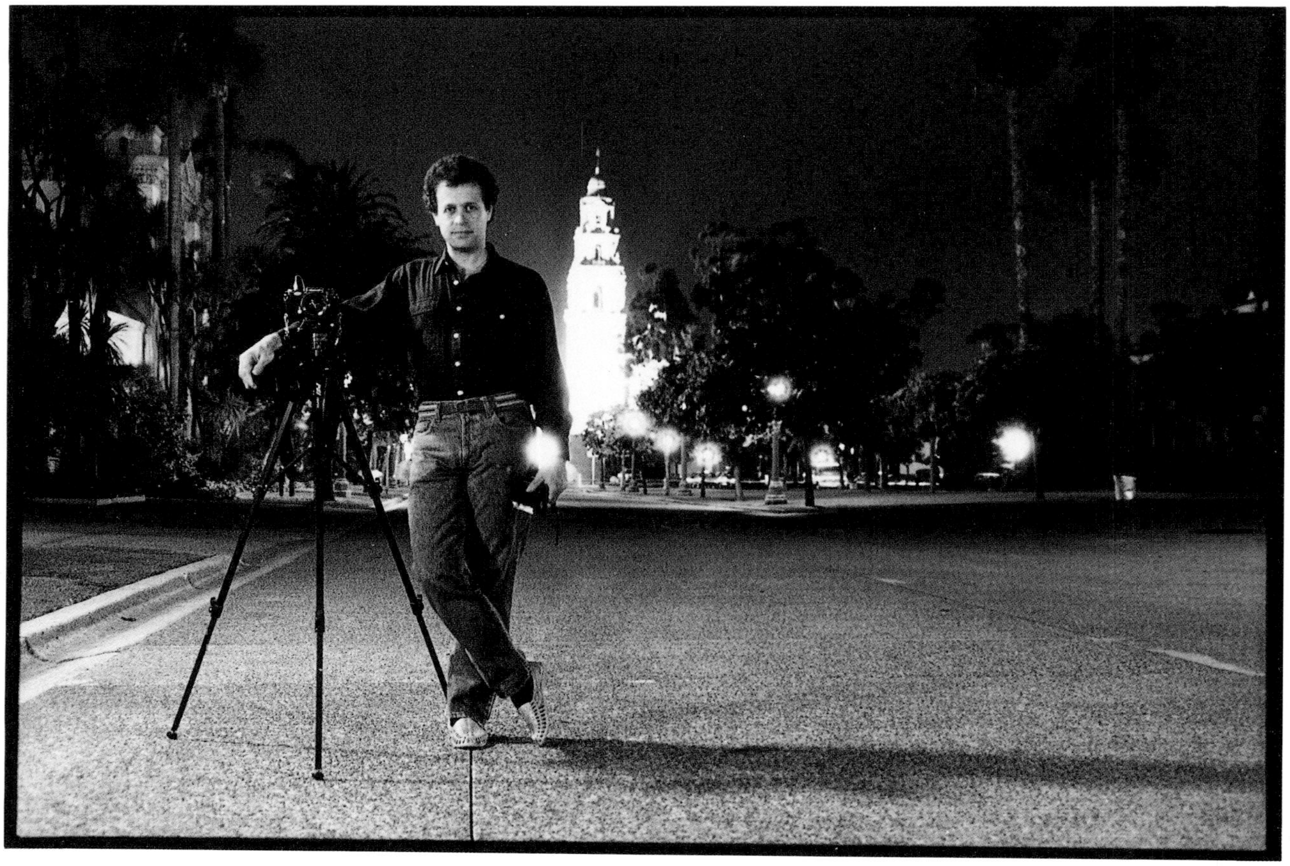

I think a lot of art comes from mutations, the things you don't expect that intrigue you about your work. I love to pick up those threads.

In his director's office in the white-walled contemporary space of the Museum of Photographic Arts in Balboa Park, Arthur Ollman admits to the difficulty of spending as much time on his art as he did when establishing himself as a prominent artist/photographer. Yet his observations of his current life as an administrator remain those of an artist in search of new material. Since 1969, in addition to following earlier themes, he has been photographing senior photographers such as Max Yavno, Arnold Newman, and Ansel Adams, having maintained close contact with them through curating exhibitions of their photographs.

Adamant about the need for artists to contribute to art beyond their own work, Ollman was a founder in 1976 of Camerawork Gallery in San Francisco and later president of the board of directors. Since coming to San Diego he has curated and written extensively on fine art photography and his night photographs have been included in numerous books on contemporary color photography and California photographers.

Ollman and his two brothers, a poet and a musician-turned-stockbroker, were raised by his mother and a writer/father. He decided to become an artist at six years of age. He is married to Leah Goldman Ollman, a writer on the arts.

My works that are best known and collected by major museums are all night explorations of urban environments in various parts of the world. I worked outdoors late at night in many cities doing very long exposures. I feel that the vulnerability was very useful to me – being open to what I'm experiencing. An artist has to be vulnerable to his perceptions. Sometimes that takes the very concrete form of being physically vulnerable.

I've never had to run for my life, never had my camera stolen, fortunately. Certain places are more trouble than others but sometimes there's not much you can do. I was arrested in Marrakesh, for photographing late at night in the Casbah and had a very difficult time talking my way through that since I don't speak Arabic and my French is frail and they didn't speak English. They didn't want to believe I was just photographing at night. They had seen photographers running around there but had never seen one do that before. More often it's the police rather than the drunks that make the trouble. But the most dangerous thing is not that I might get beat up at night, it's that I might not be included in a major show.

Ever since I picked up a camera I was interested in night. I've always liked night. Maybe I prefer to sleep during the day. It's a circadian rhythm I guess. But the first role of film I ever made when I was sixteen or seventeen had a night exposure or two on it. It's what I was most excited by. It's been one of the consecutive themes in my work.

Doing the night photographs was building up a lot of tension, just physical tension about being in tough places and so I moved to working interiors. One of the reasons I worked interiors was related to the fact that while shooting at night I would also come inside to warm up after a long time outside or to change a role of film. I'd come into a bar or restaurant or hotel and have two shots left on a role of film and rather than wait I would shoot them off inside, change the film and go back out. Over the years I'd look at the ends of a bunch of rolls of film and there were dozens of these pictures, some of which I was really intrigued by. I began to follow that mutation from my original intent. I think a lot of art comes from mutations, the things you don't expect that intrigue you about your work. I love to pick up those threads.

As a museum director I've got a lot of entertaining I'm supposed to do, taking people out, visiting guests at hotels. I've gotten intrigued by the artificiality of these places, the way people inhabit the space and behave in public. People will go to a restaurant and behave as though they were invisible, be seen with people who they should not be seen with, behave in indiscreet ways. You can see this drama taking place because it seems they're in a romantic little nook and meanwhile people are going by. There's a lot of danger. Some of that is interesting to watch, people behaving or misbehaving in public. I'm enjoying the theater of it, I feel like a moviemaker.

So some of my pictures – because they're shot in dim interiors – might be ten seconds long instead of the half hour exposure needed to make outdoor photographs at night. Ten seconds with a little bit of movement looks more active than did half an hour on a tripod when the building involved didn't move. It's more hit and run. I can shoot a whole role of film in a night. I'm more spontaneous. I can sit and order a drink, set my camera on the table and make pictures of everything that goes on around me. Certainly I'm more relaxed than standing in the shadows between a couple of buildings in a tough neighborhood. And the results are interesting. There's a lot of pretense out there. People are in a theater. They all behave as though they were actors, so I enjoy that.

I'm convinced of the necessity of artists giving something back to their scene. Good poets never expect to earn any money. I don't know of any poets who just do their poetry. They also do anthologies, journals, newsletters, teach, run readings, run a small press.

I've always liked to get a couple of people together and make something happen, but I never expected to wear a tie and sit down at a desk. My friends from other parts of my life see me with a tie on sitting behind a desk and they think it's funny. I'm not worried about the threads, that doesn't matter much. I'm more interested in what can be done and I find more and more colleagues feel the same way.

We used to get an alternative space for a hundred bucks a month, put up art, and people would come. That was good at a certain time. But now we're all thinking about insurance and electricity and how to raise money to pay bills and give honorariums to artists and make the program interesting and make sure the staff is well paid and happy and the public educated and the best facility available when people come here. There are a lot of other interests and concerns but I don't think that has anything to do with what we learned at art school.

SELECTED BIOGRAPHY

BIRTHPLACE

Milwaukee, Wisconsin

EDUCATION

University of Wisconsin, Madison, BA in Art History, 1969
San Francisco Art Institute, 1974
Lone Mountain College, San Francisco, MFA, 1977

SOLO EXHIBITIONS

Grapestake Gallery, San Francisco, 1979
Centre Georges Pompidou, Musee National D'Art et De Culture (Beaubourg), Paris, 1979
Institute of Contemporary Arts, Boston, 1984
Michelle Chomette Gallery, Paris, 1988
"Arthur Ollman, Night," Kodak Gallery, travelling to Tokyo and Osaka, Japan, 1988

GROUP EXHIBITIONS

"Mirrors and Windows, American Photography Since 1960," Museum of Modern Art, New York, 1978
Biennial, Whitney Museum of American Art, New York, 1981
"Beyond Color," 1980; "New Acquisitions," 1982; "California Photography, 1945 to 1980," San Francisco Museum of Modern Art, 1984
"Nouvelle Coleur Straight," Paris Art Center, 1984
"Three Photographers," curated by Walter Cotten, travelling exhibition in Shanghai and Hangzhou, 1987

GRANTS

National Endowment for the Arts, Artists Fellowship and two research grants
California Arts Council, Special Projects grant

PUBLICATIONS

Samuel Bourne: Images of India, Friends of Photography, Carmel, 1983
Arnold Newman: Five Decades, Harcourt Brace Jovanovich, San Diego, 1986

COLLECTIONS

Metropolitan Museum of Art, New York
Museum of Modern Art, New York
Centre Georges Pompidou (Beaubourg), Paris
San Francisco Museum of Modern Art
Los Angeles County Museum of Art

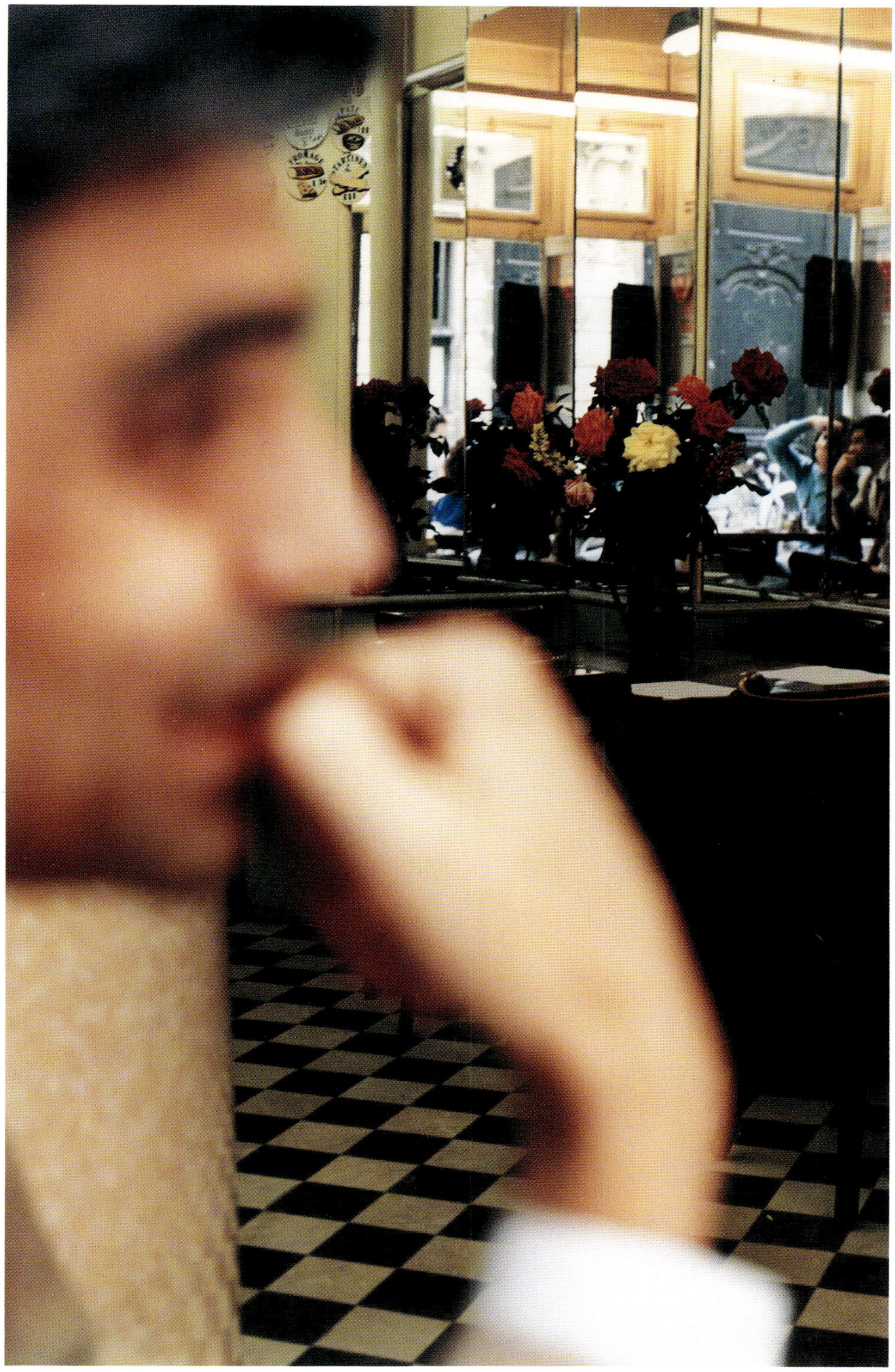

Photographer Bernard Plossu, Paris, Ektacolor print, 16"×20", 1986

Patricia Patterson

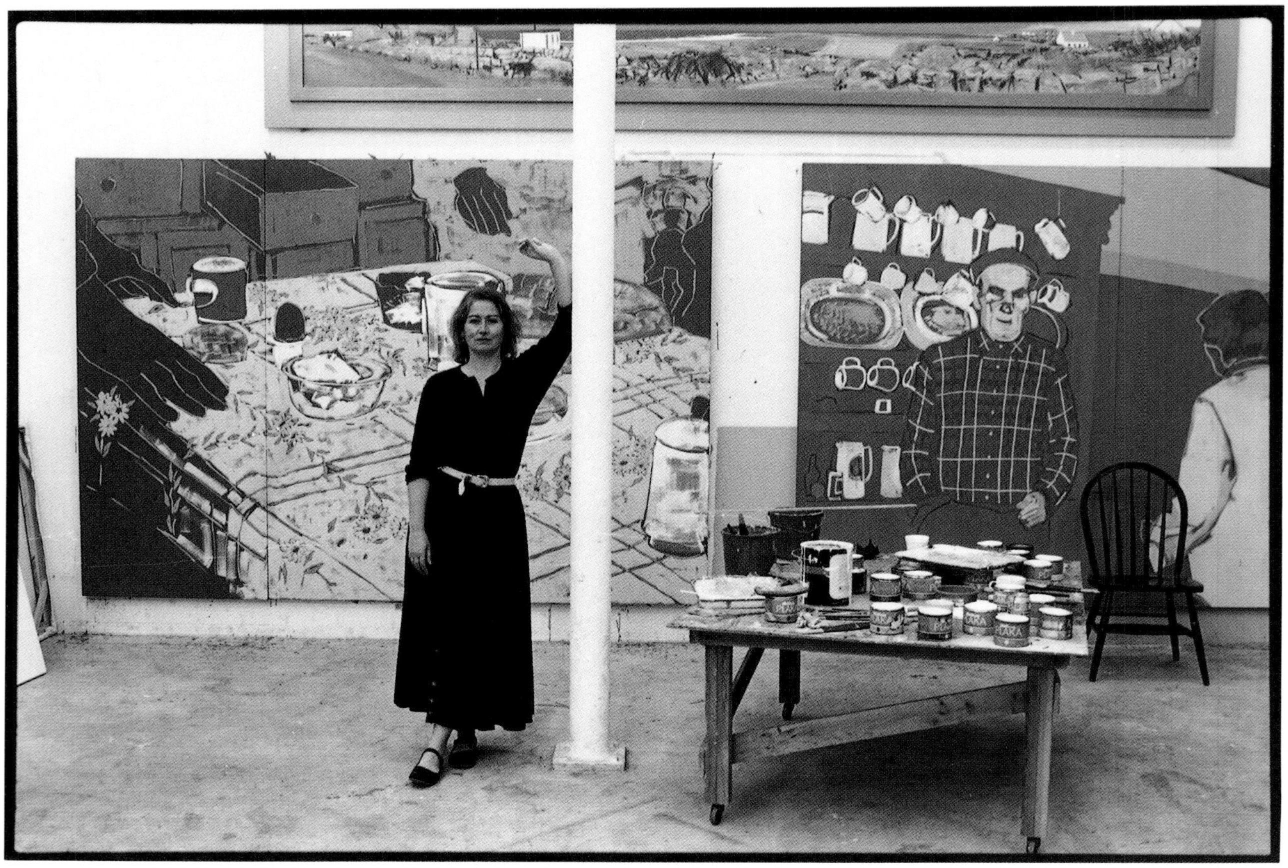

*I can't imagine not doing art . . .
life moves so fast that to make
things or objects slows it down
and puts a frame on something,
makes it concrete so that it
doesn't disappear.*

In her Water Tank studio at UCSD brightly colored frame samples hang from the edge of a stairway leading to a loft full of props. Paintings in progress stretch across two long walls. Patricia Patterson, dressed all in black, is as reticent and quiet as her work is sure and bold.

Her best known paintings and installations have been inextricably linked to her intimate perception and experience of the Aran Islands of Ireland, more specifically the village of Kilmurvey where her friends live. Patterson brings a fresh approach to these works, is sensitive to the color and space. As she expands her insights into cultural nuance and pinpoints the poignant subtleties of human interaction, these works continue to reflect that ambience.

Patterson grew up with two sisters in an Irish-American family which extended to twenty-eight first cousins, all of whom were in the same parish and with whom she attended Catholic schools. She is the only artist. After hearing endless tales about the Aran Islands during her childhood, she first visited there in 1960. She lives in Leucadia with her husband, artist Manny Farber. She collaborated with Farber on film reviews during the mid-1970s.

When I went to live on the island of Aran for two years there were a lot of problems with everyday life, keeping the fire going being the biggest one. Cóilín and his wife Nan helped me and I got to be very close and eventually moved in with them. A few years later I got to know Pat, his wife Mary, and their dog Jigs and we've been close friends ever since.

Manny has never gone. Never. In the beginning it was because he wasn't interested, but now I really insist on going alone because it's such a very intense experience and I have such a long history there I have enough to handle without him being there too. If you bring someone else into a situation it interrupts the whole balance.

I did an installation at the Los Angeles County Museum of Art called "Here and There, Back and Forth" that gives the sense of being an American artist living in California but making a lot of work about another culture. I'm really part of both and go back and forth between them. The whole piece was based on the contrast between two worlds which are so opposite. In Ireland you're right by the water but no one goes swimming. They fish but no one knows how to swim and it would never occur to them to consider the water as having anything to do with recreation. Here, of course, it's so much the opposite. Surfing, sunning, and swimming and the relation to the ocean is profoundly other. People in Ireland drink and smoke a lot and when they get sick the first thing they think of is to go to the pub and get some whiskey to cure a cold, a hot whiskey. That's unthinkable here. If you get sick you take herbal teas, you don't take whiskey. Californians have such a conviction that they live the right way, but so do the Irish. I find that very humorous to go back and forth between these two worlds and also find it very exciting material.

I listen to a lot of lyrics out of rock music while I work and lyrics out of very old traditional Irish songs. I like the contrast between them. I'm very involved in rock music. I listen to the Talking Heads and lately to a lot of African music, King Sunny Ade and Toure Kunda. I want to do some kind of work on paintings of rock musicians. I don't know any. I don't think I want to know them. I also listen to a lot of very old seventeenth and eighteenth century Irish songs that are sung partly in the English language, partly in Irish.

When I was starting out I was working with quite small figures, small paintings. In all large paintings you're actually surrounded by a field of color and I thing that makes for a greater intimacy and warmth. That kind of relation of your own physical body to the painting is very strong. The one of Pat in the Kitchen is almost the size of the kitchen. You feel what it would be like to be in that room.

Basically I used these four people, Cóilin, Nan, Pat, and Mary, and the elements of the houses for my installations. I had the stove and other elements built as a very exact copy. In the exhibits all the people in the paintings are at the same eye level as the people in the room viewing them. I want to have movement throughout the room that would be from person to person and the color elements tie it in.

There's a kind of literalness in color that I like very much, the idea of red reading very much as red – pure red – and not being cut by the illusion of the painting. I like the idea of having solid green and solid red, and it also works kinetically to move the eye around the room.

I certainly didn't have a real sense of color in any art work I did in my early years. All the emphasis was on drawing and on tone and modeling. Actually, about ten years ago I started gardening and looking at the colors in flowers – the pure color – and I fell in love with that and wanted to use that kind of color. Also they use color incredibly in Ireland, really powerful color almost like in Mexico. In Ireland the color is not outside on the austere white buildings and slate roofs, but inside. There's one color on the upper part of the wall and often a whitewash from waist level down. Usually the brightest colors are used in the woodwork and on things like tables. The floors also have two strong colors of tile that goes up behind the stove for splatter.

I can't imagine not doing art. I think it makes sense out of things that don't necessarily make sense otherwise. Also life moves so fast that to make things or objects slows it down and puts a frame on something, makes it concrete so that it doesn't disappear.

SELECTED BIOGRAPHY

BIRTHPLACE

Jersey City, New Jersey

EDUCATION

Parsons School of Design, New York, certificate, 1961

TEACHING

University of California, San Diego, 1973 to present

SOLO EXHIBITIONS

"Five Views of Cill Mhuirbigh (Kilmurvey)," installation, Nancy Lurie Gallery, Chicago, 1980
"The Rabbit and the Kiss," curated by Grant Holcomb III, San Diego Museum of Art, 1983
Tibor de Nagy Gallery, New York, 1984
"Itinerant Painter," University of Texas, Arlington, 1986
Newspace, Los Angeles, 1983, 1985 and 1986

GROUP EXHIBITIONS

"Autogeography," Whitney Museum of American Art, New York, 1975
"Proscenium," installation, curated by Anna Heis, P.S. 1, sponsored by The Institute for Art and Urban Resources, Long Island, NY, 1978
"3:1," curated by Barry Rosen, Tibor de Nagy Gallery, New York, 1982
"Setting the Stage," installation, Los Angeles County Museum of Art, 1985
"California Genre Painters," travelling exhibition, Laguna Art Museum, CA, 1988 through 1990

COLLECTIONS

Northern Trust Bank, Chicago
Eli Broad, Los Angeles
Stan and Theodora Cornyn, Los Angeles
Douglas Simay, M.D., San Diego
Richard Weston, Los Angeles

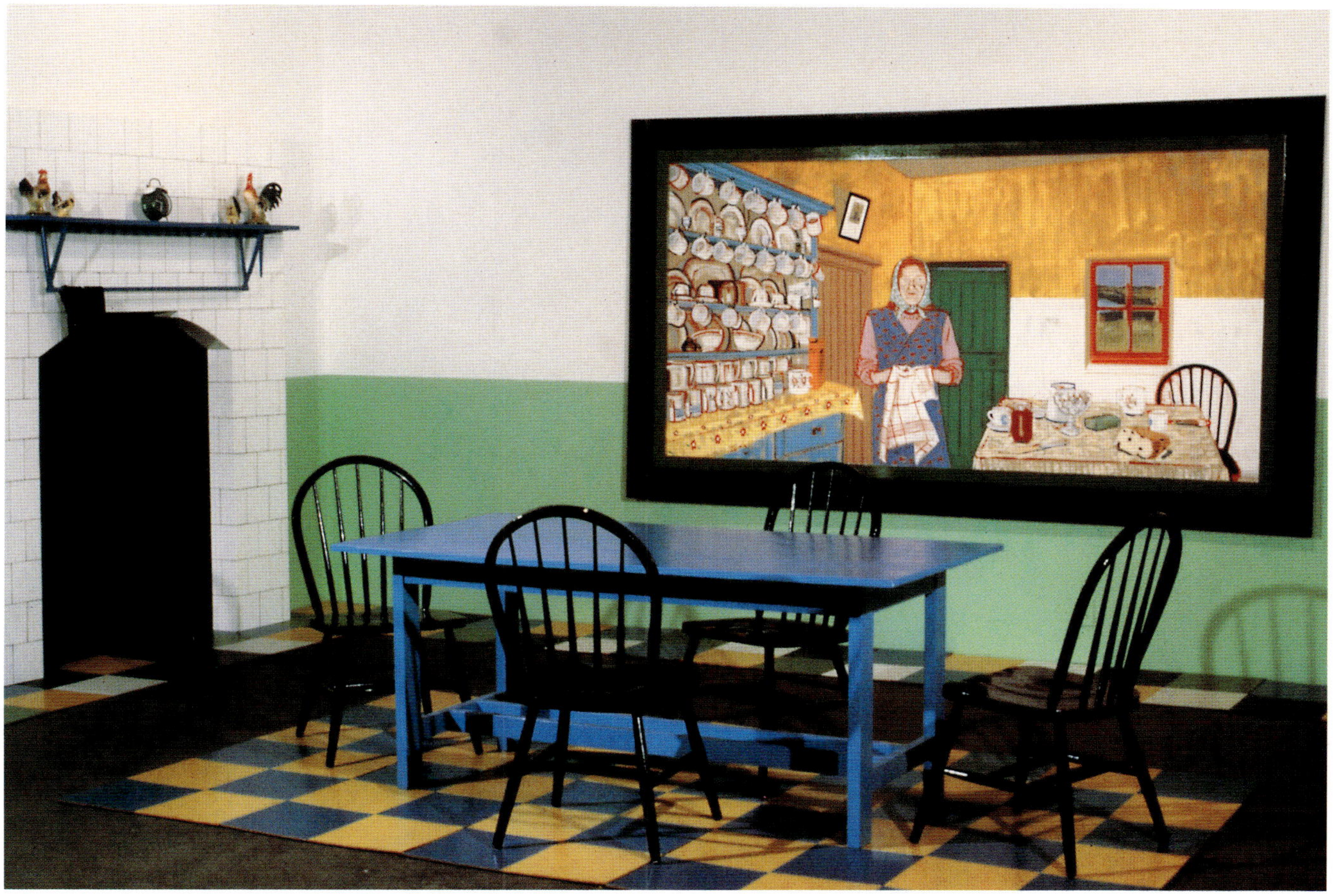

The Kitchen (Installation detail), casein/paper, canvas, Newspace, L.A., 1985

Carl Provder

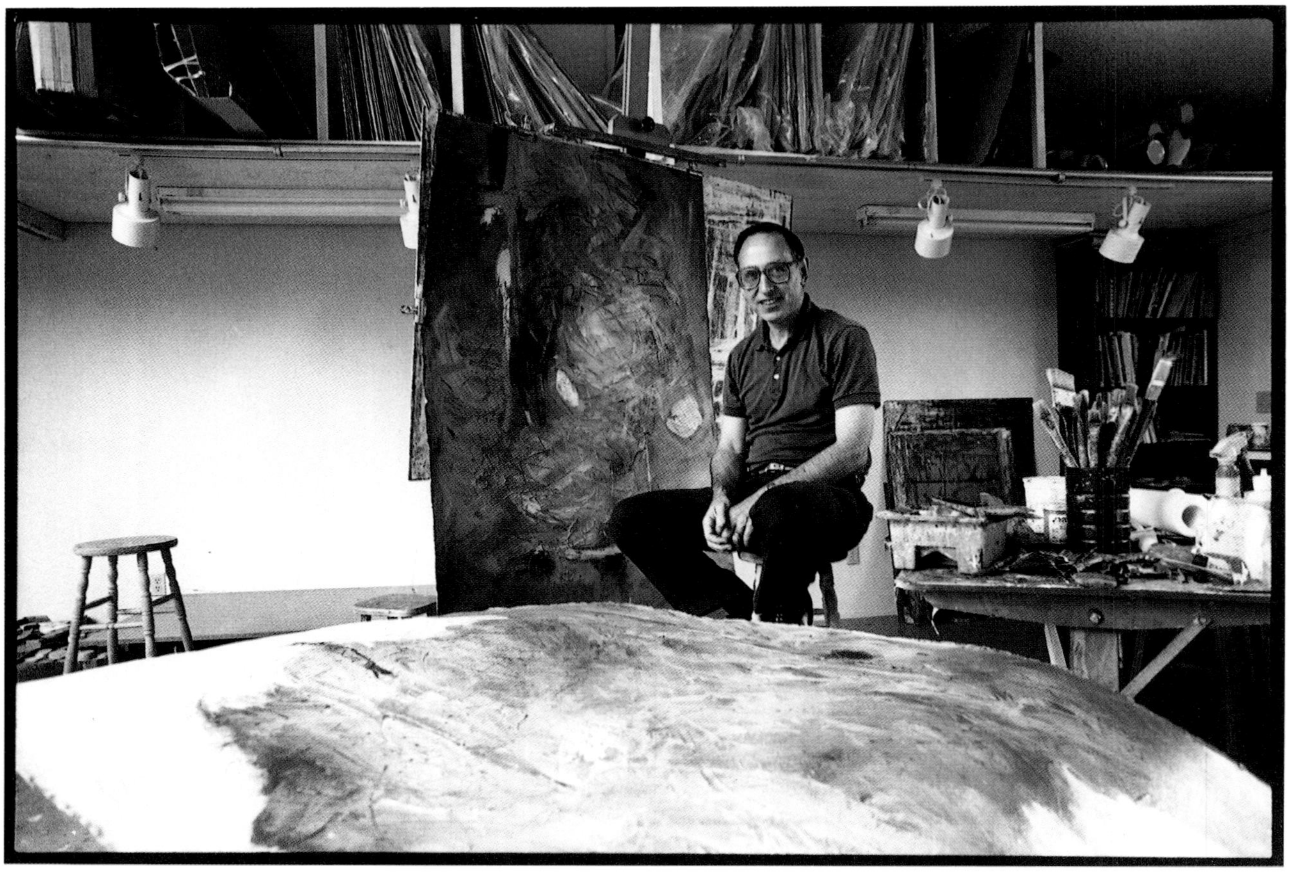

I'm not interested in putting my anger into my work. I get it out in other ways. When I was most angry I wasn't painting.

Natural light pours into the Encinitas studio above his home as Carl Provder considers the direction of his latest works. Gone is the dramatic dark tumult and stunning design of his earlier collages and no longer does he do abstracted figures in deep, emotionally applied colors. Still expressive, and ingrained with now-unconscious design principles, Provder has mellowed and developed into an artist whose work evokes a quieter emotional and spiritual response.

Firmly committed in his feelings about art, Provder has held private workshops for a number of years, influencing the development of several respected artists, among them Elizabeth King and Ann Ahlswede.

He was raised with a brother, seven years younger and a chemist, by his parents in New York City. With no art leanings themselves, they encouraged him in his art, backing him as long as he promised to get a teaching credential, reminding him "every Monday and Friday."

His first wife, the late Elinor Gurman Provder, was an accomplished artist, with whom he raised one son. He has been married since 1983 to Mandara Bechek, Ph.D., a therapist and painter.

I work in one medium for maybe a year or three years, then when I find I get stale or I get satiated and it doesn't have that excitement about it I switch to another medium.

I meditate first, then quietly look at the work. The most important thing is for me to get an immediate gut reaction. If I'm not sure, if I see something that's jarring, doesn't work, I'll put a tape down and write, "Change this, change that." Or maybe I'm not sure and I'll put it aside. I've found many times if I can't find anything glaringly wrong it might be finished.

Ever since I've been doing the mixed media collage work I've been staying away from my structured analytical self, which is my real life aside from my painter life. My painting life is my alter ego where I throw paint around like a child. Prior to this I would look at the work and say, "Okay, do I have a balance to this? Do the colors balance? Do the shapes go this way?" You know, the whole trip I'd do with my class. When I'm teaching I'm verbalizing. And when I'm working I'm working intuitively, not verbally. It's a non-verbal thing. So in the last two years I've gotten away from the analytical criticisms of my work to a gut reaction. Feelings. It's a big difference. It's an intuition based on all that I've learned through the years, but it's a feeling that hits me if it's working or not.

When I start overworking a painting I have all kinds of problems and sometimes if I really get mad at it then things happen. The best time is when I'm doing a painting and there's a great area. I don't know how it happened. I don't remember doing it in a state like that and if I can be in that state all the time (laughs) I could do some great pieces!

I didn't do any meditation until I came to San Diego, never went to a consciousness workshop. If I were still living in New York I might never have, but here I got involved in a lot of it. None of my friends in New York were or are involved. I've become more open about my feelings, not quite as closed, as rigid. I started doing meditation with the Theosophical Society about ten years ago for a year or two, then stopped and started to meditate again with the mixed media work about four years ago. I don't do it religiously everyday. I think it's part of my life. I do Northern Buddhist meditation. All are valid. Some people go into it more and some, like Mandara, use a mantra. I just do breathing. I find before painting I like to do it, to empty my mind.

I'm trying to take more risks in my work. I realize

I'm not going to be an avant garde pace setter in American art. I feel that's not me to try to do something weird or different. I just try to do a better painting and develop that painting to wherever it takes me. I have problems with a lot of paintings I see today because I'm not into bad art or ugly art. I'm still from the old school and want to do what I consider in a way beautiful paintings, not pretty, but having a beautiful spirit, beautiful feeling.

I'm not interested in putting my anger into my work. I get it out in other ways. When I was most angry I wasn't painting. It doesn't work for me to do art when I'm in pain. I find that there have been times that were very traumatic for me, the New York teacher's strike, Ellie's death. Everybody told me, "Paint, paint, it'll be a good outlet," and I just could not paint. It was nine months or a year later before I could paint again. I must have done something during that period of time. I never went that long since I started painting.

I'm not interested in doing things to promote selling my paintings, like go to every opening as if it's part of my business. It may be the difference between being an introvert and an extrovert. I put more and more energy into my painting, keep my teaching to a minimum. I'd say I'm prolific. I get a certain satisfaction when a painting comes out but I'm not really satisfied. Of course, if you get to the point where you're really satisfied and everything you do is wonderful then you can throw away your brushes because you've already accomplished that.

I'm getting more and more away from being the male problem solver. I try to hold back from giving people advice unless they come right out and ask me. I heard that the difference between Buddhism and politics is that in politics you try to change things in society; in Buddhism you try to change things within yourself. So I'm leaning more and more to trying to change things within my self and theoretically if we could all meditate everyday, try to change things within ourselves, there wouldn't be anybody that would pick up a weapon and kill somebody. It's a very Utopian theme which may not happen, but I feel the most important thing is to work on myself and that's what I'm trying to do through my art, just being conscious.

SELECTED BIOGRAPHY

BIRTHPLACE

Brooklyn, New York

EDUCATION

Pratt Institute, Brooklyn, BFA, 1955
Columbia University, New York, MA, 1970
Instituto Allende, San Miguel De Allende, Mexico, MFA, 1972

SOLO EXHIBITIONS

Gallery 84, New York, 1971 and 1972
Nassau County Museum of Fine Arts, East Meadow, New York, 1976
Paidea Gallery, Los Angeles, 1976
Riverside Museum, Riverside, California, 1976
Knowles Gallery, La Jolla, 1982 and 1986

GROUP EXHIBITIONS

147th Annual, National Academy of Design, New York, 1972
"All California," Laguna Art Museum, 1977
"Southern California Artists," travelling exhibition to Keele University and Cambridge University, 1978
"Oil Painters of Note, Invitational" San Bernardino County Museum, San Bernardino, California, 1981
Mathes Center, Felicita Foundation for the Arts, Escondido, California, 1985 and 1986

COLLECTIONS

Harcourt Brace Jovanovich, Inc., San Diego, California
Hyundai Motor America, Garden Grove, California
St. Joseph's Hospital and Medical Center, Phoenix
Drexel Burnham Lambert, La Jolla
Mandell Weiss, San Diego

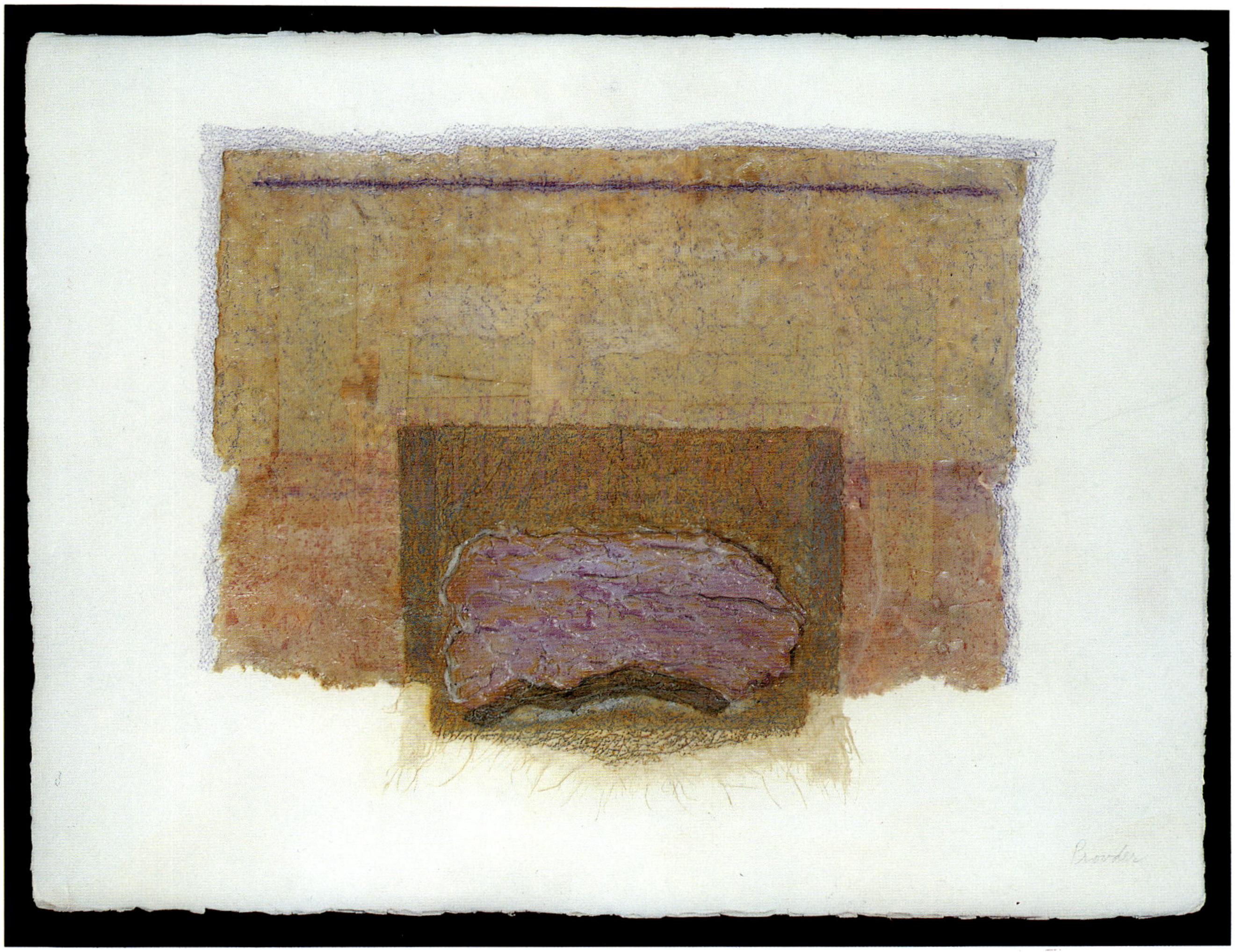

AH 22 Rejuvenation, mixed media, 23′×30′, 1986 Photo by Millie Pervis

Philipp Scholz Rittermann

If you become addicted to making art then you create all this bullshit in your life so that you require therapy through your art to get it out of your system. That's. . . .really backasswards. . . .

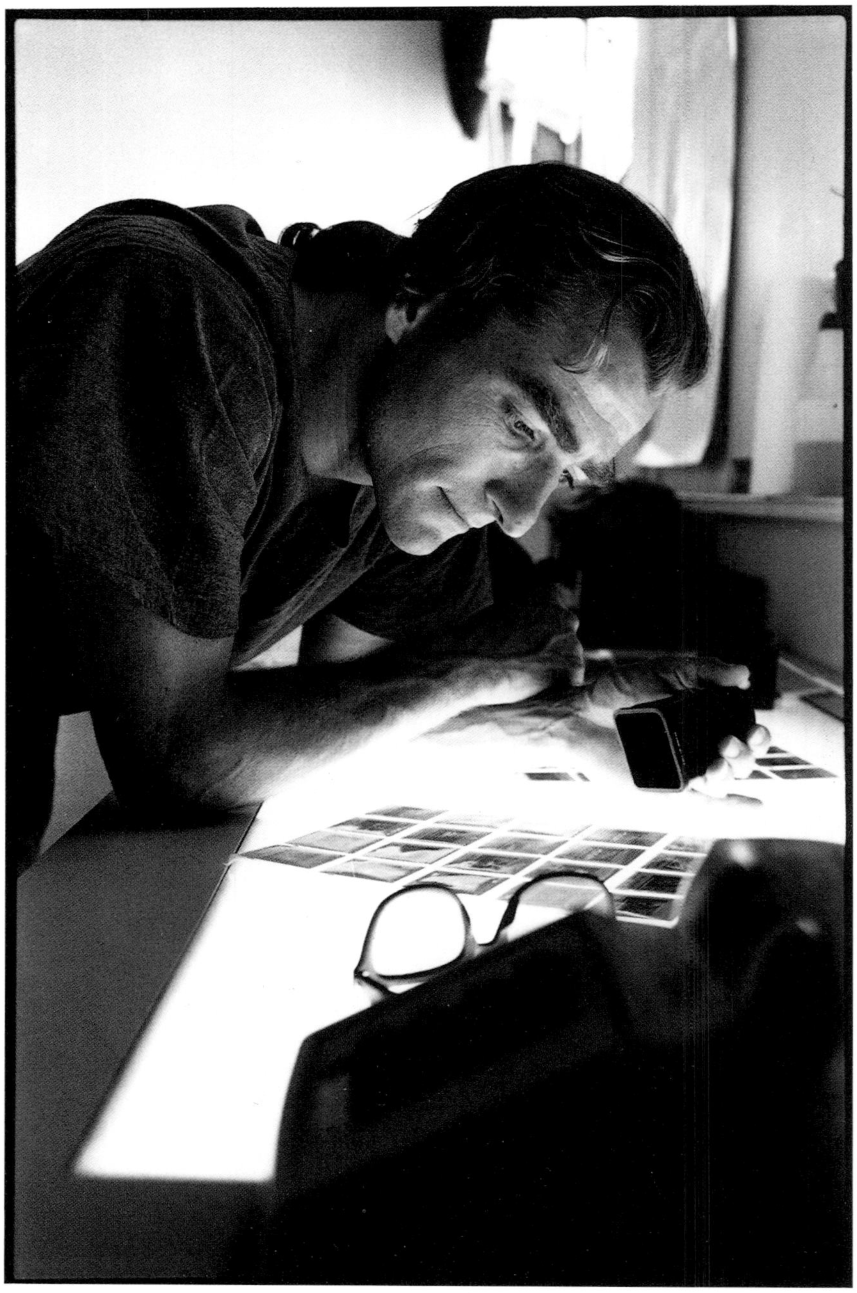

Asserting that he keeps in shape by running up stairs carrying his photographic equipment, Philipp Rittermann has already made an energetic impact on the community's art scene by contributing experimental and multicultural exhibits of both his own work and the curated shows of other artists.

Distance and light are the elements which forcefully draw the viewer to Rittermann's fine art photography. Having shot night scenes in industrial areas throughout Europe, Rittermann has long been interested in the transformations that occur from day to night. As a continuation of that interest he has recently been pursuing the idea of "drawing with light" in his works, incorporating written words executed with a hand-held flashlight and sometimes photographed from as far away as three hundred feet.

His Peruvian-born mother of German descent and his father, who was raised in Brazil and Germany, both left Germany before World War II. Rittermann was born in Peru and at fourteen, with two older brothers who now run a surf shop and teach school in the Canary Islands, moved back to Germany. There he lived on his own and at the early age of fifteen firmly resolved to become a professional photographer. He first came to the U. S. in 1981, then decided to stay.

Rittermann shares a Mission Hills studio-living space with designer Brenda Rendina.

This is the first time I've felt that I'm in a place where I can be at home. I was always a gringo in Peru where I was born and I was a weird sort of South American in Germany. I never became German and never became Peruvian. I have strong ties to both places, just by the amount of time I spent and the emotional involvement, the history you go through.

I've been working with industrial ideas since 1983 in Germany. I guess I dig into it and come back out of it, depending on the availability. When I was photographing in the NASSCO shipyards near my studio downtown, I photographed for myself but I had to submit all the negatives for approval because they didn't want to let out any secret Navy information. in doing so they chose a number of images for their offices and those happened to be some of the strongest images I'd made, not the typical grandiose view of something. That really encouraged me because a really good image is accessible at different levels, could mean different things to different people. They're still looking at them and discovering things on their own level. For me they are images about scale, the monstrous size of machinery and the relationship to humans. In one, a welder sits underneath the belly of a ship that extends as far as the eye can see. Technology really overpowering man, that's what I saw in it.

I'm also fascinated with the moving standpoint, as opposed to having the camera rock solid where something might move through the frame. I change that around, so the camera and the deck of a ship are one unit and the rest of the world revolves around the camera. The stars and moon and everything including lights swirl around me. That got to be really fun, exposing with the flash to get partially frozen movement of people and everything else going whacko. Art critic Jeff Kelly wrote that it was a very American view, that it was an egocentric view that I started when I came to the West Coast. To me it was still an investigation of the moving standpoint as against the stationary standpoint.

Along those lines, I think when we send data-collecting instruments to outer space or into the ocean, to the areas we cannot see with our own senses, I've often wondered about the parameters of that data we get back. What if it were like a moving standpoint camera, you wouldn't see the world the way it would be perceived by somebody standing and taking in the continuum. What if the time span of the sampling of each one of those information discs is completely inadequate for the occurrences that are there or the time scale that goes on in the dimensions those instruments are sampling? What if they are getting milliseconds for hours in one little unit? It makes me think about those things which are fun. I'm not saying that's visible in the image at all.

I see the size of things and how they relate and the speed with which they travel against each other. In photography you create the illusion of depth in a two-dimensional medium. What I'm doing is giving you a window to step into and walk around. That's when I think the photographs work best.

I felt very strongly about coming here and making a go of it since I first travelled to the U.S. in 1981. My experience as an artist in this country has been nothing but positive. The hierarchy isn't as sedentary and demented as it is in Europe. And for someone without a formal education to create a show at a major photography museum, for me to be teaching in colleges without the college degree in anything, that doesn't happen in Germany.

I see that the stereotypic notion of the Bohemian lifestyle is a lot of hogwash. Maybe when we're younger we need all the *angst* and *sturm* and *drang*. There have been times, like in 1982, when things were really crazy. My wife and I were involved in a near-miss plane crash, then we were separating and as I was coming to the States I had a motorcycle accident and then the apartment partly burned up. During that time I made some really powerful photographs and it was because I couldn't sleep.

I've noticed that in times of emotional upheaval or insecurity in my personal life I tend to be quite creative. That's an idea I don't like because it implies you have art as therapy. If you become addicted to making art then you create all this bullshit in your life so that you require therapy through your art to get it out of your system. That's a really backasswards way to handle things!

Recently I've done a lot of soul searching and I realize the upheaval actually fragments my time and takes time away from my center. I'd like to think that my better work comes from within and not just from some little intellectual concern. I'd like to get to the point where I could spend really focused, unfragmented time on my art and do the art for the right reasons *and* be happy.

SELECTED BIOGRAPHY

BIRTHPLACE

Lima, Peru

TEACHING

Grossmont College, El Cajon, 1983 to present
Southwestern College, Chula Vista, 1984 to present

SOLO EXHIBITIONS

Studio 666, Paris, France, 1982
ARCO Center for the Visual Arts, Los Angeles, 1983
"27 hrs., 34 min., 30 Images," Equivalents Gallery, Seattle, Washington, 1984
"Night Light Scenarios," University Art Gallery, University of Texas, Arlington, 1987
Anuska Gallery, San Diego, 1987

GROUP EXHIBITIONS

"New Black-and-White- West European Photography," curated by Lorenzo Merlo, Amsterdam, travelling exhibition to Boston, Houston, Los Angeles, 1982 and 1983
"Night Photography," Focus Gallery, San Francisco, 1984
"The European Iceberg," Art Gallery of Ontario, Toronto, Canada, 1985
"A San Diego Exhibition," La Jolla Museum of Contemporary Art, 1985
Museum of Contemporary Photography, Columbia College, Chicago, 1987

COLLECTIONS

Bibliotheque Nationale, Paris
Museum of Modern Art, New York
Metropolitan Museum of Art, New York
La Jolla Museum of Contemporary Art
Museum of Photographic Arts, San Diego

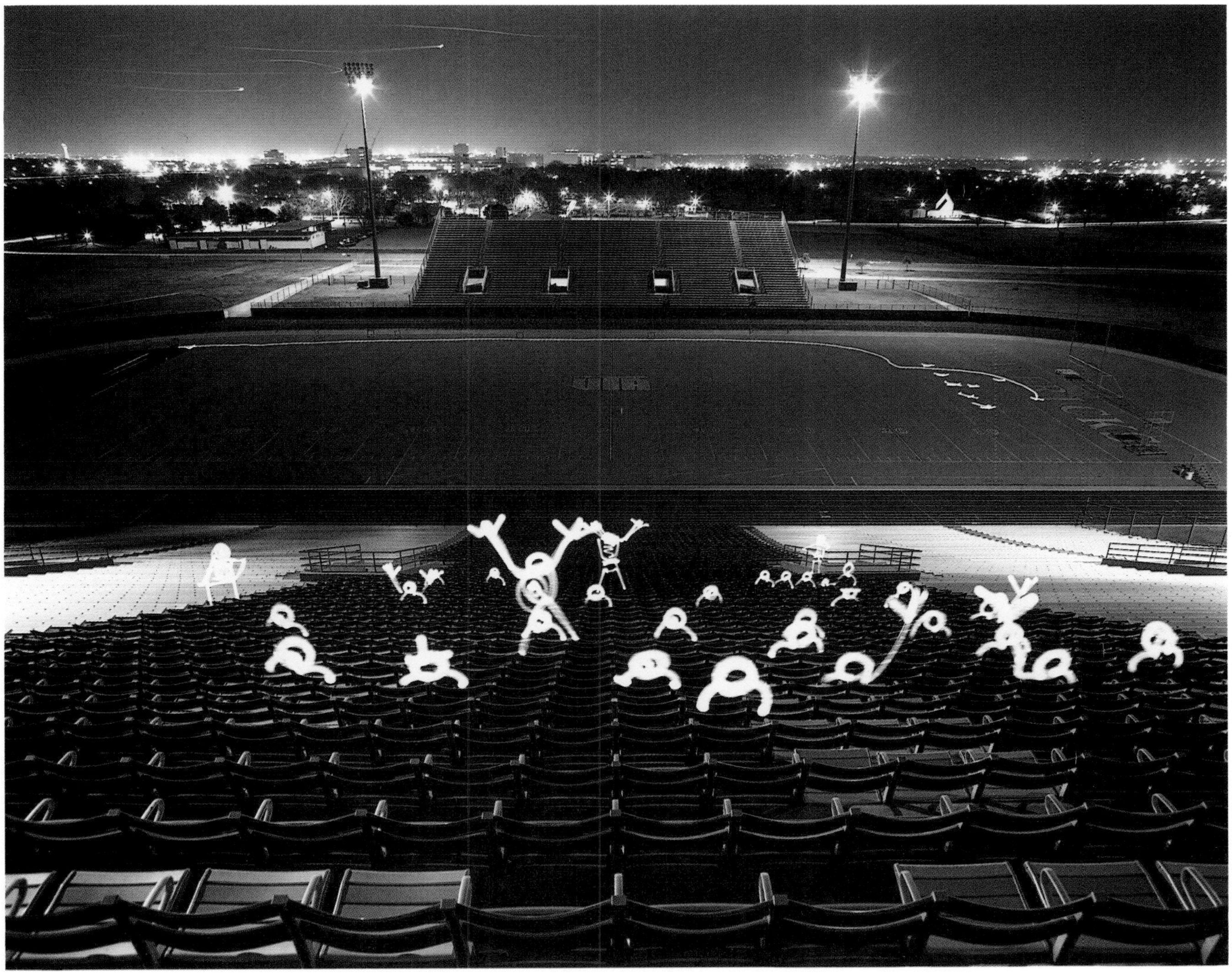

Ninety-Five Yard Touchdown, University of Texas, Arlington, black & white silver gelatin print, 40"×60", 1987

Italo Scanga

They could never pin me down. They used to say, "He's a neon artist. He's a rock artist. He's a wood artist." They classified artists with materials, like a trademark. . . . I don't want to be classified as anything.

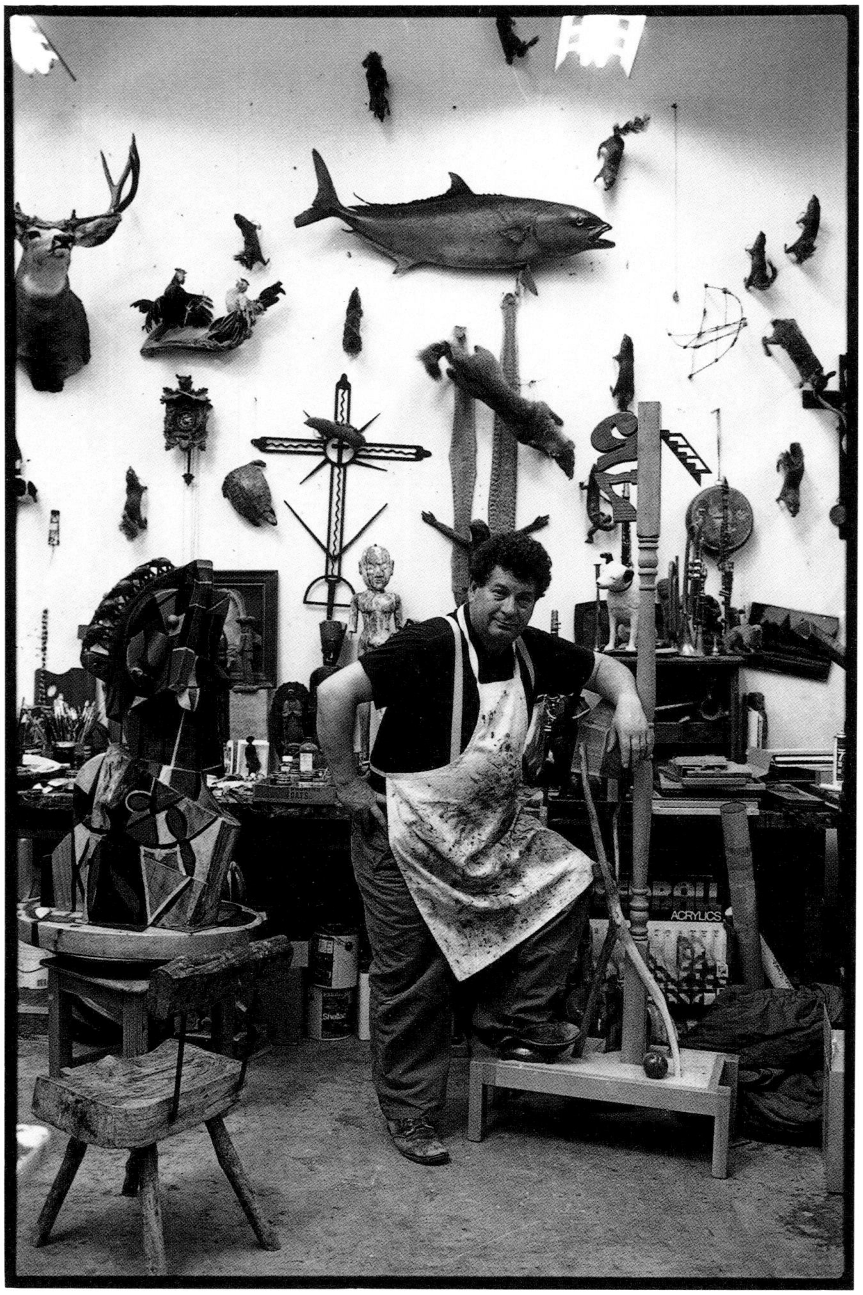

Greeting visitors, collectors, and students, answering questions of his assistants and his wife Stephanie who is fielding phone calls, Italo Scanga gives the impression of a man in his element, loving every minute of the hectic attention and pace that his sculpture generates now that the years of struggle are behind him.

*His UCSD Water Tank studio is filled with a serendipitous collection of memorabilia which supplement nearby works earmarked for museums and galleries in the United States and Europe. Scanga is an energetic man who has retained an identification with his provincial Italian roots. As a cover star (*ARTnews Magazine*, November 1984), Scanga's figurative style is uniquely his own, fashioned out of tree limbs, found objects, and roughly joined wood. His open mind and eclectic eye enable him to use and borrow from all periods of art, uninhibitedly painting and combining materials and probing moments of historical pathos to give his work an immediate, visceral impact.*

Raised in southern Italy during the war with two sisters and a brother, Scanga worked in factories and spent his days assisting a local furniture maker while his father emigrated to the United States alone. By 1947, however, Scanga was able to emigrate. Stephanie Smedley Scanga has been his assistant and manager since the mid-1970s. He has one daughter, a teacher, and a son in architecture.

I have a reputation for changing all the time. I work in series. I work on one series and then when I'm finished I work on another series. I sort of do a theme, go back to it again, reuse it and I continue until I'm exhausted, tired, bored with it. That's the crux of the matter: I get bored with the idea and I change again to something else. Like the religious work, then the fear work, then my more metaphysical work, abstract work. Now I'm doing a piece about the war again with globes, semi-political again about the world in trouble.

But I'm still working on the figure. I'm still working on cubistic heads. It's a continuous process. I put myself in, my political beliefs, my religious beliefs, my aesthetic beliefs – everything comes in. That's part of the artmaking process, it's me, what comes out of me. It has to come from within you. If you don't feel it you can't force it.

Everyone is talking now about sculpture coming from painting, or another group that says no painting comes from sculptures. Me, I'm in between. I do mass and volume and then I paint in the tradition of painters. That's a kind of duality. It's hard for a sculptor to deal with narrative if he's dealing with mass and volume. My figural pieces are more like dealing with drawing than they are about painting.

All my materials have to do with sculpture. I never use canvas. I use hard materials such as wood, glass, iron, steel. I came directly from sculpture. I do assemblage, I carve everything, I do everything. I assemble, I glue, I screw, I cover it up. You can't tell my techniques with my pieces. Probably if I lived in Italy I would be a caster. But it's difficult here. I used to cast for a long time. I was a welder for a long time. That's a trouble sculptors have, we start to depend on too much technology and materials, expenses. It's a pain in the neck. We're at the mercy of a lot of people to make things. Like glass, I can't do glass unless I have somebody blow glass for me. I have to go where they blow glass. I have to go where the furnace is. It's a very difficult process.

In the 1960s you had to work with one specific image, one specific concern. Not me. They could never pin me down. They used to say, "He's a neon artist. He's a rock artist. He's a wood artist." They classified artists with some materials, like a trademark. The rock was somebody's trademark. I don't want to be classified as anything.

I know what goes on in the world. I mean not completely. I know what goes on in the world of art. I read things, history books, contemporary books. But I do my own thing. I go into the studio and make my own decisions. Sometimes maybe I react subconsciously.

It took me a long time to exhibit my work. I didn't start to show my work until I was almost fifty. If you couldn't be classified they'd put you in a category. Now there's more of a pluralism. Now it's easier. But if you didn't do abstract paintings in the 1960s you'd never get into anywhere. You'd have a hard time. It was like a union. You'd have to stick with it and that's it. Now they expect you to change. They think – if you do the same thing over and over again – what is this guy doing? People just ignore you. You've got to come out with more change. Otherwise after a while you have a product, the same thing over and over again like a brickmaker.

I go to swap meets and pick up things. That's really to relax. It's interesting. I love to see junk, ordinary things, common things, not only artistic things. You look at things, you train your eyes, the idea of the perception of selecting. You look at all the stuff in the world and you've got to select the piece that you want. It's kitsch, it's entertainment.

It's hard to change the world through painting and sculpture, you know. I don't think we really have any political, how should I say, grip or strength. We say something, but we don't really change anything. It's a political force, but it's a small political force in comparison with other forces in the world.

I like to come to my studio. I'm crazy about my studio. I never get tired of it. I love to get up and come to my studio. If your work's in demand you want to work harder. If you're in a bad period then it's difficult, especially if nobody's paying attention to you, then you say, "what am I doing this for?" You want the world to love you. And especially to respect you.

SELECTED BIOGRAPHY

BIRTHPLACE

Lago, Calabria, Italy

EDUCATION

Michigan State University, East Lansing, BA, 1960; MA, 1961

TEACHING

University of California, San Diego, 1976 to present

SOLO EXHIBITIONS

Los Angeles County Museum of Art, 1983
La Jolla Museum of Contemporary Art, 1983
Oakland Museum, travelling to the Seattle Art Museum and I.C.A, Philadelphia, 1986 and 1987
Peggy Guggenheim Collection, Venice, Italy, 1988

GROUP EXHIBITIONS

"Depth and Presence," The Corcoran Gallery of Art, Washington, D.C., 1971
"Anxious Edge," Walker Art Center, Minneapolis, 1982
"1970 Annual Exhibition: Contemporary American Sculpture," 1970; Biennial, Whitney Museum of American Art, New York, 1983
"Projects: Pier 18," 1971; "International Survey of Recent Painting and Sculpture," 1984; "Primitivism in 20th Century Art," Museum of Modern Art, New York, 1984
"El Arte Narrativo," Museo Rufino Tamayo, Mexico City and P.S. 1, Long Island, New York, 1984

GRANTS AND HONORS

National Endowment for the Arts, Individual Artist in Sculpture grants
Howard Foundation
Copley Foundation

COLLECTIONS

Museum of Modern Art, New York
Metropolitan Museum of Art, New York
Solomon R. Guggenheim Museum, New York
Los Angeles County Museum of Art
La Jolla Museum of Contemporary Art

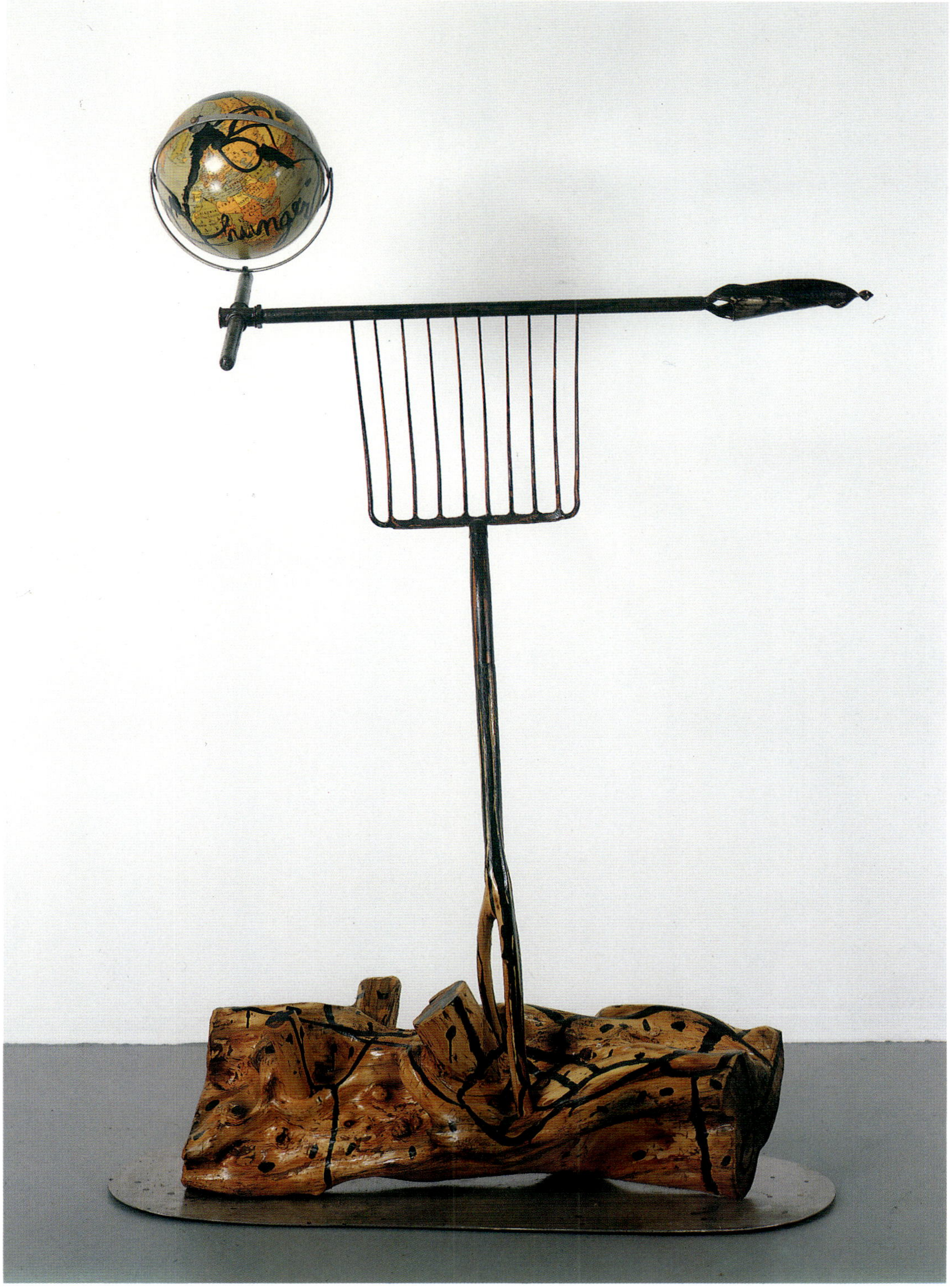

Photo by Roy Porello

Troubled Worlds, wood, steel, rake, awl, globe, 78″×50″×22″, 1987

Courtesy of Pamela Auchencloss Gallery, N.Y.

Lynn Schuette

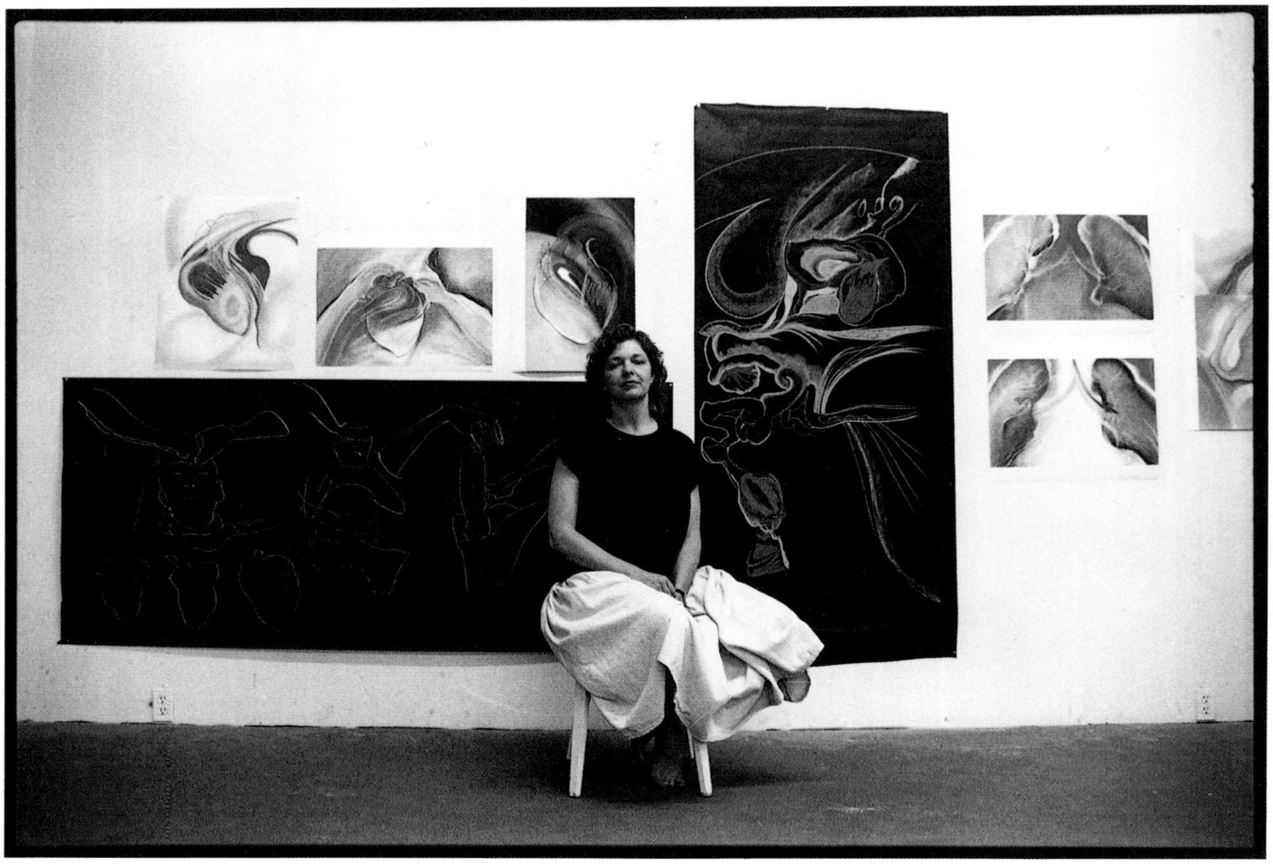

I wanted to be physical with the paintings in the way that the dancer would be physical with the floor. . . . it felt right to be working physically, using my arms in a certain way, stretching and moving like a dancer.

Marked by a purple door on Island Avenue in the downtown area, Lynn Schuette's studio bisects the first floor of an industrial building she bought and renovated with artist Gloria Poore. Schuette has established herself as a savvy and daring arts administrator, being founder and director, since 1980, of Sushi, Inc., the Eighth Avenue performance art space.

She creates Sushi's yearly program of nearly one hundred performances by visiting artists and dancers, staging solo exhibits and installations, sponsoring street festivals, public art, and the annual January Neofest, a month-long interdisciplinary arts festival of premiere works.

In her own paintings and wall pieces, Schuette has left behind some of the biting social commentary of her works of the 1970s. She now finds time to paint mainly during summer months when Sushi is hosting dance workshops. Evoking a sense of assurance, her large paintings are vibrant with sensual line and deep contrasting color.

Schuette and her younger brother were born when her mother was in her mid-thirties and her father was fifty. Though they were uneducated Illinois farmers, they supported her art interests. She was the first person in her family to attend college. With a supportive and friendly Doberman pinscher as companion, she lives and works in downtown San Diego.

Most artists, after going through an educational system, realize they've been taught a particular skill and they're structurally unemployed. What you've been taught is valuable but is not what you're going to be making a living at. Or you may make a living but it's going to be ten years down the road. You come to that climax and a personal understanding of that. It happened to me when I was about twenty-seven. I was a waitress, so forty hours a week I was waiting on tables and putting on a costume and playing this game with people to make money and then I'd go home and paint. Finally I just said, "I can't split my whole being in half. It's insane, I can't psychologically do that. I've been taught that art is something I care about, it's part of my soul, it's spiritual. I just had to make a living somehow that relates to that spirit. I can't be hypocrital at that level. I believe too deeply in my art." So I literally made art about being a waitress to come to terms with it. I talked about something beyond just what my painting was. That was good for me, to look at issues. At that point I knew my art somehow has to do with making a living and there were options and choices I'd have to make. I didn't want to turn around and paint sailboats, that was worse than being a waitress. And the painting I was doing was contemporary, there was no access for it to get sold anyway, no market, no galleries showed that kind of work.

So in my mind there were two things I could do. I could sit and complain or I could become a part of that gallery system and learn how to do it and then maybe my work would have a place to be marketed. I wound up at a regional art council, then Community Arts, doing administration and I was good at it. There was nothing that prepared me to know I could do it, nothing about being a painter that let me know I could. I wound up liking it.

Downtown in the late 1970s there were a handful of women who were friends: Marjorie Nodelman, Juliette Mondot, Susan Minnick, Gloria Poore, and I. It was a joke, we all had nicknames. Marjorie was "La Bamba" and I was Lynn "Sushi" – raw fish.

When I started Sushi in 1980 it really was my vision and I found performers who do what I wanted to do, exactly the kinds of issues I felt were relevant and that artists should be dealing with. That took the burden off my own work. I didn't have to deal with every political issue in every painting. I felt the freedom and responsibility to let go and get back and do what my painting was about.

I had a studio in proximity to the artists and the performers and they affected me on a lot of levels. I didn't think about how they affected me, but they affected me in a physical way. I had my studio backstage and it was on a wooden floor primarily used for dance so my body had a different relationship with the floor. I wanted to be physical with the paintings in the way that the dancer would be physical with the floor, so the work was large and it had a lot more movement in it. It felt right to be working physically, using my arms in a certain way, stretching and moving like a dancer.

Being an administrator part of the time I didn't have the luxury of being able to work constantly or work a little bit each day. I couldn't concentrate that way. So when I did work I found that I had to almost go into training like an athlete or a dancer. At that point the work was clean. It certainly is a pastel palette, it's soft but it's clear, it's direct and large and it has a physical strength as well as a conceptual sense.

I think I was raised with that romantic notion that artists are above the world or they're outsiders to the rest of the world and that's to be cultivated. I don't believe in that notion. I think that we have certain intuitions that are different, but they're just different, not better. At a certain point I said I don't want to be an artist starving in a garret for some ideals that don't fit in society. I like fitting into a culture. I like having a role and being an artist, saying I'm an artist. Artists fit into a culture, they're an integral part. They make a living, they pay taxes, they drive cars and do everything a normal person does. That's not to say art is mundane.

I was the first person in my family to go to college. I was like a different kind of animal. I took my mother to the Chicago Art Institute for the first time when I was about twenty. I had come home to see the Marcel Duchamps retrospective. It was the first show my mother ever saw. I gave her a ten minute pep talk about Marcel Duchamps and when she came out she said, "I think it's just wonderful. I had no idea that such things could be called art." Her open attitude affected a lot of things. If I do crazy performances at Sushi, I say, "Well, my mother would accept it. You don't need to have an edge about it. We need to come to it with an open mind."

Art's function to me is to knock people around but it can be done in very subtle ways. It doesn't have to mean you knock 'em down and kick 'em in the teeth. Shake 'em in a nice way. Go up to them very gently and rattle them. But it feels good at the same time and they go, "Oh, my mind works. Oh, that's kind of complex." Or they may have something very jarring and very cathartic happen.

I like working with performers and I love working on art in a horizontal way. I don't want to look at a painting up and down in the vertical. I like looking at dancers my same age and who have been influenced by the same things, like Bebe Miller or Karen Finley because she came out of Chicago and she's my age. While they're not painters, I think there's more similarity in my attitudes and what makes me tick as an artist than maybe the artist who has a studio across the street. That's why I wanted Sushi and why it regenerates me. I like looking at that time frame about art. The horizontal not the vertical.

SELECTED BIOGRAPHY

BIRTHPLACE

Elmhurst, Illinois

EDUCATION

School of The Art Institute, Chicago, 1969
University of Illinois, Champaign, BFA, Summa Cum Laude, 1970
University of California, Berkeley, 1970 to 1972

SOLO EXHIBITIONS

Jewish Community Center Gallery, San Diego, 1982
"Visceral Devotion," Grossmont College, El Cajon, 1987

GROUP EXHIBITIONS

Loyola University, Chicago, 1980
Boehm Gallery, Palomar College, San Marcos, CA, 1984
"Forum II, Emerging California Artists," Laguna Art Museum, CA, 1985
"New Faces," curated by Robert McDonald, Shoshana Wayne Gallery, Los Angeles, 1986
Wita Gardiner Gallery, San Diego, 1987

SET DESIGNS/DECORS

Philip-Dimitri Galas, San Diego, 1981
Poyesis Genetica, San Diego, 1984
Bebe Miller & Company, New York, 1988

COLLECTIONS

Great Western Savings Bank, San Francisco
Palomar College, San Marcos, California
San Diego National Bank
Rob Wellington Quigley, San Diego
Whoopi Goldberg, Berkeley

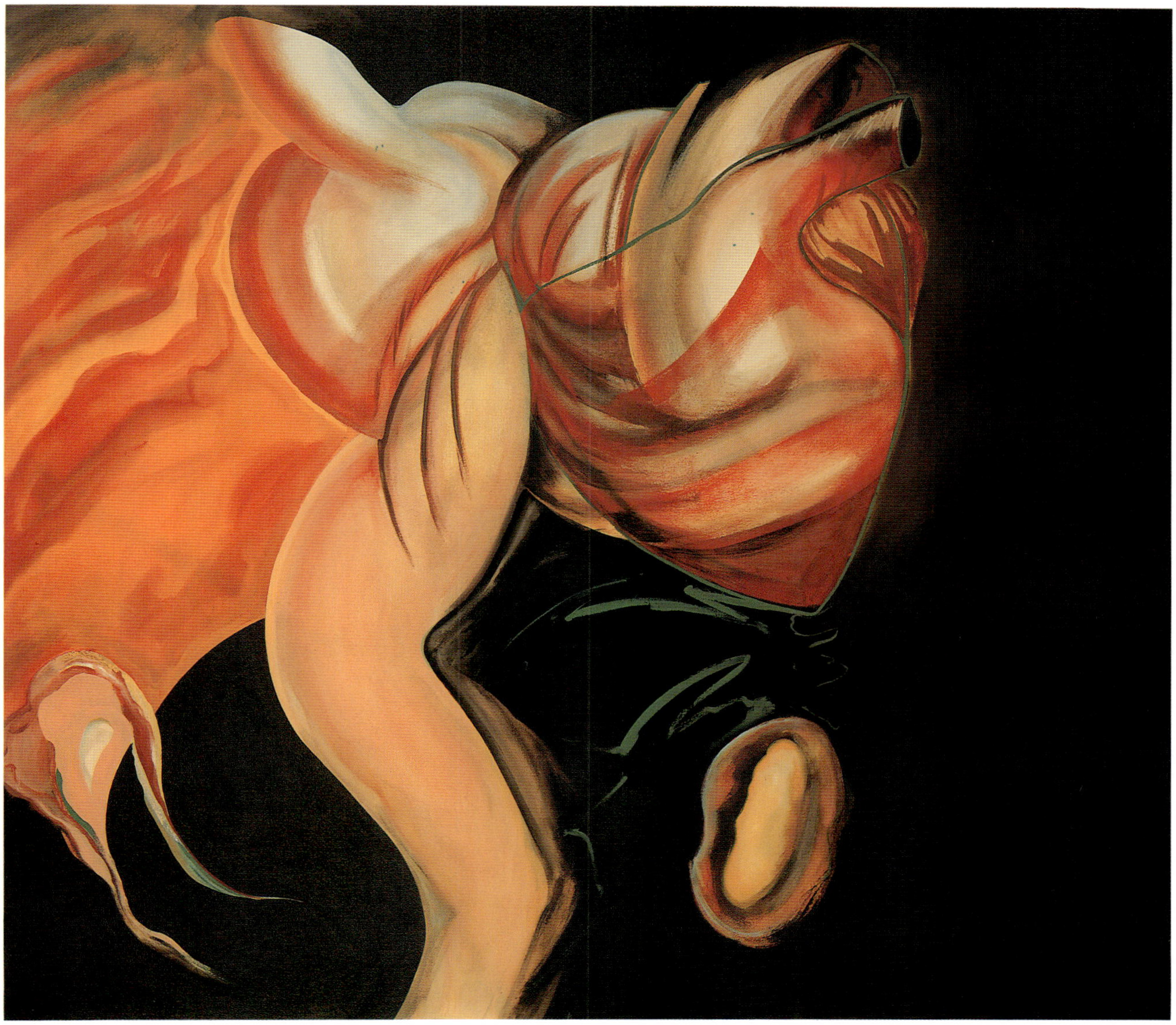

Private Performance, acrylic/canvas, 72" × 114", 1987

Photo by Becky Cohen

Reesey Shaw

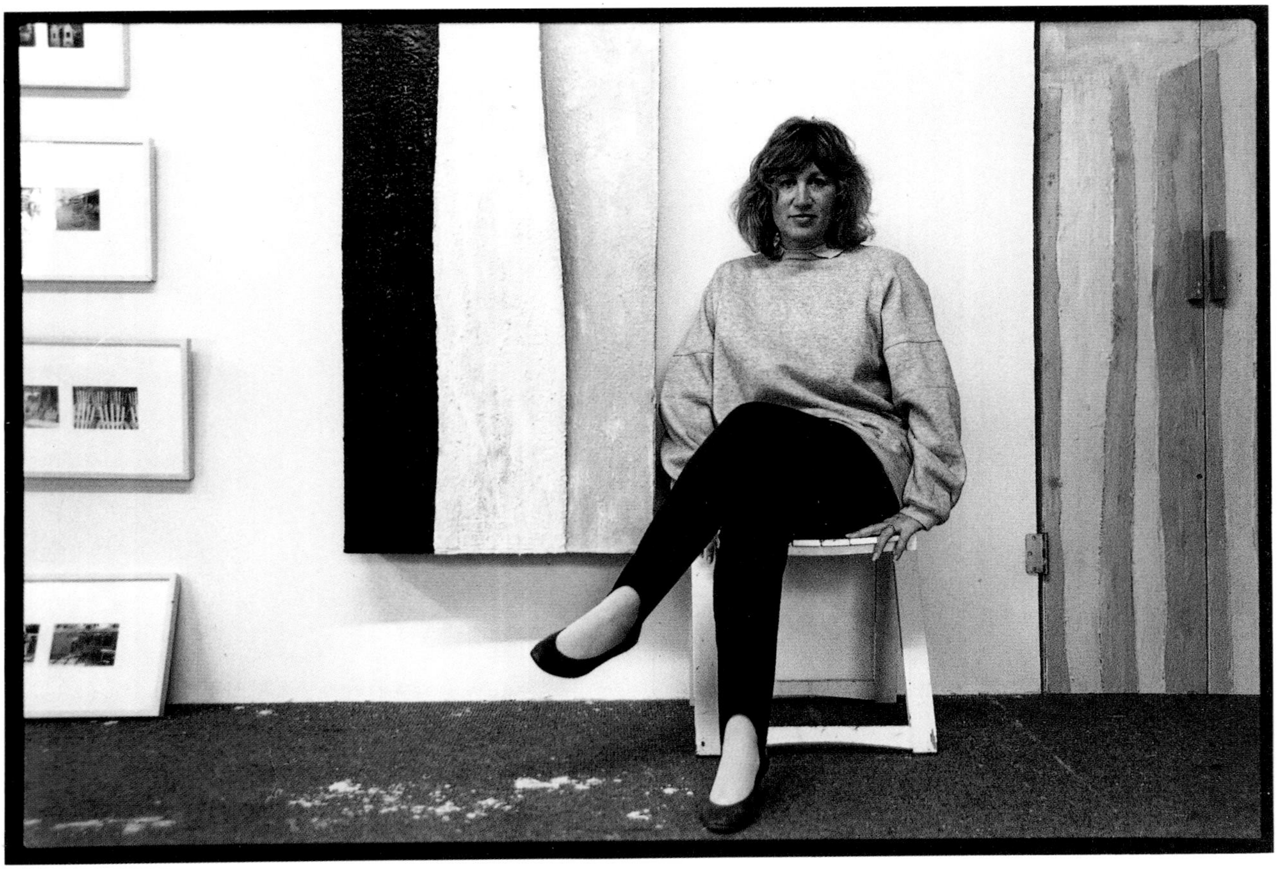

The paintings, like little kids, have been through red, yellow, and blue. Gradually they have become simplified as it becomes clearer what they are and what they need to do.

While some people think Reesey Shaw still has her studio in Venice, California, she has been back working in the large studio at her Mt. Soledad home for the last few years. But that doesn't mean this independent and expressive artist isn't in Los Angeles, San Francisco, and New York any less than she was before.

Shaw's work suggests an introverted stoicism and subdued simplicity. Shaped monochromatic canvases, small square or rectangular pieces on the wall, or freestanding monoliths work individually, as well as in strong groupings, to compliment each other. It is almost as if they are interacting in thoughtful dialogue.

She has long been active in developing a higher profile for San Diego artists, was founder of the San Diego Artist's Cooperative on India Street in 1973 along with artists Ethel Greene, Maria Lench, Flossie Cohen, Patricia McReynolds, and Lilly Hill. This cooperative later became Spectrum Gallery, now located downtown. She has currently been curating art exhibits at the elegant Gustav Anders Restaurant in La Jolla and for the Felicita Foundation in Escondido as plans develop for an art museum in San Diego's north county area.

She and her younger sister, who teaches Eurythmics, grew up in a family that collected antiques and Persian rugs as well as "weird things," such as her mother's collection of old cigar makers, shoe lasts, and original lead hat forms. Her father ran a paint and furniture business.

Shaw lives with her husband David, a UCSD cardiologist. Their two sons are in college.

I remember having the feeling that in California I was standing inside a blue cereal bowl. It was a phenomenon that I expected to end because somehow I was so used to artificial light. It was perfectly comfortable in Maryland to paint with artificial light at night, under any conditions, because the color wasn't really about natural light, it was painted color. Whereas out here, it's harder to work at night. You have to be really careful that you don't wind up having to repaint everything the next day when the light is different.

I brought my paints out on the plane when we moved from Maryland because I'd been working so hard. You know you get real attached to certain brushes and colors. I was afraid they might lose them so it was the only thing that I brought out with me on the plane to put under my feet. If it took a long time for the moving van to come I would have them right there. So I was able to start painting right away, but somehow the old subject matter didn't seem to work.

I had been going to construction sites and doing drawings and taking photographs of machinery, big earthmovers. I was using those machine shapes, the interiors, as a grid on the canvas. Moving here, that grid was no longer operable, no longer satisfying.

I started making day trips down to Mexico. Everything across the border just fascinated me, everything instantly smelled different, like the dirt streets. The terrain was so clear driving down to Rosarita Beach with the huge island off the coast, so powerful. I went down at least once a week, maybe twice a week. I started looking at and finding things in Mexico and in the landscape, the way the houses were constructed and the light and sense of space. It gradually took over as a kind of content. The man-made aspects of it seemed more human and the landscape seemed to satisfy a lot of transcendental moods, I guess.

I got interested in cemeteries. I came on one by accident going to Tecate to look for Mexican tile. There was a funeral marching down a little dirt road. There were a lot of what later turned out to be paid mourners, a lot of women in black dresses and the body was shrouded in a white bag and being carried on the shoulders of young men. I guess that's another interest in Mexico, the emotional content of what goes on there is so much clearer, both joy and sorrow. They're so much more direct with life and death experiences.

I've always been attracted to organic materials that come from the ground like wood and clay.

The final pieces I'm doing now are painted with encaustic which is a pure pigment with beeswax as a vehicle.

Ironically the paintings start out in a red, yellow, or blue but usually resolve in a much simpler way. People who aren't real familiar with painting tend to look at forms that are real simple like a lot of mine are, especially the black and white ones, and think of them as real reductive. Actually there's been a whole process that's gone on, all kinds of combinations, resolutions underneath. That's what it takes to finish the piece, almost like a human life. The paintings, like little kids, have been through red, yellow, and blue. Gradually they've become simplified as they become clearer what they are and what they need to do.

Black and white seems to be the strongest contrast and the clearest choice. It's interesting symbolically, intellectually. Black can be depressing, serious. I feel black is almost like a tree trunk. It's not muddy, yet you can put a whole lot of colors in black, a lot of layers to make that black so that it ultimately can have a lot of depth. And the same thing with white, which can have four hundred shades and it can maintain, have a kind of lucidity, whereas a lot of other colors would go muddy.

I always pursued my own work and what I needed to do very aggressively and at different times my children were amused or embarrassed. When they got older, seven, eight, nine, the boys needed to spend more time with their dad and about that time I got the studio in Venice, near Los Angeles. I knew that I could see the shows in Los Angeles, could fly up to San Francisco quickly and cheaply to see shows that would have been a major thing from home.

I really enjoyed the time with them and I didn't resent it, didn't feel, "God, when is this going to be over? When am I ever going to get to do what I want to do?" So often it's assumed that a father can travel, a father can make certain career moves but a mother can't. I suppose there were problems like any kind of move or any kind of change, but it seems to me they were resolved in a very good way. The kids got to know their dad and I didn't have to be out there constantly nagging. I think that people always feel better with whatever they're doing when their own needs are met.

In the third grade my son said, "I brought home a vocabulary word for you." I held onto my chair and he said, "Eccentric." So, yeah, that's O.K. I got a sense of myself through that and thought, well, I guess I am.

SELECTED BIOGRAPHY

BIRTHPLACE

Jacksonville, Florida

EDUCATION

Boston University School of Fine Arts, 1960 to 1962
Maryland Institute College of Art, Baltimore, BFA, 1964; MFA, 1967

SOLO EXHIBITIONS

Henri Gallery, Washington, D.C., 1978
Los Angeles Institute of Contemporary Art, 1980
Quint Gallery, San Diego, 1981, 1984, 1986
La Jolla Museum of Contemporary Art, 1974, 1986
Jeffrey Linden Gallery, Los Angeles, 1986

GROUP EXHIBITIONS

Newspace, Los Angeles, 1978
Los Angeles Municipal Art Gallery, 1977 and 1982
"Sunshine and Shadow: Recent Painting in Southern California," curated by Susan C. Larsen Martin, University of Southern California, 1985
Allan Stone Gallery, New York, 1977 and 1985
"Painting on Wood," Martina Hamilton Gallery, New York, 1987

COLLECTIONS

La Jolla Museum of Contemporary Art
American Telephone and Telegraph, New York
ARCO Corporate Collection, Los Angeles
Kaufman and Broad Collection, Los Angeles
Leslie Simon and Michael Krichman, San Diego

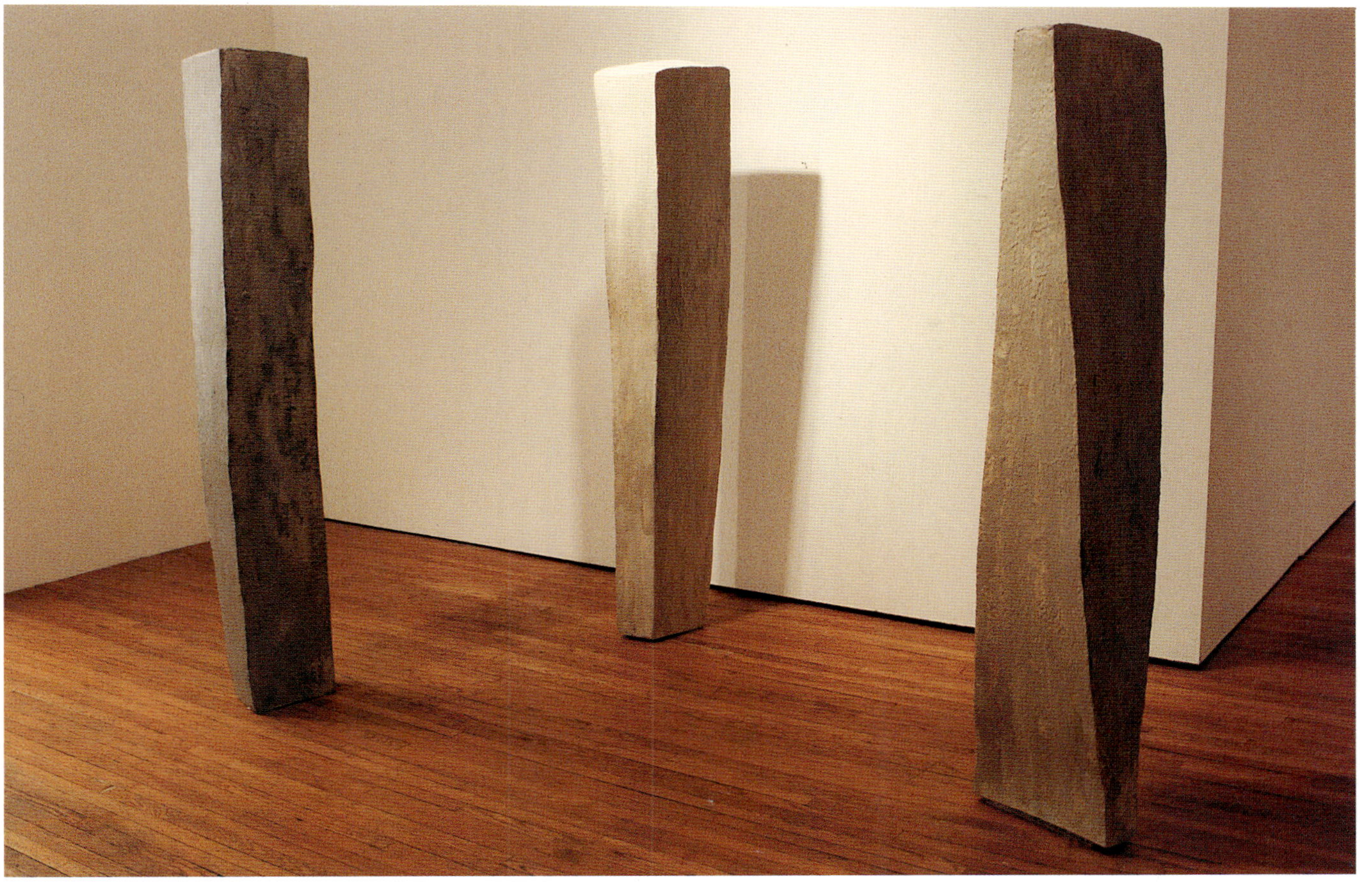

Untitled Pillar #1, *Untitled Pillar #2*, and *Anchor*, installation at Quint Gallery, wooden armature covered with poplar and painted with encaustic, #1 – 78″×10″×8″, #2 – 76″×11″×7″, Anchor – 73″×14″×5″, 1986

Ernest Silva

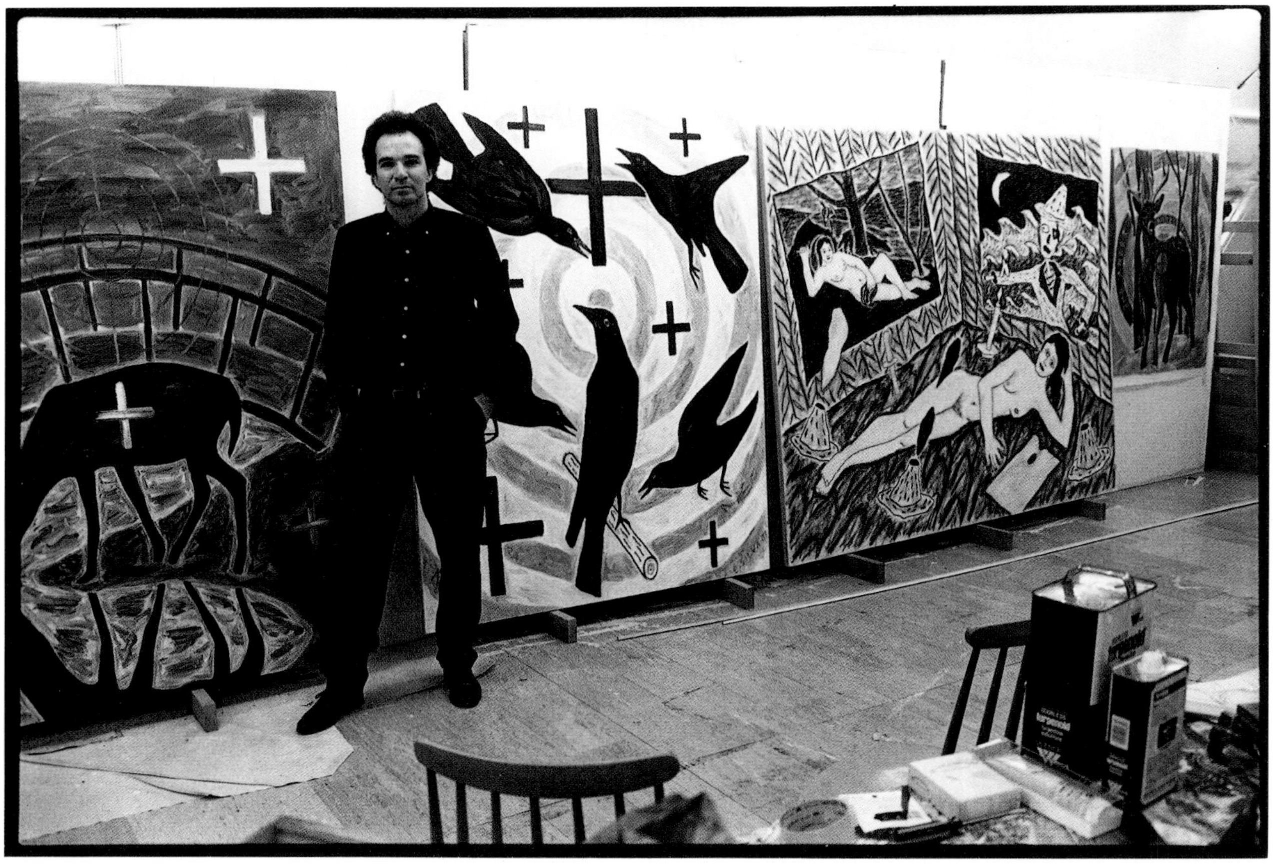

You can look at something and it may not hit you and you may look at it for thirty seconds and you remember it two years later. As soon as you make an image it implicates everyone.

Works being prepared for upcoming shows are propped against the long, curved walls of Ernest Silva's UCSD Quonset hut studio. The gentle presence of the artist is in contrast to the elemental and dramatic scenes played out in the powerfully colored paintings, shadow boxes, and cut-out forms.

Drawing from personal associations and sense memories of moments from the past, Silva's recurring themes are riderless horses, anguished bare trees, bluntly cut tree stumps, and female nudes. Archetypal in their suggestion of dream-like or nightmare experiences, these paintings refer to several sources in art history: folk art, Matisse, Henri Rousseau, and Albert Pinkham Ryder. From these he has created a narrative expressionistic style that is quite recognizably his own.

Silva has a brother three years younger who is an electrical engineer and a sister six years younger who was trained in psychology. A family where "being practical and pragmatic was really stressed," his mother "put together celebrations" and his father worked for the Veteran's Administration.

His wife, Cora Boyd, is a respected art dealer (not related to Roy Boyd, of the Los Angeles gallery). He and Cora live near UCSD.

I started working with the image of a man and a woman in about 1972 in Philadelphia. The house that I was staying in was broken into and I happened to walk in when the two people robbing the house were on their way out. I yelled at them and they jumped out of the window and I jumped out of the window and started chasing them until I realized, what would I do if I caught them? So I went back in the house. I was taking care of it for a friend of mine and the place was loaded with equipment because he was an artist who had been trading his work with the man who owned Best stores. Well I had this real fear that the people were going to come back. That night I called my girlfriend and she came over. I couldn't sleep. I woke up in the middle of the night and I did this drawing of myself as a scarecrow guarding the house. I drew the scarecrow with his arms up in the air like he was being mugged and the other part of the drawing was an image of a woman. It hit me to do an image of myself and a woman, a couple, and this became the first image that I did when I started to break away from abstraction.

I've seen poetry as a literary parallel to painting. I like works that pose a question. It seems like when you pose a question you kind of invite the viewer to go in and come up with an answer, even if it's temporary. I've been attracted to works that have a certain kind of openness, not so clear technically that you are excluded, not so polished in terms of content that you feel someone is yelling at you, telling you what to think.

A lot of imagery in my work comes out of observations that I've made from nature that are out of the ordinary enough so that they kind of strike themselves in my memory. The kinds of things that have done that to me are walking in nature and seeing clouds that had some kind of a pattern that triggered multiple associations, that were more than clouds. Or seeing trees that have some kind of abstract beauty that reminded me of something else.

Essentially what I'd like to do is put together triggers that are unconscious, triggers that I see in my own life that lead me to come to a conclusion about my own experience or about the way that I relate to the world. That seems to me really powerful, much more powerful than describing something in an analytical manner.

I've had an interest in the everyday experiences and in artists looking for exotic sources, like Picasso's interest in African art, Van Gogh's interest in Japanese prints, Gauguin's interest in Tahiti. So the images of the ocean and palm trees that I was drawing on the East Coast – when I was confronted with a place that had those things – brought out in me a different way of looking at those things. I wondered if Southern California was an exotic place I could turn into a home or if it was an imaginary paradise and how I could introduce it into my own work. The La Brea tar pits in Los Angeles, the ocean, some of the exotic color you see in Mexican folk art, I introduced into my work.

The running horse is an image that recurs in my work. I used to ride. I was holding on for dear life when the horse took off once. There was a mix of exhilaration and absolute terror. The moment goes from play to being out of control. I think play is very much like being out of control, pleasantly out of control and then at the next moment you'd like to be able to control it. I use the image of the galloping horse as something that could go either way, either out of control or exhilarating. Carried to an extreme you get thrown from the horse, you get hurt, and on the other extreme there is this vicarious experience, this unleashing of power, like temporary and joyful and in the wrong circumstances it's really catastrophic. Part of this image is from my own experience and part is from the painting "War" by Henri Rousseau where he has this very unusual image of war with this large goddess child riding on horseback.

My work is the way I see the world. I'd like to state it in a way that other people can understand. I dig into my own experience, try to state it as truthfully as possible and as clearly as possible without either of those things compromising each other. You can look at something and it may not hit you and you may look at it for thirty seconds and you remember it two years later. As soon as you make an image it implicates everyone. It may be less disturbing in an immediate way but more disturbing to the extent that everyone can internalize it later.

SELECTED BIOGRAPHY

BIRTHPLACE

Providence, Rhode Island

EDUCATION

University of Rhode Island, Kingston, BFA, 1971
Tyler School of Art, Elkins Park, Pennsylvania, MFA, 1974

TEACHING

University of California, San Diego, 1979 to present

SOLO EXHIBITIONS

Institute of Contemporary Art, Boston, 1972
Artist's Space, New York, 1975
Vanderwoude Tananbaum Gallery, New York, 1983, 1984
Roy Boyd Gallery, Los Angeles, 1984
Quint Gallery, San Diego, 1982, 1983, 1986

GROUP EXHIBITIONS

"Contemporary American Drawings," travelling exhibition, Corcoran Art Gallery, Washington, D.C., 1975 to 1976
"Painting and Sculpture Today," Indianapolis Museum of Art, 1984
"Sunshine and Shadow: Recent Painting in Southern California," curated by Susan Larsen Martin, University of Southern California, 1985
"Three Painters," Janet Steinberg Gallery, San Francisco, 1985
"A San Diego Exhibition," and "Aspects of the Permanent Collection," 1985; "Parameters 8," 1986, La Jolla Museum of Contemporary Art

COLLECTIONS

Fogg Museum, Harvard University, Boston
Grand Rapids Art Museum, Grand Rapids
Chemical Bank, New York
Kaufman and Broad Collection, Los Angeles
Anne d'Harnoncourt, Philadephia

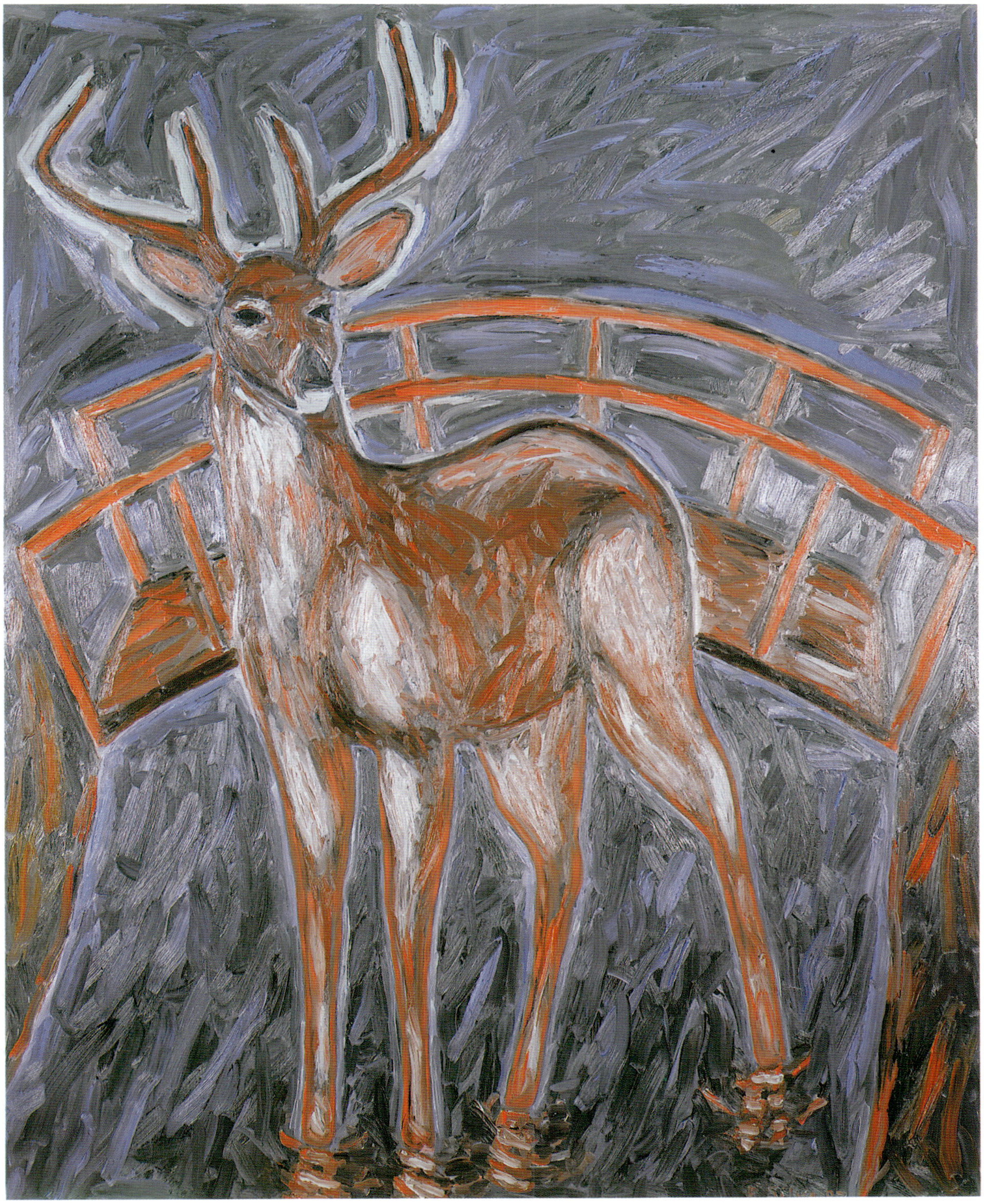

Deer and Bridge, o/c, 74″×60″, 1987

Photo by Roy Porello

Deborah Small

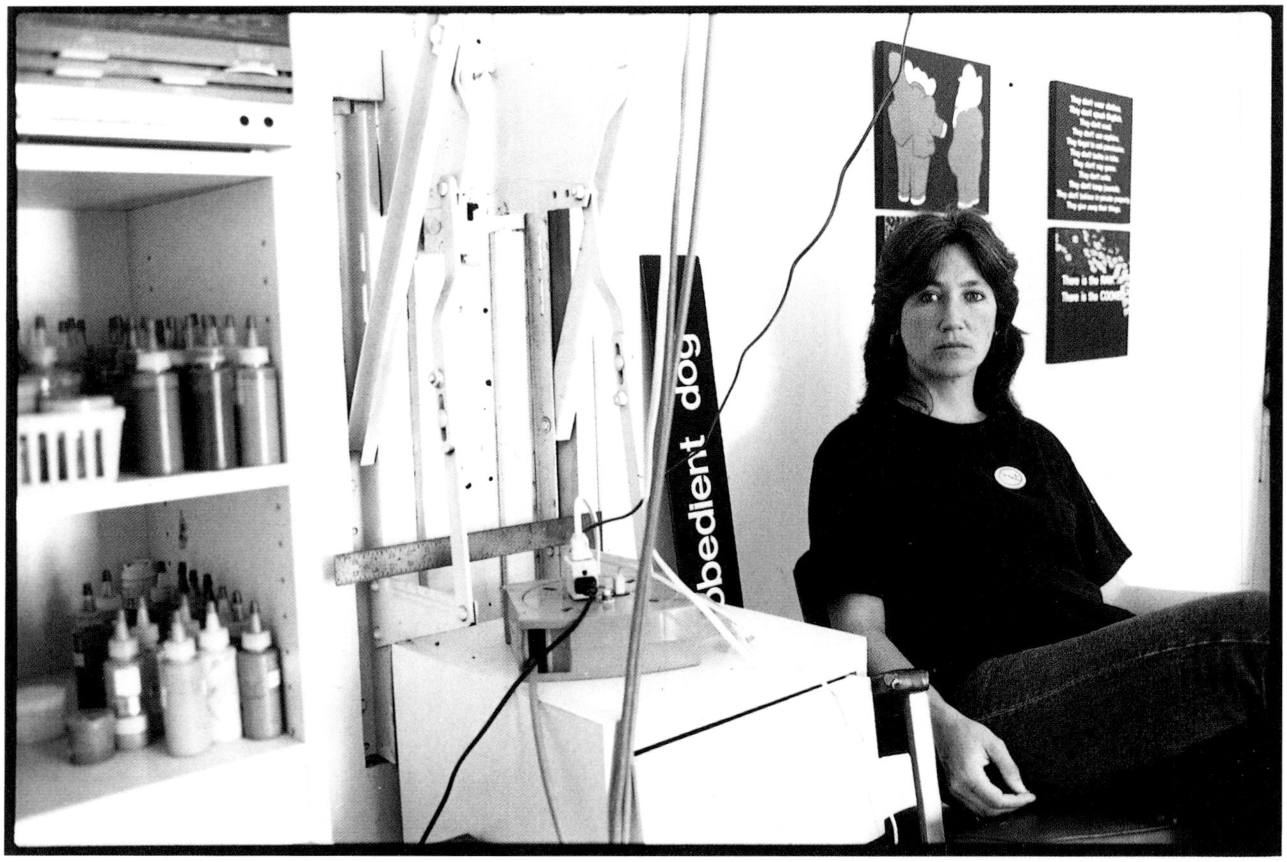

One of the challenges that I give myself is to see how I can integrate language and image and not have one function more important than the other.

In a small La Jolla cottage behind another small cottage, Deborah Small works with black and irridescent red paint in an untextured graphic style. The works under way will go off to a political fundraising art exhibit. She is concentrated and reserved as she discusses the social-political statements she makes through her art.

Small's work has taken many forms. The deductive reasonings and associational writings accompanying her installations have appeared in recent literary reviews. Child's toys such as dominoes, Babar the elephant, and letter blocks are elements in other works which are naive visual effects meant to draw attention to critically loaded subjects like the Bay of Pigs crisis, apartheid, and the nuclear bomb. Small's large, two-hundred-ten-panel installation, "1492" – a critical look at the conflicting circumstances and underlying implications of Christopher Columbus's discovery of the Americas – is in the collection of Harcourt Brace Jovanovich, Inc., and will become a permanent travelling exhibit.

She is the second of five children raised by a social worker mother and a father in government work. Her only brother is an electrical engineer, the only family member not in the helping professions. Small has a yard full of eleven cats, at last count.

The main thing I'm interested in now is trying to look at historical events, like the piece called "1492," associated with what's called the discovery of America. I tried to reconstitute this using lesser known versions of this particular event rather than the mainstream one available in grade school.

In "1492" I quote from an historian named Francis Jennings: "To call a man savage is to warrant his death." I used images that I had to get from the New York Public Library. I didn't have to say Columbus was a bad guy, I just let his words do it for him. He talked about sending slaves, about how much money could be made by the slave trade. It's not our mainstream idea of what Columbus did, how we perceive him. I use a lot of things that look like early learning devices, blocks and flashcards, repeating, playing off that kind of imagery. As an occupational therapist I worked with brain-injured adults and we used a lot of those kinds of things. In fact, I did a piece with large scale dominos that was called Spirit Influences. The formal aspect of that piece was inspired by the dominos we had people use for abstract numbers. I think that experience had an enormous influence on how I go about using art expressions.

A lot of critics talk about how didactic my work is. Well, I think that the idea of didacticism isn't necessarily a bad thing at all. When I got out of graduate school one of the things I was interested in was to present language without just sort of pasting it on a painting, to integrate it. My solution at first, at least, was to use these blocks.

Language became the image I'd use and was a predominant part of the image. In one of the pieces, "Against Apartheid," I used the official explanations of the death of South African political prisoners, like, "Slipped in shower," "Strangulation," "Fell ten floors during interrogation," and that became the image. I think it was successful. One of the challenges that I give myself is to see how I can integrate language and image and not have one function more important than the nother.

I'm not active in political party politics. I try to use my artwork as it can be used. I've done posters for various groups, apartheid rally posters, Central America. But I'm not involved in city politics. I get excited sometimes when I think that the work can have a function.

I don't necessarily have everything worked out and then do an artwork. In a sense I learn as I'm going along. One of the reasons I'm interested in using historical events is to reconstitute American history, relearning as I'm going along.

Some of my works come directly from my interaction with students. Somehow Auschwitz came up in a writing class at UCSD and I discovered that some of them had never heard of it. So I did a piece called "A is for Auschwitz" which used a Theodore Adorno quotation that says, "To write poetry after Auschwitz is barbaric." That was one of the texts on the blocks, then on another shelf it says, "What's Auschwitz?" To me that kind of ahistorical education students are growing up with is horrifying. Poor Adorno will be rolling in his grave. Our culture is so unhistorical; our president obliterates the past and you can't be critical of him if you don't understand what the past is.

One person whose writing I think had an enormous influence on me is Jim Scully. I've become interested in how one reframes things. Angela Davis does this in her book, *Women, Race, and Class.* It's like a radical reframing of history. You can almost palpably feel her doing it, showing that these people who are slaves are not victims. They might be beaten and practically mutilated but they get up and they fight back. Throughout the book she shows slavery as a series of resistances. You feel the power, the resistance. I think the number of resistances, rebellions is probably underplayed. It's not taught us as youngsters that from the moment slavery began it was a struggle. Someone like Scully or Davis shows that.

If people are only shown images of the victim and not the sense of the struggle, even if ostensibly unsuccessful, then people are saying there's no way that I can intervene, there's no way anything I do will matter. That's one thing I want to express more. It's hard to know what the repercussions are of what you do. You don't know who you are affecting.

SELECTED BIOGRAPHY

BIRTHPLACE

Mariemont, Ohio

EDUCATION

University of California, San Diego, MFA

TEACHING

University of California, San Diego, Department of Literature, 1983 to present

SOLO EXHIBITIONS

"No One Sends a Postcard from Bikini Atoll," Atomic Survivors Conference, San Francisco, 1984
"I Hear America Singing," Reed College Art Gallery, Portland, Oregon, 1985
"1492," Anuska Gallery, San Diego, 1986
"The Right Tie Can Change Everything," Sushi, San Diego

GROUP EXHIBITIONS

"A San Diego Exhibition," La Jolla Museum of Contemporary Art, 1985
"On the Horizon," part of Passages: A Survey of California Women Artists 1945 to present, Fresno Art Center and Museum, Fresno, California, 1987
"Emblem," 1984 and "Variations III," travelling exhibition, 1987, Los Angeles Institute of Contemporary Art
"Image and Text," Woman's Building, Los Angeles, 1988
"UNKNOWN SECRETS: Art of the Rosenberg Era," travelling exhibition, Muhlenberg College, Allentown, Pennsylvania, 1988

GRANTS

National Endowment for the Arts, Visual Artists Fellowship
NEA/COMBO Visual Artists Fellowship

PUBLICATIONS

1492, with Maggie Jaffe, self-published, 1986

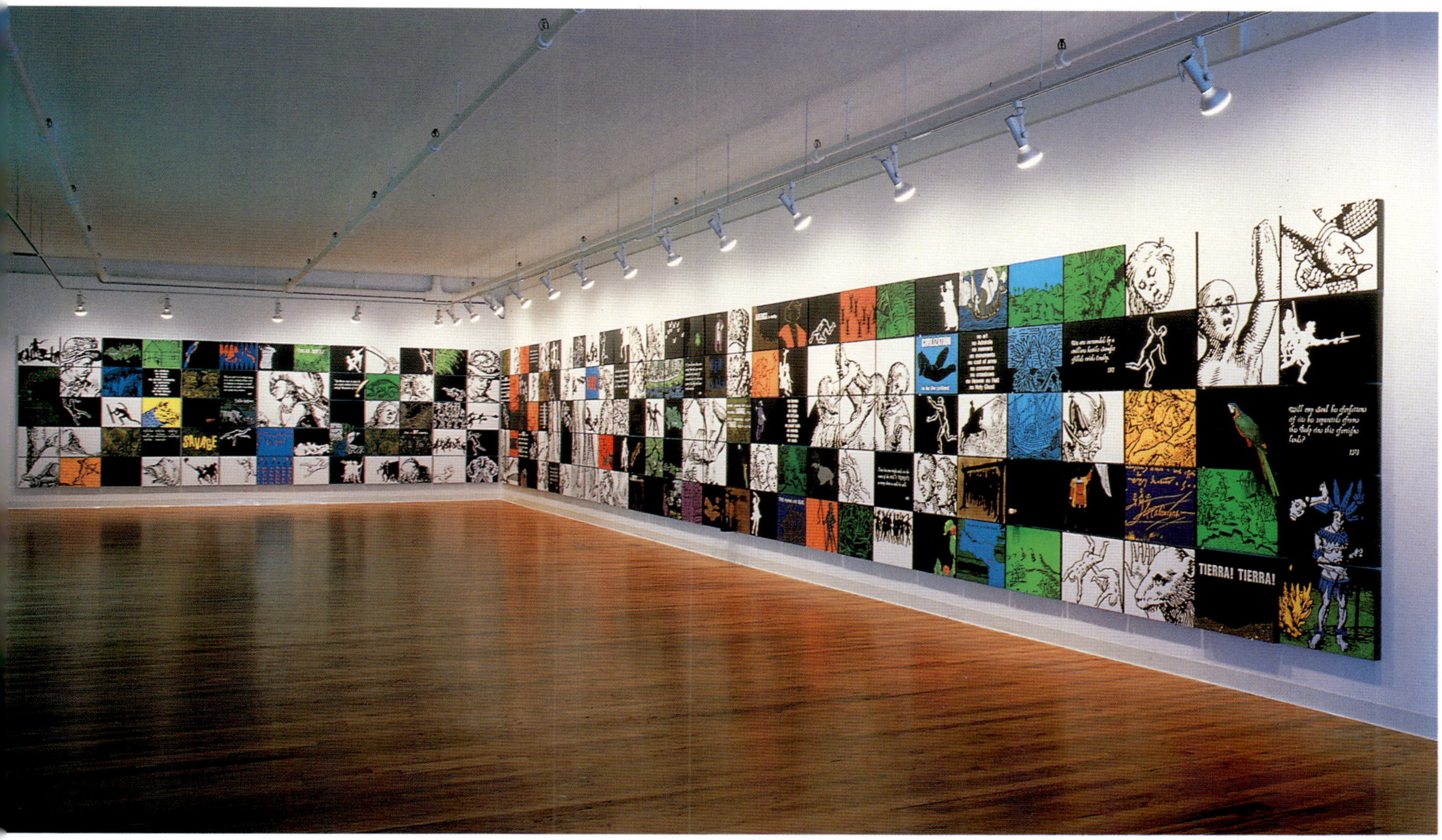

Photo by Philipp Scholz Rittermann

2, mixed media, 6'3" × 20'6" × 46', 1986

Collection of Harcourt-Brace-Jovanovich, San Diego

Ron Tatro

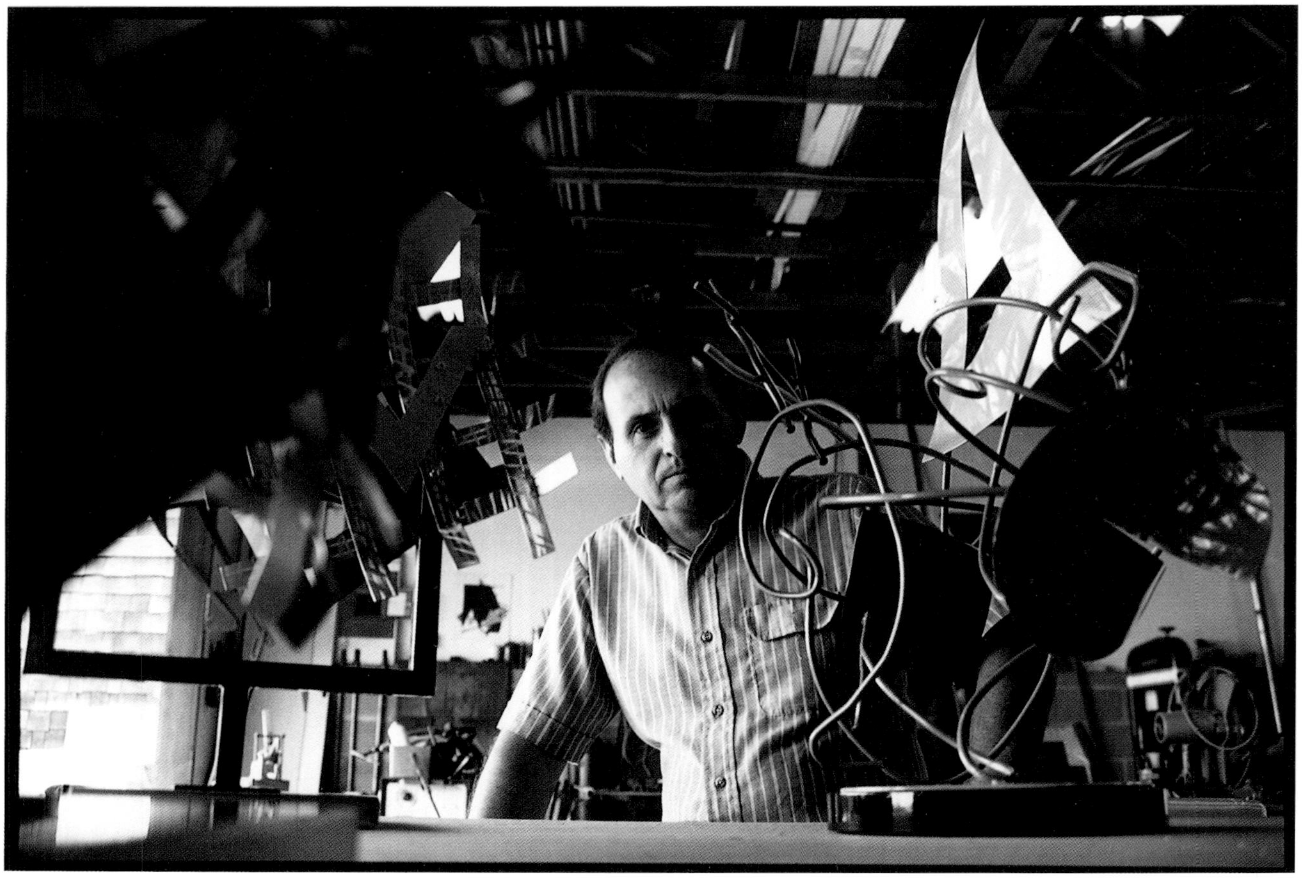

I see my work dealing very strongly with the dynamics of opposition, the dynamics of balance, because I feel that life is just this precarious, very fragile thing.

Southeast of San Diego in the hilltop town of Crest, Ron Tatro's welded metal sculptures are discovered among the manzanita bushes as the visitor meanders along dirt paths. Through the negative spaces formed by his larger-than-life abstract pieces one may temporarily focus on surprising vistas of the unpopulated valleys below.

Tatro's sculptural interest shifted in the early 1980s from these large, weathered, outdoor abstractions to smaller, delicately unbalanced pieces which are constructed of the simplest shapes connected by metal wire. These assemblies are loose and fluid, as if they were spontaneous line drawings. In a studio shared with sculptor Jeff Laudenslager in nearby El Cajon, Tatro polychromes these welded steel forms with a lasting enamel in bright, primary colors in a non-textured glaze.

An only child, Tatro was four years old when his father died and he was raised by his mother, a teacher who also conducted after-school art classes. He lives with his wife Janice and their school-age son in a home that overlooks the outdoor sculptures and several separate work spaces.

The reason I started to make welded steel sculpture was that it was collage-like, a very fast material as opposed to casting where you have to develop a wax, then make a mold, and finally make the casting. Assembly was natural to me. If you didn't like the shape there you could cut it off, like a big scissors, in a way. It was maybe more demanding physically, but nonetheless you could just cut it and put it back somewhere else. When I started out that's the way I handled steel. It was very close to what I had done and experienced as a painter.

In about 1980 I tired with it. I felt it was too intellectual. I started a real self-examination about what I was doing as an artist in terms of what I think about art, where my ideas come from. Somewhere along the line you say, "Wait a minute, I was trained this way, why?" I was thirty-eight. I thought, now I know how I see the world, but my art is not really reflecting totally the way I'm seeing it, parts of it, but I'm going to risk it and I'm going to do what I do whether it fits the art world, art history, the art market, or an intellectual mainstream.

I developed a very tight set of parameters for myself in terms of a vocabulary. I felt that what was most important was to make art that had some kind of emotional impact and I started to make decisions about what I like. People say, "I don't know a lot about art but I know what I like." I started to pay attention to that statement. I thought, there's something to that. I mean, who the hell am I to think I have to educate everybody all the time? Can't people just like something? Does art have to be so pontifical and so intellectual for anybody to look at it and say "I like it."?

I don't like art that you have to read. I don't like Hieronymous Bosch, for example. So I don't make art that you have to read. My work has an immediate and spontaneous look, but it's not made that way. It takes a long period of time, but that's not the point, the point is what does it look like. I wanted to have an immediate kind of engagement, for the viewer to be struck instantly. That's one of the reasons for limiting the palette. I like color very much. The pieces start with materials like paper, wood, and flexible copper wire that bends easily. When I was making steel early on it was so physically difficult to make a piece that sometimes you would do something that would not be in your aesthetic simply because the material starts to take over and becomes an overpowering thing.

When I was twelve years old I was in a fire and was burned badly and was laid up for a year recuperating. When I got out of the hospital my grandparents bought me a set of paints I had seen for four dollars. My mother was off to work and I had nothing to do all day and I started painting. I never changed from that point on because I found that was what I wanted to do. I found it was a way I could experience my own ideas about the world, I guess, about the self. Because I was handicapped from the fire I didn't have the opportunity to play sports like the other kids. And I was an only child. I was always alone.

In high school I saw a photo display from *Life* Magazine about Willem DeKooning, Jackson Pollack, and Picasso. I was totally taken by that. I grew up in a town where there wasn't any art, an industrial town. But I would stand and look at the painting from the WPA on the post office wall. Every town had one.

I see my work dealing very strongly with the dynamics of opposition, the dynamics of balance, because I feel that life is just this precarious, very fragile thing. One minute we're here doing our thing and the next minute we're gone. When a human being dies it's permanent and it's a strange kind of overwhelming presence of nature. You go along in your world thinking that it's a well-balanced, very well organized, very stable situation without thinking about the fact that anything can mess it up. People can create imbalances or nature creates imbalances and gives us a flood, a volcano, an earthquake. It's an ongoing process, a search for dynamic balance, order, a yin-yang kind of thing.

The fragility of life, the precariousness. I like my work to have these kinds of emotional qualities in them. I make the work with very bright colors, but formally the form of the work has a chaotic quality to it.

It's almost like life has a sugar coating, that sense of order always being at the edge of falling over into disorder and chaos and total uncontrol, instability. It's like candy. It's so sweet and so deadly, so tasty but it does bad things to you. I like that kind of contrapuntal, contradictory quality that one thing is covering up another thing, that things aren't as they appear.

SELECTED BIOGRAPHY

BIRTHPLACE

Kankakee, Illinois

EDUCATION

Southern Illionis University, Carbondale, BA, 1965; MFA, 1966

TEACHING

Grossmont College, El Cajon

SOLO EXHIBITIONS

San Diego Museum of Art, 1979
Maple Gallery, San Diego, 1985
Harcourts Contemporary, San Francisco, 1986
Lever/Myerson Galleries, New York, 1987
Ianetti/Lanzone Gallery, San Francisco, 1988

GROUP EXHIBITIONS

"All California," Laguna Art Museum, Laguna Beach, 1984
Two-person, Art Space Gallery, Los Angeles, 1984
Permanent Collection Exhibit, San Jose Museum of Art, San Jose, California, 1983, 1985, 1986
Art 17, 1986, and Art 18 (solo), 1987, Basel Art Fair, Switzerland
"Concept and Reality," University Art Gallery, Pepperdine College, Malibu, California, 1987

COLLECTIONS

San Jose Museum of Art, San Jose, California
San Diego County Annex Building
Saddleback College, Mission Viejo, California
Fluor Corporation, Irvine, California
Barbara Walbridge, La Jolla

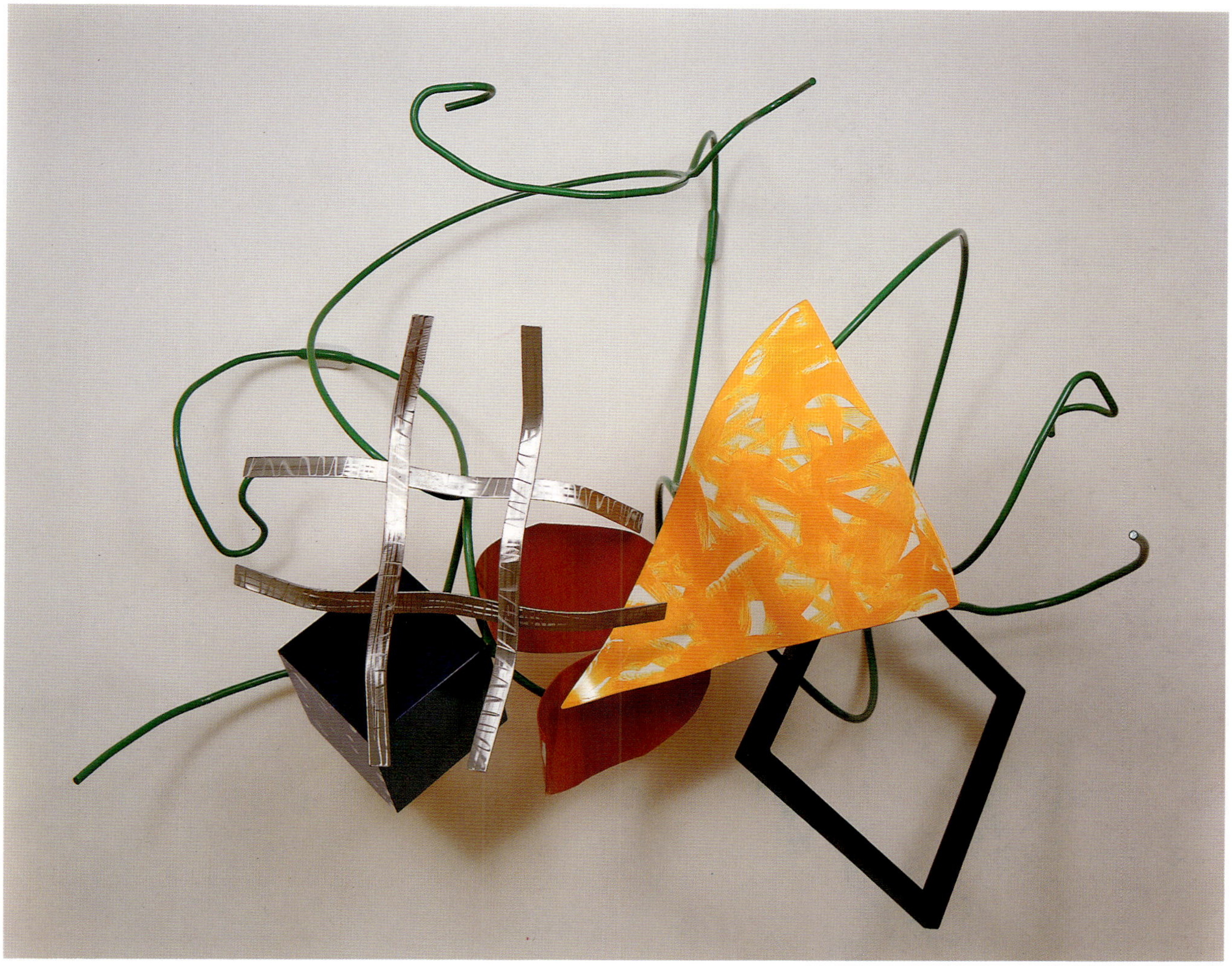

Wall Scribble #8, polychrome, steel, stainless steel, 40″×55″×24″, 1987

Photo by Joan Dixon

Gillian Theobald

I feel we're a batch of molecules and we're here to support them in becoming. It has to do with a sense of self and connectedness to other molecules. We're all one thing.

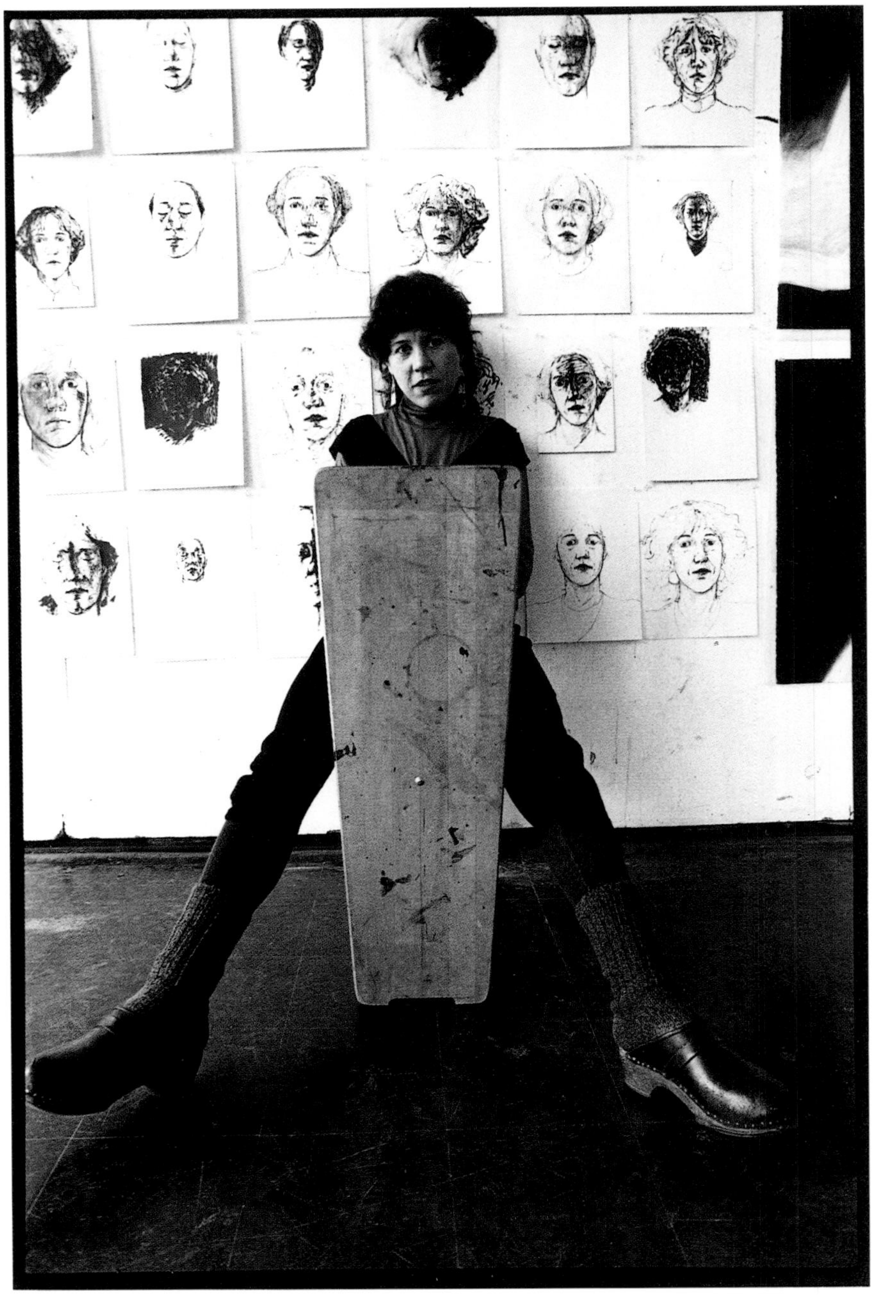

At the end of each week Gillian Theobald commutes from San Diego to her studio in a downtown Los Angeles industrial building. Gypsy-like in her individualistic clothes, she seems adapted to this commuting lifestyle which keeps her on the road between the two cities that nourish her.

Theobald's work is imbued with her sensitivity to spiritual sources of inspiration. Through drawings that have expressive, energetic line and paintings with smoothly textured, glowing colors, Theobald has earned the respect of a large community of downtown San Diego artists.

Assisting students at SDSU since 1978, Theobald developed Art ETC., an art supply store located in the University art complex. She supervises nine people and offers a wide range of specialized art material and media problem-solving expertise.

Theobald grew up with two older brothers in a highly cultural and intellectual atmosphere with her mother, a watercolor painter, and her father, a poet and SDSU professor. Since 1984 she has lived in Los Angeles each week from Thursday through Sunday.

In 1982 I started doing self-portraits because I wanted to experiment with inks and I looked around the studio and decided to do myself. They had a crudeness and a directness to them that was immediately exciting to me. I kept doing them and got hooked into it because it was really different from anything else I'd ever done. The early ones looked very German-expressionistic, real dark. After a while I realized I hadn't been looking in the mirror for some time. I became aware that the whole process was meditative. They didn't necessarily look like me.

I realized after doing a hundred or so that the process is very similar to the process of my painting. Ever since I went to New Mexico I kind of fell into a place where I mentally go there. Not that it was a direct source, but when I was there I was really impacted by New Mexico. There was something about the sense of space in New Mexico, a sense of geologic time. In the desert there's nothing covered up by greenery. My paintings aren't specifically about that geology, but I get a feeling it is a result of that kind of environment having to do with mass and scale. If one listens to Bach cantatas one has a similar sense of scale and mass. It is that sensation that is really moving to me.

I go to New Mexico about once a year. I just kind of need to be there. My lifestyle involves city to city to city commutes along a corridor of asphalt and concrete and I think that part of mentally going to that place has to point to a place in reality. It also has a strong spiritual impact on me.

Recently my work has been about water, derived from imagery from there, maybe river gorges through seemingly arid country. My commute to my studio in Los Angeles happens at night and it's a wonderful time for me and I realize that imagery is also in my paintings. As though it's not a car, it's water weaving, dealing with light and movement and going towards something. I hadn't realized consciously that was an element in my work until recently. Like most painters, I don't like to get down and define exactly what it is.

I've done a lot of thinking about landscape recently and it's been clear to me that they are more in the tradition of abstraction than landscape painting. I think there are some expectations about landscape painters to address the issue of our perception about landscape in this age with all this concrete. I don't argue with that, but I think these paintings are more in the tradition of Barnett Newman. They aren't about perception, they're about MY perception. My paintings tend to be more experiential. My experience is in there, but I don't take a position that I figure out and try to implement.

San Diego is important to me, but when I get up to Los Angeles I am so glad to be there. There's something really important to me about being in Los Angeles that doesn't have anything to do with the artistic community. It has felt like the lotus, this beautiful flower comes up and blooms on the top of the water and is rooted in the mud. There's something lyrical about San Diego, and some energy power about Los Angeles.

I've had the studio in Los Angeles for about three years. I go up on Thursday and come back Sunday night. My studio has this exquisite view of downtown. It looks out over the warehouse rooftops, towards the really tall buildings about half a mile away. Every time I look out I have to open the reticulated glass window. There is no screen because it's an industrial space, so the air comes in. Every time I look out that window it's a tangible, physical experience of what it looks like and the feel of the air at the same time. It's had a physical impact on me that is most treasured, though other people wouldn't respond the same way.

There is some spiritual reason why I do art. It is my vehicle. I feel we're a batch of molecules and we're here to support them in becoming. It has to do with a sense of self and connectedness to other molecules. We're all one thing.

Sometimes I have doubts about art, that it isn't interactive and participatory, like a play that's written and never acted isn't fully a play and a painting that is made and stored away isn't fully all that it can be. I owe it to the work to put it out there. But sometimes that's a painful process.

SELECTED BIOGRAPHY

BIRTHPLACE

La Jolla

EDUCATION

Byam Shaw School of Drawing and Painting, London, 1964 to 1965
San Diego State University, BA, 1967; MA, 1971

SOLO EXHIBITIONS

552 Gallery, San Diego, 1981
Installation Gallery, San Diego, 1982
Mira Costa College, Oceanside, California, 1984
Patty Aande Gallery, San Diego, 1987
Cirrus Gallery, Los Angeles, 1983, 1986, 1987

GROUP EXHIBITIONS

"A San Diego Exhibition," La Jolla Museum of Contemporary Art, 1985
"To the Astonishing Horizon, L.A.V.A.," curated by Peter Frank, Los Angeles Design Center, 1985
Chicago International Art Exposition, 1985
"Scapes," University Art Museum, University of California, Santa Barbara, 1985
"Vistas," curated by Peter Frank, G.W. Einstein, New York, 1987

COLLECTIONS

Capitol Group, Los Angeles
Security Pacific Bank Collection, Los Angeles
Mobil Oil Corporation, New York
Chemical Bank, New York
Irene Williams and Michael Dunsford, San Diego

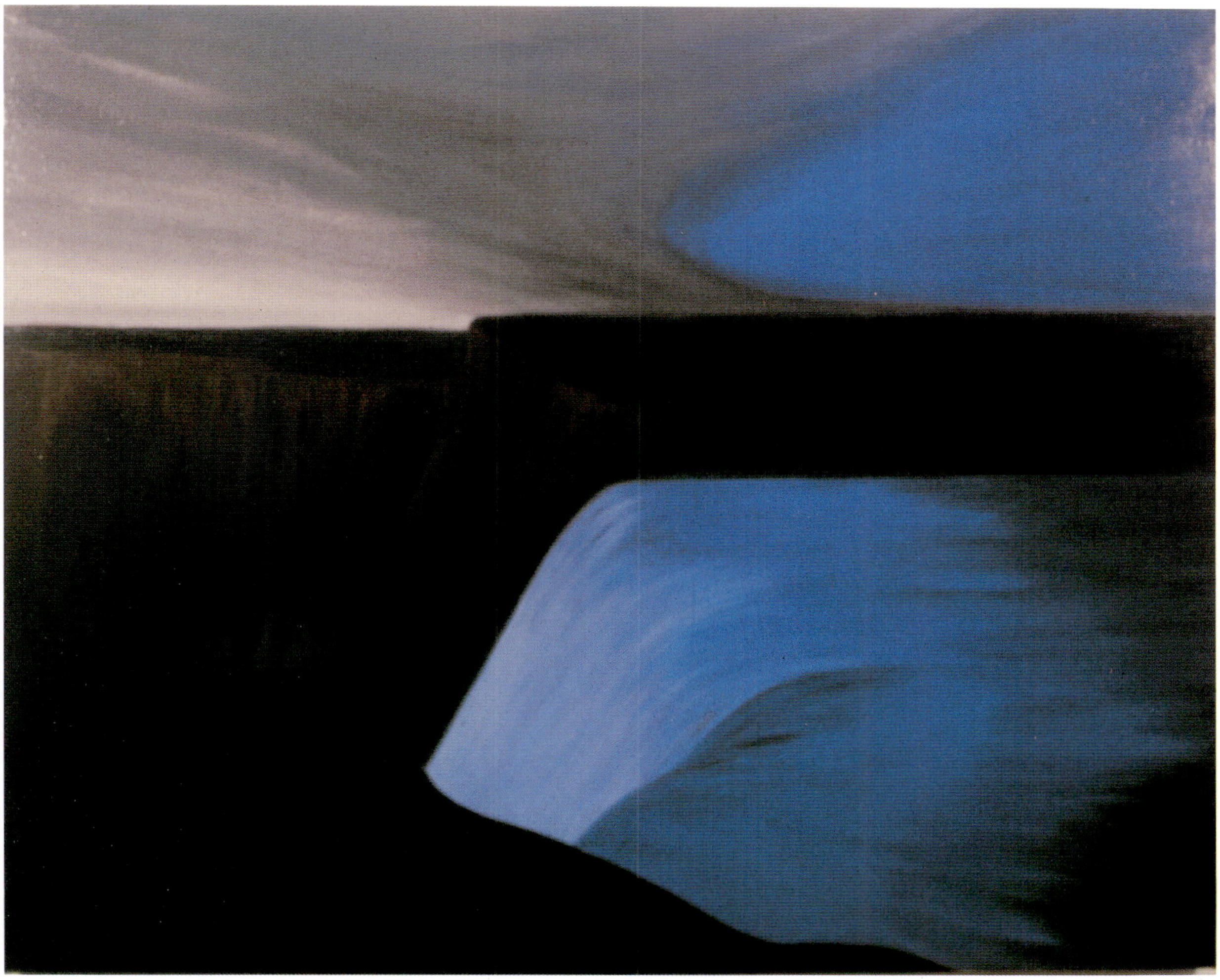

Blue River, enamel/canvas, 35" × 45", 1987

Barbara Weldon

You're never the same today as you were a week ago because things are either layered onto your mind or things constantly change, add to, or erode.... that's what the collages are all about.

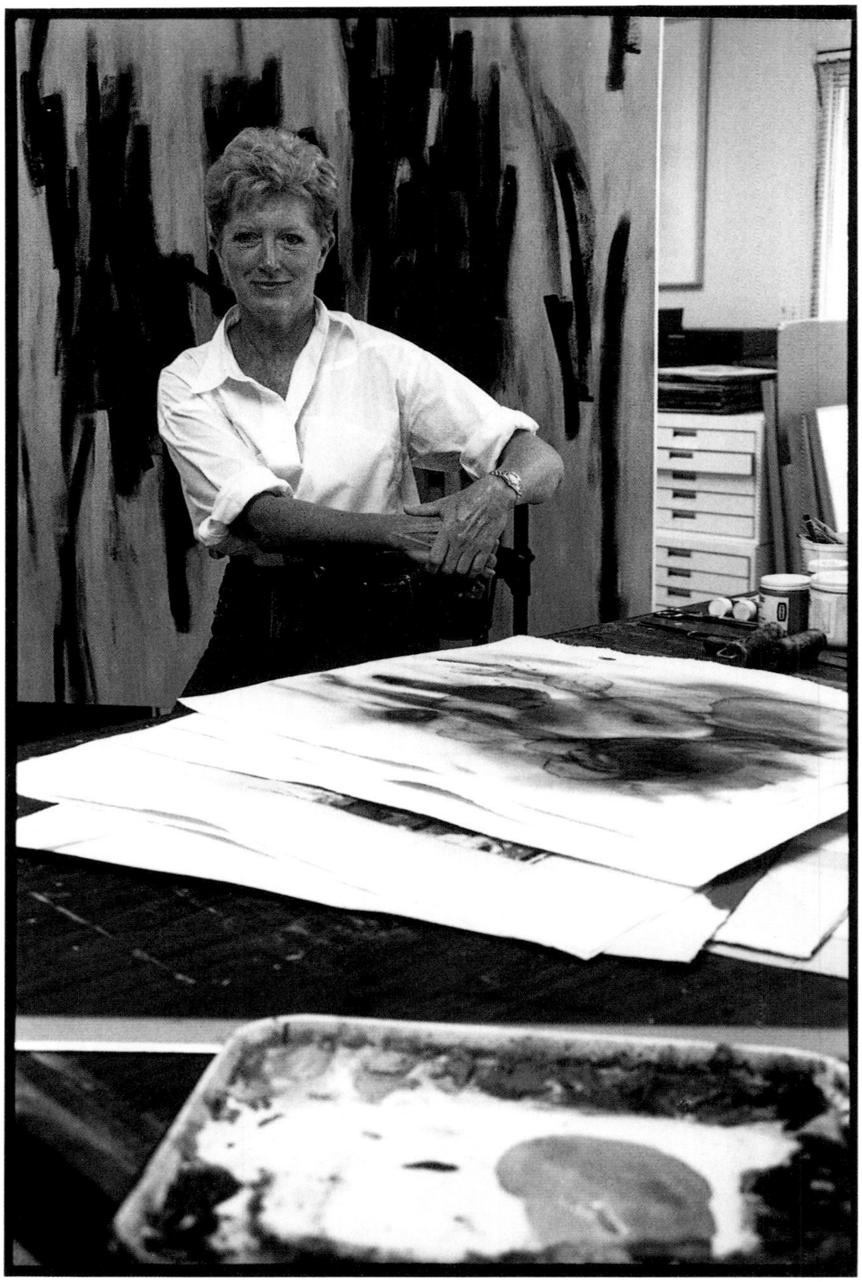

A well-lit studio is the focal point in Barbara Weldon's home. Layers of paintings on both paper and canvas lean against each other between several large work tables. She speaks in a gentle voice which is barely heard over the jazz and classical music playing in the background, but what she expresses in her work and life speaks loudly for her dedication to an art career.

Weldon is one of the most collected painters in San Diego, an artist who has made difficult life and career transitions in her developmental processes. One of the few artists to move successfully through a reputation as a watercolorist into an exploring of other media, Weldon's mixed media collages have become standards by which other area artists measure their use of color and sense of design.

*Admired by critic Robert McDonald (*The Los Angeles Times, *April 15, 1986) for her "lyrical abstractions," Weldon's work is perhaps richest when exploring the flow of large gestural strokes and the restrained palette of her "Tango" series that has, somewhat tentatively, recurred in recent years.*

After her father died when she was six, Weldon and two older sisters were raised by a strong, practical, working mother. Since the late 1970s, she has remained a close friend of Thomas Babeor, director of the Thomas Babeor Gallery in La Jolla. She has a grown daughter and a son in college.

For several years I did a lot of transparent watercolors. I was fascinated with the spontaneity, but bored with it after a while. I gradually began adding some ink lines and layers of rice paper and then very delicately, subtly washing color a bit and adding more layers of paper, so that I gradually got away from the traditional idea of watercolor. The rice paper layers were replaced by pieces of early prints of mine, intaglios. I have an etching press and I had done etching quite a bit. I have very few intaglios left now because I just kept digging into them for the collages. I liked printmaking because of the multiple process except that I found just doing that alone was just technical and not as spontaneous as I liked. In the last couple of years I've added actual materials that I brought back from the Orient and Indonesia.

I think you are all the layers that just keep adding onto you, that change you. You're never the same today as you were a week ago because things are either layered onto your mind or things constantly change, add to, or erode. I think that's what the collages are all about. It's not for decoration, although I think some people interpret it that way. I have a hard time responding to someone's work where there's just one layer of paint on it, that's hard edge. It might be interesting to me, but I don't really relate to it.

When I was married and had two small children I wasn't thinking, oh, I'm going to become a professional artist. It was just a need to do art that had to be satisfied. It became more than a profession. Once I was no longer married I had choices to make about whether to abandon art or whether to give it my all. My children were still in elementary school. It was a major commitment and it was kind of scary. There were a few opportunities along the way to teach at community colleges, but I have watched friends who taught and painted and they didn't really have much time or enthusiasm for painting while teaching.

I have a lot more time now to seriously devote to my painting now that my children are grown, although when they were young I was seriously committed and worked long hours, it's just that the art had to be broken up with commitments to other things, so I would work into the wee hours of the morning. I have more choice now about how I structure my time. I probably produce more now than I could then. I can afford to experiment more and my attention isn't being pulled in two different directions.

There's a part of me that's very organized and

there's a part that needs freedom, that cannot be controlled by anyone else. I know that one reason I've been able to make it as an artist is that disciplined side. I keep files on every painting I do. Every painting has a card that gives a rundown of everything I need to know about it with a photo on the back and when it's sold it's marked with who purchased it, the cost and then it's filed away. I hate taking care of these details but I just find a day and I do it because it's necessary. When a young artist asks how to get from wanting to paint to being in a good gallery and earning a living, you forget all the things that happen along the way. But I think a lot of artists have problems because they're unable to be disciplined about these things. I think it's very hard to make it unless you can be disciplined a day at a time.

Among people who are not really involved in the art world there is a mystique, an awe. In some cases there is an assumption that you have to be sort of strange. There are all kinds of preconceived ideas people have about artists, maybe fostered by the artists themselves who feel they have to have a certain image. I think you should be whoever you are. You shouldn't be trying to be what you think the art world is supposed to be.

SELECTED BIOGRAPHY

BIRTHPLACE

Yuma, Arizona

EDUCATION

San Diego State University
University of California, San Diego

SOLO EXHIBITIONS

San Diego Museum of Art, 1976
Clark Gallery, Lincoln, MA, 1979, 1980
Laguna Art Museum, Laguna Beach, 1984
Ivory/Kimpton Gallery, San Francisco, 1982, 1983, 1984, 1986, 1988
Thomas Babeor Gallery, La Jolla, 1980, 1982, 1983, 1984, 1986, 1988

GROUP EXHIBITIONS

"San Diego Artists," Yokohama Citizen's Gallery, Japan, 1979
National Academy of Design, William A. Patton prize, New York, 1979
Newport Harbor Art Museum, Newport Beach, California, 1981
Mulvane Art Center, Washburn University of Topeka, Kansas, 1984
Sheila Nussbaum Gallery, Millburn and Princeton, New Jersey, 1984 to 1987

COLLECTIONS

35 paintings, Marshall Fields Stores, Chicago, Dallas and San Antonio, Texas
Bank of America World Headquarters, San Francisco
Security Pacific Bank Collection, Los Angeles
Copley Memorial Library, La Jolla and Copley Publishers, San Diego
Elizabeth and Mason Phelps, La Jolla

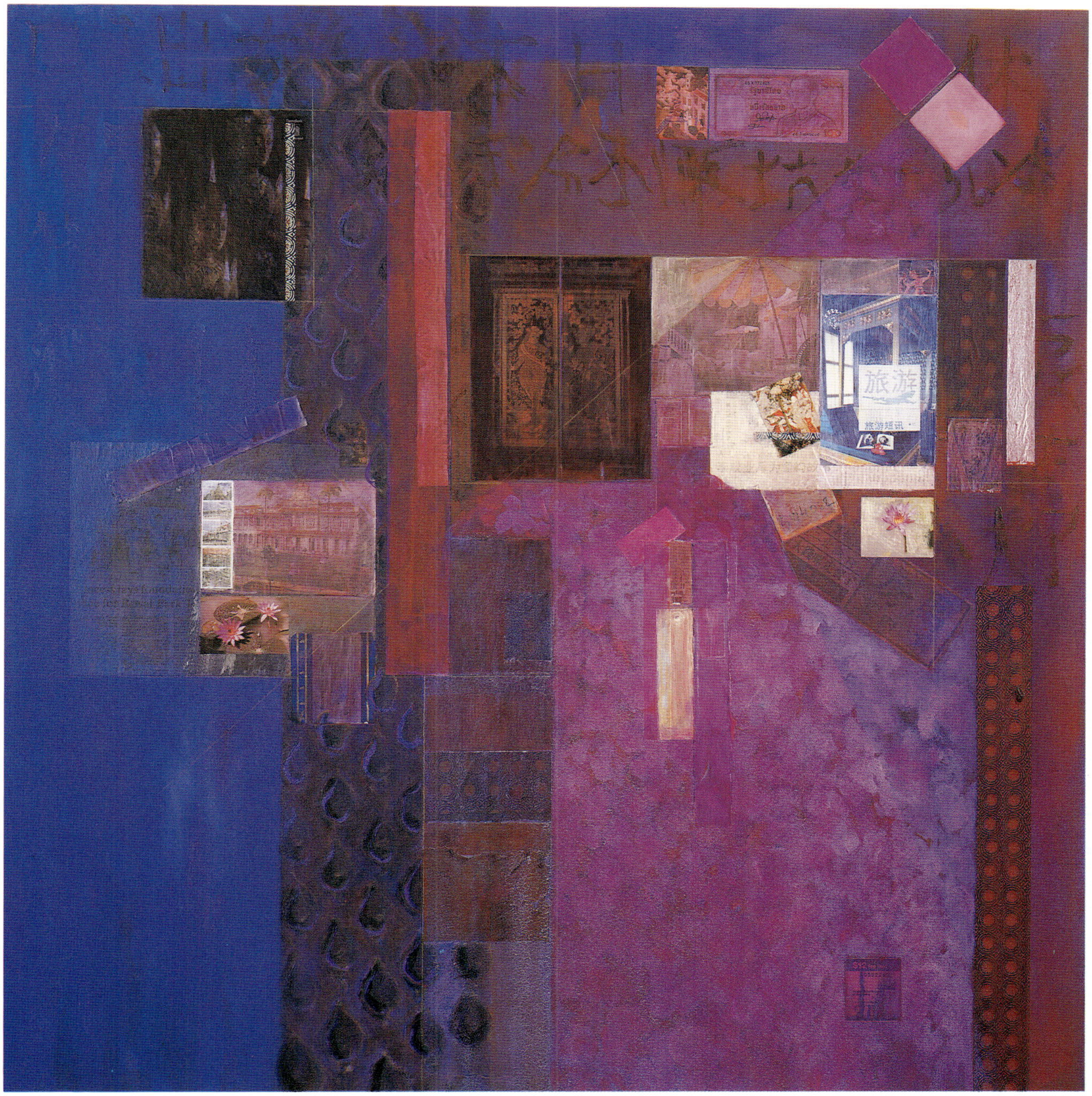

Oriental Series, acrylic and collage/canvas, 48″×48″, 1987

Ron Wigginton

The artists I respect the most are dealing in some way with how things are put together.... I have more interest in talking to a good physicist about subatomic particles than.... talking to an artist.

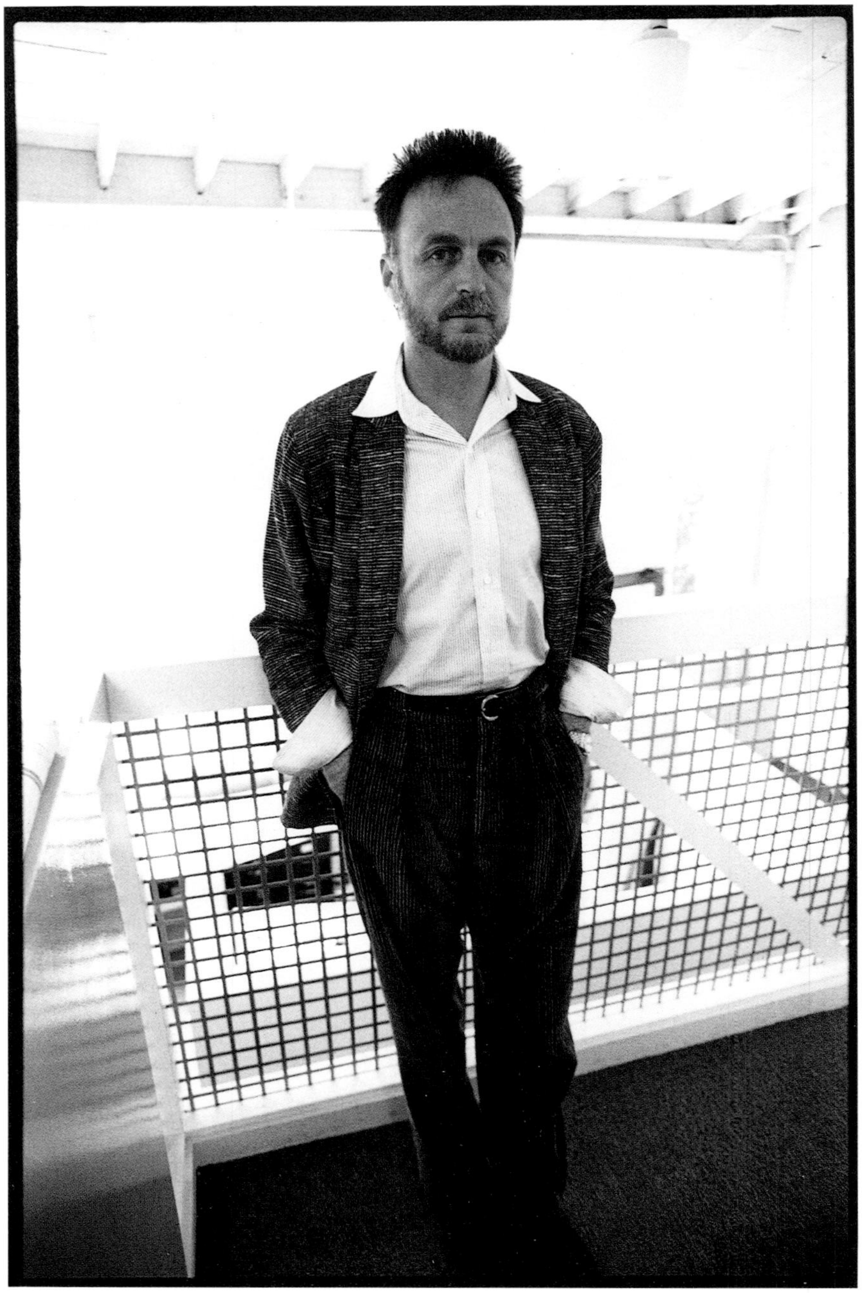

The unusual design of a platform area above the drafting tables in Land Studio, downtown, is a reflection of Ron Wigginton's personal vision of a world of "high platforms to lift the collective mind that much closer to the stars." With a design sense that extends to the choice of drafting tables, reading chairs, lamps, and the library, Wigginton's all encompassing personal aesthetic approaches landscape architecture as pure potential.

Ron Wigginton/Land Studio was founded in 1981 as a natural expression of the artist's views as they related to site-oriented environmental statements long expressed in his sculpture maquettes and drawings. With a diverse group of eight others assisting, Wigginton's concepts are becoming realized throughout San Diego county. As of this writing, several projects for the Golden Triangle area are in the planning stages and will be constructed in the next few years.

Wigginton had a grandfather who was an architect but otherwise declines further biographical notes.

Back in school when I was studying sculpture, I had a natural predilection for going to the library and reading about the glory of Japan. I felt here I've come home, here's how I've lived and here's a whole nation that lives like this, at least they did in the Momayama period. The Momayama period so impressed me that I took it all in, everything from tea mas. . rs – particularly Rikyu – to ceramic masters, the political-social wars, the Buddhism, all of it. I just adopted it instantly because I felt it was something I already knew. But that was all through the eyes of somebody who was creating in a studio atmosphere, so it was understandably in a totally different way than a historian or somebody who was interested in the stories. I was watching man creating things which I was creating at the same time but under different circumstances.

In 1970 I jumped a ship and went to Japan and hitchiked through Japan and met up with Shoji Hamada, a potter who is a National Treasure. I was able to travel through the central spine of the country tracking down the ancient dragon kilns and meeting masters, very unusual people, very inspiring. I met the artist Agnes Martin there as well.

I've found that a lot of people evolve disciplines by coming out of left field, it's not their discipline originally, they come from somewhere else. It's a very unknowing thing. What they do is bring a different mind to it and that results in some new progress.

All countries are having a difficult time right now and if I had a grand dream it would be to inspire poetic wars to get people to back off, back away from a sense of being driven by this machine that produces war equipment and homes that are deadening to the mind and the eye. If we could start some poetic wars like Rikyu was trying to do, we could put the same energy and thought behind the same evolution and the same successes and make the same amount of money. Poetic competition could create people who love good music, pull in millions of people from other countries, get a real free flow of people around the earth and make a connection between the earth and the solar system.

Anything autobiographical is very distasteful to me, a very low form of art. The artists I respect the most are dealing in some way or other, whether expressed or not with how things are put together. The real stuff flows easily into society and moves forward, the other on an autobiographical level does something else. If you have an injured psyche and dwell on it a lot you use up your life span.

When I'm creating designs they are really created in just a few seconds. The thoughts come instantaneously, the conceptual work takes a little longer and I enjoy that the most, imagining the world that's taking place around the real thing as it's drawn. I'm usually seeing it from all sides.

A lot of people in the profession of landscape architecture are interesting in that they're flexible, their thoughts are flexible. I was telling someone in Land Studio the other day that there are differences between art and landscape architecture, as we all know, but the one that strikes me frequently is that in art there is just one solution. When I'm painting a painting it's not done until it's done, but in design there are multitudes of solutions and that's more difficult.

I've developed a palette which is different from the way some landscape architects approach landscape design. I don't swing stylistically from tropical to arid or whatever. I just have a palette with which that I can convey meaning and tell a story. This palette is not as large as some others use. It's just right to me. I'm using everything I need to achieve a goal and anything else would be excess.

I see the big triangle between the Far East, Seattle, and San Diego – and the points in between – as a *place*, they're not different places. I haven't found a landscape that hasn't affected me. The very center of my work goes back to this awe of the landscape. I can't say just landscape either, because I have a tremendous desire to know what other planets are composed of, what the solar system is composed of, what subatomic particles are composed of. And I approach these concerns in a phenomenological way. I have more interest in talking to a good physicist about subatomic particles than I would talking to an artist. I think a lot of artists really feel that way too. Talking shop is very boring.

What you really want to know is what makes things and why, where do they come from, what are we doing here, where are we going. Gauguin's questions and Einstein's questions, those are the important ones.

SELECTED BIOGRAPHY

BIRTHPLACE

Oakland, California

EDUCATION

University of Montana, Missoula, BFA, 1967
University of Oregon, Eugene, MFA, 1968
California Registered Landscape Architect, 1982

SOLO EXHIBITIONS

Anneburg Gallery, San Francisco, 1973
"Tsukubai," Foster/White Gallery, Seattle, 1974
"Landscape Puzzle," Tokyo/American Club, Tokyo, 1977
"Sources of Power," 1982; "City Forest," installation, Quint Gallery, San Diego, 1985

GROUP EXHIBITIONS

"Awards Annual," Louis Comfort Tiffany Foundation, New York, 1966
"Northwest Artists," 1974; "Works on Paper," 1975, Seattle Art Museum, Seattle
"American Painters in Paris," Palais Des Congress, Paris, 1975
"To the Astonishing Horizon, L.A.V.A.," curated by Peter Frank, Los Angeles Design Center, 1985
"SIX VIEWS Contemporary Landscape Architecture," California State University, Fullerton, 1986

HONORS

Dorland Mountain Colony Resident Artist Fellowship
Award of Merit, "Forecast 80's" project, 1982; Award of Honor for Excellence in Design, "Miraflores, Fairbanks Ranch," with Rob Wellington Quigley Architects, 1987, American Institute of Architects, San Diego
National Merit Award, "Starwalk" project, 1984; "City Forest" and "Visual Productions Incorporated," 1986, American Society for Landscape Architects
First Award, "Wheat Walk" project, 1988; International Design Arts Competition, National Endowment for the Arts, University of California Arboretum, Davis

COLLECTIONS

Seattle Art Museum, Seattle
Oakland Museum, Oakland
Site design, Oliver McMillan Business Center, Tempe, Arizona
Site design and fountains, California First Bank Plaza Golden Triangle, San Diego
Site design and fountain, Escondido Surgery Center, Escondido, California

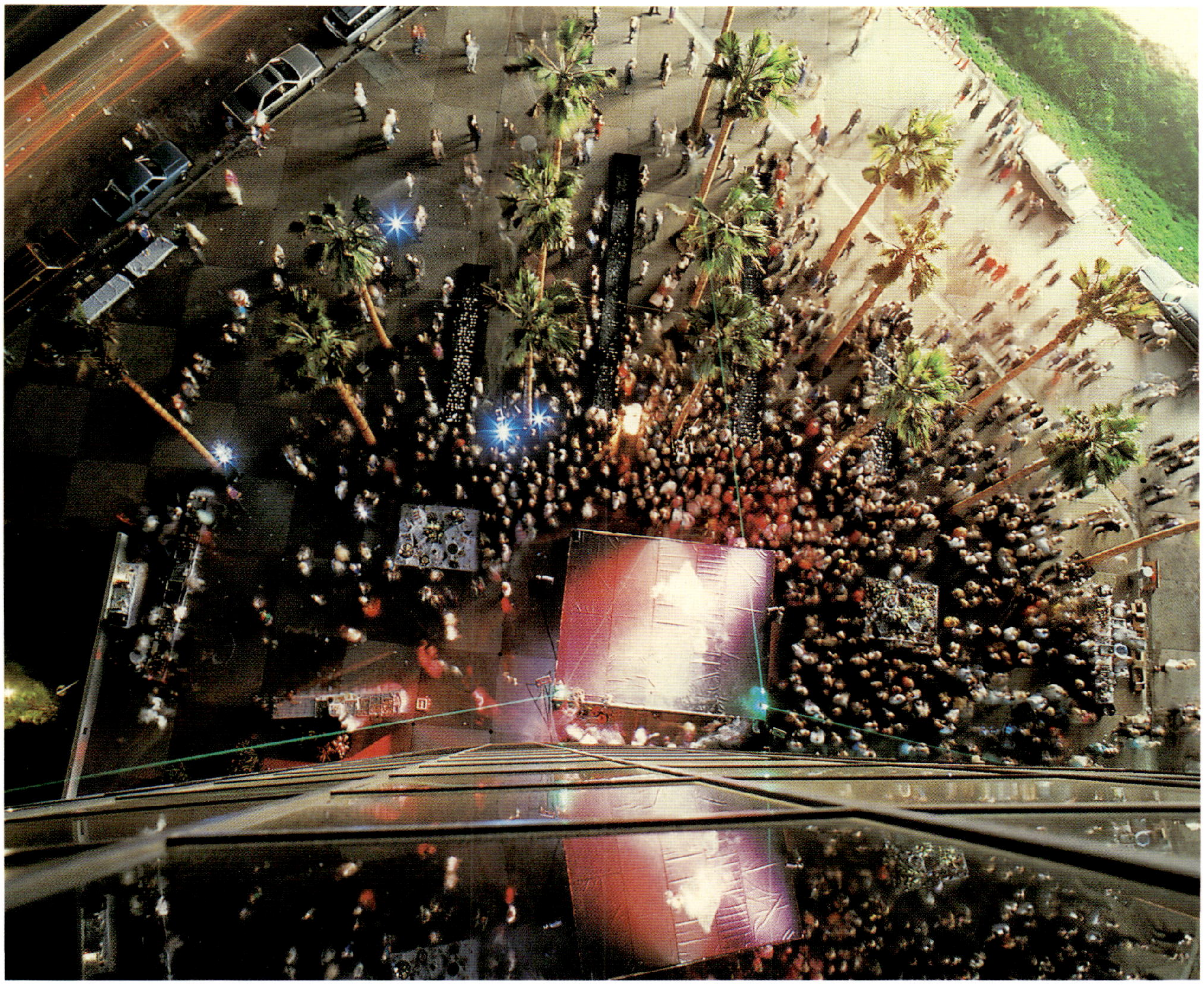

Star Troughs at California First Bank, 1986

Photo by Philipp Scholz-Rittermann

W. Haase Wojtyla

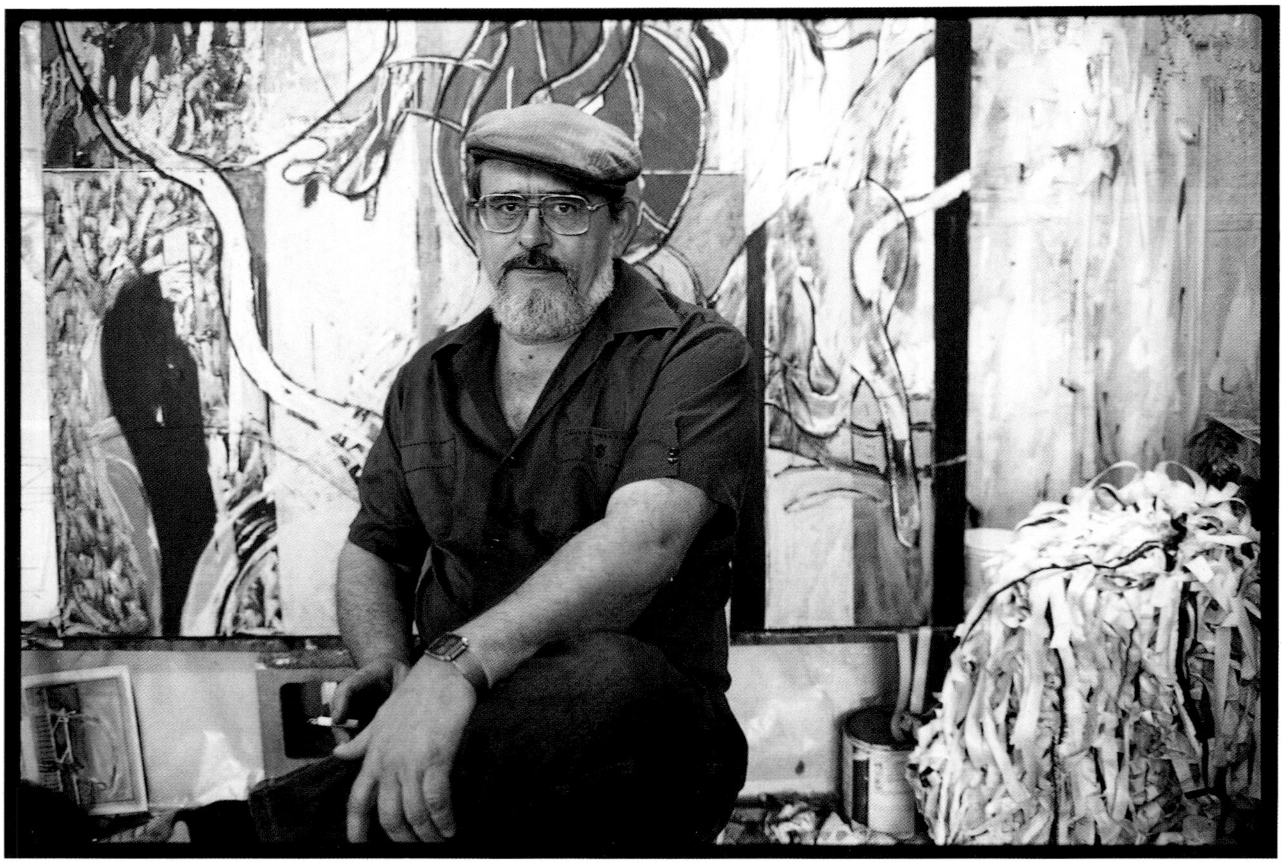

...I've been brought up on oil paintings. It's a different feel. I like the canvas, the bounce of the canvas.

On the first floor of an apartment house on Twenty-second Street near downtown, W. Haase Wojtyla (more popularly known as "Walter") paints with a vengeance – and with remnants of torn canvases, used paint tubes, and exhausted paint rags which have accumulated in silent testimony to his years of work. The studio has long been too small to serve the artist's needs; he is closed in by table tops, books, and a huge store of large canvases, most of which are off their stretcher bars, having been rolled up and stacked wherever space would allow. Against one clear area of wall a painting is in progress and can be scrutinized from one of two chairs in the room.

Seemingly determined to keep his works among the best kept secrets in the art world, limiting their viewing to the co-op Spectrum Gallery, SDMA's Artist's Guild annual, and a few other local exhibits, Wojtyla maintains a disarmingly naive approach to his art which flies in the face of the powerful and sophisticated expressiveness of a remarkable body of work. Evoking the spirit and independence of Francis Bacon, Wojtyla's paintings have long been recognizable as solely his. The writhing, bizarre imagery at once grips and repels, fascinates and disturbs. These complex distortions only seem to reaffirm the artist's private world view.

Wojtyla's older brother, like Van Gogh's, is a collector of his work and is an economist. His younger brother is a musician. They were raised by a bookworm mother and a violin-playing father. During his Army stint in France Wojtyla traveled throughout Europe, painting outdoors on weekends with a local artist. Their favorite spot was Perigoux and the Dordogne caves. He lives alone and has one son in college.

My main series were the Nudes in the Shower and the Murder series. I don't know about these off-shoots, like the Tennis or Religious series I did. Religious things don't sell, neither do Giraffes. I thought they brought out interesting shapes, going off the canvas with their necks extended. Can't get their necks in there. Nobody likes giraffes. Dogs. Dogs are good. Nudes in the shower are good.

I think I sold one Murder piece. I was always fascinated with murders and crimes. Especially true crimes. I've got a whole bunch of books on my shelves on crime stories. My mother used to read a whole lot of that, *True Detective Magazine*. For a while my dad was an undertaker, that has to do with the murders, finally he was working for the government. Fascinating, so I thought I'd give it a try. I like the Murder scenes because there's an interaction between the true life and the painting. You have the story and you want to make a painting and there's sort of a reality and non-reality that I like.

I think the paintings I'm happiest with are Nudes in the Shower. I just love working on them. I guess because I see so many possibilities the way the water falls, even the change in the water. I did my first one a long time ago in Illinois and sent it to the Chicago Art Institute and got a little prize. It had a certain kind of design, like a step-down design. I don't consciously do it, sometimes it shows up in my paintings. I don't know, it seems to work for me.

I did do some film, some underground filmmaking in New York. I like film a lot but it's costly and you've got to buy film and all the equipment and it takes a lot of time. I did all the editing myself and it took me over a year to put together one piece of film, a 16mm film that was on the Brooklyn Bridge. It won a prize at a film festival in Ann Arbor, Michigan and at one of the museums, and was shown in New York at this big loft where there was a Roy Lichtenstein on the wall. In the 1960s my camera was stolen. That was the end of my film career.

You can't help but be influenced by your surroundings. Like I went to Mexico for three years. If I say that, some people will say I got my color from Mexico. But I always thought it didn't matter where I was. I feel perhaps I'm painting the same thing I'd paint in New York, maybe not the same things the same way. Color was never a big hang-up for me. I always thought I had a good color sense so I never really studied color. The form is more important. I use primarily basic colors, not exotic colors. Forms, shapes, composition are important to me.

I enjoy art. When one comes off, that's nice. It's the only thing I can do, I guess. I like to be alone. I guess you have to if you're a writer or a painter. Getting assistants to do the work, like Robert Motherwell, that wouldn't work for my kind of painting, it's too personal, it changes all the time. I don't make sketches, I draw on the canvas. I use oils. Maybe because I've been brought up on oil paintings. It's a different feel. I like the canvas, the bounce of the canvas.

I like to work directly on canvas, make a lot of changes and kind of build it up. That makes a statement too. I don't like things to look finished. That's why I feel I don't take it to the nth degree. I think I'd like to get more muddier, more dirtier on the canvas, not so much nice color. So maybe my next painting will be like that, a little more raw. I think my paintings are finished when I start saying, "Well, I'll do a little bit here, a little bit there, a little cosmetic stuff." You shouldn't do that. It makes it too sweet. I always like a little imperfection. I like that. It's gutsy. I like gutsy paintings.

I never thought about making a living off it. You just go from day to day. I've worked in banks, all kinds of odd jobs. When I was in New York I was working at the bank. They were going to give me a promotion and I knew it would sock me into the bank and I refused it. After that it was down the drain for me! (laughter) But I didn't want to do that. I wanted to paint. I can't think of doing anything else. I think I have a feel for it.

I don't think much about anything. I'm not involved with politics. Maybe I'm living in an ivory tower. Something catches my eye, I do a painting, then it's all on the canvas. I never got involved in other issues. That's the way I am.

Well, maybe I'll turn around and become myself. Maybe I've seen too many other artists. I'll give it a try.

SELECTED BIOGRAPHY

BIRTHPLACE

Chicago

EDUCATION

Art Institute of Chicago, 1952 to 1954
University of Illinois, Urbana, BFA, 1956
Brooklyn Museum of Art, New York, 1956 to 1957 (Max Beckmann Scholarship)
University of Cincinnati, MFA, 1967

SOLO EXHIBITIONS

Key Gallery, New York, 1962, 1963, 1966
Galeria Chapultapec, Mexico City, Mexico, 1972
San Diego Museum of Art, 1975
Spectrum Gallery, San Diego, 1978, 1980, 1983
East Gallery, Claremont Graduate School, Claremont, California, 1983

GROUP EXHIBITIONS

"Art in America Invitational," The Lighthouse, New York, 1962
"All California," Laguna Art Museum, Laguna Beach, 1975, 1976
"San Diego Artists," Yokohama Citizen's Gallery, Yokohama, 1979
"Humor in Art," A.R.T. Beasley Gallery, San Diego, 1984, 1986
San Diego Museum of Art, 1976, 1978, 1979, 1981, 1983, 1985, 1987

COLLECTIONS

National Institute of Fine Arts, Mexico City
Illini Union, University of Illinois, Urbana
Linda and Irving Baran, M.D.s, San Diego
Sandra and Arnold Berlin, M.D., San Diego
Susan Leonard, San Diego

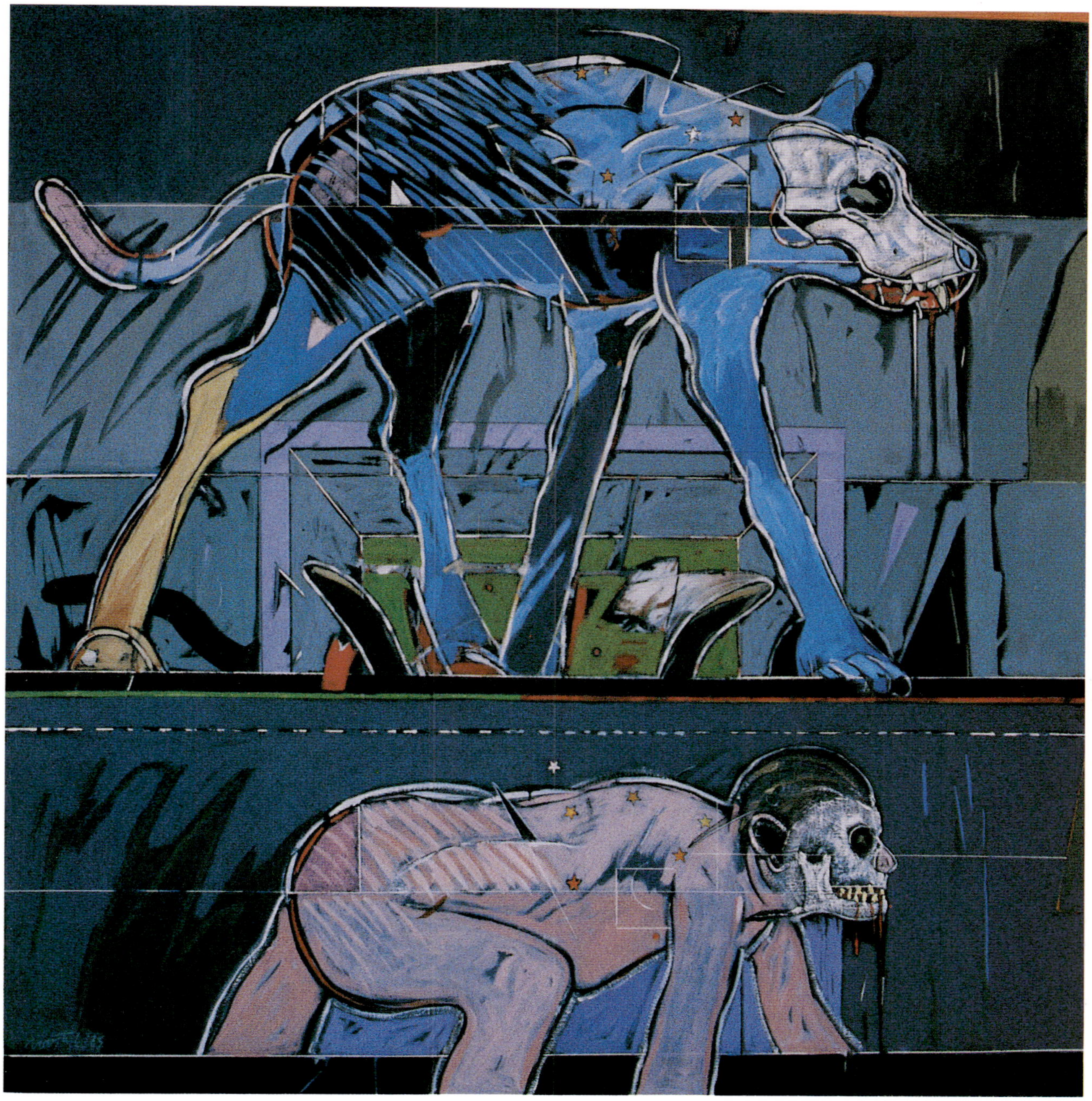

Night Stalker, oil/canvas, 54"×54", 1985 Collection of artist